Lecture Notes in Computer Science 7646

Commenced Publication in 1973
Founding and Former Series Editors:
Gerhard Goos, Juris Hartmanis, and Jan van

T0216172

Editorial Board

Yang Xiang   Mukaddim Pathan   Xiaohui Tao
Hua Wang (Eds.)

Internet and Distributed Computing Systems

5th International Conference, IDCS 2012
Wuyishan, Fujian, China, November 21-23, 2012
Proceedings

 Springer

Volume Editors

Yang Xiang
Deakin University
School of Information Technology
Burwood, VIC, Australia
E-mail: yang@deakin.edu.au

Mukaddim Pathan
Media Distribution
Telstra Corporation Limited
Melbourne, VIC, Australia
E-mail: mukaddim.pathan@team.telstra.com

Xiaohui Tao
The University of Southern Queensland
Department of Mathematics and Computing
Toowoomba, QLD, Australia
E-mail: xtao@usq.edu.au

Hua Wang
The University of Southern Queensland
Department of Mathematics and Computing
Toowoomba, QLD, Australia
E-mail: hua.wang@usq.edu.au

ISSN 0302-9743   e-ISSN 1611-3349
ISBN 978-3-642-34882-2   e-ISBN 978-3-642-34883-9
DOI 10.1007/978-3-642-34883-9
Springer Heidelberg Dordrecht London New York

Library of Congress Control Number: 2012951309

CR Subject Classification (1998): C.2.4, C.2, H.3-4, J.1, D.2, D.4.6, K.6.5

LNCS Sublibrary: SL 3 – Information Systems and Application, incl. Internet/Web
and HCI

Typesetting: Camera-ready by author, data conversion by Scientific Publishing Services, Chennai, India

Printed on acid-free paper

Springer is part of Springer Science+Business Media (www.springer.com)

Preface

IDCS 2012, the 5th International Conference on Internet and Distributed Computing Systems, was held in Wuyishan, Fujian, China, during November 21–23, 2012, jointly with the 6th International Conference on Network and System Security (NSS 2012) and the Third International Conference on Data and Knowledge Engineering (ICDKE 2012). IDCS 2012 was organized and supported by the School of Mathematics and Computer Science, Fujian Normal University, China.

IDCS is a series of events aimed at promoting research in diverse fields related to the Internet and distributed computing systems. The target audience includes researchers and industry practitioners who are interested in different aspects of the Internet and distributed computing systems, with a particular focus on practical experiences with the design and implementation of related technologies as well as their theoretical perspectives.

Following the previous four successful editions of IDCS: IDCS 2008 in Khulna, Bangladesh, IDCS 2009 in Jeju Island, Korea, and IDCS 2010 and IDCS 2011 in Melbourne, Australia; IDCS 2012 was the fifth event in its series. In response to the call for papers, 22 papers were selected for inclusion in the proceedings out of 80 submitted papers (acceptance rate: 27.5%).

We are very grateful to Al-Sakib Khan Pathan and Christian Vecchiola, for their selfless effort during the conference promotion, paper assignment and review decision-making process; and the founder of Daily Positive, Jubaer Arif, for sponsoring the best paper award.

Last but certainly not least our thanks go to all authors who submitted papers and all attendees. We hope you enjoy the conference proceedings!

November 2012

Yang Xiang
Mukaddim Pathan
Xiaohui Tao
Hua Wang

IDCS 2012 Organization

General Co-chairs

Al-Sakib Khan Pathan   International Islamic University, Malaysia
Yang Xiang   Deakin University, Australia

Program Co-chairs

Mukaddim Pathan   Telstra Corporation Ltd., Australia
Christian Vecchiola   IBM Research and Development, Australia

Program Committee

Jemal Abawajy	Deakin University, Australia
Tarem Ahmed	IIUM, Malaysia and BRAC University, Bangladesh
Falah Ali	University of Sussex, UK
Hani Alzaid	King Abdulaziz City for Science and Technology, Saudi Arabia
Giuseppe Amato	ISTI-CNR, Italy
Cosimo Anglano	Università del Piemonte Orientale, Italy
Marcos Dias De Assuncao	IBM Research and Development, Brazil
Doina Bein	Pennsylvania State University, USA
Ladjel Bellatreche	ENSMA, France
Angelo Brayner	University of Fortaleza, Brazil
Rajkumar Buyya	University of Melbourne, Australia
Massimo Cafaro	University of Salento, Italy
Rodrigo N. Calheiros	University of Melbourne, Australia
Marco Canini	EPFL Lausanne, Switzerland
Valeria Cardellini	Università di Roma "Tor Vergata", Italy
Andre Carvalho	Universidade de Sao Paulo, Brazil
Emiliano Casalicchio	Università di Roma "Tor Vergata", Italy
Luca Caviglione	CNR-ISSIA, Italy
Tania Cerquitelli	Politecnico di Torino, Italy
Ruay-Shiung Chang	National Dong Hwa University, Taiwan
Yue-Shan Chang	National Taipei University, Taiwan
Tzung-Shi Chen	National University of Tainan, Taiwan
Mauro Coccoli	University of Genova, Italy
Carmela Comito	University of Calabria, Italy
Antonio Coronato	ICAR-CNR, Italy
Raphaël Couturier	University of Franche Comte, France

Mustafa Mat Deris	Universiti Tun Hussein Onn, Malaysia
Susan Donohue	University of Virginia, USA
Zongming Fei	University of Kentucky, USA
Giancarlo Fortino	University of Calabria, Italy
Karl Fuerlinger	Ludwig Maximilian University, Germany
Jinzhu Gao	University of the Pacific, USA
Joaquin Garcia-Alfaro	TELECOM Bretagne, France
Jose Daniel Garcia	Carlos III University of Madrid, Spain
Alex Gerbessiotis	New Jersey Institute of Technology, USA
S. K. Ghosh	IIT-Kharagpur, India
Harald Gjermundrod	University of Nicosia, Cyprus
Victor Govindaswamy	Texas A&M University-Texarkana, USA
Ragib Hasan	University of Alabama-Birmingham, USA
Houcine Hassan	Universidad Politecnica de Valencia, Spain
Mohammad Mehedi Hassan	King Saud University, Saudi Arabia
Xuming He	NICTA, Australia
Ching-Hsien Hsu	Chung Hua University, Taiwan
Yo-Ping Huang	National Taipei University of Technology, Taiwan
Jaehoon Paul Jeong	Brocade Communications Systems, USA
Dimitrios Katsaros	University of Thessaly, Greece
Muhammad Khurram Khan	King Saud University, Saudi Arabia
Ram Krishnan	University of Texas at San Antonio, USA
Changhoon Lee	Hanshin University, South Korea
Deok Gyu Lee	ETRI, South Korea
Hae Young Lee	ETRI, South Korea
Keqin Li	SAP Research, France
Keqin Li	State University of New York-New Paltz, USA
Pengfeng Li	National Taiwan University, Taiwan
Kai Lin	Dalian University of Technology, China
Pangfeng Liu	National Taiwan University, Taiwan
Timothy Lynar	IBM Research and Development, Australia
Jamie Lloret	Polytechnic University of Valencia, Spain
Carlo Mastroianni	ICAR-CNR, Italy
Muhammad Mostafa Monowar	University of Chittagong, Bangladesh
Amiya Nayak	University of Ottawa, Canada
Surya Nepal	CSIRO, Australia
Marco Netto	IBM Research and Development, Brazil
George Pallis	University of Cyprus, Cyprus
Suraj Pandey	CSIRO, Australia
Apostolos Papadopoulos	Aristotle University of Thessaloniki, Greece
Rubem Pereira	Liverpool John Moores University, UK
Dana Petcu	West University of Timisoara, Romania
Thomas Repantis	Akamai Technologies, USA
Pedro Pereira Rodrigues	University of Porto, Portugal

Casiano Rodriguez-Leon   Universidad de La Laguna, Spain
Caspar Ryan   RMIT University, Australia
Erich Schikuta   University of Vienna, Austria
Seetharami Seelam   IBM T. J. Watson Research Center, USA
Edwin Sha   University of Texas at Dallas, USA
Riaz Ahmed Shaikh   University of Quebec-Outaouais, Canada
Ramesh Sitaraman   University of Massachusetts, USA
Giandomenico Spezzano   ICAR-CNR, Italy
Domenico Talia   University of Calabria, Italy
Kerry Taylor   CSIRO, Australia
Jichiang Tsai   National Chung Hsing University, Taiwan
Parimala Thulasiraman   University of Manitoba, Canada
Gennaro Della Vecchia   ICAR-CNR, Italy
Spyros Voulgaris   Vrije Universiteit Amsterdam, The Netherlands
Cho-Li Wang   The University of Hong Kong, Hong Kong
Chen Wang   CSIRO, Australia
Ziyuan Wang   IBM Research and Development, Australia
Qishi Wu   University of Memphis, USA
Bin Xie   InfoBeyond Technology, USA
Lexing Xie   Australia National University, Australia
Chao-Tung Yang   Tunghai University, Taiwan
Norihiko Yoshida   Saitama University, Japan
Rui Zhang   University of Melbourne, Australia
Xiangmin Zhou   CSIRO, Australia
Sotirios Ziavras   New Jersey Institute of Technology, USA

Table of Contents

IDCS: Ad-Hoc and Sensor Networks

IDCS: Internet and Web Technologies

IDCS: Network Operations and Management

IDCS: Information Infrastructure

IDCS: Resilience, Fault Tolerance, and Availability

An Efficient Detection Model of Selective Forwarding Attacks in Wireless Mesh Networks

Shapla Khanam, Habibullah Yusuf Saleem, and Al-Sakib Khan Pathan

Department of Computer Science, International Islamic University Malaysia
Gombak 53100, Kuala Lumpur, Malaysia
{shapla_iiu,habib_2869}@yahoo.com, sakib@iium.edu.my

Abstract. Wireless communications technologies have seen a great degree of advancements and sophistication in the past decade. Different research works have tried to solve various issues related to different wireless Ad hoc networks, many of which are yet to find standardized solutions. Among different classes of Ad hoc networks, Wireless Mesh Networks (WMNs) are becoming a popular choice now-a-days, which offer flexible, fast and inexpensive connectivity for communities, homes, municipalities, and other similar premises. While different research issues are being extensively dealt with for WMN, security flaws and attacks are turning out to be a significant concern as relatively less attention has been dedicated to this topic so far by the research community. Because of the structural formation and mode of operation of WMN, routing security is one of the prime concerns in WMN. An efficient method of detecting selective forwarding attack could largely ensure better and secure routing for which we have taken this as our research motivation. In this paper, we present a model for detecting selective forwarding attacks with a game theory-based approach to analyze the attack model, where the main goal of player 1 is to maximize its throughput and the goal of player 2 is to minimize the throughput of network. In our approach, we also propose a multi-hop acknowledgement based algorithm to analyze and detect the malicious behavior to defend against selective forwarding attacks in WMNs. We present our mathematical model and analyze it in detail to illustrate the efficiency of the proposed approach.

Keywords: Attacks, Behavior, Forwarding, Malicious, Selective, WMN.

1   Introduction

With the rapid advancements of various wireless network technologies, Wireless Mesh Networks (WMNs) have come forward as a usable technology that may bring the dream of a seamlessly connected world into reality [1], [2], [3], [4]. The concept of wireless mesh area network was developed from the idea of next-generation network, where it was expected to make the network available to everyone regardless of the location. Due to the self-configuration and self-healing characteristics of WMN, it is envisioned as a reasonably practical network paradigm to build up a large scale wireless commodity network. In fact, this type of network can easily, effectively and wirelessly connect large geographical vicinity to include cities and municipalities

Y. Xiang et al. (Eds.): IDCS 2012, LNCS 7646, pp. 1–14, 2012.

using inexpensive and existing technologies where traditional networks rely on wired access points or wireless hotspots to connect end users [5], [6]. In WMNs, the network connection is spread out among hundreds of wireless mesh nodes that communicate with each other to share the network across a large area.

The mesh architecture of wireless network concentrates on the emerging market requirements for building networks that are highly scalable and cost effective. However, wireless mesh networks lack efficient security guarantees in various protocol layers [7]. There are a number of factors that come into the consideration. Firstly, all communications go through the shared wireless nodes in WMNs which make the physical security vulnerable. Secondly, the mesh nodes are often mobile, which move to different directions and often change the topology of the network. Finally, since all communications are transmitted via wireless nodes, any malicious node can provide with the misleading topology updates and those updates could spread out over the whole network topology [6], [8].

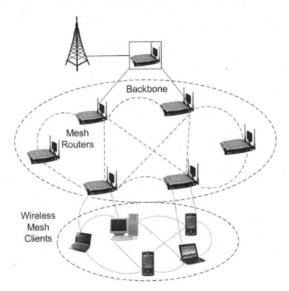

Fig. 1. Infrastructure of a WMN

WMNs consist of mesh routers and mesh clients, where mesh routers form the backbone of the network that provides network access to both the mesh and conventional clients. Mesh clients can either connect (see Figure 1) to a backbone or among each other. Hence, mesh client can access the network through the mesh router in a multi-hop fashion. Therefore, any malicious node can attack the network in the forms of blackhole attack, grayhole attack, and Sybil attack [1], [6]. In all of these attacks, the routing packets are deliberately misled towards wrong destinations or network entities. Once the malicious node or the attacker has control over the packet after getting it in its trap, the packet could be modified, fabricated, dropped, or forwarded (arbitrarily); all of which are considered the major obstacles for secure and guaranteed routing in WMN. Although, based on the precise operational methods, different attacks are given different names to clearly identify them (with slightly different operational methods), most of the routing attacks are related to selective forwarding (or, use it as an underlying method), which means that the received trapped packets are manipulated either to forward selectively (with or without modification or fabrication) or could be dropped. Selective forwarding could be the eventual result of all these attack attempts. Hence, from our analysis of the related issues, we are motivated to focus on mitigating selective forwarding attack by detecting it using some useful and efficient approach.

In this paper, we mainly analyze the selective forwarding attack and propose a solution to tackle it in a WMN setting. We discuss a game theoretic approach to study the performance of mesh topology in the presence of malicious node(s) and propose an algorithm to detect the existence of malicious activities.

The remainder of this paper is organized as follows: related works and motivation are presented in Section 2. Our approach is presented in Section 3. Section 4 contains the analysis and discussion; and finally, Section 5 concludes the paper noting the future directions of research on this topic.

2   Related Works and Motivation

Although many different security schemes have been proposed for wireless mesh networks in recent years, in most of the cases, they are yet to reach satisfactory level. Also, most of these existing works focus on other security issues than selective forwarding attacks. It should be noted that because of the structural and operational differences, the security mechanisms built for other classes of Ad hoc networks may not work directly in WMN in many cases. In this section, we note some previous works which especially focus or influence the security issues in WMN. The limitations of these works have motivated us to devise our approach to deal with selective forwarding attack which has been discussed before.

Lundberg's findings [9] provide useful information about the criteria of a secure routing protocol, types of vulnerabilities and associated types of attacks in the field of Ad hoc routing protocols. The study shows a comparative demonstration of existing routing protocols based on their application requirements. A short analysis of two routing protocols has been exhibited to discuss protective solutions of the information routing system. However, discussion of the possible solutions is not proven and no extensive performance analysis has been provided.

In [7], the authors propose an algorithm to specifically defend against security attacks in WMNs where the algorithm makes use of counter threshold to find threshold value. This threshold value will be compared with the actual number of data packets delivered. If the actual data packet is less than the threshold value, then the route is declared to contain malicious node(s) which implies the packet loss is always due to the malicious node(s). Therefore, the path will be excluded from route selection. However, the packet loss may occur due to other factors such as mobility and battery power. If we keep excluding the route by assuming that the poor performance routes contain malicious nodes, then we may end up with few routes or no routes for communications at the end. This method may work on specific settings but is not efficient to encounter security attacks in dynamic topologies of WMNs.

The authors in [10] advocate using PANA (Protocol for carrying Authentication for Network Access), to authenticate the wireless clients. The PANA model also provides the cryptographic materials necessary to create an encrypted tunnel with the associated remote access router. However, the authentication procedure presented in the paper is tedious and resource-consuming. Although the framework talks about protection of the confidentiality of exchanged information and the overall approach is analyzed, it has not been tested in a detailed manner that could convince the readers about the efficiency of the approach in practical implementation cases.

The authors in [11] propose a framework of non-cooperative zero-sum game between genuine and malicious mesh routers and use mathematical tools and models for their approach. This game model solves the problem of grayhole attack where the malicious node drops a subset of packets that it receives. The game has a source node as the target and malicious node as the attacker; who compete with each other for limited resources and each node gains depending on the strategy of itself and that of the other. The attacker gains benefit from dropping packets and the target gains from forwarding packets successfully. Our approach adopts similar game theoretic model as a part of the total solution. However, the difference is that we circumvent the flaws of this paper's idea by using our own mathematical model and choosing appropriate parameter values. As an example, [11] takes 50% of the packet arrival rate to send buffer based on which the gains of both nodes vary. Therefore, it may be impractical because in reality higher packet arrival rate is expected to minimize packet delay as well as large number of nodes should be involved in communications in any wireless mesh networks.

A novel algorithm named Channel-Aware Detection (CAD) has been adopted in the work presented in [12]. The authors in this paper use two different strategies to detect the grayhole attacks. Their approach detects a potential victim mesh node (i.e., which can be attacked) by hop-by-hop loss observation and traffic overhearing. A comparative performance analysis has been shown to detect and isolate the selective forwarding attackers in multi-hop network scenario. The probability of miss detection or false alarm is analyzed and a design is proposed to limit these to certain threshold. However, the approach is complicated, focuses on narrow set of attacks, and is applicable only in some restrictive scenarios. This work basically focuses on the communication and signaling aspects in physical layer but is related to our work in the sense that some of the ideological concepts helped us in the formulation of our approach, which we will discuss later.

Several attentions have been devoted to investigate the use of cryptographic techniques to secure the information transmitted through the wireless network. Some other preliminary solutions have been addressed in Ad hoc, sensor and wireless mesh networks to prevent different types of malicious attacks [13], [14], [15].

None of the above frameworks, nevertheless, embark upon all the security issues of wireless mesh networks. In fact, most of the previous works deal with security weaknesses related to specific malicious activities. Keeping these in mind, in this paper, we propose a game theoretic approach to analyze the performance of the mesh network and propose acknowledgement based detection model to detect the malicious node in the transmission route. The objective is to defend WMN against selective forwarding attack which could prevent many types of attacks that more or less rely on this particular strategy of dealing with traffic packets.

3   Our Proposed Approach

There are mainly two phases in our proposed approach. The first phase is (i) *Game theory based attack model*, and the second phase is (ii) *Detection of malicious behavior*. The following sub-sections illustrate our approach in detail.

3.1   Game Theory Based Attack Model

Game theory [16] can be defined as the statistical model to analyze the interaction between a group of players, who act strategically. In this section, we propose the first phase of our approach, *game theory based attack model*. Figure 2 introduces a usual attack model where there are two players involved namely Player 1, which is the source node S and Player 2, which is the malicious/attacker intermediate node A. Let D be the destination node and N be the finite set of all players. We limit our game to non-cooperative, incomplete information, where a single player is involved on both sides with no relevant information, for example utility, strategy of its opponents. In this paper, we considered a zero-sum game model where if one player wins then, the other player must lose, equaling to sum of the gain and loss to be zero [17]. The attacker tries to minimize the throughput of the network by dropping the packet. The attacker should spend more than the target to drop any packet and eventually the attacker has to pay heavily for its actions.

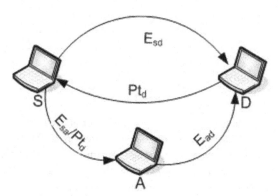

Fig. 2. S sends packet directly and S sends packets via A

Let P_i be the probability to defend the ith node in the network. We assume that v_i is an intermediate node and v_{i-1} and v_{i+1} are the upstream and downstream nodes respectively. The total probability of defending all N nodes is, $\sum_{i=1}^{N} P_i$. The energy spent for utility cost is: $E_{sd} = \sum_{i=1}^{N} P_i$, because the amount of energy is needed as the same amount of probability for defending all nodes. The interaction of different players and their total probabilities are constructed based on their individual probability. The energy probability is the sum of probability of individual nodes or player and their energies.

The remaining energy is: $E_r = 1 - \sum_{i=1}^{N} P_i$ where, $\sum_{i=1}^{N} P_i \leq 1$. Our objective is that the energy that needs to be spent by the attacker in order to compromise the nodes must be more than the energy spent by the target. The energy of the sender to send via the attacker could be noted by the equation: $E_{sa} = \propto \sum_{i=1}^{N} P_i$, where $\propto$ is a constant. The successful attack depends on the value of $\propto$. If $\propto > 1$, the attack succeeds. If $\propto = 1$, the energy spent by the attacker equals to that of the target. When $\propto = 0$, the attacker cannot attack, and $\propto < 1$ means that the attacker cannot drop any packet.

The state of the game is (m, n), where m is the sending buffer of Player 1 and n is the dropping buffer of Player 2. If one packet is present in the sending buffer of m of Player 1, then m will take a value of 1 and n can take value 0 or d, depending on whether any packet is dropped or not. We also denote μ as the probability that a new packet arrives at the sending buffer of Player 1. There are four possible states of the game and they are: $k_1 = (0,0), k_2 = (0, d), k_3 = (1,0), k_4 = (1, d)$. Therefore, the transition probabilities from one state to another state are calculated as follows:

When $(m = 1)$,

$$P_{(m,n)(m+i,n)}(x) = \begin{cases} (1 - \mu)(p_d + p_a q_f) & ; if\ i = -1, n = 0 \\ (1 - \mu)(p_a q_d) & ; if\ i = -1, n = d \\ \mu(p_d + p_a q_f) & ; if\ i = 0, n = 0 \\ \mu(p_a q_d) & ; if\ i = 0, n = d \end{cases} \tag{1}$$

When $(m = 0)$,

$$P_{(m,n)(m+i,n)}(x) = \begin{cases} (1 - \mu) & ; if\ i = 0, n = 0 \\ (\mu) & ; if\ i = 1, n = d \end{cases} \tag{2}$$

where, μ is the arrival rate of packets in the send buffer and x is the joint strategy.

For example, assume that the current state of system is $(1,0)$. Player 1 (i.e, S) has packet in its send buffer. It uses two strategies: transmit packet directly or transmit via A. If S transmits packet directly to D, then the states are $(0,0)$ or $(1,0)$ with probability p_d. Otherwise, it transmits packets via Player 2 (i.e., A) with probability, p_a. A either drops the packet or forwards it to D. If it drops, then the states become $(0, d)$ or $(1, d)$. If A forwards the packet, then the next states will be $(0,0)$ or $(1,0)$. However, any strategy combination which any player chooses is coupled with payoffs and since this is a zero-sum game, the payoffs are calculated as: payoffs of player 1 = - payoffs of player 2.

The strategy set for Player 1 is $S_1 = \{s_1, s_2\}$, meaning that Player 1 forwards the packet either directly to destination D (s_1) or via A (s_2). Mixed strategies that correspond to S_1 are $\pi_s(s_1, s_2) = (p_d, p_a)$, where $p_d + p_a = 1$. The strategy set of Player 2 is $A_2 = (a_1, a_2)$. Mixed strategies corresponding to the action of A_2 are $\pi_a(a_1, a_2) = (q_f, q_d)$ where, $q_f + q_d = 1$. Here, q_d = probability of dropping the packet. Hence, $x = (\pi_s, \pi_a) = (p_d, p_a, q_f, q_d)$.

The destination D gives some points to source S for the transmitted packet. When the source node S sends the packet through the path $S \rightarrow D$, node S receives some points of Pt_d from D. When S transmits packets via A, it receives points of Pt_d from D and it gives A some points, Pt_{sa}. If S does not receive any point from D for the transmitted packet, it means that the packet did not reach to D successfully. Each packet transmission from v_i node to v_{i+1} node causes an energy spending Ev_iv_{i+1}. Therefore, depending on the energy spent and points received by the source and attacker, the nodes S and A will remain with the following net utility:

$$U_s = \begin{cases} Pt_d - E_{sd}; & S \text{ transmits directly to } D. \\ Pt_d - Pt_{sa} - E_{sa}; & S \text{ transmits to } D \text{ via } A. \\ -Pt_{sa} - E_{sa}; & \text{node } A \text{ drops the packet.} \end{cases} \quad (3)$$

If $(-Pt_{sa} - E_{sa}) < (Pt_d - E_{sd}) < (Pt_d - Pt_{sa} - E_{sa})$, the utility of S will decrease if A drops the packet compared to the utility it receives when a packet reaches to D.

$$U_a = \begin{cases} Pt_{sa} - E_{ad}; & A \text{ forwards the packet to } D. \\ Pt_{sa} + \beta; & \text{node } A \text{ drops the packet.} \end{cases} \quad (4)$$

where β is the profit earned by node A. If $(Pt_{sa} - E_{ad}) < (Pt_{sa} + \beta)$, the utility earned from dropping the packet is higher than the utility received from S for transmitting the packet. However, the utility can be calculated from the equations below based on the probability of dropping and forwarding the packets.

$$U_s(x) = \mu(1 - \mu \times p_a q_d)\{p_d(Pt_d - E_{sd}) + p_a(q_f(Pt_d - Pt_{sa} - E_{sa}) + q_d(-Pt_{sa} - E_{sa}))\} + \mu^2 \times p_a q_d\{p_d(Pt_d - E_{sa}) + p_a(q_f(Pt_d - pt_{sa} - E_{sa}) + p_a(q_d(-Pt_{sa} - E_{sa}))\}$$

$$(5)$$

And,

$$U_a(x) = \mu(1 - \mu \times p_a q_d)\{p_a(q_f(Pt_{sa} - E_{ad}) + q_d(Pt_{sa} + \beta))\} + \mu^2 \times p_a q_d\{p_a(q_f(Pt_{sa} - E_{ad}))\} + \mu^2 \times p_a q_d(p_a q_d(Pt_{sa} + \beta))$$

$$(6)$$

3.2   Detection of Malicious Behavior

In this section, we introduce a Multi-hop Acknowledgement Based algorithm to detect malicious node(s) of selective forwarding attack. We know that selective forwarding attack is one of the most dangerous attacks because the packets are dropped randomly which may contain sensitive data. In this algorithm, multiple nodes need to be selected as acknowledgement points in WMNs. This means that those mesh nodes are responsible for sending an ACK packet after receiving a packet from a source node or nearest intermediate source nodes. We assume that the WMNs are operating under an ideal channel quality and majority of the mesh routers are normal-behaving. We are considering that the packet loss appears only due to malicious activity. Moreover, since there may be multiple existing routes from a source mesh node to a destination mesh node and a source node may receive multiple route replies of each of its route requests, we encourage the source node to keep record of each route for future references. It should be noted here that dealing with physical layer or channel-level matters are out of the scope of this work as we focus on the theoretical framework and mathematical model of the operational concept.

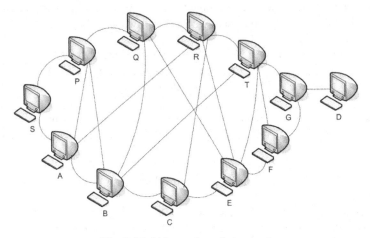

Fig. 3. Multi-hop acknowledgement

In Figure 3, we show the structure of a wireless mesh network where S is the source node and D the destination node. We assume N is the total number of mesh nodes in the forwarding path. M is the number of malicious nodes among N. Let X be the normal-behaving nodes between each two malicious nodes and Y be the number of acknowledgement points in the forwarding path. We consider Z as the percentage of randomly selected check points.

When the source node S sends a route request, it receives several route replies. Let us consider that S chooses the route SABCEFG→D, where E is the malicious node. We are considering two selected acknowledgement points (i.e., Y=2) namely B and F. B and F will acknowledge back after they receive the packets from the source mesh nodes. Therefore, the following possibilities may occur if:

Case 1: One of the nodes is malicious in the forwarding path.
Case 2: One or more nodes are malicious in the forwarding path.
Case 3: Both the Acknowledgement points B and F are malicious
Case 4: Either B or F is malicious.

This algorithm uses two approaches: hop-by-hop loss observation and traffic overhearing to detect malicious node on the path of data flow. More specifically, we assume v_i as an intermediate node and v_{i-1} and v_{i+1} as the upstream and downstream nodes respectively. v_{i+1} receives a packet from v_{i-1}, then it updates itself with the packet count history and with the corresponding packet sequence number and then buffers the link layer acknowledgment (ACKs) that it receives for each packet and then forwards it to v_{i-1} (i.e., upstream node). We denote w_s as the total number of packets that are successfully sent-received by the source S to destination D. $n_{v_i \rightarrow v_{i+1}}$ is the number of packets received successfully by v_{i+1} (i.e., this is the number of successfully received packets from any intermediate node to its downstream node).

Two operations are performed when the mesh router forwards a packet to the downstream node as explained in this paragraph. When each packet is relayed to the downstream traffic, the mesh router or upstream node buffers the ACKs and overhears the downstream traffic to check whether it (downstream node) forwarded or tampered the packet. The upstream node observes these two operations and then makes a simple analysis of the scenario.

The downstream node maintains two parameters. They are; (a) probability of acknowledgment (ACK) which we denote as P_{Ack} and (b) probability of no-acknowledgment (NACK), P_{NAck}. Probability of ACK (P_{Ack}) is computed as $P_{Ack} = 1 - P_{NAck}$ and the probability of no-acknowledgment is computed as $P_{NAck} = (n_t + n_d)/n_f$, where n_t is the number of tampered packets, n_d is the number of dropped packets, and n_f is the number of total forwarded packets.

We introduce two packets: PROBE packet and PROBE_ACK to detect the malicious routers. The PROBE packet is used by the source node S with every w_s data packets to the destination node D. When the source node S sends the PROBE packet through the path, each node in the path marks the PROBE packet with the detection parameters and this is termed *packet marking*. A PROBE packet sent to destination by the source node is also marked by it (i.e., S) with the number of packets that will be transmitted to a particular destination node. When the PROBE packet is passed along the path, each node v_i attaches a mark of its opinion to the downstream node (v_{i+1}). The opinion is calculated by observing the downstream node's behavior by the transmitter node. The opinion of downstream node is calculated as follows:

If ($P_{NAck} > t_m$), it means malicious behavior.
If ($P_{NAck} < t_m$), it means normal behavior.

where t_m is the monitoring threshold and it carries values between 0 and 1. As the PROBE packet is passed through the path, the node also appends the behavior parameter to the PROBE packet. The behavior parameter represents the observation of node v_{i+1} about the behavior of the upstream node, v_i. The behaviour of the node is calculated by determining the loss rate of the packets over the link, v_i to v_{i+1} . It is calculated by the following formulae:

If ($L_{v_i \rightarrow v_{i+1}} > t_l$), malicious behavior is detected.
If ($L_{v_i \rightarrow v_{i+1}} < t_l$), normal behavior.

where, $(L_{v_i \to v_{i+1}} = 1 - (n_{v_i \to v_{i+1}}/n_{v_{i-1} \to v_i}))$ is the loss rate of the link that is observed by the node, v_{i+1} . t_l is the loss rate threshold that can take any value between 0 and 1. The algorithm will detect the malicious behavior with higher probability with the lower values of t_l and t_m.

4   Performance Analysis and Discussion

For the game theoretic analysis, we substititute the values for required energy to transmit packets from S to D either directly or via A and the points earned by source S and A as follows: $E_{sd} = 0.6$, $E_{sa} = E_{ad} = 0.05$, $Pt_d = 1$, $Pt_{sa} = 0.3$. We assume that the packet arrival rate μ to send buffer is quite fast; $\mu = 0.8$, and $\beta = 0.2$. However, the parameter settings are chosen based on probabilities. The closer the probability to one, the higher the utility will be.

Using equation (5) and (6), we obtained the utitilty of Player 1 and Player 2. We represented Figures (4 to 8) of utility of S and A as a function of drop probability using MATLAB. The packet dropping probabilitiy is chosen between 0 and 1. It is observable from the Figures (4 to 8) that the utility of S is decreasing and utility of A is increasing with the increase of dropping probability.

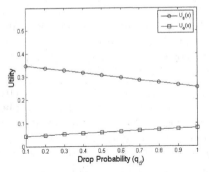
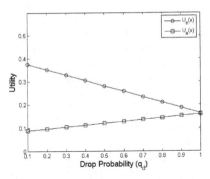

Fig. 4. Increasing the utilities of A and decreasing the utilities of S with respect to different drop probabilities of q_d when $p_a = 0.8$ and $p_a = 0.2$

Fig. 5. Increasing the utilities of A and decreasing the utilities of S with respect to different drop probabilities of q_d when $p_d = 0.6$ and $p_a = 0.4$

Player 2 reaches the maximum utility when source S transfers all the packets via A with the highest dropping probability. It can be seen from Figure 8 where $p_a = 1$ and $q_d = 1$, the maximum utility of $U_a = 0.4$. On the other hand, for $q_d = 1$, Player 1 has its maximum utility $U_s = 0.256$, when the probability of sending packets direcly to D increases. The maximum utility of S is shown in Figure 4 where $p_d = 0.8$ and $q_d = 0.1$. Figures 9 to 13 represent the utility of S and A as a function of forward probability to A, p_a. The forward probability is chosen between 0 and 1.

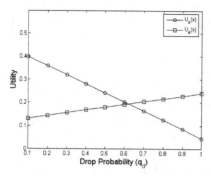
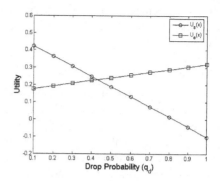

Fig. 6. Increasing the utilities of A and decreasing the utilities of S with respect to different drop probabilities of q_d when $p_d = 0.4$ and $p_a = 0.6$

Fig. 7. Increasing the utilities of A and decreasing the utilities of S with respect to different drop probabilities of q_d when $p_d = 0.2$ and $p_a = 0.8$

The forward probabilities are $q_f = 1$ and $q_f = 0.75$ and the drop probabilities are $q_d = 0$ and $q_d = 0.25$ in the Figure 9 and Figure 10. It is clear that in Figure 9, the utilities of S and A are increasing. The maximum utility of S is 0.5 and the maximum utility of A is 0.2. In Figures (10, 11, 12, 13), the utility of S is overall decreasing (with a slight bent increase and going down) and the utility of A is increasing and the maximum utility of A is 0.4 ; the forward probabilities are, $q_f = 0.75$, $q_f = 0.5$, $q_f = 0.25$, and $q_f = 0$ and the drop probabilities are $q_d = 0.25$, $q_d = 0.5$, $q_d = 0.75$, and $q_d = 1$.

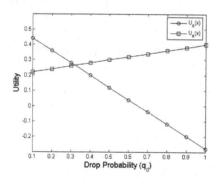
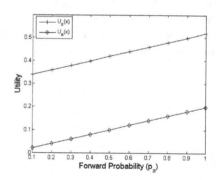

Fig. 8. Increasing the utilities of A and decreasing the utilities of S with respect to different drop probabilities of q_d When, $p_d = 0$ and $p_a = 1$

Fig. 9. The increase of utility S and A as a function of p_a with respect to $q_f = 1$ and $q_d = 0$

All these graph plots show how our mechanism behaves when different parameters have different values. It is understandable that in some cases, it may be unsuitable for communicating via the intermediate node when the utility of S goes down and A gets higher profits.

In the malicious behavior detection phase, the following possible scenarios may occur when the upstream and downstream nodes are combined to detect malicious activities:

Scenario 1: If $P_{NAck_{v_i \to v_{i-1}}} > t_m$ and $L_{v_i \to v_{i+1}} > t_l$.

The node v_i either drops or tampers the packets. The probability of NACK is greater than the monitoring threshold, t_m. The node v_{i-1}, the upstream node will observe node v_i on whether it drops the packets or tampers it. Node v_{i-1} will increase n_d which is the number of dropped packets and also n_t which is the number of tampered packets. The downstream node, v_{i+1} will observe if loss rate is greater than the threshold t_l, loss rate threshold. The upstream and downstream will observe if node v_i is misbehaving.

Scenario 2: If $P_{NAck_{v_i \to v_{i-1}}} < t_m$ and $L_{v_i \to v_{i+1}} > t_l$.

In this scenario, the monitoring threshold is greater than the probability of NACK from node v_{i-1} to v_i. The node v_i is behaving normally. If the observed loss rate of link from v_i to v_{i+1} is greater than the loss rate threshold, node v_i is misbehaving. According to the upstream node, node v_i is normal but on the other hand the downstream node can detect if node v_i is misbehaving. To overcome this problem, we need to verify link layer acknowledgments that is received by the upstream node v_{i-1} for each packet that is forwarded successfully by the node, v_i.

Scenario 3: If $P_{NAck_{v_i \to v_{i-1}}} > t_m$ and $L_{v_i \to v_{i+1}} < t_l$.

In this case, the upstream node v_{i-1} has a greater probability of NACK and is greater than the monitoring threshold, t_m. In this case, there is a misbehaving activity at the node v_i. On the other hand, the observed loss rate link from v_i to v_{i+1} is lower than t_1, which is the loss rate threshold. According to upstream node v_{i-1}, the node v_i is misbehaving and downstream node will consider node v_i as normal. To overcome

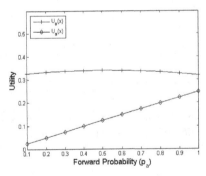 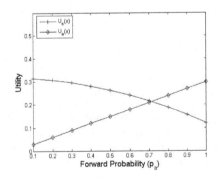

Fig. 10. The increase of utilities S and A as a function of p_a with respect to $q_f = 0.75$ and $q_d = 0.25$

Fig. 11. The increase of utility A and decrease of utility S as a function of p_a with respect to $q_f = 0.5$ and $q_d = 0.5$

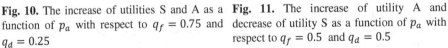

this issue, the upstream node can detect the misbehaving node v_i by observing false information in the PROBE packet.

Scenario 4: If $P_{NAck_{v_i \to v_{i-1}}} < t_m$ and $L_{v_i \to v_{i+1}} < t_l$.
The downstream and the upstream nodes do not detect any misbehaving node.

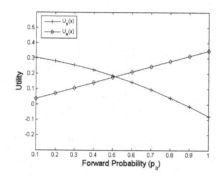
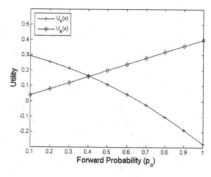

Fig. 12. The increase of utility A and decrease of utility S as a function of p_a with respect to $q_f = 0.25$ and $q_d = .75$

Fig. 13. The increase of utility A and decrease of S as a function of p_a with respect to $q_f = 0$ and $q_d = 1$

5   Conclusions and Future Works

WMNs have gained noticeable attention and emerged as a promising technology recently due to its variety of applications as local area networks, community networks, home and neighborhood network and others. However, the major challenge of these self-organizing networks is the vulnerability to various security attacks. Selective forwarding attack is one of the most difficult ones. In our work, we have formulated a zero-sum non-cooperative game based approach to detect the presence of such attacker(s) in WMNs and we introduced a multi-hop acknowledgment based algorithm to identify the malicious behavior during the transmission of packets. As our future work, we would like to investigate cooperative selective forward attacks in Wireless Mesh Networks.

Acknowledgments. This work was supported in part by NDC Lab, KICT, IIUM projects.

References

1. Pathan, A.-S.K.: Security of Self-Organizing Networks: MANET, WSN, WMN, VANET. Auerbach Publications, CRC Press, Taylor & Francis Group, USA (2010) ISBN: 978-1-4398-1919-7

2. Wireless Mesh Networks and Applications in the Alarm Industry. WhitePaper, AES Corporation (2007), http://www.aes-intellinet.com/documents/AESINT-WhitePaper.pdf (last accessed January 09, 2012)

3. Schrick, B., Riezenman, M.: Wireless Broadband in a Box. IEEE Spectrum Magazine 39(6), 38–43 (2002)

4. Hay, R.: Introduction to Wireless Mesh Networking. Presentation Slides, Canadian Telecommunications Consultants Association, Toronto (April 6-8, 2006), http://home.cogeco.ca/~rmhay/WirelessMeshIntro_20060312.pdf (last accessed January 09, 2012)

5. Bruno, R., Conti, M., Gregori, E.: Mesh Networks: Commodity Multihop Ad Hoc Networks. IEEE Communications Magazine 43(3), 123–131 (2005)

6. Akyildiz, I.F., Wang, X.: A survey on wireless mesh networks. IEEE Communications Magazine 43(9), S23–S30 (2005)

7. Shila, D.M., Anjali, T.: Defending Selective Forwarding Attacks in WMNs. In: IEEE International Conference on Electro/Information Technology 2008 (EIT 2008), Iowa, USA, May 18-20, pp. 96–101 (2008)

8. Deng, H., Li, W., Agrawal, D.P.: Routing Security in Wireless Ad Hoc Networks. IEEE Communication Magazine 40(10), 70–75 (2002)

9. Lundberg, J.: Routing Security in Ad Hoc Networks. Helsinki University of Technology, HUT TML, Tik-110.501 Seminar on Network Security, 1–12 (2000)

10. Cheikhrouhou, O., Laurent-Maknavicius, M., Chaouchi, H.: Security Architecture in a Multi-hop Mesh Network. In: 5th Conference on Safety and Architectures Networks, SAR 2006, Seignosse, Landes, France, pp. 1–10 (June 2006)

11. Shila, D.M., Anjali, T.: A Game Theoretic Approach to Gray Hole Attacks in Wireless Mesh Networks. In: Proc. IEEE MILCOM, San Diego, CA, November 16-19, pp. 1–7 (2008)

12. Shila, D.M., Cheng, Y., Anjali, T.: Channel-Aware Detection of Gray Hole Attacks in Wireless Mesh Networks. In: The Proceedings of IEEE Globecom 2009, Honolulu, HI, USA, November 30-Decemebr 4, pp. 1–6 (2009)

13. Parno, B., Perrig, A., Gligor, V.: Distributed Detection of Node Replication Attacks in Sensor Networks. In: Proceedings of the 2005 IEEE Symposium on Security and Privacy (S&P 2005), May 8-11, pp. 49–63 (2005)

14. Sanzgiri, K., Dahill, B., Levine, B.N., Shields, C., Belding-Royer, E.M.: A Secure Routing Protocol for Ad Hoc Networks. In: Proceedings of the 10th IEEE International Conference on Network Protocols (ICNP 2002), November 12-15, pp. 78–87 (2002)

15. Salem, N.B., Hubaux, J.P.: Securing Wireless Mesh Networks. IEEE Wireless Communication 13(2), 50–55 (2006)

16. Srivastava, V., Neel, J., MacKenzie, A.B., Menon, R., DaSilva, L.A., Hicks, J.E., Reed, J.H., Gilles, R.P.: Using game theory to analyze wireless ad hoc networks. IEEE Communications Surveys & Tutorials, Fourth Quarter 2005 7(4), 46–56 (2005)

17. Javidi, M.M., Aliahmadipour, L.: Game theory approaches for improving intrusion detection in MANETs. Scientific Research and Essays 6(31), 6535–6539 (2011)

Effective Ad Hoc Social Networking on OLSR MANET Using Similarity of Interest Approach

Teerapat Sanguankotchakorn[1], Shradha Shrestha[1], and Nobuhiko Sugino[2]

[1] School of Engineering and Technology, Asian Institute of Technology, Thailand
teerapat@ait.asia, shres.shradha@gmail.com
[2] Interdisciplinary Graduate School of Science and Engineering,
Tokyo Institute of Technology, Japan
sugino.n.aa@m.titech.ac.jp

Abstract. Recently, social networking over MANETs has attracted the attention of research community, due to its flexibility, cost saving and infrastructure-less architecture. However, various problems namely, to efficiently find nodes of similar interest and network partition, exist in such environment. For enabling ad hoc social networking in an intermittent network scenario, Delay Tolerant Network (DTN) emerges as one of the solution. This paper proposes a novel algorithm allowing users to find friends of similar interest both in their neighborhood and in entire network by using DTN on OLSR MANET. We investigate and compare the similarity of users interest using four similarity metrics: Cosine Similarity, Jaccard, Correlation and Dice Coefficient. We simulate the algorithms assuming that users change their interest at fixed and random time (normal and uniform distribution). The simulations results show that Cosine Similarity provides the highest number of similar interest matching. In addition, by implementing the proposed algorithm on DTN with the normal distributed users interest-changing time, the success ratio of finding matches increases significantly.

Keywords: MANETs, OLSR protocol, ad hoc social networking, interest matching, similarity metrics, DTN (Delay Tolerant Network).

1 Introduction

A large number of people have colossal interest in social networks over past several years. Social networking applications like Facebook, Twitter, Hi5, Google+, MySpace, etc., have millions of participants, for sharing information, making friends and etc. Such online applications and social networking services rely on infrastructure connectivity. However, in practice, rather than pre-established social network, there exists a wondrous need of constructing social networks that rely upon opportunistic connections between mobile devices.

When it comes into social networking, abundant people are associated with web-based social networking services. These social sites are pre-built networks

Y. Xiang et al. (Eds.): IDCS 2012, LNCS 7646, pp. 15–28, 2012.

implemented on central server. These types of social networking are mainly operated in somewhat pre-registering mode. In addition to these conventional networks, there exists a social networking enabling people to communicate with each other on demand without the need of Internet or infrastructure, called ad hoc social network. Usually, this type of social network is implemented on infrastructure-less network such as Mobile Ad Hoc Network (MANET). Ad hoc social network is, therefore, a MANET consisting of wireless devices (called nodes) equipped with Wi-Fi and Blue-tooth, which can move freely in any direction and are connected with each other via some similar social patterns such as interests. Ad hoc social networks implemented on MANET are useful mainly due to the following reasons: (a) It can be implemented in any places where deployment of network infrastructure is expensive/not possible, (b) It is free of charge, if this feature was added in any wireless devices (mobile-phones, laptops, etc.). Since people can easily share their information with each other around them in the ad hoc manner. This would be a remarkable contribution.

The major objective of ad hoc social network is to find persons for a given user whose interest is best matching. The network should be embedded with the efficient and smart enough algorithm to search friends of similar interest for each given user. There are several methodologies proposed to discover friends of similar interest in ad hoc environment [1]~[7]. Most of the existing proposal has adopted the complicated algorithm leading to the high computational complexity, low success ratio of finding the similar interest matching and high energy consumption. One of the good example is the semantic-based social network[2].

The motivation of this research is to provide the efficient and simple algorithm in searching the matching of the people who have the same interest in ad hoc social network under realistic situation given that the ad hoc social network is implemented mainly on the MANET which usually has the energy constraint.

Therefore, the contribution of this work is the framework allowing the users to identify their interest and to find the people on the social network who have the similar interest using the simple and efficient algorithm in the ad hoc manner. In addition, four well-known computation schemes namely, Cosine Similarity, Jaccard Coefficient, Correlation and Dice Coefficient are verified and compared within the same environment to find the most efficient one. The environment considered here is quite realistic, that is, the cases where the users' Interest Changing Time are fixed, randomly normal distributed and uniform distributed. The proposed system is implemented on typical MANET OLSR network and MANET OLSR with DTN in order to find the most efficient one. Based on our proposed algorithm, the success ratio of finding the match can be improved without any modifications to the existing protocols. Finally, the cost of implementation in terms of query overhead comparing to the existing algorithm is also illustrated.

This paper is structured as follows: Section 2 describes the related previous works. Section 3 describes the proposed system model, algorithm as well as the similarity computation techniques. Section 4 provides the detailed parameters and simulation scenarios while the simulation results and discussion are provided in section 5. We conclude our work in section 6.

2   Related Works

Recently, many ideas and prototypes regarding the ad hoc social networks have been developed and deployed. The prototypes are mainly implemented on touch screen mobile phones supporting the ad hoc IEEE 802.11b. We can list some prototypes as follows:

In year 2008, a prototype of a social networking application to operate in a multi-hop ad hoc network [6] was proposed. The demonstration for this prototype is carried out using three Motorola e680 mobile phones executing on an embedded Linux platform. In the same year, Rahnama, H., et al,[4] proposed a novel architecture based on peer-to-peer communication procedure. It is capable of creating matching engine to search without any user participation and without the need of any centralized architecture. The user interface is developed on a Java enabled mobile phone. In year 2009, some software platforms such as AdSocial [5] and MobiClique [3] were proposed. In AdSocial, a user can search for friends with matching interest using only strings. AdSocial has been deployed using 10 to 15 Nokia N810 Internet Tablets based on OLSR routing protocol to establish multi-hop ad hoc network environment. In the same year, a first semantic-based social network called MobiSN (Mobile Social Network) [2] was proposed. Users can search friends of similar interest, share resources, browse profile and send text messages using semantic-based matchmaking method as a searching mechanism. The prototype is fully implemented using 12 SonyEricssonK750 phones in Java 2 Micro Edition (J2ME).

In year 2010, a social ad hoc networking system called TWIN [7] was implemented. It supports various applications namely detection of nearby users, multimedia sharing, community-based communication, search friends of common interest, chat, radar view of other users, event log view and message board services. 250 users were employed in the field study of TWIN. In year 2011, Lee, J., and Hong, C.S. [1] proposed a novel system utilizing the information from users' mobile devices to form an ad hoc social network. The information from mobile device refers to URLs browsed, images or file downloaded by user are used to identify users interest. To determine the similarity between users, the vector space model and cosine similarity are adopted. The simulation of the system has been carried out using Omnet++.

3   System Model

3.1   Proposed OLSR HELLO Message and Similarity Index Computation Procedure

In order to build ad hoc social network on MANET, it is necessary that nodes should be able to find the other nodes with the similar interest. In OLSR, HELLO message is generally generated every 2 seconds (default value) to discover neighbors and for link sensing [8]. In this work, the interest of any users are carried in the "Reserved" field within the HELLO message without any modification of the original message format as shown in [9].The mechanism of building such a network using HELLO message can be divided simply in 3 steps and the detailed Similarity Index computation in each step can be described as follows:

(i) Exchange the Interest using HELLO message
  - Node A sends HELLO message carrying its interest to node B, B, then, computes similarity index of their interests for four main categories, namely Sports, Movies, Shopping and Food by using defined measurement metrics.

(ii) Determine Similarity Index at Category Level
  - If the similarity index is greater than pre-defined threshold value, B will checks the similarity for sub-category of matching category, else B discards the message.
  - If they are categorically matched, the normalization of weights of categories will be performed to determine category of interest.
  - In normalization process, each category set is divided by the highest weight of each individuals interest (note: the highest weight of As interest may not be equal to highest weight of Bs interest). That is, each category of node As interest is divided by node As highest weight and similarly for node B.
  - Then, normalized values of each category are summed up such that the category with the highest sum is considered to be the one that both nodes are interested in.

(iii) Determine Smilarity Index at Subcategory Level
  - Next, for interested categorical event, the similarity between their respective sub- categorical values is determined by using defined measurement metrics.
  - Again, if similarity index is greater than pre-defined threshold value, then we perform normalization to determine their present interest in the same way as we perform to judge the common interest in the category level.
  - Finally, we can judge the similarity in the sub-category level. If similarity is found, node B sends response message to node A, otherwise, node B discards HELLO message sent by A.

3.2   Interest Matrix

In this work, we propose to define the individuals current interest profile by using the two-dimensional vector space as shown as an example in Table 1. The assignment of interest into vector for all nodes is done randomly to build their interest matrix without destructing defined vector laws. Each individuals interests are categorized into four main categories: Sports, Movies, Shopping and Food. Each of these categories is further sub-divided into four sub-categories.

The main interest categories vector $I = \{Sports, Movies, Shopping, Foods\}$ is defined. And we define the weight of users interest level on them as $W_I = \{w_1, w_2, w_3, w_4\}$ such that $\sum w_i = 1$. Similarly, for sub-categories of each category, we represent them as vector, $I_{sub} = \{I_{sub1}, I_{sub2}, I_{sub3}, I_{sub4}\}$ and define

Table 1. An Example of Interest Matrix with their Weights (in parenthesis)

Sport (0.1)	Football (0.5)	Basketball (0.3)	Swimming (0.1)	No Interest (0.1)
Movies (0.2)	Drama (0.4)	Sci-Fi (0.4)	Horror (0.0)	No Interest (0.2)
Shopping (0.5)	Mall-X (0.7)	Mall-Y (0.2)	Mall-Z (0.1)	No Interest (0.0)
Foods (0.2)	Pizza (0.2)	KFC (0.2)	Subway (0.2)	No Interest (0.4)

users interest level on them as $W_{sub} = \{w_{sub1}, w_{sub2}, w_{sub3}, w_{sub4}\}$ such that $\sum w_{subi} = 1$.

In general, the interest of people changes with time. To be more realistic, therefore, we consider two scenarios of users Interest Changing Time (ICT): fixed time (5, 10, 15 minutes) and random time (uniform and normal distribution) in two type of networks: OLSR and OLSR+DTN to determine efficiency of the similarity computation metrics.

3.3   Interest Similarity Index Computation

When a node receives a HELLO message, it extracts the interest matrix of sender node and compares with its own interest. To determine the similarity of the users' interest, we investigate four similarity measurement metrics namely, Cosine Similarity, Jaccard Coefficient, Correlation and Dice Coefficient defined as follows:

$$Cosine\ Similarity = \frac{\sum_{i=1}^{N} A_i B_i}{\sqrt{\sum_{i=1}^{N} A_i}\sqrt{\sum_{i=1}^{N} B_i}} \tag{1}$$

$$Jaccard\ Coefficient = \frac{\sum_{i=1}^{N} A_i B_i}{\sum_{i=1}^{N} A_i^2 + \sum_{i=1}^{N} B_i^2 - \sum_{i=1}^{N} A_i B_i} \tag{2}$$

$$Correlation = \frac{N \sum_{i=1}^{N} A_i B_i - \sum_{i=1}^{N} A_i \sum_{i=1}^{N} B_i}{\sqrt{\left[N \sum_{i=1}^{N} A_i^2 - \left(\sum_{i=1}^{N} A_i\right)^2\right]}\sqrt{\left[N \sum_{i=1}^{N} B_i^2 - \left(\sum_{i=1}^{N} B_i\right)^2\right]}} \tag{3}$$

$$Dice\ Coefficient = \frac{2 \sum_{i=1}^{N} A_i B_i}{\sum_{i=1}^{N} A_i^2 + \sum_{i=1}^{N} B_i^2} \tag{4}$$

Where N is the total number of nodes in the network, A_i and B_i denotes the interest of node A and node B, respectively.

4   Simulation Scenarios and Parameters

4.1   Simulation Network Scenarios

In ad hoc networking, due to the absence of centralized server, node discovery has always been a great challenge. In our system, we have implemented and simulated two network scenarios:

- OLSR only: a node can compare its interest only with its 1-hop neighbors.
- OLSR+DTN: the store-and-forward mechanism, where each node keeps record of previously interacted nodes, is implemented. When a node meets another node, in addition to HELLO message and its interest, it also forwards the interests of previously interacted nodes. If receiving node has already encountered any of these nodes before, then it ignores that corresponding nodes interest. when interest of any node changes, its records of previously met nodes are discarded.

The interest of nodes usually changes periodically. In this work, we consider three types of ICT (Interest Changing Time): Fixed, Normal and Uniform Distribution.

4.2   Simulation Parameters

The proposed system is simulated using Network Simulator (NS2). The simulation parameters are shown in Table 2. The simulation results are illustrated with 95% confidence interval.

Table 2. Simulation Parameters

Parameters	Value		
Area (sq.m)	1000 x 1000		
Node Placement	Random		
No. of Node (N)	2, 5, 10, 15, 20, 30, 40, 50		
Speed of Node (V) (m/s)	1, 3, 5, 8, 10, 15, 20, 30		
Transmission Range of Node (m)	250		
Interest Changing Time (ICT) (min)		Fixed	Random
		5, 10, 15	Normal and Uniform Distribution in the range [0,30] with mean=15 and standard deviation (SD)= 8
Node Pause Time (s)	0		
Threshold Value	0.5		
Simulation Time (min)	60		
No. of Simulation per Data point	20		

4.3   Performance Evaluation Matrix

The following two metrics are used:

- **Similarity Index:** the similarity measurement metric that can efficiently discover the similarity between two corresponding nodes.
- **Success Ratio:** the times that any node finds another node with common interest in the network. Mathematically, it can be represented as follows:

$$Success\ Ratio = \frac{Number\ of\ Matches\ found}{Number\ of\ Message\ sent} \qquad (5)$$

In OLSR network, total number of message refers to the total number of HELLO messages generated by all nodes in the observation period. Every node broadcasts a HELLO message every 2 seconds (default value) to all its neighboring nodes at once. Even though there is not any neighbors for a node, HELLO message is still broadcasted. Therefore, in considering the total number of messages in the network, the number of broadcasted HELLO messages that are not received by any nodes should also be put into account. This is called overhead.

5   Results and Discussion

5.1   Similarity Index

Here, we show the result graph of Similarity Index of four kinds of similarity measurement metrics. In general, we can say that among the four measurement metrics, the best metric is considered to be the one that is capable to find the highest number of matches (similarity index) of the users.

- **Similarity Index vs Speed of Nodes**

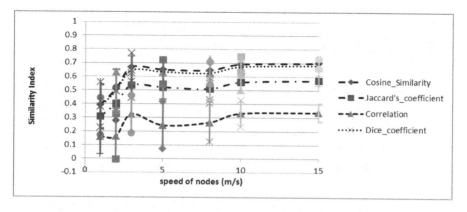

Fig. 1. Similarity Index vs Speed of Nodes (V) (No. of Nodes=2)

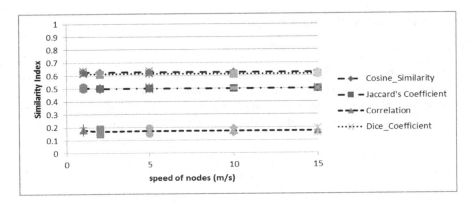

Fig. 2. Similarity Index vs Speed of Nodes (V) (No. of Nodes=20)

Fig. 1 shows various similarity measurement metrics versus speed of nodes. When number of node is 2, it is apparent that similarity index increases with nodes mobility. Since, when speed of node increases, the opportunity of inter-action between two nodes also increases. This results in increasing number of matches found. However, when the density of node increases to some certain level, as shown in Fig. 2, regardless of speed of node, the chances of node encountering the other nodes are almost identical. That is, in dense network, opportunistic meeting of nodes doesnt depend on node mobility but depends highly on number of nodes. This fact is confirmed by the results illustrated in Fig. 3.

• **Similarity Index vs Number of Nodes**

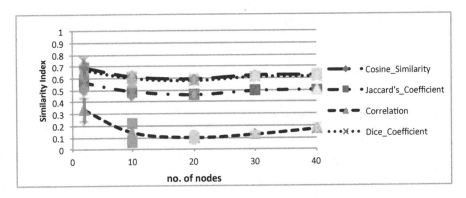

Fig. 3. Similarity Index vs No. of Nodes (Speed = 10 m/s)

According to simulation results illustrated in Fig. 1 and 2, it is found that Cosine Similarity has the highest similarity index, followed by Dice Coefficient, then Jaccard Coefficient and finally Correlation. If similarity index is greater

than threshold value, then nodes are said to be matching. When value of similarity index is higher, any users can find more friends whose interests are similar
and have more chance to interact with them. Thus, we can conclude that Cosine
Similarity performs better in finding relevant friends than the other metrics.

5.2   Success Ratio

Here, two types of network: typical OLSR an OLSR with DTN are considered.
Within each type of network, we perform the simulations based on two scenarios
of ICT: fixed time (ICT=5, 10, 15 minutes) and random time (Normal and Uniform Distribution) in OLSR network with and without DTN. However, since all
the results of the fixed ICT have the same trend, therefore, we illustrate only the
result of fixed ICT=10 minutes. In addition, we actually perform simulations by
varying the speed of nodes. However, since all results also have the same trend
for different speed, therefore, we show the results only at speed 10 m/s here.

- **Network with only OLSR**

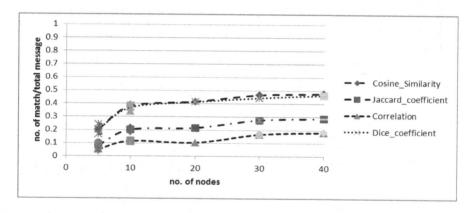

Fig. 4. Success Ratio vs No. of Nodes (Speed = 10 m/s), ICT=15

From Fig.4-Fig.6 which illustrate the simulation results of network with only
OLSR, it is obvious that the success ratio of all type of ICT distributions (fixed,
normal and uniform distribution) follow the same trend. That is, the success
ratio increases with the increasing number of node and it almost un-changes
when the number of node is large enough. Because nodes have large opportunity
to interchange the interest profile when the density of node is large. In addition,
it is found that Cosine Similarity is capable of finding highest number of matches
in the network. The next is Dice Coefficient, Jaccard Coefficient and Correlation,
respectively. All four metrics are capable of finding more matchings in network
when number of node increases.

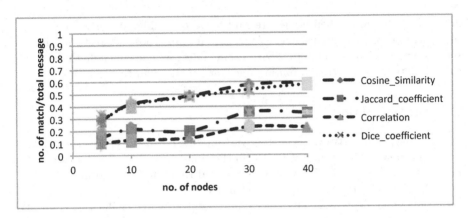

Fig. 5. Success Ratio vs No. of Nodes (Speed = 10 m/s), ICT=Normal Distribution

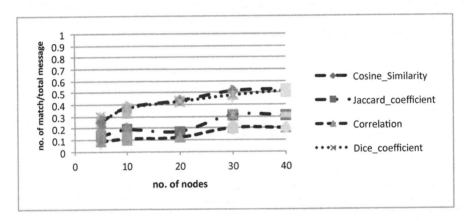

Fig. 6. Success Ratio vs No. of Nodes (Speed = 10 m/s), ICT=Uniform Distribution

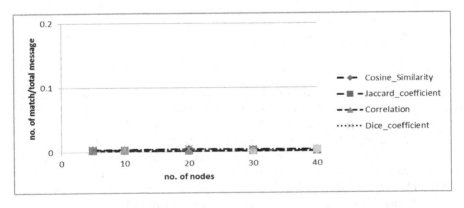

Fig. 7. Success Ratio vs No. of Nodes (Speed = 10 m/s), ICT=15

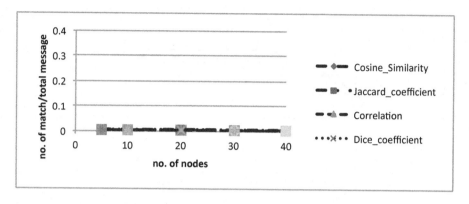

Fig. 8. Success Ratio vs No. of Nodes (Speed = 10 m/s), ICT=Normal Distribution

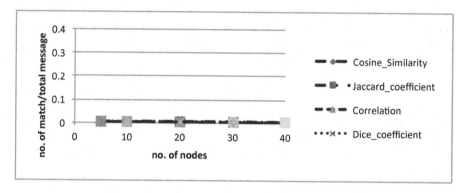

Fig. 9. Success Ratio vs No. of Nodes (Speed = 10 m/s), ICT=Uniform Distribution

• Network with OLSR+DTN

In Fig.7-Fig.9 which illustrate the success ratio of the OLSR implemented on DTN. It is obvious that the success ratio of OLSR implemented with DTN is very low regardless of the ICT distribution (fixed, normal and uniform distribution). Because, in this network, when any sender node receives interest profiles of its neighboring and the other nodes that sender node had previously interacted with, if receiver has already heard from any of these nodes before, then it discards their messages. The process of interest comparison of each node with remaining nodes finishes within a short period of time and the number of matches found is unchanged. However, HELLO messages are still generated continuously from each node in every 2 seconds. As a result, the number of matches will be much lower than that of number of messages generated.

To study the effect of nodes mobility on a network performance, we illustrate only the results of Cosine Similarity, because it outperforms the other metrics as shown in the previous simulation results.

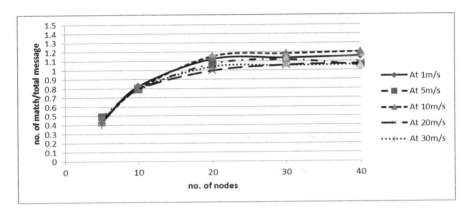

Fig. 10. Cosine Similarity Index: Success Ratio vs No. of Nodes

From Fig.10, we can conclude that number of matches is irrelevant with speed of nodes, but depending on number of nodes in the network.

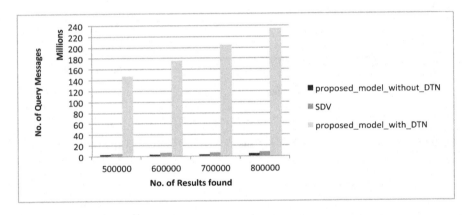

Fig. 11. Query Overhead (with and without DTN) comparing to SDV [2]

Fig. 11 compares the Query Overhead of our proposed model (with and without DTN) with the method implemented in [2]. It is found that Query Overhead of our proposed model without DTN is smallest while it is largest in case of with DTN. The reason, as explained previously, is due to continuously generated HELLO messages.

6   Conclusion and Future Works

In this research, we consider an ad hoc social networking in OLSR MANET. We proposed an algorithm that is simple and efficient to find persons of similar interest for any user. We implement and investigate four types of similarity index computation namely, Cosine Similarity, Jaccard Coefficient, Correlation and Dice Coefficient in network with only OLSR and OLSR+DTN. We evaluate the performance of our proposed algorithm using two evaluation metrics: Similarity Index and Success Ratio. Among these four metrics, Cosine Similarity is found to be the most effective one. In addition, it is found that the Success Ratio of finding matches of interest by using store-and-forward mechanism of DTN is very low and irrelevant with the model of ICT (fixed, normal and uniform distribution). Since, no matters the model of ICT is, the number of queries increase drastically while number of matches remains almost unchanged. This results in very small success ratio.

In this work, we have simulated scenarios for pause time of 0 seconds. Further performance evaluation and analysis can be done on varying pause time of nodes. In addition, only the concept of interest matching in an intermittent network is considered. The virtual communication or implementation of system in real life environment can be performed to evaluate the effectiveness of the proposed algorithm.

Acknowledgement. The authors wish to thank National Institute of Information and Communication Technology (NICT), Japan for providing funding to support this research.

References

1. Lee, J., Hong, C.S.: A mechanism for building Ad-hoc social network based on users interest. In: The 13th Asia-pacific Network Operatens and Management Symposium (APNOMS 2011), pp. 1–4 (2011), doi:10.1109/APNOMS.2011.6076997
2. Li, J., Khan, S.U.: MobiSN: Semantics-Based Mobile Ad Hoc Social Network Framework. In: The IEEE Global Telecommunications Conference (GLOBECOM 2009), pp. 1–6 (2009), doi:10.1109/GLOCOM.2009.5425993
3. Pietiläinen, A.-K., Oliver, E., LeBrun, J., Varghese, G., Diot, C.: MobiClique: middleware for mobile social networking. In: Proceedings of the 2nd ACM Workshop on Online social Networks, pp. 49–54. ACM, New York (2009), doi:http://doi.acm.org/10.1145/1592665.1592678
4. Rahnama, H., Madni, A.M., Sadeghian, A., Mawson, C., Gajderowicz, B.: Adaptive context for generic pattern matching in ad hoc social networks. In: The 3rd International Symposium on Communications, Control and Signal Processing (ISCCSP 2008), pp. 73–78 (2008), doi:10.1109/ISCCSP.2008.4537195
5. Sarigöl, E., Riva, O., Stuedi, P., Alonso, G.: Enabling social networking in ad hoc networks of mobile phones. Proc. VLDB Endowment 2(2), 1634–1637 (2009), Retrieved from http://dl.acm.org/citation.cfm?id=1687553.1687611
6. Smith, N., Bonta, J.: Prototype of a social networking application in a multi-hop autonomous ad hoc network. In: The 5th IEEE International Conference on Mobile Ad Hoc and Sensor Systems (MASS 2008), pp. 535–537 (2008), doi:10.1109/MAHSS.2008.4660081

7. Väänänen-Vainio-Mattila, K., Saarinen, P., Wäljas, M., Hännikäinen, M., Orsila, H., Kiukkonen, N.: User experience of social ad hoc networking: findings from a large-scale field trial of TWIN. In: Proceedings of the 9th International Conference on Mobile and Ubiquitous Multimedia, pp. 1–10. ACM, New York (2010), doi:http://doi.acm.org/10.1145/1899475.1899485

8. Kas, M.: OLSR-Aware Cross-Layer Channel Access Scheduling in Wireless Mesh Network. Thesis of degree in Master of Science, Bilkent University (June 2009)

9. Clausen, T., Jacquet, P.: Optimized Link State Routing Protocol (OLSR), Experimental, Project Hypercom, INIRIA (October 2003)

Distributed Algorithms for the Creation of a New Distributed IDS in MANETs

Paulo M. Mafra[1], Joni da Silva Fraga[1], and Altair Olivo Santin[2]

[1] Departamento de Automação e Sistemas
Pós-Graduação em Engenharia de Automação e Sistemas
Universidade Federal de Santa Catarina (UFSC)
Caixa Postal 476 – CEP 88040-900 – Florianópolis – SC – Brazil
{mafra,fraga}@das.ufsc.br
[2] Pontifícia Universidade Católica do Paraná (PUC-PR)
R. Imaculada Conceição, 1155 – CEP 80215-901 – Curitiba – PR – Brazil
santin@ppgia.pucpr.br

Abstract. A great effort for the development of new communication technologies has been witnessed in the last decade. Among these new technologies are the Mobile Ad Hoc networks (MANETs), which form highly dynamic environments without the presence of concentrator units. As this new technology depends upon the cooperation of his entities for transmission and routing, any malicious or faulty node can spoil all the communication in these environments. Intrusion detection systems (IDS) have been applied as a possible solution. However, the proposed IDSs do not tolerate the presence of malicious or faulty nodes among the IDS nodes. Most of the studies in the literature does not employ the use of cryptographic mechanisms in the communication of IDS nodes, even if this communication depends on the cooperation of nodes that do not belong to the IDS. In this paper we propose a set of distributed algorithms for an IDS model that can support the presence, up to a established threshold, of malicious or faulty nodes at any IDS level. We employ distributed systems and fault tolerance techniques together with cryptographic mechanisms to detect and punish malicious or faulty nodes. We describe the proposed model, making a comparison with major efforts in the literature on distributed intrusion detection systems for MANETs and present the results of tests obtained with an implementation of the proposed model.

1 Introduction

The last decade has witnessed a great evolution in communication technologies such as the Mobile Ad Hoc Networks. In this technology, there are no concentrator units and the environment is highly dynamic with nodes entrances and departures at any time [1]. However, such technology is susceptible to a great variety of attacks. The challenge that arises is to maintain the mobile ad hoc networks free from the activity of malicious or faulty nodes. In the face of the

Y. Xiang et al. (Eds.): IDCS 2012, LNCS 7646, pp. 29–42, 2012.

difficulty of avoiding the effects of malicious activities, mechanisms are necessary to at least minimize such effects. Intrusion detection systems (IDSs) can be used as one of these mechanisms [2]. The key question in these IDSs is to ensure that applications in mobile Ad Hoc environments can always evolve despite of failures, attacks by malicious entities or their own mobility.

Works in this area deals mainly with problems applied to routing protocols in MANETs (mobile ad hoc networks)[3] and some works focus on problems of malicious behavior [2,3,4,5]. These works are limited to monitoring the communications in MANETs and the proposed IDS models usually have centralized elements and do not admit intrusions in their elements. There are no mechanisms to protect their own information.

The communication among entities in MANETs can be monitored by distributed components of an IDS in order to detect faulty or malicious behavior and to improve security and reliability of these dynamic environments. In this paper we propose a secure and fully distributed IDS model for mobile Ad Hoc networks. We apply concepts of distributed systems and dependability. The use of these concepts allows, within certain limits, the construction of an IDS less subject to restrictions than those present in other IDS models. The algorithms presented in this paper define an IDS with functions performed by sets of components (fully distributed executions) and with mechanisms and techniques that are tolerant to malicious activities of their own components.

The greatest contribution of this study, separating it from others present in literature, is the use of distributed systems concepts and dependability concepts applied to develop a new IDS model for MANETs. The use of these concepts permitted - within certain limits - the development of a model less subject to restrictions. The proposed system is able to deal with various faulty or malicious nodes without there being interference in the network's normal behavior. Unlike the other works in literature, this IDS also uses cryptographic mechanisms to guarantee the messages authentication between IDS elements. IDSs normally developed for MANETs, in the literature do not have mechanisms to protect their own information and do not tolerate intrusions into its various components. The approach introduced in this paper aims to build an IDS infrastructure that tolerates malicious actions. Beyond this, our system is able to identify a large number of different attacks or variations of known attacks. In section 2 we describe the IDS organization, defining its components and their roles in the proposed model. In section 3 we introduced the algorithmic base that supports our secure IDS. In section 4 we present an analysis of the costs involved in the communication of IDS nodes and some results of performed tests in a simulator. Following (section 5), related work are presented and compared to our propositions. We finally present our conclusions and future studies.

2   Architecture Description

Communication protocols in MANETs depend upon collaboration from equipment which form these network nodes. As such, we also assume this collaborative environment. However, we do not limit this collaboration. I.e. all the network nodes participate in the intrusion detection. The proposed IDS model is distributed and should assume a hierarchical stratification in order to attend the diverse IDS functions. The differentiation of functions and their distribution among nodes in this collaborative environment establish two classes of nodes: the "leader nodes", which perform higher level functions such as analysis; and the "collector nodes", which assume lower level functionalities such as sensors, collecting data for future analysis. We also assume that all the network nodes possess at least $2f + 1$ neighbors, where f is the failure or intrusion limit that our algorithms should support[1].

2.1 Topology and Component Description

The hierarchical topology of the model introduces the idea of clusters, as well as in [3,4]. However, in our model, we consider each cluster to have various "leaders". These various leaders form what we denominate as "leadership". The leaders are chosen by its connectivity and available energy, but if it is necessary to maintain the number of $2f + 1$ leaders, any node could be chosen as a leader. These leaders which form a leadership in a cluster use "secure channels" to exchange information and alerts among themselves. The collecting nodes send a summary of the data collected to the leaders also through "secure channels". The leadership which define the domains of a cluster are instituted based on $2f + 1$ leaders. Leadership and, consequently, the corresponding cluster no longer exist as of the moment in which a leadership has less than $2f + 1$ leaders.

The collecting nodes constitute the largest part of the cluster. In order to belong to a cluster, the collecting nodes need to possess secure channels with at least $f + 1$ leaders of the cluster. It is also assumed that communication among the collecting nodes (messages which do not belong to the IDS) occur in an insecure manner. The IDS messages are always encrypted and authenticated in secure channels ("collector - leader" and "leader - leader"). The data collected by the collectors always considers its neighborhood. I.e. the collecting nodes capture the data from each neighbor and store the information in them for subsequent dissemination in leadership. This information may be, for example, the quantity of packets received and sent by the neighboring node i.

The leader nodes analyze the data sent by the collecting nodes related to the same cluster. Based on the analysis of this monitoring information, they make their decisions concerning malicious nodes. These decisions are in turn registered in local lists (ex. malicious nodes list) and later shared, compared, and synchronized with the remaining leader nodes which make up the same leadership of the corresponding cluster. Since the leadership has at least $2f + 1$

---

[1] This limit f is used in our approach of a threshold for the occurrence of abnormalities which, once they are not surpassed, the IDS and its distributed functions will continue to supply the correct and expected behavior. At this limit, malicious and faulty nodes present in the cluster and further, departures of nodes out of a predefined period are accounted for.

leaders, the same choice of $f + 1$ leaders about the behavior of a given node is sufficient for this decision to be considered by the leadership.

2.2   Cryptographic Mechanisms

IDS communication, which occurs among (collector - leader) and (leader - leader) cluster nodes makes use of cryptography. Encrypting messages is done with the use of session keys and symmetric encryption. Key distribution involves the public keys (pair of asymmetric keys) for each participating node. The public key of each node is signed by the committee that manages the system, generating a certificate for node's authentication. These asymmetric cryptography keys are one of the prerequisites for any participating node in the system and in the IDS.

The leadership also authenticates its messages. These leadership authentications are founded in the threshold signature scheme (TSS) [6]. The public key of the leadership (E_l) will always be known by all the cluster nodes and is used in verifying leadership signatures. The corresponding private key (D_l), used to generate the leadership signatures, possesses guaranteed secrecy through threshold cryptography. In other words, the key D_l is not available in any moment in the system. Its use is through a K set of partial keys ($|K| = m, K = SK_1, SK_2, ..., SK_m$) derived from D_l using threshold cryptography. In this model, generating and verifying partial signatures is completely non-interactive, without needing messages exchanges to execute these operations. In the proposed IDS, each one of these m partial keys is delivered to a specific leader from leadership. Any operation with D_l is only possible through the participation of at least $f + 1$ leaders and their partial keys, this ensures that for each signature the malicious nodes need one non-malicious node which is not possible. These keys are generated during the activation of a cluster, executing an algorithm for distributed key generation [7]. The public key of the leadership, used to verify the signatures generated, is available in any cluster node.

2.3   The System Dynamics

Collectors send data monitoring summaries to leadership. Such data is sent upon concluding a time period called the transmission time (Tt). The leaders analyze the data sent from collectors at the end of each (Tt). We call epoch the periods in which each cluster "freezes" its composition. In other words, during one epoch it is assumed that the composition of the cluster does not change. At each epoch there are several data collections (several Tt's). The transmission time (Tt) occurs n times in each epoch ($Tt = epoch/n$).

The changes which occur in the system during this period are not updated. I.e. possible system changes (within an epoch) such as faults, node entrances or departures, node exclusion, etc. are not taken into consideration in composing the cluster during that time. At the conclusion of each epoch, the cluster must synchronize itself. Thus, the updating round (UR) is initiated. These updating rounds define a time period where cluster leaders exchange information in order to update their knowledge concerning the present state of the cluster. Therefore,

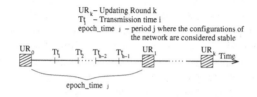

Fig. 1. Temporal relation among updating rounds

in each synchronizing period (one updating round), the changes that occur in the cluster at last epoch are considered. Then, the composition for the new epoch is defined. During these updating rounds are also defined new roles for cluster nodes. The decisions taken during updating rounds will always depend upon the agreement of $f + 1$ leaders. The ratio of these periods of time is illustrated in Figure 1. At the end of the UR a new epoch is initiated.

3   Algorithmic Support for the IDS

We developed a set of distributed algorithms to provide for the proposed model an infrastructure that allows the IDS to tolerate up to f malicious nodes.

3.1   Data Analysis

Data analysis is performed in each updating round. This analysis takes into account available data from neighbors of a node and is implemented based on the system OctopusIIDS [8]. Each leader makes the analysis of each network node based on the data that it received from collectors. If the statistical analysis of $f + 1$ nodes points node i as suspect, then it is considered suspect by the corresponding leader.

This analysis is done by all the leaders present in a leadership. The comparison (through the exchange of encrypted and authenticated messages) among the results obtained in analysis from these leaders is made concrete as well as in the leadership. The results obtained by these comparisons will be considered by the cluster as a whole. With $f + 1$ leaders agreeing upon the analysis results, these results will be considered by the leadership. If there are at least $2f + 1$ leaders, the cluster will always decide upon any analysis result, even in the presence of f malicious leaders.

3.2   Data Dissemination

Each leader will only be connected to a cluster if it possesses routes to at least $f + 1$ leaders of that cluster, just as any node in the network. In order to the messages reach leadership, there must always be dissemination in leadership based on the correct leader. [9] proposed a dissemination algorithm. Based on that algorithm, our $Disseminate()$ works as follows. A node j disseminates a message msg_j in the

Leadership$_j$ which corresponds to its knowledge about the leaders that form the cluster's leadership. Upon receiving the message msg_j, each leader in turn sends it to its respective leadership knowledge. In this algorithm, at least one correct leader is reached with each resend, which returns to disseminate the message once again, using the recursion of the *Disseminate()*. As each leader is connected to at least one correct leader and if the cluster leadership does not form disjointed graphs, then the majority of leaders will be reached through such dissemination.

3.3   Synchronizing Periods: Epoch Times, and Updating Rounds

In order to deal with the dynamic aspects of the network and collecting data for the detection process, it was necessary to define times which determine the synchronization of the actions distributed throughout the system. As we work essentially with time periods, synchronizing the clocks is not necessary for the nodes to initiate synchronized operations. Using their local clocks, the periods are controlled with their respective deadlines with timers which aid corresponding operational activation.

At these synchronizing periods it is stipulated a period d and at the end of this period a leader node start sending a *sync* message to the leadership. Upon receiving this message, the node saves it and checks how many *sync* messages he has received from different leaders. If the number of messages is greater than $f + 1$ then this node sends again a *sync* message for the other nodes in order to force them to get in synchronizing period, if they still have not received $f + 1$ messages. After this last send, the sender starts participating in the updating round (UR).

3.4   Transmission Times

Algorithms for the activities corresponding to transmission time (Tt) periods and updating round (UR) periods were defined. In the $Tt()$ algorithm, a deadline in which each collector node must send a summary of collected data during the last period (time between Tt -1 and Tt) to the leadership was established through the Disseminate() protocol (lines 4-9 of algorithm 1). Upon receiving the message, the leader node verifies if the message is not older and saves it (lines 10-12). If the number of received messages in this Tt were greater or equal to the number of collectors minus f or if the *timeout* has been achieved (line 13), then the leader node sets the reached timeout and starts analyzing each cluster node by checking in the received data if the node is suspect by most of its neighbors (lines 14-19). In such case, this suspected node is inserted into the list of suspects from that leader node (lines 17-18).

In this system, for the purpose of estimating the time when the majority of messages sent by collectors arrive at leader nodes, we apply an adaptive timeout that can auto-adjust over time. This adaptive timeout is based on the timeout used in TCP protocol proposed by Jacobson [10]. In it, each sent message involves the sender estimating a time interval to receive of an acknowledgment from the destination. This adaptive timeout is implemented in the *EstimatedTime()*

Algorithm 1. Tt(Tt_i)

```
1: Init :
2:     γ ← time()
3:     Collected_data_l, suspects_List_l ← ∅

4: upon ((time() − γ) ≥ p) at node i do                    % p is the period between two Tts
5:     if (i ∈ Collectors_i) then
6:         Disseminate(< monitoring_data_i, Tt_i, γ_i, id_i >, Leadership_i)
7:         Tt_i ← Tt_i + 1
8:         γ_i ← time()
9:     end if

   % leader l receives data from collector i
10: upon receive(< monitoring_data_i, Tt_i, γ_i, id_i >) at l : l ∈ Leadership_i) do
11:     if Tt_i = Tt_l then
12:         Collected_data_l ← Collected_data_l ∪ {< monitoring_data_i, Tt_i, γ_i >}
13:         if (| Collected_data_l | ≥ | Collectors_l | −f) ∨ ((time() − γ_i) ≥ timeout) then
14:             reachedTimeout ← (time() − Tt_i ∗ p)
15:             for all node n ∈ Cluster(Leadership_l) do
16:                 analysis_l^n ← Data_Analysis(Collected_data_l, id_n)
17:                 if analysis_l^n ∈ is_suspect then
18:                     suspects_List_l ← suspects_List_l ∪ {id_n}
19:             end for
20:             Tt_l ← Tt_l + 1
21:             Collected_data_l, suspects_List_l ← ∅
22:             timeout ← EstimatedTime(timeout, reachedTimeout)
23:         end if
```

function, in which the observed error from last timeout was first calculated and the next value for the timeout then estimated.

3.5 Updating Rounds

An updating round (UR) is defined as a period of time where the cluster nodes update their views about the cluster. This view is composed by a set of lists (malicious nodes, leaders, collectors, etc). During these URs, the information about suspected nodes is shared among cluster leaders. In an UR node entrances and departures are also processed. Following, we explain how UR() works.

In UR() algorithm the list of suspects generated from last epoch during (Tts) is sent to other leaders through the Disseminate() protocol. Upon receiving this list, the leader node checks if the message is not older. If the number of received messages is greater than or equal to $2f + 1$, then the leader node executes the function *identifies_Suspect()* in which an analysis of each node is performed searching for nodes reported to be suspicious by at least $f + 1$ leaders. These nodes are included in the malicious node's list of the leader. In the sequence, the leader node disseminates a message asking for the election of a new coordinator. These messages are saved and when the number of messages reaches $(| Leadership | /2) + 1$, a leader is elected as coordinator.

The coordinator then processes the node entrance and departure requests in the cluster, generates a new view of the cluster (with new nodes) and broadcasts this view to all the nodes in the cluster. Upon receiving the new view of the cluster, it checks the message validity. If the message is valid then the node updates its view and its list of neighbors, starting a new epoch. If it is not valid, a message asking for new coordinator is spread throughout leadership again. The algorithm (UR) were not included in this paper because it is very extensive.

3.6 Route Discovery and Update

In this model we adopted the DSR routing protocol [11], an on demand routing protocol widely used in MANETs with a local routing cache. We adapted the DSR algorithm to update the local routing cache, inserting $f + 1$ disjoint routes[2] to the leadership.

Algorithm 2. RouteUpdate(Leadership$_i$) at node i

1: **Init**
2: $\quad Routes_i, RouteCache_i, newLeadership_i \leftarrow \emptyset$

3: **for all** $l \in Leadership_i$ **do**
4: $\quad RouteCache_i \leftarrow RouteDiscovery(l)$ % finds all routes from i to l
5: $\quad$ **for all** $r_{il} \in RouteCache_i$ **do**
6: $\quad\quad$ **if** $(l \notin newLeadership_i)$ **then**
7: $\quad\quad\quad newLeadership_i \leftarrow l$ % add l to new leadership
8: $\quad\quad$ **if** $\exists \, r_{il} : disjointRoute(r_{il}, Routes_i)$ **then**
9: $\quad\quad\quad Routes_i \leftarrow Routes_i \cup r_{il}$ % add route r_{il} in $Routes_i$
10: $\quad\quad\quad$ **if** $i \in Collectors_i$ **then**
11: $\quad\quad\quad\quad$ **if** $| Routes_i | \geq f + 1$ **then**
12: $\quad\quad\quad\quad\quad$ **exit**   % get out, the number of routes is enough
13: $\quad\quad\quad\quad$ **end if**
14: $\quad\quad\quad$ **end if**
15: $\quad\quad$ **end for**
16: **end for**
17: $updateDSRRoutes(Routes_i)$ % update local cache used by DSR
18: $Leadership_i \leftarrow newLeadership_i$ % update the list of leaders

---

This adapted algorithm (Algorithm 2) also updates the list of leaders from the node that is running it. In this algorithm, all the existing routes from i to a leader l are obtained (through the Route Discovery mechanism in the DSR). If the node that is running this algorithm is a leader, it attempts to get the maximum number of disjoint routes to the leadership as possible ($f + 1$ at least). Otherwise (the node is a collector), it gets just $f + 1$ disjoint routes[3].

3.7 Identification, Entrance, and Departure of Nodes

The node identification process in the network should be secure enough so that it cannot create multiple identities. Thus, it is possible to prevent attacks like the Sybil [12]. In our model, node identification is carried out with the use of certificates. A certifying authority (CA) considered to be known and reliable by the network nodes generates a certificate for the public key for each node when it joins the system. The role of the CA in our model is assumed by a certifying

---

[2] A set of routes that only have the initial node in common are considered disjoint.
[3] The collector nodes need to reach just one correct leader that will disseminate the message through the leadership.

entity[4]. With this model, we may define the user and his/her equipment. There will not be users using multiple equipment on the network.

Algorithm 3. Entrance of node i into the cluster

```
1:   CN_i ← neighborsUpdate()                          % node i updates its neighbor's list
2:   broadcast < REQIN, id_i, cred_i > to j                          % broadcast REQIN

3: upon receive < REQIN, id_i, cred_i > at node j do
4:     if VerifiedSignature(cred_i) ∧ (i ∉ black_List_j) then    % node j verifies the credentials of i
5:         Disseminate(< REQIN, id_i, cred_i >, Leadership_j)
6:         if (j ∈ Leadership_j) ∧ (< REQIN, id_i, cred_i >∉ inactive_nodes_j) then
7:             inactive_nodes_j ← inactive_nodes_j∪ < REQIN, id_i, cred_i >
8:     end if                          % node i wait for a response of the leadership in next UR

9: upon receive < view, tUR_l, id_c > at node i do
10:     if VerifiedValidity(cert_i : cert_i ∈ view.certificates) then
11:         if i ∈ view.Lead then
12:             role_i = leader
13:         else if i ∈ view.Col then
14:             role_i = collector
15:         end if
16:         black_List_i ← view.black_List
17:         Leadership_i ← view.Lead
18:         Collectors_i ← view.Col
19:         listNeighbors_i ← (neighborsUpdate() ∩ view.Col ∪ view.Lead\view.black_List)
20:         RouteUpdate()
21:         tUR_i ← view.tUR_l + 1
22:         Tt_i ← view.Tt_l + 1
23:         Synchronization(tUR_i)                       % starts a new epoch synchronized
24:         Tt(Tt_i)
25:     end if
```

Algorithm 3 presents the steps involved to insert a new node within a network cluster. Upon entrance, a new node i must update its list of neighbors (through the function $neighborsUpdate()$) and broadcast an entrance request message (REQIN). A neighbor, upon receiving REQIN, verifies the message signature and if the node is not in black list. If the verification succeeds, it disseminates the message to the leadership and saves a copy of it. This message, which should reach the cluster leadership informs its identification (node id) and its credential (its public key in certificate form) (lines 2-7 of algorithm 3). The new node i, upon receiving the new view of the leadership verifies the view's validity and initializes its view of the cluster, assuming the role assigned to it by the leadership[5]. After that, the new node update its list of neighbors and routes to the leadership, its counters of transmission time and updating round, executes the synchronization algorithm and starts a transmission time (lines 9-25 of algorithm 3).

Algorithm 4 presents the steps that involve the departure of a node from the system. In this algorithm, the node that want to leave the cluster, disseminate a message REQOUT to the leadership. Upon receiving the message, each leader node adds the message in a list of leaving nodes (*leaving_nodes*). In the next UR,

---

[4] This certifying entity will not necessarily need to be an official PKI. It may be a system management commission, an administrator, etc.

[5] The role of a new node is defined based on the need of leaders to maintain the cluster, node's connectivity and available energy.

Algorithm 4. Departure of node i

1: $Disseminate(< REQOUT, id_i, cred_i, tUR_i >, Leadership_i)$

2: **upon receive** $< REQOUT, id_i, cred_i, tUR_i >$ **at** node l **do**
3:     **if** $l \in Leadership_i$ **then**
4:         $leaving\_nodes_l \leftarrow leaving\_nodes_l \cup \{< REQOUT, id_i, cred_i >\}$
    % node i waits a response from leadership in next UR
5: **upon** $receive < view, tUR_l >$ **at** node i **do**
6:     **if** $VerifiedSignature(cert_i : cert_i \in view.certificates))$ **then**
7:         node i leaves the system
8:     **end if**

---

when the node that want to quit receive the new view, it checks the signature and can then leave the system. The entrances and departures of the system are always considered during periods of updating rounds. If a node leaves the system disrespecting this process, in the middle of an epoch, the system will consider it as a malicious node.

4   Results and Corresponding Analysis

4.1   Communication Costs

The communication costs of the algorithms proposed in this model depend principally upon the size of the cluster and its leadership. As such, we calculate these costs in terms of the messages sent from each algorithm. Table 1 presents these costs for each algorithm, in which: n is the number of nodes; l is the number of leaders in the cluster; c represents the number of collectors in the cluster. We adopted the limit of $f = (l - 1)/2$. In other words, the number of malicious or faulty nodes is half minus one of the cluster's leader nodes (it is the limit of anomalies that the IDS supports to operate properly). In this calculation, we also assume the costs of the cryptographic mechanisms, presented in [13].

Table 1. Communication costs

Entrance of a node in the network	$c + (l^2 + 10l + 1)/4$
Transmission time (Tt)	$cl/2 - c/2 + (l^2 + 2l + 1)/4$
Updating Round (UR)	$(l^3 + 2l^2 + l)/4$

In the entrance process of a node in the network (Algorithm 3), this node sends a request to his neighbors (c in the worst case). Upon receiving the request, each neighbor node resends the request to the other leaders of leadership using the protocol Disseminate(). The cost of this protocol is given by $D = (f+1)*(f+1)$ where $f = (l-1)/2$. In this calculation, we arrive at $D = (l^2 + 2l + 1)/4$. Thus, the total cost for a node gets into the network is then $(c+D)$, or $c+(l^2+2l+1)/4$. In calculating the costs for transmission time (Tt), each collecting node sends a message with monitoring data to $f + 1$ leaders and the first leader to receive the message executes the Disseminate() protocol. As such, we arrive at $c*(f+1)+D$. Through substitution, we arrive at $cl/2 - c/2 + (l^2 + 2l + 1)/4$. In calculating an updating round, each leader disseminates, into the leadership, a message containing the result of its analysis concerning each cluster node $(l * D)$ or $((l^3 + 2l^2 + l)/4)$.

Based on this calculation we can estimate the costs (in terms of messages) for the entrance operations of a network node, transmission time and updating rounds. With the use of communication cost information obtained, it is always possible to find more adequate values for the number of leaders in a cluster. In a 100-node network forming merely one cluster, the ratio between adequate leaders and collectors should be approximately 20 leaders. We note that as of 20 leaders, the ratio between the number of necessary messages for updating round operations (UR) grow exponentially. This same behavior is not noticed when the considered algorithms are transmission time (Tt) and entrance of a new node into the network. This algorithms are not as dependent on their costs in terms of messages as the updating round regarding the size assumed for the leadership.

4.2   Implementation and Tests

We performed tests to verify the simulated limits the system would support. This tests were performed through the Omnet++ version 4.1 simulator with a Mixim version 1.1 wireless network module in a 300 x 400 meter rectangular environment. The period for transmission time was established at 60 seconds, and each epoch's time was set at 300 seconds. These amounts were obtained based on simulator tests, in such a way as to not saturate the system with messages generated during transmission times and updating rounds. The total simulation time was limited to 6010 seconds (20 URs). This total time was found to be sufficient to observe the proposed model's results. The node mobility rate in mps (meters per second) was defined at 2.0 mps. These values are similar to those employed in [14] where tests with MANETs were performed.

The malicious activity was defined considering that nodes with malicious behavior fulfill their functions in randomly routing messages. In other words, sometimes they transmit, other times they omit messages in routing. This behavior in our simulations follows a uniform distribution, in which 80% of the cases of the messages are discarded by the malicious nodes. In the other 20%, they participated in routing correctly. We chose this type of behavior as it is more difficult to detect than simply a node which discards all the messages it receives, or than nodes which retransmit only to similar (routing messages merely to a list of nodes which possess the same behavior pattern).

In these tests we measure the rate of messages lost in communications (collector - leader) and (leader - leader). This showed us the network's behavior in terms of failures. Following that, we observe message delivery in leadership as to the use of the Disseminate() protocol. In other words, we observe whether a message is delivered within leadership when it arrives to at least one correct leader sent through its leadership knowledge of the cluster and after that, each leader in $Leadership_j$ fulfilling the algorithm resends the messages to its leadership knowledge. Finally, we verify the detection rate of the system's malicious nodes. In order to obtain data measured, three tests were carried out: the first

100 nodes were used (Table 2), the second and third began with 100, but then varying node entrances and departures rates (Tables 3 and 4).

Table 2. Results of tests

Observed Feature	0% mal.	10% mal.	20% mal.	30% mal.	20% surp. f	30% surp. f
Loss of messages	6.52%	13.56%	20.63%	29.67%	29.69%	35.43%
Disseminated msg	100%	100%	100%	99.99%	99.68%	98.03%
Detection rate	100%	100%	100%	96.03%	95.08%	91.26%

In the first test, three distinct conditions were observed: without malicious nodes; 10%, 20%, and 30% of the malicious nodes respecting the $2f+1$ leadership limit; and with 20% and 30% of the malicious nodes, but keeping the leadership set at 10% (surpassing the f limit). The results of this test are presented in Table 2. This test showed us that even with the occasioned loss of messages through network problems, node mobility, or malicious activity, the message dissemination rate among leaders remained very close to 100% (even when the f limit was surpassed). Consequently, the malicious activity detection rate was rather high. As such, even exceeding the limits supported by the presently proposed model, the system continues to work without the guarantee of message delivery.

Table 3. Results of tests without malicious nodes

Observed Feature	5% dep.	10% dep.	15% dep.	20% dep.
Loss of messages	5.0%	5.09%	14.53%	15.91%
Disseminated msg	100%	100%	93.66%	92.06%
Detection rate	100%	100%	97.13%	97%

In the second and third tests, two distinct conditions were observed, respectively, without malicious nodes and with 10% of the malicious nodes (therefore, respecting the $2f+1$ leader limit in leadership). In these tests, we adopted a fixed entrance of nodes at 10% to each updating round, but varying the departure in 5%, 10%, 15%, and 20%. With these tests, we observed the system's behavior with the node entrances and departures. The results of these tests are presented in Table 3 and Table 4.

Table 4. Results of tests with 10% of malicious nodes

Observed Feature	5% dep.	10% dep.	15% dep.	20% dep.
Loss of messages	11.94%	11.41%	20.46%	22.71%
Disseminated msg	100%	100%	93.37%	93.05%
Detection rate	100%	100%	97.07%	96.73%

Through these tests, we were able to observe that system message loss was greater with 10% malicious nodes than without any. However, the rate of messages spread throughout leadership was similar (with 10% maliciousness, and without any). We also observe that with a departure rate greater than its entrance rate, some messages were not widespread among leadership. This may be explained by the low network density over time. With such density, the nodes possess fewer connections. As a result, some messages may not arrive to any correct leader (the probability of this happening increases with reduced network density). In the detection rate factor, one observes behavior similar to message diffusion rates. If some messages are not spread throughout leadership, the detection system will end up erring. Finally, we judge the set of tests to be satisfactory and that it evidences the limits and effectiveness of our proposals.

5   Related Studies

Intrusion detection systems for MANETs were proposed in [3,2]. These systems use clusters to collaboratively detect intrusions. Each cluster possesses a leader which monitors all the traffic within its cluster. These studies have not used cryptography in message exchange, thus making it possible for various types of attacks to occur in the intrusion detection process. Nor have these systems assumed their leaders were alone in their clusters, with malicious behavior.

In another IDS [15], the node which detects suspect activity requests opinions from its neighbors concerning this suspect activity. After analyzing each neighbor's vote, the node makes a decision and informs it to the participating nodes who voted. However, this voting mechanism is vulnerable to message violation from and collusion with malicious nodes. In another study [16], a node hierarchy organizational model was developed on various levels, where the lowest level collects the data and the higher levels correlate the data sent to them. This study, to the contrary of the others cited here, permits the detection of several malicious nodes at the same time. However, the malicious nodes may only belong to the lower levels of the proposed hierarchy. In our proposal, any node may have malicious behavior, whether leaders or collectors. The only limitation to guarantee efficiency in our model is that the number of malicious nodes cannot exceed the f limit.

Studies concerning IDS for MANETs show that the majority of the systems proposed are capable of identifying few types of attacks or some routing protocol problems for these networks [5]. In our proposal we adopted a detection model based on anomalies. Thus we are able to identify and neutralize a large set of types of attacks and routing problems described in literature. Just as the architectures presented in [2,3,16], our model also assumes a hierarchical stratification. In these models, the hierarchical topology introduces the idea of clusters. The majority of studies in literature do not deal with the entrance aspects, departure aspects, or node mobility within the network. In no related study were we able to find simulated test results or real environment test results. In [3] a time period was established for the network to reorganize itself, in which the leaders could be re-elected through a voting process. Merely some of the IDS presented ([17,16]), indicate the use of cryptographic mechanisms to secure properties such as authenticity, confidentiality, and the integrity of messages exchanged between the IDS nodes.

6   Concluding Remarks

In this paper, we presented our efforts to develop an IDS model for dynamic environments together with distributed algorithms that support this model. This proposal is centered on a hierarchical malicious behavior detection model for

MANETs. This model follows the concepts of dynamic distributed systems, permitting the presence of various non-malicious entities. We presented the complexity of the proposed algorithms in terms of messages (calculating the number of messages necessary for each operation). The proposed model permits the correct functioning of the network while the faulty or malicious node limit is not exceeded. However, tests showed us that even with the f limit exceeded, the system continues to function. In such a case, there is no guarantee that our algorithms always work correctly. The prototype developed, base on the proposed model, shows the viability of this model. Unfortunately, we were not able to find other related studies in IDS mobile ad hoc networks which presented simulation tests or real environment tests to serve as a comparison for the results obtained.

References

1. Djenouri, D., Khelladi, L., Badache, A.: A survey of security issues in mobile ad hoc and sensor networks 7, 2–28 (2005)
2. Kachirski, O., Guha, R.: Effective intrusion detection using multiple sensors in wireless ad hoc networks, 1–8 (January 2003)
3. Ahmed, E., Samad, K., Mahmood, W.: Cluster-based intrusion detection (cbid) architecture for mobile ad hoc networks, Australia, pp. 1–11 (May 2006)
4. Bononi, L., Tacconi, C.: Intrusion detection for secure clustering and routing in mobile multi-hop wireless networks. Int. J. Inf. Secur. 6(6), 379–392 (2007)
5. Nadeem, A., Howarth, M.: Protection of manets from a range of attacks using an intrusion detection and prevention system. Special Issue on Mobile Computing Technologies of Telecommunication System Journal, 1–12 (2011)
6. Shoup, V.: Practical threshold signatures, pp. 207–220. Springer (1999)
7. Pedersen, T.P.: A Threshold Cryptosystem without a Trusted Party. In: Davies, D.W. (ed.) EUROCRYPT 1991. LNCS, vol. 547, pp. 522–526. Springer, Heidelberg (1991)
8. Mafra, P.M., Moll, V., da Silva Fraga, J., Santin, A.O.: Octopus-iids: An anomaly based intelligent intrusion detection system. In: ISCC, Italy, pp. 405–410 (2010)
9. Chandra, T., Toueg, S.: Unreliable failure detectors for reliable distributed systems. J. ACM 43(2), 225–267 (1996)
10. Jacobson, V.: Congestion avoidance and control. SIGCOMM Comput. Commun. Rev. 18(4), 314–329 (1988)
11. Johnson, D.B., Maltz, D.A., Broch, J.: DSR: The Dynamic Source Routing Protocol for Multi-Hop Wireless Ad Hoc Networks. Addison-Wesley (2001)
12. Vora, A., Nesterenko, M., Tixeuil, S., Delaët, S.: Universe detectors for sybil defense in ad hoc wireless networks. CoRR abs/0805.0087 (2008)
13. Pereira, F.C., da Silva Fraga, J., Custódio, R.F.: Self-adaptable and intrusion tolerant certificate authority for mobile ad hoc networks. In: AINA (2008)
14. Böse, J.H.: Atomic transaction processing in mobile ad-hoc networks. Master's thesis, Freie Universität Berlin (2009)
15. Razak, S.A., Furnell, S.M.: Friend-assisted intrusion detection and response mechanisms for mobile ad hoc networks. Ad Hoc Netw. 6(7), 1151–1167 (2008)
16. Sterne, D., Lawler, G.: A dynamic intrusion detection hierarchy for manets. In: Sarnoff Symposium, SARNOFF 2009, pp. 1–8. IEEE (April 2009)
17. Zhang, Y., Lee, W., Huang, Y.: Intrusion detection techniques for mobile wireless networks. ACM/Kluwer Wireless Networks Journal 9(5) (September 2003)

Practical Privacy for Value-Added Applications in Vehicular *Ad Hoc* Networks

Lei Zhang[1], Qianhong Wu[2,3], Bo Qin[2,4], and Josep Domingo-Ferrer[2]

[1] Shanghai Key Laboratory of Trustworthy Computing,
Software Engineering Institute
East China Normal University, Shanghai, China
[2] UNESCO Chair in Data Privacy, Dept. of Comp. Eng. and Maths
Universitat Rovira i Virgili, Tarragona, Catalonia
[3] Key Lab. of Aerospace Information Security and Trusted Computing
Ministry of Education, Wuhan University, School of Computer, China
[4] Department of Maths, School of Science, Xi'an University of Technology, China
`leizhang@sei.ecnu.edu.cn`, {`qianhong.wu,bo.qin,josep.domingo`}`@urv.cat`

Abstract. Advances in mobile networking and information processing technologies have triggered vehicular *ad hoc* networks (VANETs) for traffic safety and value-added applications. Most efforts have been made to address the security concerns while little work has been done to investigate security and privacy for value-added applications in VANETs. To fill this gap, we propose a value-added application, specifically, a security and privacy preserving location-based service (LBS) scheme for VANETs. For each LBS transaction, the scheme provides authentication, integrity and non-repudiation for both the service provider and the user. A user can obtain the service in an anonymous way and hence user privacy is well protected. However, a tracing procedure can be invoked to find malicious users, thereby efficiently preventing users from abusing the anonymity provided by the system.

Keywords: Information security, Vehicular *ad hoc* networks, Location based service, Conditional privacy.

1   Introduction

Vehicular *ad hoc* networks (VANETs) consist of computers mounted on vehicles and road infrastructures, and they are emerging as the first commercial mobile *ad hoc* networks. This kind of networks allow vehicle-to-vehicle and vehicle-to-roadside communications by means of on-board units (OBUs) installed in each vehicle as well as roadside units (RSUs) deployed alongside roads. The development of VANETs is expected to improve traffic safety and management efficiency by allowing information on current traffic conditions to be shared in quasi-real time; obvious benefits will be driver assistance, traffic management, and handling of traffic jams and emergencies. To this end, a large body of proposals (e.g. [7,10,15,16]) have been proposed to guarantee trustworthiness of vehicle-generated messages and address the security concerns in VANETs.

Y. Xiang et al. (Eds.): IDCS 2012, LNCS 7646, pp. 43–56, 2012.
© Springer-Verlag Berlin Heidelberg 2012

In addition to safety applications, VANETs may enable a broad range of value-added applications. Among them, LBSs are expected to open substantial business opportunities. However, to let LBSs be widely deployed in VANETs, specific security and privacy requirements have to be met. For instance, any LBS user should be authentic and any transaction must be non-repudiable to guarantee that providing LBSs is profitable. Also, user privacy[1] should be ensured against a malicious LBS provider to prevent maliciously tracing or profiling users. In traditional wired networks, sophisticated cryptographic technologies have been developed to protect parties in value-added applications including LBSs. However, all these protocols are only suitable for a full connectivity scenario. VANETs are very dynamic and their communications are volatile, which makes those complex protocols unsuitable.

Related Work. In recent years, a number of papers have dealt with security and privacy in VANETs [7,10,15,16]. However, few efforts have been made to address the security and privacy issues of value-added applications attracting drivers to use VANETs. To fill this gap, Sampigethaya et al. [12] proposed a scheme called AMOEBA. In their scheme, the group concept is introduced to provide anonymous access to LBSs and prevent a malicious service provider from profiling any target vehicle. However, as remarked by the authors, there are several limitations left unsolved in their scheme. For instance, due to the dynamic and volatile connections in VANETs, the groups in this kind of networks might be hard to maintain. Even if the group can remain, the privacy of the group leader is sacrificed to achieve privacy for the group members, because the leader has to continually reveal his identity and locations. Also, the use of the leader as a proxy for LBS access implies lack of end-to-end connectivity between the service provider and group members. Their scheme relies on public key cryptography in the PKI (public key infrastructure) setting and pseudonyms are required to achieve anonymity. However, no details are provided to manage these anonymous certificates for vehicles, which has been shown to be an obstacle to achieve practical anonymity in VANETs. Finally, their scheme does not provide anonymity revocability, which may not suit some applications in which anonymity must be revoked for the prevention, investigation, detection and prosecution of serious criminal offences.

In [14], the authors presented a secure data downloading (a specific LBS application) protocol in VANETs. This protocol overcomes the weaknesses in [12]. However, in [14], a single authority is employed to authenticate the vehicles and issue private/public key pairs for vehicles. Therefore, the system has the bottleneck of generating the key pairs for all the vehicles. Further, to download the data, the protocol requires five rounds of communication. Hence, it is not suited for real time applications. In [6], an anonymous batch authenticated and key agreement scheme for LBS in VANETs was presented. However, this scheme was shown to be insecure against a conspiracy attack [13].

---

[1] Privacy in VANETs usually denotes that an attacker cannot trace a vehicle according to the messages sent/received by a vehicle.

Contributions. We investigate the security and privacy concerns in LBSs for VANETs and propose a practical LBS scheme. For each LBS transaction, the scheme provides authentication, integrity and non-repudiation to both the service provider and the user. This guarantees the system's security. A user can obtain the service in an anonymous way and hence user privacy is well protected. However, if a user abuses the service, a tracing procedure can be invoked to find the malicious user, thereby efficiently preventing users from inappropriately leveraging the anonymity provided by the system. These two features are achieved with the help of group signatures. Our system does not depend on the grouping approach, which seems expensive in VANETs due to volatile connections. Instead, we propose that properly distributed RSUs in a VANET play a role similar to the one of the group leader in the AMOEBA protocol. This ensures that our system is robust in the sense that users can access LBSs and preserve their privacy without being affected by the vehicle density. To implement the scheme securely, we propose RSUs and the LBS provider to use their recognizable identities as their public keys. On the vehicle side, only a secret member key is needed to generate a group signature for authentication of data regarding the request of LBSs. This approach eliminates the certificate management overhead, noting that, as remarked above, neither identity based cryptosystems nor group signatures require public certificates. Analysis shows that cryptographic operations in our scheme introduce a very light overhead to the underlying VANET. Membership revocation is a critical issue in group signature based systems. The above system also suffers from the membership revocation problem. To handle this problem, we extend our system with hierarchical technology HKMK (see Section 6). With this technology, our system can also host a large number of LBS users.

2   System Architecture and Design Goals

2.1   System Architecture

The system architecture is illustrated in Figure 1. In the system, there are key generation center(s) (KGC(s)), RSUs, vehicles and providers of location based services (LBS providers):

- A KGC is a trusted third party. It generates private keys for vehicles and LBS providers and it issues secret member keys for vehicles. In addition, the KGC is assumed to be able to determine the real identity of vehicles and LBS providers.
- RSUs are equipped with on-board sensory, processing, and wireless communication modules, and they are distributed along the roadside. They are connected to LBS providers by a wired network. RSUs are assumed to be semi-trusted (*i.e.*, some of them might be compromised).
- Vehicles move along the roads, sharing environmental information with each other and/or querying LBSs through RSUs using the DSRC protocol [1]. Each vehicle is equipped with on-board sensory, processing, and wireless communication modules.
- LBS providers process the data forwarded by RSUs and offer LBSs to vehicles.

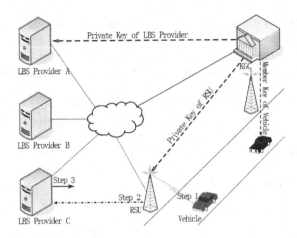

Fig. 1. System architecture

2.2 Design Goals

The design goals of our LBS scheme are summarized as follows.

- **Security.** Authentication, integrity and non-repudiation should be provided for both the service provider and the user. The transcripts of a successful execution of the LBS protocol can be used as evidence to prove that both parties have been involved in that transaction. If a user abuses the service, the real identity of the user can be traced.
- **Privacy.** An attacker cannot trace or profile any specific user by monitoring all the public communications in the system or data mining her received data.
- **Robustness.** Users should be able to access intended LBSs anytime anywhere, provided that the underlying VANET is available and the LBSs are open for providing services. The service quality and privacy of the requestor should not be affected by vehicle density.

We further decompose our design goals into security requirements. We first show the communication model of an LBS protocol. As illustrated in Figure 1, an LBS protocol can be described in three steps. In the first step, a vehicle sends its request to a nearby RSU in a single-hop or multi-hop manner. In the second step, the RSU receives the request from the vehicle and detects what kind of services the vehicle is asking for; then it forwards the request to the corresponding LBS provider. In the last step, the LBS provider authenticates the vehicle. If the vehicle is a subscriber, the LBS provider returns the requested service to the vehicle by routing his response through RSUs neighboring the RSU the vehicle request came from. Within the above model, the design goals can be achieved by meeting the following security requirements.

[Security requirements at Step 1] In this step the security requirements are:

- **Message Confidentiality.** An LBS request may contain sensitive information of a vehicle. For instance, if a vehicle requests a priced service, the e-cash may be included in the query. If the vehicle sends this request to the LBS provider through an RSU, anyone can learn the e-cash information and an attacker can steal the e-cash by disabling the communication from the requesting vehicle to the RSU. Hence, message confidentiality is required. Message confidentiality at this step has two levels. Level 1 provides confidentiality when the attacker does not know the private key of the RSU. It requires that only the vehicle and the RSU be aware of the information exchange. Level 2 provides confidentiality even if the attacker learns the private key of the RSU. In this case, we require that no one but the vehicle and the designated LBS provider can learn the content of the LBS request.
- **Vehicle Privacy.** Privacy in this step has also two levels. Level 1 guarantees privacy when the attacker does not know the private key of the RSU. It requires that it be computationally hard for everyone (except the message generator or some trusted third party) to decide whether two different messages were generated by the same vehicle. Level 2 guarantees privacy even when an RSU is compromised by an attacker. In this case, we require that the attacker can only learn the service type a vehicle is requesting.

[Security requirements at Step 2] In our system, an RSU serves as a router. For an LBS protocol in VANETs, an RSU only needs to know the service type that a vehicle is requesting so that it can forward the request to the right LBS provider. Hence, in our design, we only let RSUs learn the kind of service the vehicle wants to access. This step needs to meet the following security requirements:

- **Message Confidentiality.** No one but the vehicle and the designated LBS provider can learn the content of the message forwarded by the RSU.
- **Vehicle Privacy.** It is computationally hard for everyone (except the message generator or some trusted third party) to decide whether two different messages were generated by the same vehicle.

[Security requirements at Step 3] This step has the following requirements:

- **Vehicle Authentication.** The LBS provider must be sure that the request is from some registered vehicle, *i.e.*, a subscriber.
- **Vehicle Privacy.** The LBS provider only learns that a vehicle is querying the LBS but it cannot learn the vehicle's identity. Furthermore, the LBS provider cannot decide whether two different requests were generated by the same vehicle.
- **Vehicle Traceability.** In VANETs, the privacy of a vehicle should be conditional. That is, if necessary, some trusted third party should be able to revoke the anonymity of doubtable vehicles. Otherwise, a malicious vehicle might send fake messages to jeopardize the system without fear of being caught. In this paper, KGC is endowed with the ability to trace the real identity of dishonest vehicles sending fake messages to LBS providers in order to disrupt services.

3   Technical Preliminaries

3.1   Bilinear Maps

Bilinear maps are widely used in many cryptosystems, *e.g.*, identity-based cryptography (IBC) and group signature schemes. We briefly review them here.

Let $\mathbb{G}_1, \mathbb{G}_2$ be two cyclic groups of prime order q and $\mathbb{G}_T$ be a multiplicative cyclic group of the same order. Let g_1 denote a generator of $\mathbb{G}_1$, g_2 a generator of $\mathbb{G}_2$, ψ a computable isomorphism from $\mathbb{G}_2$ to $\mathbb{G}_1$, with $\psi(g_2) = g_1$. A mapping $\hat{e} : \mathbb{G}_1 \times \mathbb{G}_2 \longrightarrow \mathbb{G}_T$ is called a bilinear mapping if $\hat{e}(g_1, g_2) \neq 1$ and $\hat{e}(g_1^\alpha, g_2^\beta) = \hat{e}(g_1, g_2)^{\alpha\beta}$ for all $\alpha, \beta \in Z_q^*$.

Such a bilinear map $\hat{e}$ can be constructed with the modified Weil pairing [3] on elliptic curves. ψ can be a trace map as described in [3], and when $\mathbb{G}_1 = \mathbb{G}_2$ and $g_1 = g_2$, ψ can be the identity map. For simplicity, in this paper we will take $\mathbb{G}_1 = \mathbb{G}_2 = \mathbb{G}$ and $g_1 = g_2 = g$.

3.2   Identity-Based Cryptography

Identity-based cryptography (IBC) [2] was introduced to simplify certificate management procedures of public key infrastructures (PKI). In IBC, the public key of an entity is some unique public information about the identity of the entity (*e.g.*, the entity's location information). Therefore, the need for public key certification can be eliminated. The private key of an entity is generated by a trusted third party, Key Generation Center (KGC).

In VANETs, since we need not consider the privacy of RSUs and LBS providers, we can use the location information and service type as the identity of an RSU (and LBS provider). For instance, if an RSU is located at street A in city B, then we can use '$RSU, streetA, cityB$' as the identity of this RSU; for an LBS provider who provides online map service in city B, we can use '$onlinemap, cityB$' as the identity of the LBS provider.

3.3   Verifier-Local Revocation Group Signatures

Group signatures [5] allow the members of a group to sign on behalf of the group. Everyone can verify the signature with a group public key while no one can know the identity of the signer except the group manager. Further, except for the group manager, it is computationally hard for anyone to decide whether two different signatures were issued by the same group member.

Member revocation is needed to disable members who left the group or whose secret member key and/or member certificate were/was compromised. Most group signatures suffer from inefficient member revocation. Recently, an efficient approach to membership revocation in group signatures was proposed, called verifier-local revocation [4]. The idea is that only verifiers are involved in the revocation mechanism, while signers have no involvement. This approach is especially suitable for mobile environments where mobile signers (*i.e.*, the vehicles in our case) have much less computational power than the verifying servers (*i.e.*, the LBS providers).

In this paper, we use the optimized verifier-local revocation group signature scheme in [9] to achieve 'Vehicle Authentication', 'Vehicle Privacy' and 'Vehicle Traceability'. Pairing operation is the most time consuming operation in the scheme in [9]. By our optimization, to generate and verify a group signature, the number of pairing operations needs to compute can be reduced from 5 and 6 to 1 and 2 respectively.

4   A Privacy-preserving LBS Proposal

In this section, we propose a privacy-preserving LBS scheme in VANETs. We define the following notations to simplify the description. $\mathcal{V}$: a vehicle; $\mathcal{R}$: an RSU; $\mathcal{L}$: an LBS provider; $ID_{\mathcal{A}}$: the identity of entity $\mathcal{A}$; $S_{\mathcal{A}}$: the secret key of $\mathcal{A}$; ||: message concatenation operation; Des: the description of an LBS request; Add: the addresses of some RSUs near $\mathcal{R}$ through which the LBS response to $\mathcal{V}$ will be routed; TP: a time stamp; IEK: the identity enrolment key, used to generate private keys for RSUs and LBS providers; MEK: the member enrolment key, used to issue member keys for vehicles; $\mathcal{E}_K(\cdot)/\mathcal{D}_K(\cdot)$: a symmetric key encryption scheme (*e.g.*, AES), with $\mathcal{E}_K(\cdot)/\mathcal{D}_K(\cdot)$ being the corresponding encryption/decryption algorithms, and K being a key which specifies the particular transformation of plaintext into ciphertext during encryption, or vice versa during decryption.

4.1   High Level Description

This section outlines the basic ideas of our LBS system for application in VANETs. We refer to the three steps mentioned in Section 2.2 and shown in Figure 2.

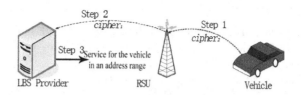

Fig. 2. The LBS protocol

In the first step, $\mathcal{V}$ first prepares a request of the form $Des||Add||TP||Sig$ and encrypts this request under $\mathcal{L}$'s identity to generate a ciphertext $cipher_1$, where Sig is the verifier-local revocation group signature on $Des||Add||TP$. Then it encrypts $TP||ID_{\mathcal{L}}||cipher_1$ under the identity of its nearby RSU to generate the ciphertext $cipher_2$. Finally, $cipher_2$ is sent to the RSU. In the second step, when the RSU receives $cipher_2$ from $\mathcal{V}$, RSU decrypts the ciphertext $cipher_2$ to get $TP||ID_{\mathcal{L}}||cipher_1$. If TP is fresh, RSU forwards $cipher_1$ to the LBS provider with identity $ID_{\mathcal{L}}$. In the last step, the LBS provider decrypts the ciphertext $cipher_1$ to get $Des||Add||TP||Sig$. It then checks whether TP is fresh and Sig is a valid signature on $Des||Add||TP$. If TP is fresh and Sig is valid, the LBS provider provides the corresponding service in Des to Add.

4.2   The Concrete Scheme

Our concrete LBS scheme consists of the following five stages.

[System Setup]

At this stage, KGC initializes the system-wide parameters as follows:

1. Choose a cyclic group $\mathbb{G}$ and a cyclic multiplicative group $\mathbb{G}_T$ of the same order q, so that there exists a bilinear map $\hat{e} : \mathbb{G} \times \mathbb{G} \rightarrow \mathbb{G}_T$, where $\mathbb{G}$ is generated by g; choose also $u_0, u_1 \in \mathbb{G}$.
2. Pick $\kappa, \rho \in Z_q^*$ as KGC's master secret key, and compute $u_2 = g^{\kappa}, u_3 = g^{\rho}$ as KGC's master public key. Hereafter, we will also denote κ as IEK and ρ as MEK.
3. Compute $Y_0 = \hat{e}(u_0, u_3), Y_1 = \hat{e}(u_0, g), Y_2 = \hat{e}(u_1, g), Y_3 = \hat{e}(g, g)$.
4. Choose a symmetric key encryption scheme $\mathcal{E}_K(.)/\mathcal{D}_K(.)$. We assume that the bit-length of K is λ.
5. Select cryptographic hash functions $H_0(\cdot) : \{0,1\}^* \longrightarrow \mathbb{G}, H_1(\cdot) : \{0,1\}^* \longrightarrow \mathbb{Z}_q^*$ and $H_2(\cdot) : \mathbb{G}_T \longrightarrow \{0,1\}^{\lambda}$.
6. Publish the system parameters as $\Psi = (\hat{e}, q, \mathbb{G}, \mathbb{G}_T, g, u_0, u_1, u_2, u_3, H_0, H_1, H_2, Y_0, Y_1, Y_2, Y_3, \mathcal{E}_K(\cdot)/\mathcal{D}_K(\cdot))$. Ψ is assumed to be pre-loaded in each vehicle, RSU and LBS provider.

The KGC also maintains a member list ML and a revocation list RL, where ML is kept secret while RL can be accessed by the LBS providers. We will define these lists later.

[Registration]

Before a vehicle, an LBS provider or an RSU joins a VANET, it registers with the KGC. The KGC generates a secret key or a member key for them using the following algorithms.

RSUJoin: This algorithm is used to generate the secret key for an RSU. Suppose that the identity of an RSU $\mathcal{R}_i$ is $ID_{\mathcal{R}_i}$. The KGC computes $S_{\mathcal{R}_i} = H_0(ID_{\mathcal{R}_i})^{\kappa}$.

ServiceJoin: This algorithm is used to generate the secret key for an LBS provider. Suppose that the identity of an LBS provider is $ID_{\mathcal{L}_i}$. The KGC computes $S_{\mathcal{L}_i} = H_0(ID_{\mathcal{L}_i})^{\kappa}$.

VehicleJoin: This algorithm is used to generate the member key for a vehicle. The KGC maintains a member list ML of tuples $(ID_{\mathcal{V}}, w, x, v)$, where $v = u_1^x$. When a vehicle wants to join the system, the KGC accepts a vehicle's identity $ID_{\mathcal{V}_i}$ and generates the member key as follows:

1. Select $x_i \in \mathbb{Z}_q^*$, compute $w_i = g^{1/(\rho+x_i)}$ and set (w_i, x_i) as $\mathcal{V}_i$'s member key.
2. Add $(ID_{\mathcal{V}_i}, w_i, x_i, v_i)$ to ML, where $v_i = u_1^{x_i}$ is the revocation token of $\mathcal{V}_i$.

[LBS Protocol]

As discussed in Section 2.2, an LBS protocol consists of three steps.

Step 1: The first step is the vehicle-to-RSU communication. Suppose that $\mathcal{V}_i$ wants to access the LBS provider $\mathcal{L}_k$ and its nearby RSU is $\mathcal{R}_j$. $\mathcal{V}_i$ chooses $s \in \mathbb{Z}_q^*$ and computes $C_1 = g^s$, $SK_1 = H_2(\hat{e}(u_2^s, H_0(ID_{\mathcal{L}_k})))$, where SK_1 will be the key of the symmetric key encryption scheme $\mathcal{E}_K(\cdot)/\mathcal{D}_K(\cdot)$, sets $m_1 = Des||Add||TP||Sig$, and computes $C_2 = \mathcal{E}_{SK_1}(m_1)$, where Sig is the signature on $m_0 = Des||Add||TP$ which is generated using the following SigGen algorithm:

1. Randomly select $\alpha, \beta, \gamma \in \mathbb{Z}_q^*$ and compute $\delta = x_i\alpha, \zeta = x_i\beta, \eta = x_i\gamma$.
2. Compute $t_1 = w_i u_0^\alpha, t_2 = g^\alpha u_0^\alpha, T_3 = Y_2^\eta$ and $t_4 = g^\gamma$.
3. Select $r_\alpha, r_\beta, r_\gamma, r_{x_i}, r_\delta, r_\zeta, r_\eta \in \mathbb{Z}_q^*$ at random.
4. Compute $R_1 = g^{r_\alpha} u_0^{r_\beta}, R_2 = t_2^{r_{x_i}} g^{-r_\delta} u_0^{-r_\zeta}, R_3 = \hat{e}(t_1, g)^{-r_{x_i}} Y_0^{r_\alpha} Y_1^{r_\delta}, R_4 = Y_2^{r_\eta}, R_5 = g^{r_\gamma}, R_6 = t_4^{r_{x_i}} g^{-r_\eta}$.
5. Compute $c = H_1(\Psi, m_0, t_1, t_2, T_3, t_4, R_1, ..., R_6)$.
6. Compute $s_\alpha = r_\alpha + c\alpha, s_\beta = r_\beta + c\beta, s_\gamma = r_\gamma + c\gamma, s_{x_i} = r_{x_i} + cx_i, s_\delta = r_\delta - c\delta, s_\zeta = r_\zeta + c\zeta$ and $s_\eta = r_\eta + c\eta$.
7. Output the group signature $Sig = (t_1, t_2, T_3, t_4, c, s_\alpha, s_\beta, s_\gamma, s_{x_i}, s_\delta, s_\zeta, s_\eta)$.

$\mathcal{V}_i$ chooses $t \in \mathbb{Z}_q^*$ and computes $C_3 = g^t$, $SK_2 = H_2(\hat{e}(u_2^t, H_0(ID_{\mathcal{R}_j})))$, sets $cipher_1 = C_1||C_2$, $m_2 = TP||ID_{\mathcal{L}_k}||cipher_1$, computes $C_4 = \mathcal{E}_{SK_2}(m_2)$, and sends $cipher_2 = (C_3||C_4)$ to $\mathcal{R}_j$.

Step 2: When $\mathcal{R}_j$ receives $cipher_2 = (C_3, C_4)$, it computes $SK_2 = H_2(\hat{e}(C_3, S_{\mathcal{R}_j}))$, $m_2 = TP||ID_{\mathcal{L}_k}||cipher_1 = \mathcal{D}_{SK_2}(C_4)$. It checks TP to decide whether the request is fresh. If it is, it sends $cipher_1 = (C_1, C_2)$ to $\mathcal{L}_k$; otherwise it aborts.

Step 3: When $\mathcal{L}_k$ receives $cipher_1 = (C_1, C_2)$, it computes $SK_1 = H_2(\hat{e}(C_1, S_{\mathcal{L}_k}))$, $m_1 = Des||Add||TP||Sig = \mathcal{D}_{SK_1}(C_2)$. If TP is not fresh, it aborts. Otherwise, it extracts $Sig = (t_1, t_2, T_3, t_4, s_\alpha, s_\beta, s_\gamma, s_{x_i}, s_\delta, s_\zeta, s_\eta)$, and checks whether Sig is a valid group signature on $Des||Add||TP$ using the following SigVer algorithm:

1. Compute $R_1 = g^{s_\alpha} u_0^{s_\beta} t_2^{-c}, R_2 = t_2^{s_{x_i}} g^{-s_\delta} u_0^{-s_\zeta}, R_3 = \hat{e}(t_1, g^{-s_{x_i}} + u_3^{-c}) Y_0^{s_\alpha} Y_1^{r_\delta} Y_3^c, R_4 = Y_2^{s_\eta} T_3^{-c}, R_5 = g^{s_\gamma} t_4^{-c}, R_6 = t_4^{s_{x_i}} g^{-s_\eta}$.
2. Check $c \stackrel{?}{=} H_1(\Psi, m_0, t_1, t_2, T_3, t_4, R_1, ..., R_6)$.
3. Output $valid$ if the signature passes the above check.

If the signature is valid, $\mathcal{L}_k$ provides the service to Add according to Des^2.

---

[2] In Des, an AES key and an identifier (e.g., a random number) can be included. The outcome could be encrypted by the LBS provider under that AES key and broadcasted with the identifier, so that only the vehicle who generated the request needs to decrypt the encrypted outcome and any other vehicles can not read the content of the outcome.

[Revocation]

Two mechanisms are suggested to tackle the revocation problem. Firstly, the KGC maintains a revocation list RL. Under normal circumstances, when a vehicle $\mathcal{V}_i$ is compromised, the KGC first finds the corresponding $(ID_{\mathcal{V}_i}, w_i, x_i, v_i)$ in ML and then adds v_i to the revocation list RL. To detect whether a group signature $Sig = (t_1, t_2, T_3, t_4, s_\alpha, s_\beta, s_\gamma, s_{x_i}, s_\delta, s_\zeta, s_\eta)$ is generated by a revoked vehicle, the LBS provider checks $T_3 \overset{?}{=} e(t_4, v_j)$ for all $v_j \in$ RL. If none of the equations holds, it means that the vehicle is not revoked. Secondly, when there are too many revoked vehicles in RL, we may allow the KGC to choose a threshold τ; and when the number of revoked vehicles in RL is greater than τ, the KGC updates its MEK and corresponding public key, and re-issues member keys for all the vehicles. This mechanism gives a tradeoff between revocation checks by LBS providers and key updates for entities in a VANET. The key updates may cause heavy overhead in case of a very large-scale VANET. In Section 6, we further propose a hierarchical approach to alleviate the overhead so that the system can stay efficient even if the VANET hosts a large number of vehicles.

[Trace]

Let $Sig = (t_1, t_2, T_3, t_4, s_\alpha, s_\beta, s_\gamma, s_{x_i}, s_\delta, s_\zeta, s_\eta)$ be a valid group signature. To trace a vehicle, the KGC checks $T_3 \overset{?}{=} e(t_4, v_i)$ for the tuple $(ID_{\mathcal{V}_i}, w_i, x_i, v_i)$ on ML. If this equation holds, KGC outputs $ID_{\mathcal{V}_i}$.

5   Evaluation

5.1   Security Analysis

The following analysis shows that the proposal meets all the security requirements described in Section 2.2.

Firstly, we show that the message confidentiality and the vehicle privacy of Step 1 are satisfied.

- *Level 1 message confidentiality and vehicle privacy.* At this step, the ciphertext $cipher_2$ is generated by using the basic identity-based encryption (IBE) scheme which was proven secure by Boneh and Franklin [2]. Therefore, the level 1 message confidentiality naturally follows. Furthermore, in each session of the protocol, a random value t is chosen. Therefore, in each session, C_3 and C_4 are different and independent from those in other sessions.
- *Level 2 message confidentiality and vehicle privacy.* In our protocol, the content of the LBS request is encrypted under the LBS provider's identity in $cipher_1$ using the Boneh and Franklin IBE scheme [2]. Only the designated LBS provider owns the secret key corresponding to this identity. Hence, even if the private key of the RSU is leaked to the attacker, no one except the vehicle and the designated LBS provider can read the content of the LBS request. Furthermore, in each session of the protocol, a random value s is chosen. Therefore, in each session, C_1 and C_2 are also different and independent from those in other sessions.

In Step 2, the RSU can decrypt $cipher_2$ to get $TP||ID_{\mathcal{L}_k}||cipher_1$. From $ID_{\mathcal{L}_k}$, the RSU can learn what kind of service the vehicle wants to access. However, since the RSU does not know the private key of the LBS provider, it cannot learn the content of $cipher_1$. Therefore, 'Message Confidentiality' for this step is met. Furthermore, $cipher_1$ is also generated under the Boneh and Franklin IBE scheme. The 'Vehicle Privacy' for this step accordingly follows.

Finally, we show that our protocol meets 'Vehicle Authentication', 'Vehicle Privacy' and 'Vehicle Traceability' of Step 3 defined in Section 2.2. In this step, the LBS provider first decrypts the ciphertext $cipher_1$ to get $Des||Add||TP||Sig$. If Sig is a valid group signature, then the LBS provider is sure that the request comes from a registered vehicle. Hence, 'Vehicle Authentication' is satisfied. Furthermore, the KGC can recover the identity of the vehicle, so 'Vehicle Traceability' is satisfied. As to 'Vehicle Privacy', since anyone can generate $Des||Add||TP$, it is easy to see that $Des||Add||TP$ may not help the LBS provider to trace a vehicle. It remains Sig for the LBS provider to trace a vehicle. However, the verifier-local revocation group signature has the property that it is computationally hard for anyone but the trusted third party (KGC in our scheme) to decide whether two different signatures were issued by the same member. Hence, Sig cannot help the LBS provider to trace a vehicle.

5.2   Transmission Overhead

In this section, we examine the transmission delay incurred by the security and privacy mechanism. We will only deal with the delay in Step 1, which has a relatively crucial bandwidth limitation.

From our LBS protocol, it is easy to see that the length of an LBS request is equal to the length of $C_3||TP||ID_{\mathcal{L}}||C_1||Des||Add||TP||Sig$ in Step 1. Excluding $Des||Add$[3], it remains to see the length of $C_3||TP||ID_{\mathcal{L}}||C_1||TP||Sig$. According to [3] and [9], the length of a point in $\mathbb{G}$ and the length of Sig are 171 bits (about 22 bytes) and 362 bytes respectively. In addition, the length of TP is 4 bytes and the length of $ID_{\mathcal{L}}$ is 20 bytes. Hence, the length of $C_3||TP||ID_{\mathcal{L}}||C_1||TP||Sig$ is about 434 bytes. According to DSRC [1], the minimal data rate in DSRC is 6 Mbps. Hence, we have that the maximal transmission delay caused by security and privacy mechanism at Step 1 is $\frac{434\times8}{6\times1024\times1024}$ s ≈ 0.55 ms. This delay is very low for vehicles in VANETs.

5.3   Computational Overhead

This section discusses the computational overhead at each step in our protocol. In the sequel, we will only consider the costly operations (*i.e.* pairing and point exponentiation operations). According to the execution time results shown in [7], the measured processing time for one bilinear pairing operation is about 1.87 ms and the time for one point exponentiation operation is about 0.49 ms.

---

[3] These data are required even without any security and privacy mechanism. It is clearer to see the cryptographic overhead without considering these data.

In the first step, we notice that all point exponentiation operations can be pre-computed off-line. Therefore, this step only needs to compute two pairing operations on-line. The time is about 3.74 ms. In the second step, an RSU only needs to compute one pairing operation to decrypt the ciphertext $cipher_2$. The time is about 1.87 ms. For the last step, the LBS provider needs to calculate 17 point exponentiation operations and 2 pairing operations. The total time is about 12.07 ms. Therefore, the total computational overhead for all the steps is about 17.68 ms. This is affordable for vehicles wishing to access LBS.

6   Hierarchical KGC and Multi-issue Key

In our basic system, we use a single KGC to generate private keys for RSUs and LBS providers, and issue member keys for vehicles. However, if there is a huge number of users in a VANET, the KGC may become a bottleneck: the KGC needs not only to generate private keys or member keys for a large number of users, but also to verify the identities of the users. Furthermore, as the number of vehicles in the revocation list grows, the performance of the system might decline. To let the system remain efficient even if a large number of vehicles are revoked, we introduce an approach referred to as hierarchical KGCs and multi-issue key (HKMK). The idea of HKMK is illustrated in Figure 3.

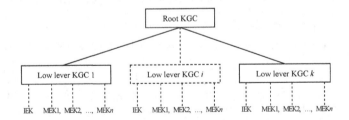

Fig. 3. Hierarchical KGC and multi-issue key

In this approach, we use a two-level hierarchical KGC. A root KGC is used to issue certificates for low-level KGCs. As in our basic system, each low-level KGC has a single identity enrolment key (IEK) which is used to generate private keys for RSUs and LBS providers. However, unlike in our basic system, each low-level KGC has n different member enrolment keys (MEKs). When a vehicle joins the system, the low-level KGC randomly chooses one of its MEKs and generates a member key for this vehicle. In this way, vehicles in a domain are separated into n sub-groups and, when a vehicle contacts an LBS provider for the LBS, the LBS provider can only learn that the vehicle belongs to a sub-group.

In what follows, we show how to set up the system parameters in the *System Setup* stage. We reformulate this stage into two sub-stages: *Root KGC Setup* and *Low-Level KGC Setup*. The description of each sub-stage comes as follows.

[Root KGC Setup]

The root KGC initializes the system-wide parameters as follows:

1. Choose $\hat{e}, \mathbb{G}, \mathbb{G}_T, q, \mathcal{E}_K(\cdot)/\mathcal{D}_K(\cdot), H_0, H_1, H_2$ as those in the System Setup stage in Section 4.2.
2. Choose $u_0, u_1 \in \mathbb{G}$ and compute $Y_1 = \hat{e}(u_0, g), Y_2 = \hat{e}(u_1, g), Y_3 = \hat{e}(g, g)$.
3. Publish the system-wide parameters $\Psi = (\hat{e}, q, \mathbb{G}, \mathbb{G}_T, g, u_0, u_1, H_0, H_1, H_2, Y_1, Y_2, Y_3, \mathcal{E}_K(\cdot)/\mathcal{D}_K(\cdot))$. Ψ is assumed to be pre-loaded in each low-level KGC, vehicle, RSU and LBS provider.

[Low-Level KGC Setup]

After seeing the system-wide parameters, a low-level KGC generates its own parameters as follows:

1. Pick $\kappa \in Z_q^*$ as its identity enrolment key (IEK) and n member enrolment keys (MEKs) $\rho_1, ..., \rho_n \in Z_q^*$.
2. Compute $u_2 = g^\kappa$ and $u_{3i} = g^{\rho_i}, 1 \leq i \leq n$ as its master public key.
3. Compute $Y_{0i} = \hat{e}(u_0, u_{3i}), 1 \leq i \leq n$.
4. Publish the parameters as $\Omega = (u_2, u_{31}, ..., u_{3n}, Y_{01}, ..., Y_{0n})$.

The low-level KGC also maintains n member lists $\mathsf{ML}_1, ..., \mathsf{ML}_n$ and revocation lists $\mathsf{RL}_1, ..., \mathsf{RL}_n$ corresponding to the n MEKs, respectively. To deal with the revocation problem more efficiently, similarly to our basic system, a low-level KGC chooses a threshold τ. If a vehicle $\mathcal{V}_i$ is compromised (we assume the member key of $\mathcal{V}_i$ is issued by using the j-th MEK, $1 \leq j \leq n$) and the number of vehicles in RL_j is not greater than τ, the low-level KGC first finds the revocation token of $\mathcal{V}_i$ in ML_j, then adds the revocation token to RL_j. Otherwise, the KGC updates its j-th MEK and corresponding public key u_{3j} and $Y_{0j} = \hat{e}(u_0, u_{3j})$, and re-issues member keys for all the vehicles in j-th sub-group.

Acknowledgments and Disclaimer. This work was supported in part by the the NSF of China under Grants 61202465, 61021004, 11061130539, 60970114, 60970115, 91018008, 60970116, 61173154, 61003214, 61173192, 61103222; EU FP7 under Projects "DwB" and "Inter-Trust"; the Spanish Government under Projects CTV-09-634, PTA2009-2738-E, TSI-020302-2010-153, TIN2009-11689, TIN2011-27076-C03-01, CONSOLIDER INGENIO 2010 "ARES" CSD2007-0004, and TSI2007-65406-C03-01; the Government of Catalonia under Grant SGR2009-1135; the Fundamental Research Funds for the Central Universities of China under Project 3103004; the Open Project of Shanghai Key Laboratory of Trust-worthy Computing (No. 07dz22304201101); the Shanghai NSF under Grant No. 12ZR1443500, 11ZR1411200; the Shaanxi Provincial Education Department under Scientific Research Program 2010JK727 and the Shanghai Chen Guang Program (12CG24). J. Domingo-Ferrer was supported in part as an ICREA-Acadèmia researcher by the Catalan Government.

References

1. Dedicated Short Range Communications (DRSC) home,
   http://www.leearmstrong.com/Dsrc/DSRCHomeset.htm
2. Boneh, D., Franklin, M.: Identity-Based Encryption from the Weil Pairing. In: Kilian, J. (ed.) CRYPTO 2001. LNCS, vol. 2139, pp. 213–229. Springer, Heidelberg (2001)
3. Boneh, D., Lynn, B., Shacham, H.: Short Signatures from the Weil Pairing. In: Boyd, C. (ed.) ASIACRYPT 2001. LNCS, vol. 2248, pp. 514–532. Springer, Heidelberg (2001)
4. Boneh, D., Shacham, H.: Group signatures with verifier-local revocation. In: ACM Conference on Computer and Communications Security, pp. 168–177 (2004)
5. Chaum, D., van Heyst, E.: Group Signatures. In: Davies, D.W. (ed.) EUROCRYPT 1991. LNCS, vol. 547, pp. 257–265. Springer, Heidelberg (1991)
6. Huang, J., Yeh, L., Chien, H.: ABAKA: An anonymous batch authenticated and key agreement scheme for value-added services in vehicular ad hoc networks. IEEE Transactions on Vehicular Technology 60(1), 248–262 (2011)
7. Jiang, Y., Shi, M., Shen, X., Lin, C.: BAT: A robust signature scheme for vehicular networks using binary authentication trees. IEEE Transactions on Wireless Communications 8(4), 1974–1983 (2009)
8. Kocher, P.C.: Timing Attacks on Implementations of Diffie-Hellman, RSA, DSS, and Other Systems. In: Koblitz, N. (ed.) CRYPTO 1996. LNCS, vol. 1109, pp. 104–113. Springer, Heidelberg (1996)
9. Nakanishi, T., Funabiki, N.: Verifier-Local Revocation Group Signature Schemes with Backward Unlinkability from Bilinear Maps. In: Roy, B. (ed.) ASIACRYPT 2005. LNCS, vol. 3788, pp. 533–548. Springer, Heidelberg (2005)
10. Papadimitratos, P., Gligor, V., Hubaux, J.: Securing vehicular communications - Assumptions, requirements, and principles. In: Workshop on Embedded Security in Cars, ESCAR 2006 (2006)
11. Raya, M., Hubaux, J.: Securing vehicular ad hoc networks. Journal of Computer Security 15(1), 39–68 (2007)
12. Sampigethaya, K., Li, M., Huang, L., Poovendran, R.: AMOEBA: Robust location privacy scheme for VANET. IEEE Journal on Selected Areas in Communications 25(8), 1569–1589 (2007)
13. Wang, H., Zhang, Y.: On the security of an anonymous batch authenticated and key agreement scheme for value-added services in VANETs. Procedia Engineering 29, 1735–1739 (2012)
14. Yong, H., Jin, T., Yu, C., Chi, Z.: Secure data downloading with privacy preservation in vehicular ad hoc networks. In: IEEE International Conference on Communications 2010, pp. 1–5 (2010)
15. Wu, Q., Domingo-Ferrer, J., González-Nicolás, U.: Balanced trustworthiness, safety and privacy in vehicle-to-vehicle communications. IEEE Transactions on Vehicular Technology 59(2), 559–573 (2010)
16. Zhang, L., Wu, Q., Solanas, A., Domingo-Ferrer, J.: A scalable robust authentication protocol for secure vehicular communications. IEEE Transactions on Vehicular Technology 59(4), 1606–1617 (2010)

Optimizing Streaming Server Selection for CDN-Delivered Live Streaming

Zhenyun Zhuang and Shun Kwok*

Ying-Da-Ji Tech., 603 Overseas High-Tech Venture Park, Shenzhen 518057, China

Abstract. Content Delivery Networks (CDNs) have been widely used to deliver web contents on today's Internet. Gaining tremendous popularity, live streaming is also increasingly being delivered by CDNs. Compared to conventional static or dynamic web contents, the new application type of live streaming exposes unique characteristics that pose challenges to the underlying CDN infrastructure. Unlike traditional web-objects fetching, which allows Edge Servers to cache contents and thus typically only involves Edge Servers for delivering contents, live streaming requires real-time full CDN-streaming paths that span across Ingest Servers, Origin Servers and Edge Servers.

DNS is the standard practice for enabling dynamic assignment of servers. GeoDNS, a specialized DNS system, provides DNS resolution by taking into account the geographical locations of end-users and CDN servers. Though GeoDNS effectively redirects users to nearest CDN Edge Servers, it may not be able to select the optimal Origin Server for relaying a live stream to Edge Servers due to the unique characteristics of live streaming. In this work, we consider the requirements of delivering live streaming with CDN, and propose advanced design for selecting optimal Origin Streaming Servers in order to reduce network transit cost and increase viewers' experience. We further propose a live-streaming specific GeoDNS design for selecting optimal Origin Servers to serve Edge Servers.

1 Introduction

Today's web contents are increasingly being delivered by Content Delivery Networks (aka Content Distribution Networks, or CDNs) [1,2]. a typical CDN infrastructure consists of two types of servers based on their functionalities: Ingest Servers for accepting customers' web contents; and (ii) Delivery Servers for serving end web users. Live streaming is becoming increasingly popular, and it is expected to be more pervasive in the near future. Major CDN providers such as Akamai [1] and Level3 [2] are supporting delivering live streaming with their CDNs. When supporting live streaming, CDN providers provide a layered infrastructure which consists of three types of streaming servers: (i) Ingest Streaming Servers (ISS) which accept customers' live streams; and (ii) Origin Streaming Servers (OSS) which transit live streams from ingest servers to Edge Streaming Servers; and (iii) Edge Streaming Servers (ESS) that directly serve the end viewers. Depending on the scale of a CDN, the number of Origin Streaming Servers varies from several to hundreds, and Edge Streaming Servers can be even thousands.

---

* Corresponding author.

Y. Xiang et al. (Eds.): IDCS 2012, LNCS 7646, pp. 57–70, 2012.

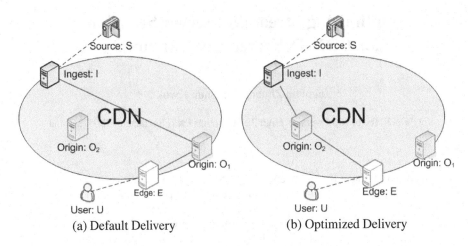

(a) Default Delivery   (b) Optimized Delivery

Fig. 1. Live streaming delivered with CDN

Unlike other traditional web-based applications, live streaming is associated with unique characteristics and in turn presents special challenges to CDN infrastructure. *First*, live streaming has to be delivered from the CDN Ingest Server to Edge Servers in a real-time fashion, which is in sharp contrast with traditional CDN-based web delivering where typically only the last hop (i.e., from CDN Edge Servers to web users) needs to be optimized. Such uniqueness requires the optimization of the entire CDN transit path which consists of two transit hops of Ingest-Origin and Origin-Edge. *Second*, live streaming often features high-bandwidth requirement. A typical live videos can easily consumes up to 3 Mbps per stream, thus there is a higher need for reducing transit cost on CDN networks. *Third*, live streaming typically is time-sensitive, and the CDN infrastructure design needs to consider such timeliness by choosing the shortest path from the streaming source to the end users.

After a live stream is ingested into the CDN infrastructure through an Ingest Server, when an end viewer requests to play a live stream, an appropriate Edge Server and an Origin Server need to be chosen, so that the player pulls the stream from the Edge Server and the Edge Server pulls the stream from the Origin Server. DNS is the standard practice for making the above server selections. GeoDNS [3], typically used by CDNs, is a specialized DNS service by taking into account geographical locations of CDN Origin/Edge servers and end users. It translates host names into IP address and redirects the requests to optimal Origin/Edge servers. Though many factors such as server loads contribute to this selection process, the critical factor is the proximity (i.e., geographical) information. For instance, in a CDN that deploys Edge Servers on both coasts of USA, an end user coming from California most likely will be served by an Edge Server located in west coast rather than east coast. Traditional GeoDNS solutions work effectively by offering the end users lower response time and higher throughput. Inside CDN infrastructure, GeoDNS is also used to determine the optimal Origin Server to serve Edge Server requests, with the goal of offering lower transit cost and response time.

When supporting live streaming, GeoDNS is used for dynamical assignment of Origin Streaming Servers in response to Edge Streaming Server requests. In this process, traditional GeoDNS only considers the properties (e.g. proximity) of Origin Servers with respect to a particular Edge Server, which may result in sub-par performance. Consider an example shown in Figure 1 where Source S is ingesting a live stream into CDN's Ingest Server I. Assuming Edge Server E needs to serve User U the live stream originating from Ingest Server I. E has two optional Origin Servers to retrieve the stream from: O_1 and O_2. Since O_1 is closer to E, default GeoDNS will assign O_1 to E's DNS request, thus resulting in a CDN transit path of $I - O_1 - E$, as shown in Figure 1(a). However, as shown in Figure 1(b), there exists a better CDN transit path of $I - O_2 - E$, which has smaller CDN transit cost in terms of stream delivery distance. In addition to less transit cost, U's viewing experience is also expected to be better, as the entire live stream path of $S - I - O_2 - E - U$ is shorter. The CDN transit path shown in Figure 1(b) can be achieved by an optimized GeoDNS solution which assigns to E the Origin Server of O_2, as opposed to O_1.

Though effectively addressing all challenges associated with live streaming requires advanced design/redesign of many aspects of CDN infrastructure, in this work, we focus on optimizing the Origin Streaming Server selection through GeoDNS, and propose a design called *Sticky-DNS* for supporting live streaming. The key idea of Sticky-DNS is that when performing GeoDNS and selecting Origin Servers to serve Edge Servers, the optimal Origin Server is determined with the consideration of two CDN hops of both Ingest-to-Origin and Origin-to-Edge rather than the single hop of Origin-to-Edge as in traditional GeoDNS.

In the following paper, we first provide some background information and motivate our design of Sticky-DNS in Section 2. We then present the problem definition and detailed design in Section 3 and Section 4, respectively. We perform prototype-based evaluation and show the results in Section 5. We present related works and conclude the work in Section 6 and Section 7, respectively.

2   Background

In this section, we first provide some backgrounds about CDN, GeoDNS, and live streaming. We then present some initial results about the popularity of live streams on Ustream.tv, a major live streaming web site. Finally, we summarize this section by providing insights into the design of new GeoDNS for live streaming.

2.1   Backgrounds

CDN: Content Delivery Networks (CDNs) can be used to deliver both static web contents and live streams. A typical CDN infrastructure consists of Ingest Servers (for accepting customer contents), Origin Servers (for serving edge servers) and Edge Servers (for serving end users directly), forming a tree-like structure. Various servers are organized into POPs (i.e., Point Of Presence).

GeoDNS: CDNs aim to deliver contents directly from Edge Servers that are closer to end users, thus minimizing the adverse impact of dynamic network path and reducing network transit cost. For this, a specialized DNS service is typically used for redirecting requesting end users to appropriate Edge Servers.

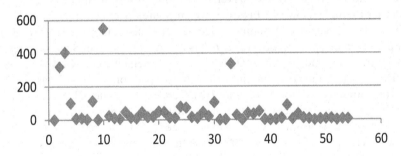

Fig. 2. Number of viewers for the first 55 streams on Ustream.tv

Live Streaming: Live streaming is a new type of application that is increasingly delivered by CDNs. Featuring different properties from static contents, live streaming typically has high bandwidth requirement which exerts pressure on the CDN infrastructure. Unlike static web contents, live streams cannot be cached and have to maintain a full path from the customer source to the end viewers (i.e., end users).

2.2 Popularity of Live Streams

On today's Internet, vast amount of live streams are being supported by CDNs. Though the sizes of viewer set vary greatly, many live streams today feature small viewer sets. Specifically, we consider a major live streaming website of Ustream.tv and study the live streams that fall into the category of "most-total-views" at a particular time. We count the numbers of viewers for each of the first 55 streams, and the results are shown in Figure 2. Note that the figure only shows the active live streams, and other streams are off-air at the particular time. We observe that though the most popular stream has more than 500 viewers, only 6 of them have more than 100 viewers. The average number of live viewers is only about 53.

2.3 Observations

As we observed from the illustrate example shown in Figure 1, CDN transit cost (i.e., Ingest-Origin and Origin-Edge paths) can be saved by assigning appropriate Origin Servers to requesting Edge Servers for live streaming applications. Instead of always assigning the nearest Origin Server to the Edge Server that issues DNS request, a specially-designed GeoDNS could determine the assignment based on the entire CDN delivery path. Such a special GeoDNS can significantly save CDN transit cost for scenarios where a live stream is not popular as they incur shorter CDN delivery paths.

Though the popularity of streams (i.e., viewer set size) varies greatly, many live streams today feature small viewer sets. On the other hand, today's major CDN providers typically have hundreds or even thousands of Edge/Origin streaming servers for supporting live streaming. The mismatch between the sizes of viewer sets and server sets motivates our design of a specialized DNS for less-popular live streams, with the benefit of reduced CDN transit cost.

For popular live streams, however, the same approach needs to be adapted to reutilize delivery path at Ingest-Origin level. Specifically, default GeoDNS practically encourages path reutilization at Ingest-Origin level since each Origin Server can aggregate the streaming requests from closer-by Edge Servers, thus reducing the CDN transit cost. Allowing each Edge Server to connect to far-away Origin Servers, on the other hand, discourages path reutilization, thus could result in larger aggregate delivery distance inside CDN. Therefore, an appropriate design of GeoDNS has to consider the popularity of a live stream, and adapts its behavior correspondingly.

3 Design of Sticky-DNS

In this section, we first formalize the problem we attempt to address. We then present the design overview of Sticky-DNS, its software structure and the entire process.

3.1 Problem Definition

We consider scenarios where a CDN provider has three types of streaming servers for supporting live streaming: Ingest Streaming Servers, Origin Streaming Servers, and Edge Streaming Servers. We use SS_I, SS_O and SS_E to denote the three server sets, respectively. The CDN provider delivers a set of live streams $\{L_m\}$. We further assume each stream L_m has a single ingesting source which connects to an Ingest Server SS_{Im}.

The problem we are addressing with Sticky-DNS design can be defined as follows. For a live stream denoted by L_m and a viewer V_n, we assume the Edge Server that serves viewer V_n is SS_{Emn}, which is determined by regular GeoDNS. Typically SS_{Emn} is the closest Edge server to the end viewer. Sticky-DNS needs to decide the optimal Origin Server SS_{Omn} to serve SS_{Emn} such that the CDN transit cost can be minimized and the end viewers' experience is not compromised. We use C_{IO} and C_{OE} to denote the transit costs corresponding to the paths of Ingest-Origin and Origin-Edge, respectively. With these assumptions, the input, output and objective function of Sticky-DNS are presented in Figure 3.

3.2 Design Overview

Sticky-DNS is a specialized DNS service designed for live streaming applications. It aims at saving CDN transit cost but not compromising end user experience. [1] Sticky-DNS achieves the cost savings by assigning proper Origin Servers to serve Edge Servers with shorter CDN delivery paths.

Sticky-DNS's operations are per-stream based, thus it maintains appropriate states for all live streams. At a higher level, Sticky-DNS adjusts its behavior as the particular live stream changes popularity. Specifically, when a live stream is not popular, Origin

---

[1] Note that for ease of presentation, we use the distance as the primary cost metric; but it would be easy to extend the cost metric to include other factors such as pricing.

Input:
1 $\{L_m\}$: Live stream set of individual stream L_m;
2 $V_m = \{V_m n\}$: Viewer set for live stream L_m;
3 SS_{Im}: The Ingest Server for live stream L_m;
4 SS_{Om}: CDN Origin Server set for L_m;
5 $SS_{Em} = \{SS_{Emn}\}$: CDN Edge Server set for L_m; // Note that each Edge Server
6   // E_{mn} for each individual viewer V_n is determined by regular GeoDNS;
7 C_{IO}: Cost arrays of all Ingest-Origin pairs;
8 C_{OE}: Cost arrays of all Origin-Edge pairs;
Output:
1 Optimal Origin Server set $SS_{Om} = \{SS_{Omn}\}$ for Edge Server set SS_{Em},
        where each SS_{Omn} is serving the Edge Server of SS_{Emn} ;
Objective Function:
1 Total CDN transit cost $\Sigma(C_{IO} + C_{EO})$ for all live streams $\{L_m\}$ is minimized;
2 Non-compromised viewer experience;

Fig. 3. Problem Definition

Servers are chosen based on the lengths of entire Edge-Origin-Ingest paths. For this, Sticky-DNS maintains the cost values of every Edge-Origin and Origin-Ingest pairs. Initially, all the costs are assigned according to certain cost-determination methods. Whenever an Origin Server is arealdy serving the live stream, the corresponding Origin-Ingest cost is set to zero to reflect the fact that serving an additional Edge Server with this Origin Server will incur no additional cost on the Origin-Ingest path.

However, as a stream becomes more popular, Sticky-DNS needs to adapt back to the default behavior determined by regular DNS for reusing Ingest-Origin paths. The reason is that when serving popular streams, since Origin Servers are more likely serving that live stream, the behavior of Sticky-DNS will more likely be that of regular GeoDNS, and the proximity-closest Origin Server is typically chosen for each Edge Server so that the Ingest-Origin paths are reutilized. To encourage this, we introduce the concept of "would-be" behavior. When an Origin Server is determined by regular DNS for Origin request issued by an Edge Server, the particular Origin is the "would-be" Origin for the Edge, while the Edge is the "would-be" Edge for the Origin. Even if a different Origin is determined by Sticky-DNS, the "would-be" state is recorded, which is used to adjust the corresponding Origin-Ingest cost. Specifically, with more "would-be" Edge Servers retrieving from an Origin, the corresponding Origin-Ingest cost is reduced further. The idea behind this treatment is that the Origin-Ingest cost is shared by all downstream Edge Servers, thus encouraging the reuse of the particular Origin-Ingest path.

These cost values will be used to choose optimal Origin Servers for incoming Origin Server DNS requests so that the smallest $\Sigma(C_{IO} + C_{EO})$ will result. To achieve this, Sticky-DNS uses the notion of "Additional Cost" when deciding on an Origin Server. Specifically, given an incoming viewer V_n and the corresponding Edge Server SS_{Emn}, Sticky-DNS always return the Origin Server that causes minimal "Additional Cost".

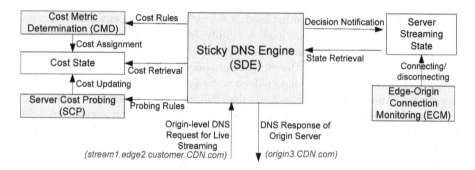

Fig. 4. Software Architecture

The additional cost is defined as the *extra* CDN transit cost that needs to be paid when serving the Edge Server with a particular Origin Server. Recall that CDN transit cost contains two parts: the Ingest-Origin cost and Edge-Origin cost. Whenever an Origin Server first connects to an Ingest Server to retrieve a live stream, CDN pays Ingest-Origin cost, but succeeding retrieval of the same live stream from the same Ingest Server to the same Origin Server will incur zero additional cost.

3.3 Software Architecture

The software architecture of Sticky-DNS is shown in Figure 4. The heart is Sticky-DNS Engine (SDE), which takes the DNS request, interacts with other components, and then decides the optimal Origin Server. Sticky-DNS assigns Origin Servers based on the cost associated with the live streaming delivery path, and the cost is CDN-specific and determined by another component of Cost Metric Determination (CMD) and updated by Server Cost Probing (SCP). Meanwhile, to accommodate network dynamics, a component of Edge-Origin Connection Monitoring (ECM) is used to update the cost state. Sticky-DNS maintains the server streaming state which basically records information of which Edge Server is serving which streams and which Origin Server is retrieving which streams. This state is updated by the events of viewers joining and leaving.

The overall process of how Sticky-DNS works is as below. When a new live streaming DNS request comes, the optimal Edge Server will be determined by regular GeoDNS. CDN will then attempt to determine the optimal Origin Server for the determined Edge Server. For this, the Edge Server issues DNS request to DNS service asking for the proper Origin Server for retrieving the live stream from. Sticky-DNS takes the Origin-Server request and returns the determined Origin Server. Meanwhile, it updates the server streaming states.

4 Sticky-DNS Components

4.1 Cost Metric Determination (CMD)

In order to perform Sticky-DNS operations, each delivery hop (i.e., Ingest-Origin and Origin-Edge) on CDN infrastructure has to be associated with quantifiable cost. Note that though physical distance is often used as the path cost, cost metrics may also include network delay, price, server load, reliability, loss rate, etc. Since different cost metrics often belong to distinct dimensions and they are often prioritized. Though how to prioritize them varies with different CDN providers and deployment scenarios, in this work we provide the following guidelines: (i) Server Load is prioritized over all other metrics. An Origin server is put into the DNS pool (i.e., available to be returned by Sticky-DNS) only if it can take more loads (i.e., serving more requests); (ii) Loss rate has to be under certain threshold. Since most live streaming (e.g., RTMP, HTTP) use TCP to transmit, large loss rate cannot sustain a reasonable level of performance; (iii) Reliability has to be above certain threshold. Live streaming requires a real-time transmission path, thus reliability is important during the stream playback; (iv) Pricing is prioritized over network delay and physical distance. Though pricing is often correlated with the latter two metrics, it is prioritized over them if they are not identical; (v) Network delay and physical distance. The impact of these two metrics are buffering time and playback delay. In reality, they can be used as the substitute for pricing metric when the latter is not available or hard to define.

Thus, with the above guidelines in mind, we propose to enforce the cost determination by keeping track of the following state information.

- An array of server load for the Origin Servers, denoted by $SL[M]$, where M is the number of Origin Servers. $SL[i]$ represents the current load of Origin Server SS_{Oi};
- A 2-D array of loss rate for each Origin-Edge path, denoted by $LR[M][N]$, where M is the number of Origin Servers and N is the number of Edge Servers. $LR[i][j]$ represents the loss rate of the path between Origin Server SS_{Oi} and Edge Server SS_{Ej}; Another array of loss rate for each Ingest-Origin pair, denoted by $LRI[M]$, assuming a single Ingest Server;
- A 2-D array of reliability for each Origin-Edge path, denoted by $RE[M][N]$, where M is the number of Origin Servers and N is the number of Edge Servers. $RE[i][j]$ represents the reliability of the path between Origin Server SS_{Oi} and Edge Server SS_{Ej}; Another array of reliability for each Ingest-Origin pair, denoted by $REI[M]$;
- Pricing is represented by $PR[M][N]$ for each pair of Origin-Edge; Another array of $PRI[M]$ for each pair of Ingest-Origin;
- Similarly, network delay and physical distance are represented by $ND[M][N]$ and $PD[M][N]$, respectively. Two other arrays of $NDI[M]$ and $PDI[M]$ are also used.

4.2   Server Cost Probing (SCP)

SCP updates the various cost state by proactively or reactively monitoring/probing the network. Specifically,

- *Origin Server Load* $(SL[M])$. The load can be obtained by installing services which monitor CPU/Memory utilization;
- *Loss rate* $(LR[M][N]$ and $LRI[M][N])$. Loss rate monitoring between servers can be obtained by observing existing connections' behaviors (e.g., TCP loss recovery behaviors) or proactively sending test packets. When a network path (e.g., Ingest-Origin-Edge) consists of two network hops, the aggregate loss rate of path $SS_{Ei} - SS_{Oj} - SS_I$ can be calculated as $LR_{ij} = (1 - (1 - LR[j][i])(1 - LRI[j]))$;

Core Algorithm:
    Initialize all cost states;
    For an incoming new viewer V_n requesting L_m, determine the Edge Server SS_{Emn};
1 If SS_{Emn} is already serving L_m;
2   Return; //No Origin Server request since the Edge Server is serving L_m now;
3 Else
4   Determine the candidate Origin Server set based on load, loss rate, etc.;
5   For every Origin Server SS_{Oi}, if $(SL[i] \leq \alpha$ and $LR_{j,k} \leq \beta$ and $RE_{j,k} \geq \gamma$, where
6   α, β, γ are the respective threshold values), SS_{Oi} is a candidate Origin Server;
7   Determine the optimal Origin Server SS_{Oq} that has the smallest aggregate
8   cost of C_{IO} and C_{OE} for SS_{Emn};
9    $NV[q][m]{+}{+}$;
10// Update $AD[q][m]$;
11 If $(NV[i][j] \geq 1)$
12    $AD[i][j] = 0$;
13 Else
14   If $(WB[i][j] ==0)$: $AD[i][j]$ = initial cost;
15   Else : $AD[i][j] = \frac{initialcost}{WB[M][T]+1}$
If Edge Server SS_{Ei} is disconnecting from SS_{Oj} for live stream L_m:
1 // Update $NV[I][J]$ and $AD[I][J]$;
2 $NV[j][m]{-}$;
3 If $(NV[j][m] \geq{=}1)$: $AD[j][m] = \frac{Initialcost}{(NV[j][m]+1)}$;
4 Else : $AD[j][m] = \{initialcost\}$.

Fig. 5. Core Algorithm

- Similarly, *reliability* ($RE[i][j]$ and $REI[i][j]$) can be obtained by monitoring the path up/down time. The aggregate reliability of path $SS_{Ei} - SS_{Oj} - SS_I$ can be calculated as $RE_{ij} = (RE[j][i] * REI[j])$;
- *Pricing* ($PR[M][N]$ and $PRI[M][N]$) can be adjusted by business logics. Whenever the CDN operators change the network pricing rates, the pricing used by Sticky-DNS can be correspondingly adjusted.
- Network delays ($ND[M][N]$ and $NDI[M]$) and physical distances ($PD[M][N]$ and $PDI[M]$) are easy to obtain with known techniques.

4.3 Edge-Origin Connection Monitoring (ECM)

ECM is used to keep the server streaming state maintained by OSS fresh, in the sense that the additional cost associated with each Origin Server is up-to-date, and the popularity state of a stream on all Origin Servers is up-to-date. For all Origin Servers, there is a server streaming state. The server streaming state is an array, and each element corresponds to an Origin Server and is defined as the Additional Cost of using the particular Origin Server to serve a stream. The state can be realized by a 2-D array of AD[M][T],

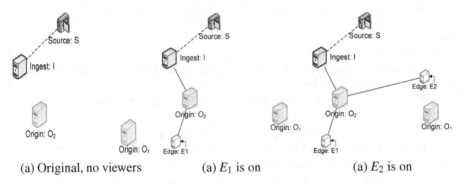

(a) Original, no viewers   (a) E_1 is on   (a) E_2 is on

Fig. 6. An illustrative example (I)

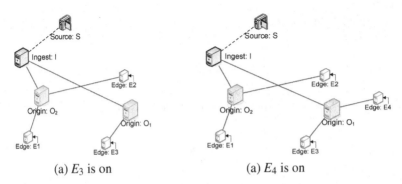

(a) E_3 is on   (a) E_4 is on

Fig. 7. An illustrative example (II)

where M is the number of Origin Servers and T is the number of streams. AD[i][j] records the additional cost of using Origin Server SS_{Oi} to serve stream L_j. The values of AD[M][T] are based on whether an Origin Server serves a stream or not.

Two other 2-D arrays are used: NV[i][j] records the number of Edge Servers Origin Server SS_{Oi} is serving stream L_j to. WB[M][T] is used to indicate the stream popularity on a particular Origin Server. The indicator uses the number of "Would-be" Edge Servers for each Origin Server. ECM monitors the connecting/disconnecting events between Origin and Ingest Servers for all live streams. Whenever the events occur, CVM updates NV[M][T], WB[M][T] and AD[M][T] correspondingly.

4.4   Sticky DNS Engine (SDE)

Dynamic DNS Engine (SDE) performs the actually computation and comparison of costs, then selects the most appropriate Origin Server given a live streaming DNS request. The algorithms are shown in Figure 5. SDE handles the joining of an Edge Server (i.e., begins to serve a stream) and the leaving (i.e., begins to drop a stream) separately. For both events, it updates the *AD* and *NV* states.

4.5   An Illustrative Example

We use the following example to illustrate how Sticky-DNS works. Assuming there are one Ingest Server (I) and two Origin Servers (O_1 and O_2), as shown in Figure 6. When the first end-viewer joins and is bound to Edge Server E_1, E_1 needs to decide which Origin Server (O_1 or O_2) for E_1. Assuming the distance is the cost metric, O_2 is chosen since the additional cost of pulling from O_2 (i.e., sum of $I - O_2$ and $O_2 - E_1$) is smaller.

When the second Edge Server E_2 requests an Origin Server, though it is closer to Origin Server O_1, the additional cost of pulling from O_1 (i.e., $I - O_1$ and $O_1 - E_2$) is larger than that of pulling from O_2 (i.e, only $O_2 - E_2$, since $I - O_2$ has cost of being zero). Thus E_2 chooses O_2 as the optimal Origin Server. Note that since E_2 is the "would-be" edge of O_2, the cost of $I - O_1$ is reduced in half to reflect the benefit of path reuse. When the third Edge Server E_3 joins, as shown in Figure 7, it compares the additional costs of pulling from O_1 and pulling from O_2. Since the cost of $I - O_1$ is not in half, assuming the cost sum of $I - O_1$ and $O_1 - E_3$ is smaller than the cost of $O_2 - E_3$, E_3 chooses O_1 to be the optimal Origin Server. Finally, when Edge Server E_4 joins, it chooses O_1 as the Origin Server.

5   Evaluation

To gain concrete understanding of GeoDNS regarding the impact on both CDN and viewers, we consider the following simplified scenario to quantify the saving on CDN transit cost and the performance experienced by end viewers. We assume an USA mainland CDN provider which has 1 Ingest POP (Point of Presence) and 10 Origin POPs, where each POP has only a single streaming server. We further assume that Edge Servers have to retrieve live streams from Origin Servers, which then retrieve from Ingest Server. For simplicity, we consider a performance metric of physical distance in the unit of thousand-miles (i.e., KMiles) for both CDN transit-cost saving and live-stream viewers. Thus, the larger the distances are, the higher cost both CDN and viewers pay.

We built a prototype with Adobe Flash Media Server (FMS) 4.0. The prototype consists of 11 servers deployed in 11 cities, all running Windows Server 2008 R2. One of the servers serves as the Ingest Server and receives a live stream from a stream source, and the other 10 servers serve as Origin Servers and are relaying the live stream to end viewers. We then invoke 10 stream viewers from different locations. Since viewers are always bound to the closest Edge Servers, we use viewers to mimic the edge servers in typical CDN setup as they need to decide the origin servers to pull stream from.

We first consider the default regular DNS, which directs each viewer to the closest Origin Server. For comparison, we also consider an optimized DNS which directs each Edge POP to the closest Origin POP that leads to smallest CDN transit path (i.e., from Ingest Server to Edge Server).

CDN Transit Cost: For both scenarios, we count the lengths of Ingest-Origin paths, Origin-Edge paths, and aggregated CDN delivery path. As shown in Figure 8, the blue bars show the default scenario, while the red bars show the optimized scenario. The aggregated CDN delivery distance is the sum of all Ingest-Origin and Origin-Edge paths. Specifically, first, the aggregated Ingest-Origin distances are 10.48 Kmiles and 1.81

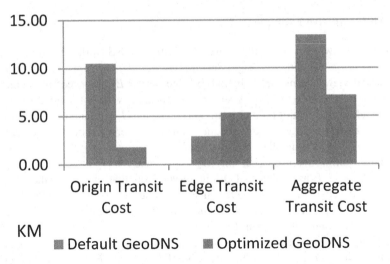

Fig. 8. CDN Transit Cost

Kmiles for two scenarios, respectively. The reason for reduced distance in optimized-DNS scenario is that some Origin POPs are not serving any Edge Servers, thus they are free from stream delivery. Second, the aggregated Origin-Edge distances are 2.92 Kmiles and 5.40 Kmiles, respectively. Since Edge Servers in optimized-scenarios may connect to far-away Origin POPs, the Origin-Edge paths are inflated. Third, the aggregated path distances, which correspond to the CDN transit cost, are 13.41 Kmiles and 7.17 Kmiles, respectively. We see that for the particular setup, optimized-DNS results in much smaller CDN transit cost (more than 46% reduction).

These results suggest that CDN is able to gain significant transit cost saving by optimizing GeoDNS inside CDN. Note that in this simple scenario, we assume each POP only has a single Edge Server. With more servers, the saved transit cost can be more significant as each server will incur a separate delivery path. Note that with shorter delivery paths, end viewers also see shorter playback buffers and better viewing experiences.

Viewers' Experience: Since each live stream has to delivered from the stream source all the way to the end users in a real-time fashion, the end-users' performance is heavily impacted by the length of the entire delivery path. In other words, though there are other factors impacting live-stream users' performance, it is generally acceptable to claim that the longer path an end user relies on, the worse performance the user experiences. For both scenarios, since the distances from streaming sources to the Ingest Server and from Edge Server to end viewer are the same, we now focus only on the CDN delivery distance from Ingest Server to Edge Server for each viewer and show them in Figure 9. We observer that all paths in optimized-DNS scenario are shorter, which is not surprising since Edge Servers choose the Origin Servers that result in shortest paths. The aggregated distances are 13.41 Kmiles and 10.35 Kmiles, respectively, or 23% decrease. These results suggest that end viewer's experience can also improved with optimized GeoDNS.

Money Talks: Taking a more direct business perspective, we now compare the transit cost with respect to pricing of bandwidth usage. Depending on subscription

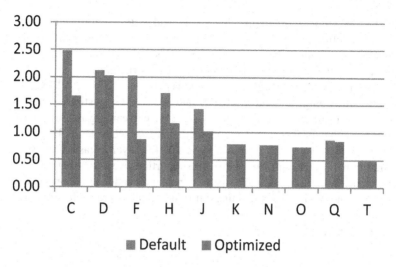

Fig. 9. Stream Delivery Paths

packages, CDN providers may pay ISPs for the bandwidth used. We assume each live stream is 3Mbps. In the above scenario where only 4 Origin Servers are delivering the same live stream, the saved bandwidth per day would be 0.20 TB*Kmiles (or 73.74 TB*KMiles per year). With 2000 streams, the saved bandwidth would be 400 TB*Kmiles (or 147.47 PB * Kmiles per year). Simply assuming the transit cost of 0.10 per GB/Kmile, optimized-DNS can help save $14.74 Million per year with 2000 streams, or about $7K per stream, as shown in Table 1.

6   Related Work

Content Delivery Networks (CDNs) have been carried out by various providers to expedite the web access [1]. The techniques used by CDNs for delivering conventional web contents are explained in related writings [4]. Despite the popularity and pervasiveness of CDNs, many research problems and system-building challenges persist for optimizing CDN infrastructure and addressing challenges associated supporting various types of applications. For instance, as we demonstrated in this work, how to efficiently support the application of live streaming with CDNs deserves more study.

Though various network architectures have been proposed and utilized for different deployment scenarios with the rapid development of Internet technology [5, 6], CDN providers typically apply layered structure (e.g., ingest-layer, origin-layer and edge-layer) due to the caching-property of delivering static web contents tracing back to

Table 1. Bandwidth/Cost Saving of Sticky-DNS

Number of streams	Daily BW Saving	Yearly BW Saving	Yearly Cost Saving
1	0.20 TB	73.74 TB	$7K
2000	400 TB	147.47 PB	$14.74M

Day-1 of CDN industry. Realizing that CDNs and P2P can complement each other, many research efforts also attempt to integrate these two realms into one [7]. Unlike these works that combine the merits of both CDNs and P2P, our work takes an inside perspective and attempts to refine CDN delivery infrastructure.

Live streaming has been studied from various perspectives [8–10]. The unique properties of live streaming, coupled with CDN-assisted delivery, justifies a specialized design of CDN infrastructure that specifically serves live streaming and saves CDN transit cost. One work [11] proposes to combine the benefits of CDN and P2P to enhance live streaming. Another work [12] proposes to build a flat-layer infrastructure (as opposed to the traditional 3-layer infrastructure) for supporting live streaming with CDNs. To our best knowledge, this work is the first to consider and address the problem of saving transit cost for delivering live streaming with traditional layered-infrastructure CDNs.

7   Conclusion

In this work, we optimize CDN streaming server selection to better support live streaming with CDN. The proposed design dynamically selects streaming servers based on the popularity of the live stream. Significantly improving both the CDN transit cost saving and end viewers' experience, the design can be deployed with a specialized GeoDNS.

References

1. "Akamai technologies", http://www.akamai.com/
2. "Level 3 communications, llc", http://www.level3.com/
3. "Bind geodns", http://www.caraytech.com/geodns/
4. Verma, D.C., Calo, S., Amiri, K.: Policy based management of content distribution networks. IEEE Network Magazine 16, 34–39 (2002)
5. Stoica, I., Morris, R., Karger, D., Kaashoek, M.F., Balakrishnan, H.: Chord: A scalable peer-to-peer lookup service for internet applications. In: SIGCOMM: Proceedings of the 2001 Conference on Applications, Technologies, Architectures, and Protocols for Computer Communications, San Diego, CA, USA (2001)
6. Ratnasamy, S., Francis, P., Handley, M., Karp, R., Schenker, S.: A scalable content-addressable network. In: SIGCOMM: Proceedings of the Conference on Applications, Technologies, Architectures, and Protocols for Computer Communications, San Diego, USA (2001)
7. Yin, H., Liu, X., Zhan, T., Sekar, V., Qiu, F., Lin, C., Zhang, H., Li, B.: Livesky: Enhancing cdn with p2p. ACM Trans. Multimedia Comput. Commun. Appl. (August 2010)
8. Sripanidkulchai, K., Maggs, B., Zhang, H.: An analysis of live streaming workloads on the internet. In: Proceedings of the 4th ACM SIGCOMM Conference on Internet Measurement, Ser. IMC 2004 (2004)
9. He, J., Chaintreau, A., Diot, C.: A performance evaluation of scalable live video streaming with nano data centers. Comput. Netw. 53, 153–167 (2009)
10. Vicari, C., Petrioli, C., Presti, F.L.: Dynamic replica placement and traffic redirection in content delivery networks. SIGMETRICS Perform. Eval. Rev. 35 (December 2007)
11. Lu, Z.H., Gao, X.H., Huang, S.J., Huang, Y.: Scalable and reliable live streaming service through coordinating cdn and p2p. In: Proceedings of the 2011 IEEE 17th International Conference on Parallel and Distributed Systems, Ser. ICPADS, Washington, DC, USA (2011)
12. Zhuang, Z., Guo, C.: Optimizing cdn infrastructure for live streaming with constrained server chaining. In: Proceedings of the 2011 IEEE Ninth International Symposium on Parallel and Distributed Processing with Applications, Ser. ISPA, Washington, DC, USA (2011)

A Novel Hybrid IP Traceback Scheme
with Packet Counters

Tomoyuki Karasawa[1], Masakazu Soshi[2], and Atsuko Miyaji[3]

[1] Internet Initiative Japan (IIJ) Inc.
tomoyuki-k@iij.ad.jp
[2] Hiroshima City University
soshi@hiroshima-cu.ac.jp
[3] Japan Advanced Institute of Science and Technology (JAIST)
miyaji@jaist.ac.jp

Abstract. In this paper we shall propose a novel hybrid IP traceback scheme with *packet counters*. In our scheme, a (packet) counter is used to improve correlation of packet sampling in order to reconstruct the attack tree efficiently. Our scheme has the remarkable advantages: (1) it is simple and efficient, (2) it is significantly resistant to attacks, (3) it requires a lower sampling rate compared with previous work, e.g., only 1% is enough, (4) its false positive/negative rates are also lower.

1 Introduction

One of the most serious threats to the Internet security is a *DoS (Denial of Service) attack*, where an attacker attempts to make a target host (called a *victim*) fail by sending a huge number of packets to the host [1]. In particular, in recent years, a *DDoS (Distributed DoS) attack*, where there are many attackers scattered over the Internet, has become more prevailing [1]. Such a DDoS attack can be represented by an *attack tree*, the leaves and the root of which are the attackers and the victim, respectively. Furthermore, we call a path along which an attack packet traverses from one attacker to the victim an *attack path*.

A promising countermeasure against DoS/DDoS attacks is called *IP traceback* [2,3,4,5,6,7,8]. In IP traceback schemes, each router on attack paths stores information about the paths on itself or on packets. Then the victim uses the information to recover the attack tree and to find out the attackers.

IP traceback schemes are roughly classified two-fold: *probabilistic packet marking* (PPM for short) protocols and *logging* ones. In PPM protocols, each router probabilistically writes path information onto the packets it receives [3,6]. On the other hand, logging IP traceback protocols make each participating router sample packets and store path information on itself [4,7]. PPM and logging protocols have some advantages, although, they have serious disadvantages (discussed in Sect. 2). Therefore to take advantages of PPM and logging approaches, *hybrid IP traceback schemes* have attracted much attention these years [2,5].

In this paper we shall propose a new hybrid IP traceback scheme. A novel idea of our scheme is the introduction of a *counter* on each packet header. Such a

Y. Xiang et al. (Eds.): IDCS 2012, LNCS 7646, pp. 71–84, 2012.

counter is used to improve correlation of packet sampling in order to reconstruct the attack tree efficiently. Our scheme has the following remarkable advantages: (1) it is simple and efficient, (2) it is highly resistant to attacks, (3) it requires a lower sampling rate compared with previous work, e.g., only 1% is enough, (4) its false positive/negative rates are lower than those of Li et al. [5]. To show these advantages theoretically, we conduct information theoretical analysis of our scheme in detail. Furthermore, we make simulation experiments to investigate the performance of our scheme in practical environments. These theoretical and practical evaluations of our scheme show that our scheme is truly effective.

This paper is organized as follows. We discuss related work in Sect. 2 and shall propose a novel IP traceback in Sect. 3. Then we thoroughly evaluate our scheme in Sect. 4 and Sect. 5. Finally we give conclusion in Sect. 6.

2   Related Work

As stated in Sect. 1, IP traceback schemes are roughly classified into *probabilistic packet marking* (PPM) protocols [3,6] and *logging* ones [4,7]. PPM does not need storage resource of routers, although, it generally requires the victim to receive a large number of packets before he can reconstruct the attack tree. On the other hand, in logging schemes, the number of packets for attack tree recovery can be small. However, logging schemes impose heavy load and require extremely large storage space on the routers.

Now, for a recent example of IP traceback protocols, let us consider the work by Yu et al. [8]. The protocol exploits entropy variation for IP traceback and is very interesting itself. However, the proposed flow monitoring algorithm and IP traceback algorithm are rather intricate. Furthermore, the false positive/negative rates in the traceback process are not discussed in detail in [8].

In summary, we still do not have an established IP traceback scheme. However, we consider *hybrid IP traceback schemes* to be promising because they can take advantage of both PPM and logging approaches [2,5]. In particular, Li et al. proposed one of the most important hybrid IP traceback schemes [5]. The protocol of Li et al. was successful in improving sampling correlation. Unfortunately, they consider only the correlation between neighboring routers. In this paper, we shall show that we can develop a highly efficient IP traceback scheme *by considering correlation of packet sampling all over a whole attack path.*

3   Our Proposed Protocol

In this section we propose a novel hybrid IP traceback scheme.

3.1   Basic Idea

First of all, we briefly give a basic idea of our proposed scheme. Our scheme attempts to improve correlation of packet sampling over a whole attack path for efficient recovery of the attack tree. For that purpose, we designate five bit space on each packet header as a *counter*[1]. Throughout the paper, we denote the counter of packet P by $P.counter$.

In our scheme, if a router on an attack path decides to sample a packet P with some probability[2], then it increments $P.counter$ by one, stores some information on itself, and finally passes the packet to an adjacent router. Consequently, *the greater the value of $P.counter$ is, the larger the number of routers on the attack path that store information of P is*. In other words, a packet with a large counter value is *useful* when we recover the attack tree. Therefore, when we sample a packet, if we *probabilistically* prefer a packet with a larger counter value to one with a smaller value, then we can improve the correlation factor of packet sampling and have more useful packets for traceback later.

3.2 Sampling

Based on the discussion in Sect. 3.1, in this section we shall propose a novel sampling algorithm as in Fig. 1. Each participating router R executes the sampling algorithm when it receives a packet P. It is really interesting that such a simple sampling algorithm as ours is highly effective, as shown later in this paper.

Sampling procedure at router R:
for each packet P
    x is chosen uniformly at random between 0 and 1
    $p \leftarrow$ compute_prob($P.counter$)   ▷ 'compute_prob' is discussed later
    if $(x < p)$ **then**   ▷ i.e, with probability p
        $P.counter \leftarrow P.counter +1$
        Store digest of P ▷ discussed in Sect. 3.3

Fig. 1. Our Proposed Sampling Algorithm

Suppose that R receives a packet P. Then as depicted in Fig. 1, with a probability p, which is computed by the procedure 'compute_prob', R increments $P.counter$ by one and stores the digest of P (see also Sect. 3.3).

Next let us take a closer look at 'compute_prob' itself. As discussed in Sect. 3.1, we should preferentially sample a packet with a larger counter value. Furthermore, in order to reduce load on routers, we must make 'compute_prob' as simple as possible. In addition, it must be efficiently computable.

Therefore, in this paper we propose to implement 'compute_prob' as in Fig. 2, where $\alpha > 1$, β, and M are some constant values, which are discussed in Sect. 4.3.

As we can obviously see from Fig. 2, a sampling probability returned by 'compute_prob' becomes larger in a polynomial order of a counter value c. Note that since we assume that $\alpha > 1$, the probability grows significantly larger than the case proportional to c. Intuitively speaking, it means that *in a polynomial order*

---

[1] Dean et al. [3] have pointed out that 25 bits in each IPv4 packet header are available for IP traceback. So five bits can easily be accommodated by each packet header.

[2] How to compute this probability is vital to our scheme and is discussed in Sect. 3.2.

function compute_prob(c)   ▷ c is a counter value
    return $(c^\alpha + \beta)/M$ ▷ return the sampling probability $(c^\alpha + \beta)/M$

Fig. 2. Our Proposed Function for 'compute_prob'

of counter values, a packet with a larger counter is sampled with a higher probability, but a packet with a smaller counter is sampled with a lower probability. In this way we give a preference to a packet with a larger counter value when sampling attack packets.

3.3 Storing Packet Digests

In our sampling algorithm in Fig. 1, we compute the digest of a packet in the form of Bloom filter [9]. For a set S of packets, Bloom filter is represented by an array A of m bits, each of which is expressed as $A[i] \in \{0,1\}$ and initially every $A[i]$ is set to zero $(i = 1, ..., m)$. Moreover, we assume that Bloom filter in this paper uses k hash functions $h_1, ..., h_k$ that are independently and randomly chosen. Every hash function h_i $(i = 1, ..., k)$ has the range $\{1, ..., m\}$.

Packet digesting is carried out as follows. When we insert the digest of packet P into S, we set $A[h_i(P)]$ to one $(i = 1, ..., k)$, where $h_i(P)$ is the output of h_i when it takes as input the first invariable 28 bits of P as in [7]. Now when we want to know if a packet P' is a member of S or not, we check the bits $A[h_i(P')]$ $(i = 1, ..., k)$. If any of the bits is zero, then P' is not in S. Otherwise, i.e., if every bit is one, P' is in S with a *high probability*. That is, even in such a case, it *is* possible that P' is actually not in S.

In summary, Bloom filter cannot exhibit *false negatives*. Therefore, when P is actually in S, the Bloom filter does never report that P is not in S. On the other hand, every Bloom filter can have *false positives*. In other words, it can conclude (with a very low probability) that $P \in S$, in spite that actually $P \notin S$. Throughout the paper, we estimate that the probability of false positives in our Bloom filter is given by 2^{-k} as in [5,9].

3.4 Traceback

Our scheme traces back the attack sources as follows. Once faced with DoS/DDoS attacks, with a some predefined threshold T, the victim adds each packet P from a set $\mathcal{N}$ of its received packets to a set $\mathcal{N}'$ of packets if P.counter $\geq T$. Note that from the discussions from Sect. 3.1, we see that if the victim sets T to a large value, then he can use packets with higher sampling correlation and it leads to efficient recovery of the attack tree. On the other hand, if he makes T too large, then the number of the attack packets available in performing traceback becomes smaller. Taking into consideration the discussion, the victim can choose any T that is appropriate for his environment.

After constructing a set $\mathcal{N}'$ of packets, the victim sends $\mathcal{N}'$ to every neighboring router R. Next if R finds out that some packet in $\mathcal{N}'$ is also in its sampling log (i.e., in the form of Bloom filter), then R supposes that it is on an attack path and sends $\mathcal{N}'$ to every router R' that is adjacent to R. Such a traceback process is repeatedly performed until it cannot go any further.

3.5 Security Consideration

In this section we briefly discuss security of our scheme. First note that all attackers are supposed to be located at the leaves of an attack tree. Therefore, an attacker could affect security of our scheme *only by forging packet counters*. More specifically, all that the attacker can do is only to set to some value the counter of a packet that he injects into the network. However, such a forge by the attacker cannot be a threat to our scheme for the following reason. Namely, a large value of a packet counter given by the attacker only leads to an increase of the sampling probability of the packet, which in turn ends with increasing the correlation of packet sampling and then finally with a more efficient traceback process. Therefore, such an "attack" can *never* be an attack in a true sense, but rather it leads the victim to a situation that is more beneficial to him.

Thus a possible attack that attackers at the leaves can make would be to always set the lowest values to packet counters, that is, to always initialize the counters to zero. This is indeed the worst case scenario to our protocol because in such a case correlation of packet sampling would be forced to be as low as possible and then traceback processes later would be made more difficult.

Fortunately, again, such an attack above cannot be effective. As shown in Sect. 4.3, even if packet counters are initially zero, our scheme exhibits excellent performance (for instance, an efficient traceback process, low false positive/negative rates, and so on).

In summary, we can conclude that our scheme is highly resistant to attacks.

4 Information Theoretical Analysis

In this section, we conduct theoretical analysis of our proposed scheme based on information theory[3].

Now, let us consider the attack path from an attacker to the victim. Henceforth in the paper R_1 denotes the nearest router to the attacker on the attack path and R_2 the second nearest router, which is adjacent to R_1. We denote by R_3, ..., R_{n-1} and R_n the remaining routers on the path in order. Thus R_n is the neighboring router to the victim and n is the (maximum) number of routers between the attacker and the victim.

4.1 Formalization of Sampling

In this section we analyze the sampling procedure of our scheme. Let X_{c_i} be a random variable that represents the counter value of a packet P when P arrives

---

[3] Notice that although the analysis in this section is done in a similar manner to [5] at a glance, the former is more involved than the latter because we must take into account the probabilistic behavior of packet counters.

at router R_i. Then, in order to be fair, we shall evaluate our scheme in the worst case scenario to it. That is, as discussed in Sect. 3.5, the case where the counter value of every packet that R_1 receives is zero. Therefore we have

$$\Pr(X_{c_1} = c) = \begin{cases} 1 & \text{if } c = 0 \\ 0 & \text{otherwise,} \end{cases} \tag{1}$$

and

$$\Pr(X_{c_2} = c) = \begin{cases} \beta/M & \text{if } c = 1 \\ 1 - \beta/M & \text{if } c = 0 \\ 0 & \text{otherwise.} \end{cases} \tag{2}$$

Generally, we have

$$\begin{aligned} \Pr(X_{c_i} = c) &= \Pr(X_{c_i} = c \mid X_{c_{i-1}} = c - 1) \cdot \Pr(X_{c_{i-1}} = c - 1) \\ &\quad + \Pr(X_{c_i} = c \mid X_{c_{i-1}} = c) \cdot \Pr(X_{c_{i-1}} = c) \\ &= \frac{(c-1)^\alpha + \beta}{M} \cdot \Pr(X_{c_{i-1}} = c - 1) + \left(1 - \frac{c^\alpha + \beta}{M}\right) \cdot \Pr(X_{c_{i-1}} = c) . \end{aligned} \tag{3}$$

Note that the counter values of packets R_i receives are non-negative and the (possible) maximum of the values is $i - 1$. Thus if $c < 0$ or $i - 1 < c$, then it holds that $\Pr(X_{c_i} = c) = 0$.

Next in regard to router R_i and a packet P, we define a random variable (indicator variable [9]) X_{p_i} as below:

$$X_{p_i} = \begin{cases} 1 & \text{if } R_i \text{ samples } P \\ 0 & \text{otherwise.} \end{cases}$$

The probability distribution of X_{p_i} can be obtained as follows by using random variable X_{c_i} (Eq. (3)) and the relationship $\Pr(X_{p_i} = 1 \mid X_{c_i} = c) = (c^\alpha + \beta)/M$:

$$\Pr(X_{p_i} = 1) = \sum_{c=0}^{i-1} \frac{c^\alpha + \beta}{M} \cdot \Pr(X_{c_i} = c) . \tag{4}$$

4.2   Evaluation of Traceback

In this section we evaluate the traceback procedure in our proposed scheme using information theory.

Suppose that we are about tracing router R_{i-1} back from router R_i by one hop. As stated in Sect. 3.4, router R_{i-1} is considered on an attack path if the number of the packets sampled by both of R_{i-1} and R_i is greater than or equal to the prespecified threshold T. In the subsequent sections, we assume that T is one for brevity.

The Model. Let $\mathcal{N}$ be a set of the attack packets that the victim uses for traceback and N_p the number of the elements in $\mathcal{N}$, i.e., $N_p = |\mathcal{N}|$. Furthermore, as in [5], we set d_i to the percentage of attack packets that traverse through R_i. Although the value of d_i varies dependently on i, in this paper for simplicity we assume that d_i equals some d for all i. Moreover, the digest of each packet is stored in the form of Bloom filters and our Bloom filter is supposed to use k independent hash functions. We assume that the probability of false positives of the Bloom filter is $f = 2^{-k}$ (see Sect. 3.3). In addition, the binomial distribution with n experiments and success probability p is denoted by Binom(n, p).

Next we introduce some random variables as defined below.

- X_{t_i}: the number of attack packets that R_i samples.
- X_{f_i}: the number of false positives when querying each packet in $\mathcal{N}$ to Bloom filter of R_i. X_{f_i} follows the binomial distribution Binom($N_p - X_{t_i}, f$).
- Y_{t_i}: the number of attack packets with which we trace back from R_i to R_{i-1}. Namely, the number of attack packets sampled at both of R_i and R_{i-1}.
- Y_{f_i}: the number of false positives when querying $X_{t_i} + X_{f_i}$ to Bloom filter at R_{i-1}. Y_{f_i} has a probability distribution Binom($X_{t_i} + X_{f_i} - Y_{t_i}, f$).
- $X_i = X_{t_i} + X_{f_i}$: the number of attack packets used for a traceback process for R_{i-1}.
- $Y_i = Y_{t_i} + Y_{f_i}$: i.e., the number of attack packets both in $\mathcal{N}$ and in the Bloom filter of R_{i-1}.

Now we can define random variable Z_i, which indicates a situation where at least one of attack packets used by R_i for traceback is also sampled by R_{i-1}:

$$Z_i = \begin{cases} 1 & \text{if } X_{t_{i-1}} > 0 \\ 0 & \text{otherwise.} \end{cases} \tag{5}$$

Attack Packets. Since we can say that X_{t_i} follows the binomial distribution Binom($N_p d_i$, $\Pr(X_{p_i} = 1)$), we obtain

$$\Pr(X_{t_i} = j) = \binom{N_p d_i}{j} \cdot \Pr(X_{p_i} = 1)^j \cdot (1 - \Pr(X_{p_i} = 1))^{N_p d_i - j} . \tag{6}$$

The victim traces back from R_i to R_{i-1} by using the set $\mathcal{N}$ of attack packets. Because X_{f_i} represents the number of false positives of the Bloom filter of R_i, which occurs in querying $\mathcal{N}$ to the filter, we get

$$\Pr(X_{f_i} = \ell) = \sum_{j=0}^{N_p d_i} \Pr(X_{t_i} = j) \binom{N_p - j}{\ell} f^\ell (1 - f)^{N_p - j - \ell} . \tag{7}$$

Moreover, since $X_i = X_{t_i} + X_{f_i}$, Eqs. (6) and (7) yield the probability distribution of X_i as

$$\Pr(X_i = j) = \sum_{\ell=0}^{\min(j, N_p d_i)} \Pr(X_{t_i} = \ell) \cdot \Pr(X_{f_i} = j - \ell) . \tag{8}$$

Next we consider Y_{t_i}. If the counter value of a packet that R_{i-1} receives is c, then the probability that both R_{i-1} and R_i samples the packet is given by

$$\Pr(X_{p_i} = 1, X_{p_{i-1}} = 1 \mid X_{c_{i-1}} = c) = \frac{(c+1)^\alpha + \beta}{M} \cdot \frac{c^\alpha + \beta}{M} ,$$

which in turn yields

$$\Pr(X_{p_i} = 1, X_{p_{i-1}} = 1) = \sum_{c=0}^{i-2} \frac{(c+1)^\alpha + \beta}{M} \cdot \frac{c^\alpha + \beta}{M} \cdot \Pr(X_{c_{i-1}} = c) . \quad (9)$$

Now from Eqs. (3), (4), and (9), we can easily compute $\Pr(X_{p_i} = 1 \mid X_{p_{i-1}} = 1)$. Furthermore, we can consider that Y_{t_i} follows $\mathrm{Binom}(X_{t_{i-1}}, \Pr(X_{p_i} = 1 \mid X_{p_{i-1}} = 1))$ and its probability distribution can also be easily calculated.

Conditional Entropy of Z_i. With the random variables in Sect. 4.2 and from the definition of conditional entropy, we can compute $H(Z_i \mid X_i, Y_i)$ (for the definition, see also [5]). Notice that the smaller $H(Z_i \mid X_i, Y_i)$ is, the higher the success probability of a traceback process. Hence in order to evaluate our proposed scheme, we need to compute $H(Z_i \mid X_i, Y_i)$. For the purpose, remember:

$$\Pr(X_i = j, Y_i = m, Z_i = a) = \Pr(X_i = j, Y_i = m \mid Z_i = a) \cdot \Pr(Z_i = a) . \quad (10)$$

With respect to Z_i, as in [5] we assume

$$\Pr(Z_i = 0) = \Pr(Z_i = 1) = 1/2 . \quad (11)$$

Below we compute $H(Z_i \mid X_i, Y_i)$ in the cases that (c1) $Z_i = 1$ and (c2) $Z_i = 0$ respectively.

Case (c1): $Z_i = 1$. In this case, we can rewrite the first part of the right side of Eq. (10) to

$$\Pr(X_i = j, Y_i = m \mid Z_i = 1) = \Pr(X_i = j \mid Z_i = 1) \cdot \Pr(Y_i = m \mid X_i = j, Z_i = 1) . \quad (12)$$

Then remembering that $Y_i = Y_{t_i} + Y_{f_i}$, in regard to the second part of the right side of Eq. (12), we in turn have

$$\Pr(Y_{t_i} + Y_{f_i} = m \mid X_i = j, Z_i = 1)$$
$$= \sum_{r=0}^{\min(m, N_p d_i)} \Pr(Y_{t_i} = r \mid X_i = j, Z_i = 1)$$
$$\times \Pr(Y_{f_i} = m - r \mid X_i = j, Y_{t_i} = r, Z_i = 1) . \quad (13)$$

For a part of the right hand side of Eq. (13), we can obtain

$$\Pr(Y_{f_i} = m - r \mid X_i = j, Y_{t_i} = r, Z_i = 1) = \binom{j - r}{m - r} f^{m-r}(1 - f)^{j-m} . \quad (14)$$

Then, in order to compute Eq. (13), we need the probability:

$$\Pr(Y_{t_i} = r \mid X_i = j, Z_i = 1) \ . \tag{15}$$

So first we introduce random variable W_i, which satisfies $X_{t_i} = Y_{t_i} + W_i$. Remember that Y_{t_i} is the number of the attack packets sampled by both R_{i-1} and R_i. Therefore W_i is nothing but the number of the attack packets which are sampled by R_i, but not by R_{i-1}. This means that W_i follows $\mathrm{Binom}(N_p d_i - X_{t_{i-1}}, \Pr(X_{p_i} = 1 \mid X_{p_{i-1}} = 0))$. Here note that $\Pr(X_{p_i} = 1, X_{p_{i-1}} = 0 \mid X_{c_{i-1}} = c)$ can be easily calculated as $\frac{c^\alpha + \beta}{M} \cdot \left(1 - \frac{c^\alpha + \beta}{M}\right)$. Therefore we have

$$\Pr(X_{p_i} = 1, X_{p_{i-1}} = 0) = \sum_{c=0}^{i-2} \Pr(X_{p_i} = 1, X_{p_{i-1}} = 0 \mid X_{c_{i-1}} = c) \cdot \Pr(X_{c_{i-1}} = c)$$

$$= \sum_{c=0}^{i-2} \frac{c^\alpha + \beta}{M} \cdot \left(1 - \frac{c^\alpha + \beta}{M}\right) \cdot \Pr(X_{c_{i-1}} = c) \ . \tag{16}$$

Consequently, from Eqs. (3), (4), and (16) we can obtain $\Pr(X_{p_i} = 1 \mid X_{p_{i-1}} = 0))$ and in turn the probability distribution of W_i.

We are now in a position to compute Eq. (15). First note that

$$\Pr(Y_{t_i} = r \mid X_i = j, Z_i = 1)$$

$$= \sum_{\ell=0}^{j} \Pr(X_{f_i} = \ell) \cdot \Pr(Y_{t_i} = r \mid X_{t_i} = j - \ell, X_{f_i} = \ell, Z_i = 1) \ .$$

Therefore from Eq. (6), the binomial distributions of Y_{t_i}, and W_i, as the analysis in [5], we can compute Eq. (15) (the detail is omitted due to limited space).

Putting the discussions above together, with Eqs. (14) and (15), we can evaluate Eq. (13). Then from the Eqs. (8) and (13), we are now able to compute Eq. (12).

Finally, from Eqs. (10), (11), and (12), we can calculate:

$$\Pr(X_i = j, Y_i = m, Z_i = 1) \ . \tag{17}$$

Case (c2): $Z_i = 0$. In this case, it is easy to see that

$$\Pr(X_i = j, Y_i = m \mid Z_i = 0) = \Pr(X_i = j)\binom{j}{m} f^m (1 - f)^{j-m} \ . \tag{18}$$

Therefore from Eqs. (8), (11) and (18), we can compute:

$$\Pr(X_i = j, Y_i = m, Z_i = 0) \ . \tag{19}$$

Computation of $H(Z_i \mid X_i, Y_i)$. $\Pr(X_i = j, Y_i = m)$ can be obtained as follows:

$$\Pr(X_i = j, Y_i = m) = \Pr(X_{t_{i-1}} = 0) \cdot \Pr(X_i = j, Y_i = m \mid Z_i = 0)$$
$$+ \Pr(X_{t_{i-1}} > 0) \cdot \Pr(X_i = j, Y_i = m \mid Z_i = 1) \ . \tag{20}$$

Thus from Eqs. (6), (12) and (18), Eq. (20) can be computed.

We have so far obtained Eqs. (17), (19) and (20). Therefore from the definition of conditional entropy, we can compute $H(Z_i \mid X_i, Y_i)$, which is the goal of this section.

4.3 Numerical Computation of Theoretical Results

In this section we shall conduct a numerical analysis of our proposed scheme in order to evaluate its performance and behavior in a more concrete manner.

How to Determine α, β and M. As discussed in Sect. 3.2, when the router receives a packet with counter value c, it holds that

$$p = (c^\alpha + \beta)/M . \tag{21}$$

Here we discuss how to determine the values α, β and M.

First, regarding a packet P, we consider the maximum and minimum value of P.counter. Since by assumption there are at most n routers on any attack paths and initial values of packet counters are zero as discussed in Sect. 4.1, the maximum value of the counters is $n - 1$. In most literature on IP traceback schemes, the maximum length of attack paths is supposed to be less than or equal to 16 (for example, see [6]) and therefore we also suppose that the maximum counter value is 16, which means that $n = 17$. Note that as we will see below in detail, even if a hop count of some packet exceeds 16, it causes almost no problems in our scheme. From an implementation point of view, as discussed in Sect. 3.1, it is fairly easy to allocate 5 bit space in each header to the counter.

For each packet P, the sampling probability p is less than or equal to one when P.counter is maximized. Hence from Fig. 2, α, β and M must satisfy:

$$p = (16^\alpha + \beta)/M \leq 1 . \tag{22}$$

However, note that as discussed in Sect. 3.5 and later in this section, in general sampling probabilities in our scheme are far below one, namely, just 1% or so.

Next we consider the minimum value of a packet counter, i.e., zero. Let p_I be the sampling probability p when the counter c is zero, that is, $p_I = \beta/M$ (see Eq. (21)). In order to be fair when we evaluate performance of our scheme, we set p_I to a smaller value than, for example, the sampling probability of the scheme of Li et al. [5], i.e, 3.3%. More specifically, we set $p_I = \beta/M = 0.01$.

From the discussion above, in this paper we consider the following three cases to satisfy Eq. (22) and $p_I = 0.01$:

– $\alpha = 2, \beta = 2.58586, M = 258.586$,
– $\alpha = 3, \beta = 41.3737, M = 4137.37$, or
– $\alpha = 4, \beta = 661.98, M = 66198.0$.

Actually we investigated other settings than the above, although, as we show later, we have already obtained satisfactory results in the above three settings.

Probability Distributions of Counter Values and Sampling Probability.
First we show the probability distributions of the counter values of routers R_{16}
(hop count 15) and just for reference, R_{32} (hop count 31) as depicted in Fig. 3
(a) and (b) respectively, according to Eq. (3). From Fig. 3 we see that almost all

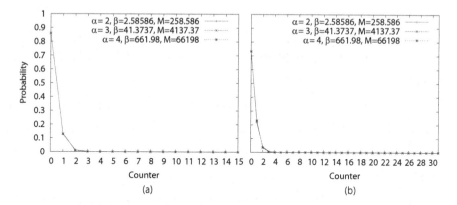

Fig. 3. Probability distributions of the counter values (Hop count = (a) 15 and (b) 31)

counter values are at most 2 with the parameters discussed in Sect. 4.3. Such a
small counter value results in a small sampling probability discussed below.

Now from Eqs. (3) and (4), we consider the average sampling probabilities,
which are depicted in Fig. 4. Fig. 4 shows that the average sampling probabilities

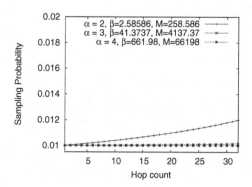

Fig. 4. Hop counts and average sampling probabilities

remain very small, that is, about 0.01, in all cases $\alpha = 2, 3, 4$. Note that the
sampling probability 0.01 is so small. For example, the scheme in [5] requires the
sampling probability 0.033, which proves how efficient our scheme is.

Evaluation of $H(Z_i \mid X_i, Y_i)$. Now we evaluate $H(Z_i \mid X_i, Y_i)$ with the parameters mentioned in Sect. 4.3 and under the conditions given below:

- $d = 0.1, N_p = 200$ (Fig. 5 (a)),
- $d = 0.2, N_p = 100$ (Fig. 5 (b)), or
- $d = 0.4, N_p = 50$ (Fig. 6).

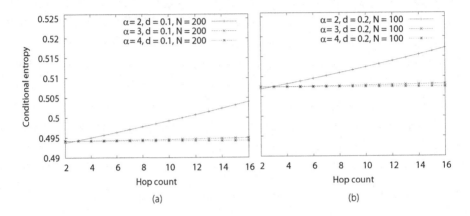

Fig. 5. Estimation of $H(Z_i \mid X_i, Y_i)$: (a) $d = 0.1, N_p = 200$, (b) $d = 0.2, N_p = 100$

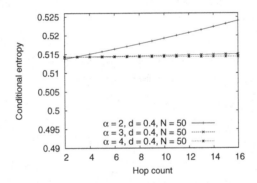

Fig. 6. Estimation of $H(Z_i \mid X_i, Y_i)$ ($d = 0.4, N_p = 50$)

That is, we set the above parameters such that the number of packets to be sampled are the same by letting $N_p d$ be 20. Remember that the smaller the value of conditional entropy $H(Z_i \mid X_i, Y_i)$ is, the smaller the number of attack packets required for traceback is.

When we compare our scheme with other work, we try to be as fair as possible as follows. First, we set k, which is the number of independent hash functions used for Bloom filters in our scheme, to 12 that is the optimum number for the scheme of Li et al. [5]. Second, we set the sampling probability p to (almost) 0.01 and the number of packets used for traceback to $N_p d = 20$. It is clear that such a setting is disadvantageous to our scheme, with comparison to the settings of Li et al. [5], where $p = 0.03$ and $N_p d = 50$. In such a setting, the optimum value of the conditional entropy of Li's scheme is about 0.63 as shown in [5].

In the above settings, in our scheme $H(Z_i \mid X_i, Y_i)$ is at worst about 0.525 as shown in Fig. 6, and is about 0.495 at best as in Fig. 5 (a). The comparison clearly shows that our scheme is superior to that of Li et al.

5   Simulation Experiments

In this section, in order to evaluate our scheme in a practical environment, we conduct simulation analysis of it. In the simulation, we utilize real world Internet topological data by Skitter project [10], which are also used in [5]. The topological data are given as follows:

- a-root: this map includes the Internet topological data on Nov. 25, 2001 from a-root.skitter.caida.org to 192,900 destinations, and
- e-root: the Internet topological data on Nov. 28, 2001 from e-root.skitter.caida.org to 158,181 destinations.

In those simulation experiments, we let the number of attackers be 1,000, and the number of attack packets N_p be 50,000. We randomly generate attack trees 1,000 times based on the above topological data and place attackers at the leaves of the trees. The lengths of the attack paths are supposed to be greater than or equal to 16 at random.

Now we give the simulation results in Figs. 7 (a) a-root and (b) e-root. In order to compare our scheme with the scheme of Li et al. [5], the relationship between the number of hash function k and the error level are given in the figures. Here

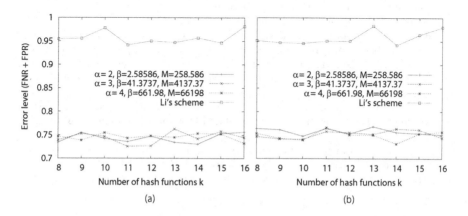

Fig. 7. Simulation results

we mean by 'error level' the sum of false negative ratio (FNR) and false positive ratio (FPR), where FNR represents the ratio of the number of routers which are not in the reconstructed tree but actually in the real attack tree to the number of the routers in the reconstructed tree. Similarly, FPR means the ratio of the number of routers which are in the reconstructed tree but actually not in the real attack tree to the number of the routers in the reconstructed tree. As we can obviously see from the results in Fig. 7, our scheme exhibits remarkably low error levels in all settings given above. The remarkable result would be mainly due to the low entropy value of $H(Z_i \mid X_i, Y_i)$, as discussed in Sect. 4.3.

6   Conclusion

In this paper we proposed a novel hybrid IP traceback scheme by using packet counters. Our scheme has the several remarkable advantages, that is, (1) it is simple and efficient, (2) it is highly resistant to attacks, (3) it requires a lower sampling rate compared with previous work, e.g., only 1% is enough, (4) its false positive/negative rates are lower than previous work.

References

1. Peng, T., Leckie, C., Ramamohanarao, K.: Survey of network-based defense mechanisms countering the DoS and DDoS problems. ACM Computing Surveys 39(1) (April 2007)
2. Al-Duwairi, B., Manimaran, G.: Novel hybrid schemes employing packet marking and logging for IP traceback. IEEE Transactions on Parallel and Distributed Systems 17(5), 403–418 (2006)
3. Dean, D., Franklin, M., Stubblefield, A.: An algebraic approach to IP traceback. ACM Transactions on Information and System Security 5(2), 119–137 (2002)
4. Gong, C., Sarac, K.: Toward a practical packet marking approach for IP traceback. International Journal of Network Security 8(3), 271–281 (2009)
5. Li, J., Sung, M., Xu, J., Li, L.: Large-scale IP traceback in high-speed Internet: Practical techniques and theoretical foundation. In: Proceedings of the IEEE Symposium on Security and Privacy, pp. 115–129 (May 2004)
6. Savage, S., Wetherall, D., Karlin, A.R., Anderson, T.: Practical network support for IP traceback. In: Proceedings of the ACM SIGCOMM, pp. 295–306 (2000)
7. Snoeren, A.C., Partridge, C., Sanchez, L.A., Jones, C.E., Tchakountio, F., Kent, S.T., Strayer, W.T.: Hash-based IP traceback. In: Proceedings of the ACM SIGCOMM, pp. 3–14 (2001)
8. Yu, S., Zhou, W., Doss, R., Jia, W.: Traceback of DDoS attacks using entropy variations. IEEE Transactions on Parallel and Distributed Systems 22(3), 412–425 (2011)
9. Mitzenmacher, M., Upfal, E.: Probability and Computing: Randomized Algorithms and Probabilistic Analysis. Cambridge University Press (2005)
10. CAIDA: Skitter project, http://www.caida.org/tools/measurement/skitter/

A Secure Mix Network with an Efficient Validity Verification Mechanism

Kun Peng[1] and Yuexin Zhang[2]

[1] Institute for Infocomm Research
dr.kun.peng@gmail.com
[2] School of Mathematics and Computer Science
Fujian Normal University, Fuzhou, Fujian, China
zhangyuexin2010@yahoo.cn

Abstract. A new mix network scheme is proposed in this paper. It adopts the so-called general verification mechanism to improve efficiency of validity verification and avoids the drawbacks of the existing general verification solutions. It can be applied to practical applications like e-voting to improve their security and efficiency.

Keywords: mix network, efficiency, robustness, e-voting.

1 Introduction

Mix network is an anonymous communication channel widely employed in popular private network applications like e-voting [18,19,3]. It consists of multiple routing nodes, who shuffle a batch of sealed messages in turn. The shuffling operation of each routing node re-orders (using a random permutation) and randomizes (e.g. re-encrypts) the sealed messages. The output of every routing node is shuffled by the next routing node. In this way, the encrypted messages are repeatedly shuffled in succession by all the routing nodes in the mix network. If at least one routing node conceals his permutation, the repeatedly shuffled encrypted messages cannot be traced. The most important application of mix network is electronic voting, which employs a mix network to shuffle the sealed votes before they are opened. A typical mix network is illustrated in Figure 1. Usually, the following four properties must be satisfied in a mix network.

1. Correctness: if all the participants are honest and do not deviate from the mix network protocol, the outputs must be a permutation of the plaintexts of the inputs.
2. Privacy: if at least one server conceals his shuffling, the permutation between the inputs and the outputs is unknown, so that the users cannot be linked to their outputs.
3. Public verifiability: honestly of the participants can be verified publicly.
4. Soundness: Passing the public verification guarantees that the outputs is a permutation of the plaintexts of the inputs.

Y. Xiang et al. (Eds.): IDCS 2012, LNCS 7646, pp. 85–96, 2012.
© Springer-Verlag Berlin Heidelberg 2012

inputs S_1 S_2 ...... S_m outputs

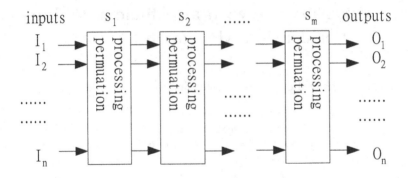

Fig. 1. Mix Network

Security of a mix network depends on the underlying shuffling operations. To convincingly show that a mix network works properly, each routing node in it needs to publicly prove that he does not deviate from the shuffling protocol. This is a basic security requirement for shuffling. When it is not satisfied, the mix network may go wrong without being detected. Of course, each routing node cannot reveal his permutation in his proof of validity of shuffling.

Since the first mix network proposed in [5], many mix network schemes [23,12,17,4,1,2,9,20,21,15,28,27,10,14,13,26,25] have been proposed. Most of them [1,2,9,20,21,15,28,27,10,14,13,26,25] requires each routing node to prove validity of his shuffling. This separate proof and verification mechanism to check validity of shuffling is inefficient as m instances of proof and verification are needed when there are m routing nodes. Some mix network schemes [17,4] use a partial proof of correctness on each routing node to improve efficiency of the separate proof and verification mechanism. However, that means some correctness is only achieved with a probability and privacy is weakened (in [17] the probability is not big enough for many applications and in [4], privacy is weakened to a dangerous level if correctness is strong enough for most applications).

Some mix network schemes [23,12] do not provide a verification of correct shuffling by each server separately. Instead, correctness of the shuffling by the whole mix network is verified after the outputs are produced in plaintext. This verification of validity of all the instances of shuffling in a mix network is called general validity verification. Obviously, this verification mechanism is more efficient than the separate verification mechanism. The structure of a mix network with general verification and is illustrated in Figure 2.

However, the existing general verification methods in mix networks have their drawbacks as shown in Section 2. In this paper, a new mix network with general validity verification is proposed. It is much more efficient than the mix networks with separate validity verification and overcomes the drawbacks of the existing general verification methods in mix networks. Our analysis illustrates that in comparison with the existing work it has advantages in efficiency and robustness. We demonstrate its application to e-voting to show its importance in practice.

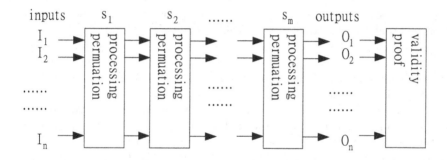

Fig. 2. General Verification Mix Network

2 Background: Existing Mix Networks with General Validity Verification

The mix network employed to implement the anonymous channel must be very efficient. So a mix network employing general verification of shuffling should be chosen. Among the three schemes in this category, Chaum's mix network [5] was the original scheme and improved by Park *et al*. So only two candidates remain: [23] by Park *et al* and [12] by Golle *et al*.

In [12], each encrypted input to the mix network is attached with a hash of it. Each server has to re-encrypt and permute the inputs together with the attachments. Each server does not need to prove that his shuffling is correct; instead he proves the product of the attachments does not change after his shuffling. This is a very efficient proof (costing $O(1)$ exponentiations) and not sufficient for the verification of validity of shuffling. Actually, it is also proved [12] that the product of the inputs does not change. However this extra proof is meaningless as even with it the validity of shuffling is not guaranteed without a final general verification. After all the inputs and their attachments are through the shuffling and decrypted to plaintext, a final check verifies that each output attachment is really the hash of the corresponding output. Golle *et al* were aware that an attack by a malicious server against the privacy of a user is possible. The server can change two or more users' inputs, so that the hash relation between the input and attachment becomes incorrect for those users while the product of the inputs and attachments is not changed. The invalidity of shuffling can be found in the final verification and the cheating server can be identified. But the attacked user's output can be traced as it is incorrectly shuffled and distinguishable from other outputs. In other words, the malicious user breaks the attacked user's privacy at the cost of being identified as a cheater. To overcome this attack, Golle *et al* employ double-encryption in their mix network. When the final verification is performed, only one layer of encryption is removed. If incorrect shuffling is found, the second layer of encryption is not removed and a SMN is employed to perform the mixing again. Correctness of this mix network is dependent on an unusual assumption: if $H()$ is a one-way and collision-resistant hash function, it is infeasible to find $\prod_{i=1}^{n} H(x_i) = \prod_{i=1}^{n} H(y_i)$ where $\{x_i | i = 1, 2, \ldots, n\} \neq \{y_i | i = 1, 2, \ldots, n\}$.

Park *et al* [23] proposed a decryption-chain mix network that employs two rounds of shuffling. In the first round, the users choose their short-term private keys and public keys and send the short-term public keys to be shuffled. The servers do not prove correctness of their shuffling in the first round. At the end of the first round, each user checks that his short-term public key is among the published results of the first round. Any user can protest if the check fails. In the second round, the users' inputs signed by their short-term private keys are shuffled and the outputs are published in plaintext. Again the servers do not prove correctness of their shuffling, which can be verified by anyone using signature verification. If any output cannot be verified to be correctly signed with one public key published in the first round, the second round of shuffling is known to be wrong. As in [12], revealing of outputs in plaintext while the shuffling is not correct is a concern. In this scheme, a cut-and-choose mechanism is used to divide every input to several pieces, which are shuffled in the second round. In the end, all pieces of the output are decrypted and verified one by one and the decryption stops whenever verification fails. So the probability the outputs are revealed when a malicious server performs an invalid shuffling is low. As decryption-chain mix network cannot achieve a good trade-off between robustness and strong privacy, a re-encryption mix network is preferred in most applications.

Both general-verification based schemes are efficient although an unproved assumption is used in [12] and cut-and-choose causes more computational cost. However, neither of them supports unconditional correctness and soundness and so they are limited in practical application. For example, they do not support an important security property, independence of input, and are not suitable for applications like e-auction and e-voting as explained in Section 4.

3   The New Mix Network Protocol

The new mix network is composed of two rounds of communication in every instance of routing (shuffling). Each user commits his inputs first and the commitments are mixed in the first round. Any user can easily verify that his commitment is shuffled correctly and protest if the verification fails. Any protest can be publicly verified and the malicious server can be identified and removed. The inputs are mixed in the second round. After the outputs are produced, they can be verified publicly against the commitments published in the first round. Both decryption chain and re-encryption can be applied to implement the shuffling. In the following, the protocol is described in detail in the case of shuffling by re-encryption.

1. An encryption algorithm is chosen for the mix network. The employed encryption algorithm can be any semantically secure encryption algorithm like

ElGamal encryption or Paillier encryption [22]. The private key of the encryption algorithm is shared among some decryption authorities, who are usually the servers in the mix network. Usually a sharing threshold is used such that decryption is feasible if and only if the number of available private key shares is over the threshold. In the case of Paillier encryption, the distributed key generation technique in [8] can be employed for key sharing. Suppose the space of the messages to be mixed is Z_M and then the message space of the employed encryption algorithm, Z_N, must be obviously larger than Z_M. For example, in the case of Paillier encryption is N is the product of two primes several hundred bits long and thus is much larger than any message in practical mix network applications (e.g. a bid in e-auction or a vote in e-voting).

2. Each user P_i chooses his input to the mix network, b_i, from Z_M and a random integer v_i from $Z_{\lfloor N/M \rfloor}$ where $\lfloor X \rfloor$ denotes the largest integer no larger than X. He calculates $a_i = v_i M + b_i$ and commits to it as $c_i = H(a_i)$ where $H()$ is a one-way and collision-resistant hash function.

3. Commitments c_i for $i = 1, 2, \ldots, n$ are encrypted to e_i for $i = 1, 2, \ldots, n$ using the employed encryption algorithm, which are submitted to the mix network.

4. Each server in the mix network randomly re-encrypts and permutes e_i for $i = 1, 2, \ldots, n$ in sequence. The servers do not need to prove correctness of the shuffling.

5. Let e'_i for $i = 1, 2, \ldots, n$ denote the shuffled outputs of the last server. The decryption authorities cooperate to decrypt e'_i into c'_i for $i = 1, 2, \ldots, n$ and publish them.

6. Each user P_i verifies that his commitment c_i is among the published shuffled commitments. Any user can complain if he cannot find his commitment in the published outputs. Any dispute is solved as follows.

   (a) The protesting user P_i challenges shuffling of his input e_i.

   (b) Each server (from the first one to the last one) has to prove his shuffling of e_i is correct by publishing his output for e_i and a ZK proof of correct re-encryption (ZK proof of knowledge of Nth root [16] if Paillier encryption is employed) of e_i to the output. If any server has performed an incorrect shuffling, it will be discovered and the next step is skipped. Otherwise, some e'_j will be revealed, which is the repeatedly shuffled result of e_i.

   (c) Each decryption authority has to prove that it has decrypted e'_j correctly using a ZK proof of correct decryption, which is detailed in [8] in the case of Paillier encryption. Any incorrect decryption can be found.

   (d) If any party fails to prove his innocence, he is removed (or replaced if necessary) and the mixing is performed again. If all the servers and decryption authorities prove their innocence, the protesting user is identified as a liar and removed.

7. Input a_i is encrypted into a ciphertext f_i for $i = 1, 2, \ldots, n$.

8. The encrypted inputs f_i for $i = 1, 2, \ldots, n$ are submitted to the servers, who perform the second round of mixing to mix them. As in the first round, shuffling in the second round is also composed of re-encryption and permutation

and not proved by the servers to be valid. Ciphertexts f_i for $i = 1, 2, \ldots, n$ are finally shuffled to f_i' for $i = 1, 2, \ldots n$ after all the shuffling operations.

9. The decryption authorities cooperate to decrypt f_i' into a_i' for $i = 1, 2, \ldots, n$ and publish them.

10. Anyone can publicly verify that every published output is correctly committed to some commitment. If $H(a_i')$ is not equal to any published commitment in the first round of mixing for an published output a_i', the problem is solved as follows.

   (a) Each decryption authority has to prove that his decryption of f_i' is correct using a ZK proof of correct decryption (see [8] for details if Paillier encryption is employed). If an incorrect decryption is found, the decryption authority performing it is identified as a cheater and the next step is skipped. Otherwise, the repeated shuffling operations leading to f_i' must be verified.

   (b) Each server (from the last one to the first one) has to prove his shuffling leading to f_i' is correct by publishing his input for the ciphertext and a ZK proof of correct re-encryption (ZK proof of knowledge of Nth root [16] if Paillier encryption is employed) of the input. If any server has performed an incorrect shuffling, he will be discovered.

   (c) If any party fails to prove his innocence, he is removed (or replaced if necessary) and the mixing is performed again. If all the servers and decryption authorities prove their innocence, the output in dispute has been traced back to an input to the mix network. The user submitting the input in dispute is identified as a cheater and removed.

11. $b_i' = a_i' \bmod M$ for $i = 1, 2, \ldots, n$ are published as the mixed messages.

12. The found cheater(s) can be punished to deter any party from cheating if there is any of them.

4 Security and Efficiency Analysis

The properties of the new mix network protocol are as follows.

1. Correctness:
   As the users do not want their inputs are tampered, they can supervise the first round of mixing is correct, namely the commitments to their inputs are correctly mixed. As the hash function is one-way and collision-resistant, incorrect shuffling by any malicious server in the second round of mixing can be detected publicly by anyone. Especially, as an random integer v_i is combined with every input message b_i before it is mixed, even if two input messages are the same (e.g. they are the same bids in e-auction or the same votes in e-voting), they are shuffled into different results and incorrect shuffling of any of them can still be found.

2. Privacy
   As threshold trust is assumed, no inputs can be decrypted before they are mixed and at least one server conceals his shuffling. So, the permutation used in the mix network is secret and privacy is achieved.

3. Robustness

As demonstrated in Section 3, dishonest servers or users can be identified. As re-encryption is employed in this mix network, the identified malicious parties can be removed while the mix can continue without them.

Although correctness of the first round mix is not publicly verifiable, any incorrect mixing of an input in the first round can be found by a user submitting the input and the dispute can be solved publicly. As a user usually does not want to be abused and is eager to protect his rights, any incorrect mixing in the first round can still be found and verified publicly. Moreover, it is highly efficient as the most costly function in a mix network —validity verification— is saved. The computational cost of the new mix network in the normal case is as follows where Paillier re-encryption is employed and there are m servers in the mix network.

- Encryption: 2 exponentiations (one exponentiation for each Paillier encryption while each input requires two instances of encryption, one for the input and one for its randomized hash function).
- Re-encryption: $2nm$ exponentiations (on every server, one exponentiation for each Paillier re-encryption while each input requires two instances of encryption, one for the input and one for its randomized hash function).

A special security property —independence of input— is also realized in our new mix network. Independence of input in a mix network means that a user cannot choose or change his inputs according to the other inputs. This property is necessary to guarantee robustness when the mix network is employed in e-auction or e-voting. In our mix network, every user's commitment is published (anonymously) before any other user's input is submitted to the mix network. So, even though a malicious user can collude with a server to change its input without being detected, this change is restricted as follows.

- During the first round of shuffling, the malicious user can collude with a server to change its commitment, thus actually changing its committed input. However, during the first round of shuffling, even if he can get collusion from all the servers the malicious user has no information about the other users' inputs if the hash function is one-way.
- During the second round of shuffling, the malicious user may get some information about the other users' inputs if he gets collusion of some parties processing the decryption key(s) of the mix network. However, if the hash function is collision-resistant he cannot change his input during the second round as his commitment has been published in the first round.

Therefore, a malicious user cannot change his input according to some other users' inputs if those users do not collude with him and the hash function is one-way and collision-resistant. This is the advantage of our new mix network over the other mix network schemes with general verification [5,23,12].

This advantage in independence of input is important as mix network is often employed in e-auction or e-voting to protect anonymity of bidders or voters. In e-auction, without independence of input, a malicious bidder can collude with some malicious auctioneers (shuffling servers) to adjust his bid according to the other bidders' bids. In e-voting, without independence of input, a malicious voter can compromise privacy of other voters as follows.

1. An innocent voter submits an encrypted vote $C = E(V)$ to the talliers where $E()$ denotes the encryption function.
2. A malicious voter wants to find out the ballot encrypted in C, and so malleates C into another ciphertext C', which is submitted as his encrypted vote. Note that the encryption algorithms usually employed in e-voting like ElGamal encryption or Paillier encryption are malleateable. For example in the case of Paillier encryption, $C' = CE(R)$ where R is an integer randomly chosen by the malicious voter.
3. After being shuffled by the talliers, neither C nor C' is traceable. However, the malicious voter's vote will be recovered as an abnormal vote as r is randomly chosen. In our Paillier-encryption-based example, his vote will be recovered as $V + R \bmod N$.
4. When noticing an abnormal vote V' in the mixed and decrypted votes, the malicious voter can find out the innocent voter's vote. In our Paillier-based example, $V = V' - R \bmod N$.

The advantage of our new mix network over the mix networks with separate verification [1,2,9,20,21,15,28,27,10,14,13,26,25] is high efficiency, which is obvious as it only needs $O(n)$ hash function operations to prove and verify validity of its shuffling and they employ $O(n)$ exponentiations in large cyclic groups for the same purpose.

5   Application to E-Voting

In this section, the new mix network is employed in an e-voting application. The new e-voting protocol supports any election rule and either decryption chain or re-encryption can be adopted in its shuffling. In the following, a detailed re-encryption-based description of the e-voting protocol is present where ElGamal encryption algorithm is employed to show that our new mix network technique can work with various encryption algorithms.

1. Preparation Phase

   – Let q be a large prime. If not specified, all the computations take place in Z_q^*. Let g be a generator of Z_q^*.
   – A public key $y \in Z_q^*$ is published, while the corresponding private key $x = \log_g y$ is generated and shared in a distributed way among the talliers by k-out-o-m publicly verifiable secret sharing [7,24,11]. Each A_j gets a share x_j while $y_j = g^{x_j}$ is published for $j = 1, 2, \ldots, m$.
   – There are n voters B_i for $i = 1, 2, \ldots, n$ and m talliers A_j for $j = 1, 2, \ldots, m$, who act as the servers in the mix network.

2. Vote submission phase
    (a) Submitting the vote commitments

    Each voter B_i chooses a vote b_i from Z_M, the vote space. In any practical election applications, q as the order of a cyclic group for ElGamal encryption is larger than M. B_i also chooses a random integer $v_i \in Z_{\lfloor q/M \rfloor}$. Each B_i calculates his commitment $c_i = H(a_i)$ and encrypts it as $e_i = (\alpha_i, \beta_i) = (g^{r_i}, c_i y^{r_i})$ where $a_i = v_i M + b_i$ and r_i is chosen randomly from Z_q^*. B_i signs e_i using a digital signature algorithm and submits it to the first server in the mix network. The signed e_i for $i = 1, 2, \ldots, n$ are published and anyone can verify that they are validly signed by the voters.

    (b) Shuffling the commitments

    Inputs to tallier A_j are $e_{j-1,i}$ for $i = 1, 2, \ldots, n$ and his outputs are $e_{j,i}$ for $i = 1, 2, \ldots, n$ while inputs to the first tallier A_1 are $e_{0,i} = e_i$ for $i = 1, 2, \ldots, n$. Tallier A_j performs the following operations:
        i. obtains input $e_{j-1,i}$ for $i = 1, 2, \ldots, n$ published by A_{j-1};
        ii. performs re-encryption $e_{j,i} = (\alpha_{j,i}, \beta_{j,i}) = (g^{r_{j,i}} \alpha_{j-1,\pi_j(i)},$ $y^{r_{j,i}} \beta_{j-1,\pi(i)})$ for $i = 1, 2, \ldots, n$ where π_j is a random permutation of $\{1, 2, \ldots, n\}$ and $r_{j,i}$ for $i = 1, 2, \ldots, n$ are randomly chosen from Z_q^*.

    (c) Decrypting the commitments

    A_m's outputs $e_{m,i}$ for $i = 1, 2, \ldots, n$ are decrypted by the talliers. Each tallier A_j publishes $d_{i,j} = \alpha_{m,i}^{x_j}$ and proves $\log_g y_j = \log_{\alpha_{m,i}} d_{i,j}$ for $i = 1, 2, \ldots, n$ using ZK proof of equality of discrete logarithms [6]. This proof of correct decryption can be publicly verified by anybody. If there exist a set $S = \{s \mid 1 \le s \le n, \ d_{i,s} \text{ is correct} \}$ larger more than k, c_i can be recovered as $c_i = \beta_{m,i} / \prod_{s \in S} d_{i,s}^{u_s}$ where $u_s = \prod_{l \in S, l \ne s} (s - l)/l$.

    (d) Checking the shuffled commitments

    Every voter checks that his commitment is among the published commitments. If a voter B_i fails in the check, he can protest by revealing his encrypted commitment (input to the mix network) e_i, his commitment (expected output of the mix network) c_i and the random value (he used in the encryption) r_i. If $e_i = (g^{r_i}, c_i y^{r_i})$, e_i is among the encrypted commitments and c_i is not among the shuffled and decrypted commitments, the shuffling is proved to be incorrect. In that case, every tallier has to prove that his shuffling and decryption is correct by zero knowledge proof of equality of logarithms. Any tallier failing to prove validity of his operations is removed. After removal of any found malicious tallier, e_i for $i = 1, 2, \ldots, n$ are re-shuffled (if necessary, a new tallier can replace the malicious tallier).

3. Tallying phase
    (a) Providing the committed votes

    Each voter B_i calculates $e_i' = (\alpha_i', \beta_i') = (g^{r_i'}, a_i y^{r_i'})$ where r_i' is chosen randomly from Z_q^*. B_i signs e_i' and submits it to the first server in the mix network. The signed e_i' for $i = 1, 2, \ldots, n$ are published and anyone can verify that they are validly signed by the voters.

(b) Shuffling the votes

Tallier A_j with $j > 1$ gets $e'_{j-1,i}$ for $i = 1, 2, \ldots, n$ from A_{j-1} and shuffles them to $e'_{j,i}$ for $i = 1, 2, \ldots, n$ while A_1 gets $e'_{0,i} = e_i$ for $i = 1, 2, \ldots, n$ from the voters and shuffles them to $e'_{1,i}$ for $i = 1, 2, \ldots, n$. Re-encryption and permutation in the shuffling are the same as in the first round.

(c) Decrypting the votes

A_m's outputs $e'_{m,i}$ for $i = 1, 2, \ldots, n$ are decrypted by the talliers. Like in the first round, if more than k talliers are honest, a_i for $i = 1, 2, \ldots, n$ can be recovered correctly.

(d) Verifying validity of the votes

Suppose $\hat{a}_i$ for $i = 1, 2, \ldots, n$ are the results of vote decryption. If $H(\hat{a}_i)$ is not among the published commitments in the first round, $\hat{a}_i$ is traced in a reverse direction through the mix network and every tallier is required to reveal his shuffling in regard to $\hat{a}_i$. Any tallier failing to prove correctness of his shuffling is removed from the mix network. If all the talliers prove correctness of their shuffling successfully, B_i is accused of submitting invalid vote and removed from the e-voting. After the malicious party (tallier or voter) is removed, e'_i for $i = 1, 2, \ldots, n$ are re-shuffled (if necessary, a new tallier can replace the malicious tallier).

(e) Counting the votes

$\hat{b}_i = \hat{a}_i \bmod M$ for $i = 1, 2, \ldots, n$ are output. After these valid votes are publicly available, they are counted according to the election rule and the election result is obtained.

As this new e-voting protocol is based on our secure and efficient mix network, it is secure and efficient. It is more efficient than e-voting based on mix networks employing separate verification and more robust than e-voting based on the existing mix networks employing general verification.

6   Conclusion

The new mix network scheme proposed in this paper has advantages in efficiency and security over the existing mix network schemes. It is more robust than the existing mix networks with general verification and much more efficient than the existing mix networks with separate verification. It can be applied to e-voting to produce a secure and efficient mix-network-based e-voting protocol.

References

1. Abe, M.: Mix-Networks on Permutation Networks. In: Lam, K.-Y., Okamoto, E., Xing, C. (eds.) ASIACRYPT 1999. LNCS, vol. 1716, pp. 258–273. Springer, Heidelberg (1999)
2. Abe, M., Hoshino, F.: Remarks on Mix-Network Based on Permutation Networks. In: Kim, K.-c. (ed.) PKC 2001. LNCS, vol. 1992, pp. 317–324. Springer, Heidelberg (2001)

3. Baiardia, F., Fallenib, A., Granchib, R., Martinellib, F., Petrocchib, M., Vaccarel-
   lib, A.: SEAS, a secure e-voting protocol: Design and implementationstar, open.
   Computers & Security 24(8), 642–652 (2005)
4. Boneh, D., Golle, P.: Almost entirely correct mixing with applications to voting.
   In: Proceedings of the 9th ACM Conference on Computer and Communications
   Security, pp. 68–77 (2002)
5. Chaum, D.: Untraceable electronic mail, return address and digital pseudonym.
   Communications of the ACM 24(2), 84–88 (1981)
6. Chaum, D., Pedersen, T.P.: Wallet Databases with Observers. In: Brickell, E.F.
   (ed.) CRYPTO 1992. LNCS, vol. 740, pp. 89–105. Springer, Heidelberg (1993)
7. Feldman, P.: A practical scheme for non-interactive verifiable secret sharing. In:
   28th Annual Symposium on Foundations of Computer Science, pp. 427–437
8. Fouque, P., Poupard, G., Stern, J.: Sharing Decryption in the Context of Voting
   or Lotteries. In: Frankel, Y. (ed.) FC 2000. LNCS, vol. 1962, pp. 90–104. Springer,
   Heidelberg (2001)
9. Furukawa, J., Sako, K.: An Efficient Scheme for Proving a Shuffle. In: Kilian, J.
   (ed.) CRYPTO 2001. LNCS, vol. 2139, pp. 368–387. Springer, Heidelberg (2001)
10. Furukawa, J.: Efficient and verifiable shuffling and shuffle-decryption. IEICE Trans-
    actions 88-A(1), 172–188 (2005)
11. Gennaro, R., Jarecki, S., Krawczyk, H., Rabin, T.: Secure Distributed Key Gen-
    eration for Discrete-Log Based Cryptosystems. In: Stern, J. (ed.) EUROCRYPT
    1999. LNCS, vol. 1592, pp. 295–310. Springer, Heidelberg (1999)
12. Golle, P., Zhong, S., Boneh, D., Jakobsson, M., Juels, A.: Optimistic Mixing for
    Exit-Polls. In: Zheng, Y. (ed.) ASIACRYPT 2002. LNCS, vol. 2501, pp. 451–465.
    Springer, Heidelberg (2002)
13. Groth, J., Ishai, Y.: Sub-linear Zero-Knowledge Argument for Correctness of a
    Shuffle. In: Smart, N.P. (ed.) EUROCRYPT 2008. LNCS, vol. 4965, pp. 379–396.
    Springer, Heidelberg (2008)
14. Groth, J., Lu, S.: Verifiable Shuffle of Large Size Ciphertexts. In: Okamoto, T.,
    Wang, X. (eds.) PKC 2007. LNCS, vol. 4450, pp. 377–392. Springer, Heidelberg
    (2007)
15. Groth, J.: A Verifiable Secret Shuffle of Homomorphic Encryptions. In: Desmedt,
    Y.G. (ed.) PKC 2003. LNCS, vol. 2567, pp. 145–160. Springer, Heidelberg (2002)
16. Guillou, L.C., Quisquater, J.-J.: A "Paradoxical" Identity-Based Signature Scheme
    Resulting from Zero-Knowledge. In: Goldwasser, S. (ed.) CRYPTO 1988. LNCS,
    vol. 403, pp. 216–231. Springer, Heidelberg (1990)
17. Jakobsson, M., Juels, A., Rivest, R.: Making mix nets robust for electronic voting
    by randomized partial checking. In: Proceedings of the 11th USENIX Security
    Symposium 2002, pp. 339–353. USENIX (2002)
18. Karlof, C., Sastry, N., Wagner, D.: Cryptographic voting protocols: A systems
    perspective. In: USENIX Security Symposium 2005. LNCS, vol. 3444, pp. 33–50
    (2005)
19. McGaley, M., Gibson, J.: A critical analysis of the council of Europe recommenda-
    tions on evoting. In: USENIX/Accurate Electronic Voting Technology Workshop
    2006, 9 pages (2006)
20. Neff, C.: A verifiable secret shuffle and its application to e-voting. In: ACM Con-
    ference on Computer and Communications Security 2001, pp. 116–125 (2001)
21. Neff, C.: Verifiable mixing (shuffling) of elgamal pairs (2004),
    http://theory.lcs.mit.edu/ rivest/voting/papers/Neff-2004-04-21-
    ElGamalShuffles.pdf

22. Paillier, P.: Public-Key Cryptosystems Based on Composite Degree Residuosity Classes. In: Stern, J. (ed.) EUROCRYPT 1999. LNCS, vol. 1592, pp. 223–238. Springer, Heidelberg (1999)
23. Park, C., Itoh, K., Kurosawa, K.: Efficient Anonymous Channel and All/Nothing Election Scheme. In: Helleseth, T. (ed.) EUROCRYPT 1993. LNCS, vol. 765, pp. 248–259. Springer, Heidelberg (1994)
24. Pedersen, T.: A Threshold Cryptosystem without a Trusted Party. In: Davies, D.W. (ed.) EUROCRYPT 1991. LNCS, vol. 547, pp. 522–526. Springer, Heidelberg (1991)
25. Peng, K., Dawson, E., Bao, F.: Modification and optimisation of a shuffling scheme: stronger security, formal analysis and higher efficiency. International Journal of Information Security 10(1), 33–47 (2011)
26. Peng, K., Bao, F.: A Shuffling Scheme With Strict And Strong Security. In: SecureWare 2010, pp. 201–206 (2010)
27. Peng, K., Boyd, C., Dawson, E.: Simple and Efficient Shuffling with Provable Correctness and ZK Privacy. In: Shoup, V. (ed.) CRYPTO 2005. LNCS, vol. 3621, pp. 188–204. Springer, Heidelberg (2005)
28. Peng, K., Boyd, C., Dawson, E., Viswanathan, K.: A Correct, Private, and Efficient Mix Network. In: Bao, F., Deng, R., Zhou, J. (eds.) PKC 2004. LNCS, vol. 2947, pp. 439–454. Springer, Heidelberg (2004)
29. Schoenmakers, B.: A Simple Publicly Verifiable Secret Sharing Scheme and Its Application to Electronic Voting. In: Wiener, M. (ed.) CRYPTO 1999. LNCS, vol. 1666, pp. 148–164. Springer, Heidelberg (1999)

DLPR: A Distributed Locality Preserving Dimension Reduction Algorithm

Mina Ghashami, Hoda Mashayekhi, and Jafar Habibi

Computer Engineering Department
Sharif University of Technology
Tehran, Iran

Abstract. Document indexing using dimension reduction has been widely studied in recent years. Application of these methods in large distributed systems may be inefficient due to the required computational, storage, and communication costs. In this paper, we propose DLPR, a distributed locality preserving dimension reduction algorithm, to project a large distributed data set into a lower dimensional space. Partitioning methods are applied to divide the data set into several clusters. The system nodes communicate through virtual groups to project the clusters to the target space, independently or in conjunction with each other.

The actual computation of reduction transforms is performed using Locality Preserving Indexing, which is a less studied method in distributed environments. Experimental results demonstrate the efficiency of DLPR in terms of preserving the local structure of the data set, and reducing the computing and storage costs.

Keywords: Dimensionality reduction, distributed systems, locality preserving.

1 Introduction

Typical databases used in data mining applications may contain millions of records and thousands of variables. In such high dimensional spaces certain highly correlated variables may exist, inclusion of which in data mining models leads to inaccurate results [1]. In addition, due to their huge volume, data objects appear dissimilar in many ways, which render common data organization strategies ineffective.

To remedy this issue, dimension reduction (DR) techniques are often employed as a pre-processing step to simplify the data model. They project data from the original high dimensional space R^u to a new, lower dimensional space $R^v (v \ll u)$, in which tasks such as classification or clustering often yield more accurate and interpretable results.

Dimension reduction techniques can be broadly classified into "feature extraction" and "feature selection" categories. Feature extraction techniques produce a new, more compact set of dimensions while attempting to preserve data characteristics of the original feature set by applying a linear or non-linear mapping [2].

Y. Xiang et al. (Eds.): IDCS 2012, LNCS 7646, pp. 97–110, 2012.
© Springer-Verlag Berlin Heidelberg 2012

Principal Component Analysis (PCA) transforms a data set such that maximum variance is preserved among data objects [3]. In multimedia data analysis a popular variant of PCA, namely Latent Semantic Analysis (LSA) is utilized [4], [5], and [6]. LSA can reveal semantic information from document co-occurrences, and it is based on the singular value decomposition (SVD) of the term-document matrix.

Locality preserving projections (LPP) are linear projective maps that preserve the neighborhood structure of the data set [7]. Theoretical analysis has shown that LPP is an optimal approximation to LDA [2] according to discrimination power. Locality preserving indexing (LPI) uses LPP for document representation and indexing. LPI is an unsupervised approach, which discovers the local geometric structure of the document space and obtains a low-rank approximation of the data space [8].

Dimension reduction techniques in literature have mostly focused on a central environment presuming all data are located in one place. However, in distributed systems, transferring data to a central server can be very communication-expensive, and also results in large storage and processing overheads. The problem becomes even more challenging in a dynamic distributed scenario, in which the target space needs to be updated in response to changes in the original data set.

In this paper, we propose DLPR, a distributed locality preserving dimension reduction algorithm which uses a hierarchical structure. DLPR partitions the original data space into several disjoint clusters. These data clusters will pose a possibly overlapping grouping of system nodes, from which a hierarchical structure is created. Nodes in each group communicate to distributedly compute the information required to extract the dimension reduced projection. The actual calculation of transformation matrix is performed by the super node, using the LPI equation. Each cluster is reduced independently or in conjunction with other clusters to reflect the global structure of data.

Many partition-based dimension reduction techniques, ignore the relation of different partitions and lack a global insight of the data space, thus resulting in degraded query processing performance. Among the dimension reduction techniques, LPI has not been studied in distributed environments, regardless of its effectiveness in preserving the local document space structure. In this paper, in addition to evaluating the performance of LPI in a distributed setting, we offer an innovative solution to preserve the global structure of data space, while reducing partitions individually. Accordingly, query processing is performed on the low dimensional space, where the best results among the clusters are returned as the response.

The rest of this paper is organized as follows: in section 2, we review the most prominent and related DR algorithms. Section 3, describes the required preliminary materials. In section 4, we present the DLPR algorithm. An experimental study is presented in section 5. Finally, in section 6 we conclude the paper and sketch future research directions.

2   Related Works

To address challenges of distributed environments, some distributed and clustering based dimension reduction methods have been proposed. Distributed LSI [9] partitions information sources regarding conceptual domains and indexes each sub collection with LSI. Zhang et al. [10] analyze the relation between truncated SVDs of a matrix and the truncated SVDs of its sub-matrices. In [11], authors propose a spherical k-means algorithm for clustering high dimensional and sparse document vectors. They partition the document space to k disjoint clusters and each cluster is represented by a concept vector. The original document matrix can be projected to the concept space spanned by the constructed matrix. Gao et al. [12] propose a clustered SVD strategy for large data sets. They cluster a large inhomogeneous data set into several smaller subsets on which they apply the truncated SVD strategy.

In another research [13], the same authors extract centroid vectors from these clusters to construct a concept matrix and use sparsification strategies to reduce storage costs. CLSI [14] is a methodology for matrix representation and information retrieval. It first clusters the term-document matrix and then executes partial SVD on each cluster. The extracted information is used to build low-rank approximations to the original matrix.

Vigna [15] proposes a distributed, large-scale LSA algorithm by combining standard search-engine algorithmic tools to compute the co-occurrence matrix of the document collection. The algorithm actually distributes the computation load among multiple nodes. MRSMO [16] is a MapReduce-based distributed SVM algorithm for automatic image annotation. It partitions the training dataset into smaller subsets and optimizes the partitioned subsets across a cluster of computers. Liu et al. [17] propose a MapReduce based distributed LSI using Hadoop distributed computing architecture to cluster the documents, and then use LSI on the clustered results.

3   Basics

In this section we give a brief review of LPP and LPI algorithms. Let $\chi = \{x_1, x_2, \ldots, x_m\}$ be the set of m document vectors, which constitute the document space. Each document x_i, is represented as a u-dimensional vector, $x_i = (x_1^i, x_2^i, \ldots, x_u^i)$. The set of terms constitutes the dimensions, and the value of each dimension for a document x_i, determines the importance of that term in x_i with respect to other terms.

Let X represent the $u \times m$ term-document matrix whose columns are document vectors. Note that in high dimensional spaces the intrinsic dimensionality of document space may be very smaller than u.

LPI aims to find a new representation of the document set, $Y = \{y_1, y_2, \ldots, y_m\}$, such that $\|y_i - y_j\|$ reflects the semantic relationship between x_i and x_j. It first executes a preprocessing step and projects the document set into the PCA subspace by discarding the smallest principal components. Let A_{PCA} denote the transformation matrix of PCA.

Next, it constructs a weight matrix W in which $w_{ij} = 1$ if either of x_j or x_j is among the k-nearest neighbours of each other, else $w_{ij} = 0$. Other methods of computing W exist, which can be found in [18]. The optimal projections, which preserve locality, are obtained by computing the minimum eigenvalue solution for the following generalized eigenvector problem:

$$XLX^T a = \lambda X D X^T a \qquad (1)$$

Where D is a diagonal matrix whose entries are column (or row) sums of W, $D_{ii} = \sum_{j=1}^{m} W_{ji}$, and $L = D - W$ is the Laplacian matrix.

Let $A_{LPP} = [a_0, a_1, \ldots, a_{v-1}]$ be the solutions of equation 1 ordered according to their eigenvalues, $\lambda_0 < \lambda_1 < \ldots < \lambda_{v-1}$. The final transformation matrix and the embedding are defined as:

$$A = A_{PCA} A_{LPP} \qquad (2)$$

$$y = A^T x \qquad (3)$$

y is a v dimensional representation of document x.

4   DLPR Algorithm

In large distributed environments, where the set of documents are distributed among nodes, computation of LPI can be very costly in terms of communication, storage, and processing costs. Constructing the document and weight matrices, X and W, requires transmission of all data to a central node, which produces a lot of communication overhead. The central node itself requires vast amount of storage and processing resources to compute equation 1. To overcome these challenges, DLPR is proposed, which consists of clustering, data preparation and reduction steps.

Assume a system of S nodes, $N = \{n_1, \ldots, n_s\}$. The system infrastructure, allows for any two nodes to communicate with each other. Each node n_j, holds a subset of the document set $\chi^j \subset \chi$. The goal is to compute a new set of document vectors in a reduced dimensional space. In what follows we describe each task of DLPR in detail.

4.1   Clustering Step

To effectively reduce various costs of executing the dimension reduction algorithm, DLPR initially partitions the document set χ, into a group of disjoint clusters $\mathbf{C} = \{C_1, C_2, \ldots, C_k\}$. The clusters pose a self-similar behavior, i.e., documents of the similar classes are grouped into the same cluster. Thus, the clusters should have high intra-cluster similarity and low inter-cluster similarity. $C(x_i)$ denotes the cluster of document x_i. Correspondingly, documents of each node fall into a subset of the overall clusters; the clusters of n_j are denoted as $\mathbf{C}^j = \bigcup_{x_i \in \chi^j} C(x_i)$.

To enable execution of DLPR, a virtual node group should be constructed per each cluster, whose members are nodes who own data in that cluster. Accordingly, a total number of k virtual groups exist in the system: $\mathbf{VG} = \{VG_1, \ldots, VG_k\}$. The set of all virtual groups which a node n_j participates in, is shown as $\mathbf{VG}^j \subset \mathbf{VG}$. Note that $|\mathbf{C}^j| = |\mathbf{VG}^j| \leq |\chi^j|$.

Each node should keep links to a subset of other nodes in each virtual group it participates in. The links can be established to random nodes in the group; however, to facilitate query processing tasks, maintaining links to nodes with semantically similar data is encouraged. After group formation, a super node should be selected for each group. A method of super node selection is proposed in [19].

The DLPR algorithm, as a general framework, does not restrict the method of clustering documents. However, due to distributed nature of documents, a decentralized clustering method is desired. In this study, we use the K-means algorithm, which is among the best known clustering methods, and has the benefit of predetermining number of clusters. This property proves beneficial in distributed setting, as better resource planning can be performed before algorithm execution.

K-means considers documents to be placed in a u-dimensional metric space with an associated distance metric δ. It partitions the data set into k clusters, where k is a user defined parameter. Each cluster C_l, has a centroid μ_l, defined as the average of all data assigned to that cluster. The algorithm relies on finding cluster centroids by trying to minimize the within-cluster sum of squares:

$$\sum_{j=1}^{k} \sum_{x_i \in C_j} \delta(x_i, \mu_j) \tag{4}$$

The formal definition of k-means is given in Figure 1. The algorithm proceeds heuristically; a set of random centroids are picked initially, to be optimized in later iterations.

Process K-means(χ, k):
　　Define k clusters $\mathbf{C} = \{C_1, \ldots, C_k\}$
　　Generate k random initial cluster centroids $\mu_1, \ldots, \mu_k$
　　repeat
　　　　$C_j = \{x | x \in \chi \ \& \ \forall i \neq j. \ \delta(x, \mu_j) \leq \delta(x, \mu_i)\}$
　　　　$\mu_j = \frac{\sum_{x \in C_j} x}{|C_j|}$
　　until $\forall j. |\mu_j^{new} - \mu_j^{old}| \leq \epsilon$

Fig. 1. The K-means algorithm

Several distributed versions of the K-means algorithm exist in the literature, e.g., [20], [21], which can be employed in the clustering step of DLPR.

4.2   Data Preparation

The main activity of the data preparation task is to distributedly construct the weight matrices and alter the corresponding term-document matrices if necessary. Each cluster C_l, has a corresponding term-document matrix X_l, and a weight matrix W_l. X_l includes the portion of X containing the documents in cluster C_l. W_l may only include intra structure of C_l or contain elements from inter structure of clusters, as well. Accordingly, the weight matrix for each partition can be constructed in two different approaches based on the portion of structure we wish to preserve. In both approaches, weight matrices are sparse and are constructed based on KNN metric. Each node n_k is responsible of calculating the non-zero values of the weight matrices per each document $x \in \chi^k$. These two weight matrix construction approaches are described below:

– **Including intra structure of cluster**
   W_l is a $|C_l| \times |C_l|$ matrix constructed based on KNN metric. Let x_i^l denote the i'th document in X^l. The value w_{ij}^l is one if and only if either of document x_i^l or x_j^l is among the K nearest neighbours of each other, and zero otherwise. To compute the values, it suffices that the node which owns x_i^l, executes a K-nearest neighbour query for this document in VG_l. To accomplish this, any of the distributed nearest neighbour execution proposals in the literature can be applied e.g., [22], and [23].

– **Including intra and inter structure of clusters**
   Let the data clusters be ordered by an associated index number. A ring structure can be set up between the super nodes of virtual node groups, such that the super node of VG_l is connected to super node of $VG_{(l+1)mod|\mathbf{C}|}$. In this case, X_l expands to a matrix of order $n \times (|C_l| + k')$, in which k' is the parameter used in the KNN metric, when constructing weight matrices of LPI. The first $|C_l|$ columns constitute the documents of cluster C_l, while the last k' columns consist of random documents from $C_{(l+1)mod|\mathbf{C}|}$. The latter documents can be obtained from the corresponding super node.
   The set of k' documents belonging to another cluster, are artificially assumed to be among k-nearest neighbours of each other. Thus, the entries of the $(|C_l| + k') \times (|C_l| + k')$ matrix W_l is computed as follows:

$$
w_{ij}^l = \begin{cases} 1 & 1 \leq i, j \leq |C_l| \wedge x_j^l \in \text{KNN of } x_i^l \\ 1 & |C_l| + 1 \leq i, j \leq |C_l| + k' \\ 0 & otherwise \end{cases} \tag{5}
$$

The entries related to documents of the current cluster, are computed distributedly by nodes in VG_l, and other entries are inserted by the super node.

Assume a specific condition where some of the attributes of the document space are discriminant in a specific cluster, and the corresponding values for documents of other clusters are constant. These attributes can bias the projection results in the latter clusters, in such a way that the global structure of the data space is violated in the reduced target space. In this condition, applying the second method discussed above, will improve the projection results.

4.3   Reduction

The complete data and weight matrices of each cluster C_l, should be constructed at the super node of the virtual group VG_l. To accomplish this, all nodes in VG_l transmit their partial entries of these two matrices to the super node, which aggregates them into the complete data and weight matrices for cluster C_l. The reduction step is performed locally at the super node. This node is able to solve the LPI equation and extract the transformation matrix of the cluster. This transformation matrix is distributed among the nodes of VG_l, so that they are able to compute the reduced version of their documents located in cluster C_l.

Considering the DLPR design, as the data preparation step is executed distributedly, the super node has only the overhead of collecting partial parts of the corresponding matrices and solving the LPI equation.

5   Query Processing

Different types of queries which can be executed on the set of documents include approximate query, range query, nearest neighbours query, etc. Given a query vector q, finding the b most similar documents to q is possible by measuring distance of q to each of the document vectors in χ. Afterwards, b documents with minimum distance are returned as the final result set. The applied distance metric is arbitrary. Other types of queries are computed in a similar fashion.

The same retrieval procedure can be executed in the reduced space, where the distance of the *reduced* query vector is computed to every *reduced* document vector. In DLPR, each cluster has its specific reduction matrix. Therefore, the query vector should be sent to some node in every virtual group. The query is then reduced using the transformation matrix of that cluster, after which b most similar documents of the cluster are extracted. Among the overall $k \times b$ retrieved documents, the b most similar ones are returned as the result.

There are some other retrieval strategies available in literature, for example in [12], a partial clustered retrieval is proposed in which k' similar documents are discovered only in clusters, whose centroids are closer to q. This procedure although reducing the accuracy, improves processing overhead of query execution.

6   Performance Evaluation

In this section, we present the experimental evaluation of DLPR, and also compare it to basic LPI and LSI algorithms.

The data sets used in the evaluations are depicted in table 1.The third data set is a large, inhomogeneous database consisting of three popular document databases (CRANFIELD, CISI, and MEDLINE). The documents of these three databases were merged. The terms of the new database were set to the union of the terms of original databases, preprocessed using stemming.

Documents of the merged data set did not have class labels. Thus, class labels were artificially assigned to the documents, by first clustering this data set into 3 partitions and then assigning a unique label to documents of each cluster. To the best of our knowledge, these data sets are among the largest data sets used for evaluation in the literature; this demonstrates our claims to the robustness and effectiveness of DLPR.

In the simulations, dimensionality is varied from 2 to 10, and number of clusters is varied from 3 to 9. Also 10% of each data set was used as the test set, while the remaining part was used as the training set. Parameter k' of the KNN metric, for constructing weight matrices, is set to 50, 10 and 6, for Covtype, Musk and merged data sets respectively. Euclidean distance was applied as the distance measure. The following metrics are used in order to assess the quality of the projection:

1. Classification Preservation Ability (CPA): This metric demonstrates the classification quality of each algorithm by measuring its capability in preserving the classification label of the KNN algorithm through projection to the target space. It is measured as the ratio of correctly classified test instances in target space, to number of test records. Values closer to 1 signify more accurate behaviour.

2. Accuracy (AC) [24]: Assume that data is clustered prior and after dimension reduction. Given a document x_i, let c_i and c'_i be the corresponding cluster label respectively. AC is defined as follows:

$$AC = \frac{\sum_{i=1}^{m} \delta(c_i, map(c'_i))}{m}, \tag{6}$$

Where m is the total number of documents, $\delta(x, y) = 1$ if $x = y$, otherwise $\delta(x, y) = 0$. $map(c'_i)$ is the permutation mapping function that maps each cluster label c'_i to some appropriate cluster label from the original data space. The best mapping can be found by using the Kuhn-Munkres algorithm [25].The AC measure basically measures number of documents which are located in the same cluster before and after dimension reduction.

3. Processing and Storage costs: These metrics demonstrate CPU time (in seconds) and storage cost (in MB) consumed by the reduction algorithms. Due to high dependency of these metrics to the implementation style, we only evaluated LPI and DLPR algorithms using the same core code. Note that time and storage of the clustering step of DLPR was not considered.

All experiments have been performed on a commodity 2.80GHz machine with 16 GB of RAM, in the Matlab environment.

Table 1. Data sets used in the evaluation

Data set	Records	Dimension	Classes	Description
Covtype	581012	54	7	Forest cover type data
Musk	6598	166	2	Molecules descriptions
Merged	3893	3303	3	consisting of Cranfield, Cisi and Medline

6.1 Classification Preservation Ability(CPA)

In the first set of experiments, we evaluated DLPR against LPI and LSI, applying both approaches of weight matrix construction in the second step of the algorithm. Figure 2 shows the CPA measure using the intra structure of clusters in the weight matrix of DLPR. As observed in Covtype and Musk data sets, DLPR has better performance than LPI. In addition, it greatly outperforms LSI. However, using 9 clusters provides best CPA performance for Covtype and Musk data sets. DLPR does not offer significant CPA values for the merged data set. This is due to the large number of features in this data set, which are only discriminant in one part of the data set. As observed later in figure 3, the performance of DLPR is significantly increased when considering inter cluster structure in the weight matrix.

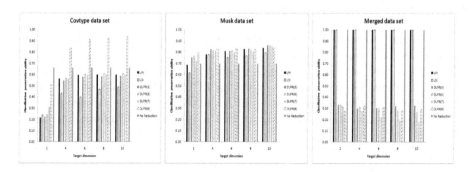

Fig. 2. Comparing CPA as number of target dimensions varies, using the intra structure of clusters in the weight matrix of DLPR. Number of clusters in K-means based clustering shown in parenthesis.

Figure 3 shows the CPA measure when weight matrix of DLPR considers both intra and inter cluster structures. Again, DLPR offers close or better performance than LPI for different number of clusters. This is also true, when comparing DLPR to LSI. As observed, CPA measure is not significantly varied for Covtype and Musk data sets. For the merged data set, however, CPA value of DLPR is increased to a high extent.

Being composed of three databases, the merged data set has a large number of features, which are only discriminant in one part of the data set. Thus, reducing each cluster independently, can mislead the dimension reduction algorithm,

into producing projections which ruin the global structure of documents in the
reduced space. Contributing the inter cluster structure in the weight matrix, can
aid to map documents into relatively correct points in the reduced space.

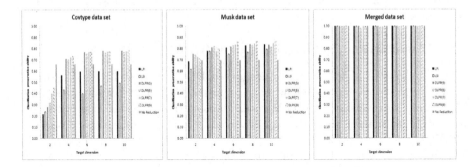

Fig. 3. Comparing CPA as number of target dimensions varies, using the intra structure of clusters in the weight matrix of DLPR. Number of clusters in K-means based
clustering shown in parenthesis.

6.2   Time and Storage Costs

Figures 4 and 5 represent the CPU time (in seconds) and storage cost (in MB)
for executing the dimension reduction algorithms on the mentioned data sets.
The average cost per each cluster is reported. As observed, DLPR consumes
much less resources compared to executing LPI on whole data set. Recalling
that DLPR offers close CPA values to LPI, and considering its reduced resource
consumption, demonstrates efficiency of DLPR specially in distributed settings.

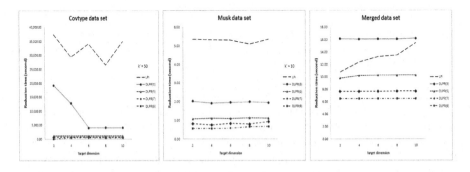

Fig. 4. Reduction processing time versus target dimension, using the intra structure
of clusters in the weight matrix of DLPR

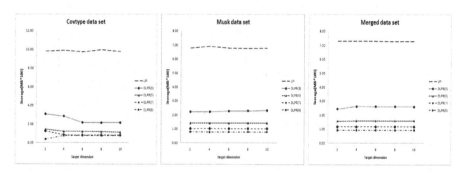

Fig. 5. Reduction storage cost versus target dimension, using the intra structure of clusters in the weight matrix of DLPR

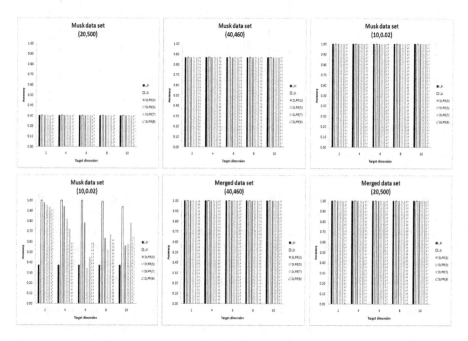

Fig. 6. Comparing AC measure when number of target dimensions varies, using the intra structure of clusters in the weight matrix of DLPR. Values of (minpoint, radius) are shown in chart title

6.3   Accuracy (AC)

In this set of expriments, we utilized Musk and Merged data sets, in order to evaluate DLPR along with its both approaches of weight matrix construction, againts LPI and LSI. In this context, we used DBSCAN algorithm [26] with different pair-values of (minpoint, radius) parameters in order to cluster data prior and after dimension reduction.

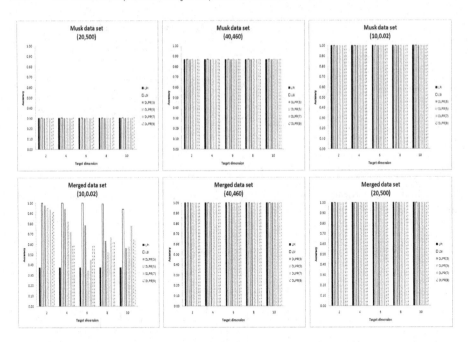

Fig. 7. Comparing AC measure when number of target dimensions varies, using the intra and inter structure of clusters in the weight matrix of DLPR. Values of (minpoint, radius) are shown in chart title

Figure 6 demonstrates the AC measure of aforementioned algorithms with an emphasis on preserving only intra structure of clusters. In DLPR, documents that are conceptually similar are clustered in a common group. This procedure decreases the inhomogeneity of the data set in each partition, which significantly contributes to the AC measure. Figure 7 shows the AC measure when weight matrix of DLPR preserves both intra and inter cluster structures.

As observed in both figures, The three algotihms have similar behavior with respect to the AC measure. This clearly shows that DLPR, although reducing each cluster separately, can preserve the overall structure of the dataset in the target space.

7   Conclusion

In this paper we presented DLPR, a distributed locality preserving dimension reduction algorithm. DLPR partitions data distributed in the network into several disjoint clusters, and projects the data of each cluster independently or in conjunction with other clusters into a lower dimensional space. Two approaches for preserving different portion of data structure are described, one of which considers intra structure of clusters, and the other also considering inter structure of clusters. To realize distributed computation of reductions, nodes are organized into virtual node groups. The queries are also processed by aggregating results derived from different virtual groups in the system. Certain most similar documents among all virtual groups are returned as the query results.

DLPR achieves quality of results comparable to the most prominent DR algorithms, while reducing storage and computation costs. It remains as future work to improve retrieval costs by selecting the best clusters to retrieve the query from, in order to prevent comparing the query against the complete data set.

References

1. Larose, D.T.: Data mining methods and models. Wiley-Interscience, Hohn Wiley and Sons, Hoboken, New Jersey (2005)
2. Duda, R.O., Hart, P.E., Stork, D.G.: Pattern Classification, 2nd edn. Wiley-Interscience, John Wiley and Sons (1995)
3. Smith, L.: A tutorial on principal components analysis. University of Otago (2002)
4. Heisterkamp, D.R.: Building a latent semantic index of an image database from patterns of relevance feedback. In: 4th International Conference on Pattern Recognition, pp. 134–137 (2002)
5. Sahouria, E., Zakhor, A.: Content analysis of video using principal componets. In: 3rd International Conference on Image Processing, pp. 541–545 (1998)
6. Smaragdis, P., Raj, B., Shashanka, M.: A probabilistic latent variable model for acoustic modeling. In: Workshop on Advances in Models for Acoustic Processing at NIPS (2006)
7. He, X., Niyogi, P.: Locality preserving projections. In: Advances in Neural Information Processing Systems 16, Vancouver, Canada (2003)
8. Cai, D., He, X., Han, J.: Document clustering using locality preserving indexing. IEEE Transactions on Knowledge and Data Engineerin 17, 1624–1637 (2005)
9. Bassu, D., Behrens, C.: Distributed LSI: scalable concept-based information retrieval with high semantic resolution. In: 2003 Text Mining Workshop, pp. 72–82. ACM Press, San Francisco (2003)
10. Zhang, Z., Zha, H.: Structure and perturbation analysis of truncated SVD for column-partitioned matrices. Matrix Analysis and Applications 22, 1245–1262 (2001)
11. Dhillon, I.S., Modha, D.S.: Concept decompositions for large sparse text data using clustering. Machine Learning 42, 143–175 (2001)
12. Gao, J., Zhang, J.: Clustered SVD strategies in latent semantic indexing. Information Processing and Management 41, 1051–1063 (2005)
13. Gao, J., Zhang, J.: Text Retrieval Using Sparsified Concept Decomposition Matrix. In: Zhang, J., He, J.-H., Fu, Y. (eds.) CIS 2004. LNCS, vol. 3314, pp. 523–529. Springer, Heidelberg (2004)
14. Zeimpekis, D., Gallopoulos, E.: CISI: A flexible approximation scheme from clustered term-document matrices. In: SIAM Data Mining Conference, Newport Beach, California, pp. 631–635 (2005)
15. Vigna, S.: Distributed, large-scale latent semantic analysis by index interpolation. In: 3rd International Conference on Scalable Information Systems, vol. 18 (2008)
16. Alham, N.K., Li, M., Liu, Y., Hammoud, S.: A MapReduce-based Distributed SVM Algorithm for Automatic Image Annotation. Computers and Mathematics with Applications 62, 2801–2811 (2011)
17. Liu, Y., Li, M., Hammoud, S., Alham, N.K., Ponraj, M.: A MapReduce based distributed LSI. In: 7th International Conference on Fuzzy Systems and Knowledge Discovery, pp. 297–298. IEEE Press, Yantai (2010)

18. He, X., Niyogi, P.: Indexing by latent semantic analysis. Neural Information Processing Systems 6, 153–160 (2003)
19. Lo, V., Zhou, D., Liu, Y., Dickey, C.G., Li, J.: Scalable supernode selection in peer-to-peer overlay networks. In: 2nd HOT-P2P Workshop, pp. 18–25. IEEE Press (2005)
20. Datta, S., Giannella, C., Kargupta, H.: K-Means Clustering over a Large, Dynamic Network. In: SIAM International Conference on Data Mining, pp. 153–164 (2006)
21. Hammouda, K.M., Kamel, M.S.: Hierarchically Distributed Peer-to-Peer Document Clustering and Cluster Summarization. IEEE Transactions on Knowledge and Data Engineering, 681–698 (2009)
22. Panigrahy, R.: Entropy-based nearest neighbor algorithm in high dimensions. In: ACM-SIAM Symposium on Discrete Algorithms (2006)
23. Mashayekhi, H., Habibi, J.: K-Nearest Neighbor Search in Peer-to-Peer Systems. In: 2nd International Conference on Advances in P2P Systems, pp. 2–5 (2010)
24. Xu, W., Liu, X., Gong, Y.: Document clustering based on non-negative matrix factorization. In: 3rd International Conference on Research and Development in Information Retreival, Toronto, Canada, pp. 267–273 (2003)
25. Lovasz, L., Plummer, M.: Matching Theory. Akadémiai Kiadó. North Holland, Budapest (1986)
26. Ester, M., Kriegel, H., Sander, J., Xu, X.: A density-based algorithm for discovering clusters in large spatial databases with noise. In: 2nd International Conference on Knowledge Discovery and Data Mining, pp. 226–231 (1996)

A Leader-Based Reliable Multicast MAC Protocol for MPEG-4 Traffic

Muhammad Khalil Afzal[1], Byung-Seo Kim[2], and Sung Won Kim[3]

[1,3] Dept. of Information and Communication Engineering, Yeungnam University, Korea
[2] Dept. of Computer and Information Communications Engineering, Hongik University, Korea
{khalil_78_pk@yahoo.com, jsnbs@hongik.ac.kr, swon@yu.ac.kr}

Abstract. Multicasting is an efficient way for group communications because one sender can transmit data to multiple receivers only by one transmission. Multimedia applications are expected to become more prevalent over mobile ad-hoc networks in the near future. Therefore, reliability in multimedia communication is an important task. However, IEEE 802.11 standard does not provide any reliable multicast. In MPEG-4, the losses of different frames have different impact on video quality. In this paper, the effects of different frame types losses on Peak Signal to Noise Ratio (PSNR) are shown, and a reliable multicast MAC layer protocol for MPEG-4 traffic is proposed to enhance video quality and reduce the probability of a collision when the traffic volume exceed the network capacity.

Keywords: MPEG-4, Multicast, Reliability, PSNR.

1 Introduction

Recently, group-oriented services have appeared as one of the primary applications i.e. video conferencing, online gaming, and video streaming. Multicasting [1][2] is the transmission of data to a group of multicast members identified by single destination address. Moving Picture Expert Group version 4 (MPEG-4) gives the better performances in terms of video streaming applications as compared to MPEG-1 and MPEG-2. While MPEG-4 makes the use of video codes to reduce the bit rate and the amount of data transmitted, it provides the same video quality as MPEG-1 and MPEG-2 does. MPEG-4 video stream consists of three types of frames; I-frame (Intra-coded frame), P-frame (Predicted frame), and B-frame (Bi-directional frame). I-frames are independently encoded from the other frames. P-frames are encoded with a reference frame, which is I-frame or P-frame. P-frames consider the closest time-preceding frames. B-frames are coded with a reference frame, which is I or P frames and are the time adjacent frames [3]. An example of the sequence of frames is shown in Figure 1.

There are a few proposals for reliable multicast [5][6][7]. However, still there is no proposal that specifically addresses MPEG-4 multimedia streaming. The higher throughput does not always mean the better quality of MPEG-4 as shown in [4]. The transmission losses on the different types of frames have a different impact on video quality. In this paper, at first, we show the effect of different frames on Peak Signal to

Y. Xiang et al. (Eds.): IDCS 2012, LNCS 7646, pp. 111–119, 2012.

Noise Ratio (PSNR) and then proposed a Leader-based reliable multicast Medium Access Control (MAC) layer protocol for MPEG4 traffic.

The rest of the paper is organized as follows. In section 2, we provide some of the research efforts carried out in the perspective related to our works. Section 3 discusses problem statement in detail. After, problem statement, loss of different frames on video quality is described in section 4. Section 5 presents proposed protocol, and finally, conclusions and future works are given in Section 6.

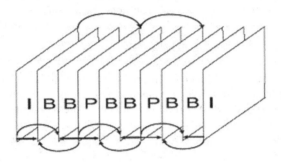

Fig. 1. I, P and B frames

2   Related Work

Kuri and Kasera [5], propose a Leader-based Protocol (LBP) to improve the reliability of multicast traffic in wireless LAN. This protocol chooses one of multicast receivers for the exchange of Clear to Send (CTS), Ready to Send (RTS), and Acknowledgement (ACK) frames. However, proposed protocol does not consider the numerous parameters associated with MPEG-4 traffic i.e. frame types, frame size.

Authors in [6] propose an extension to the IEEE 802.11 standard-based MAC, called 802.11MX, to improve link-level reliability for multicast data. They use a tone-based mechanism for the signal of negative acknowledgement (NAK) frame, so there is no collision in NAK frames. Authors further propose a dual busy tone to reduce packet collisions due to node mobility. However, the higher data throughput and reliability of 802.11MX comes at the cost of additional transceivers.

Choi at al [7], propose a Reliable multicast MAC protocol (RBMAC) by using a busy tone that improves the data throughput while guaranteeing the transmission reliability. The simulation results show that the proposed RBMAC improves the throughput up to 20 % and the receiving rate up to 49 %. To provide reliability RBMAC uses two busy tones (BTC) channels and one control tone channel (CTC) which requires extra time to monitor the status of channels.

Lee and Cho [8], proposed a multiple access collision avoidance protocol for multicast services in mobile ad hoc network. In this protocol, a sender sends a single multicast RTS frame to all the neighbors and waits for the CTS frame. The RTS frame is overloaded to contain the addresses of all multicast next hop neighbors. Thus, the RTS frame size is larger than the size of the frame in IEEE 802.11standard making the RTS frame itself prone to collision due to hidden terminals. CTS frames are transmitted in a time-based priority schedule like the ACK frames. Jain and Das [9], propose an extension to 802.11-based MAC protocol. Authors modify the RTS frame to include, at-most, four multicast next hop neighbor addresses which helps to keep the RTS frame size within bounds. However, proposed protocols are not suitable for MPEG-4 traffic because different frames require different reliability.

The works in [10] propose a reliable multicast MAC protocol (RAMP) for multi-hop networks. RAMP ensures high packet delivery ratio as well as reduce control overheads. To maintain the control overhead low, RAMP limits the use of multicast RTS and multicast CTS frames to the first packet of a multicast data flow. There is no handshaking for the following packets. The unreliable and error-prone nature of the wireless channel can cause severe degradation in performance due to such handshaking process.

Multimedia communication over wireless devices is increasing day-by-day and multicasting is an efficient way of multimedia group communication. Reliability is issue in multicast communication because IEEE 802.11 standard does not provide reliability. This motivates us to propose a reliable multicast MAC protocol for MPEG-4. Furthermore, in this paper we analyze the impact of losses of different types of MPEG-4 frames on PSNR.

3   Problem Statement

Xiao et al [4] present simulation result shows that the higher throughput does not always mean a better quality of MPEG-4 video. Losses from different frames have different effects on the video quality. During their analysis in [4], authors observed that I, P and B frames are in a decreasing order of importance. If I frames of MPEG-4 video are lost, the next N-1 frames (all P and B frames) are useless, where N is the total number of frames contained in one Group of Picture (GOP). In the case of I frame loss, the transmission of N-1 frames would also be a waste of network resources i.e. bandwidth. During our experiments, for example, we have a GOP size of 9 with one I frame, 2 P and 6 B frames, then the average bandwidth waste for 2 P and 6 B frames will be:

$$(Average\ size\ of\ P\ frames \times 2\ +\ Average\ size\ of\ B\ frames \times 6) =$$
$$(765 \times 2 + 490 \times 6)\ bytes = 4470\ bytes = 4.36\ KBytes$$

I frame is used as a starting point for the sequence of the frames (P and B frames). I frame is also used for resynchronization of the entire scene. Because the loss of I frames affects so many later P and B frames, the reliability of I frames is very important.

The 802.11 specifications [11] do not offer any MAC layer recovery on multicast and broadcast frames. There is no handshaking mechanism, such as Request-to-Send/Clear-to-Send (RTS/CTS) frames or acknowledgement (ACKS). To overcome the shortcoming of IEEE 802.11 and enhance the video quality we proposed a Leader-based reliable multicast MAC layer protocol for MPEG-4.

4   Effect of Different Frame on Video Quality

In order to test the effect of a different frame loss on video quality, we conduct simulations using video framework Evalvid [12]. Evalvid is a complete framework and tool-set for evaluating the quality of video transmitted over a real or simulated communication networks. Simulations are performed in Network Simulator 2 (NS2) version 2.35[13] over multicast-based network environments. The simulation parameters are shown in table 1. To measure the video quality on multicast receiver, PSNR is calculated with different frame loss rates. PSNR is one of the most widespread objective metrics to assess the application-level QoS of video transmissions. Such objective methods are described by ITU [14] [15], MPEG [16], and ANSI [17][18].

Table 1. Simulation Parameters

Parameter	Value
Radio Channel	802.11 a
Data rate	6 Mbps
Wmin	31
Wmax	1023
SIFS time	16μs
DIFS time	34μs
Slot time	9μs
Phy header	46bits
Mac header	24 Bytes
UDP + IP header	28 bytes
Application layer Traffic	MPEG-4
Average GOP size	3989 bytes
Average Frame sizes	I=2734 bytes, P=765 bytes, and B=490
Error Probability	0.05
Number of Nodes	5

$$PSNR(n)_{db} = 20\log_{10}\left\{\frac{V_{peak}}{\sqrt{MSE}}\right\}, \tag{1}$$

$$V_{peak} = 2^k - 1, \tag{2}$$

where V_{peak} is the maximum possible pixel value of the image, and k is number of bits per pixel i.e. when pixel are represented using 8 bits per sample, this peak value will be 255. Mean Square Error (MSE) is referred to the estimate of error variance and the value of MSE is given as:

$$MSE = \frac{\sum_{i=1}^{N_{Col}}\sum_{j=1}^{N_{row}}[Y_S(n,i,j) - Y_D(n,i,j)]^2}{N_{Col}N_{row}}, \tag{3}$$

where N_{Col} and N_{row} are the total number of columns and rows in input images, respectively, i and j indicate the current columns and rows position, and n is current frame number. Y_S is the luminous component of source image, and Y_D is the luminous component of destination image as defined in [12].

The other measure is known as subjective quality metrics. This metric of the human quality impression is usually given on a scale that ranges from 1 (worst) to 5 (best) known as Mean Opinion Score, shown in table 2.

Table 2. PSNR to MOS conversion

PSNR(db)	MOS
> 37	5 (Excellent)
31 ~ 37	4 (Good)
25 ~ 31	3 (Fair)
20 ~ 25	2 (poor)
< 20	1(bad)

The impact of I frame loss on video quality can be viewed in Fig 2. Fig. 2(a) represents the frame number 287 in the original video file and the type of frame is I frame. Fig. 2(b) shows the received video I frame, which is not fully decoded due to a missing of MAC frame delivering parts of the frame. There is multiple MAC segments for one I frame because and I frame are the bigger in size as compared to P and B frames. Fig. 2(c) and Fig. 2(d) show the propagation effect on the following P and B frames in one GOP due to a missing a I frame.

The propagation effect due can also be observed in Fig. 3. In Fig. 3, Frame number 287 (I-frame) is not decoded since some MAC frames are lost, so the following P and B frames also show lower PSNR values. The same effect can also be observed for the frame number 305 (I-frame) and 341(I-frame).

Fig. 3 also shows the effect of the losses of P and B frames on PSNR. In the case of the loss of P frame, there is less PSNR. However, there is no effect of propagation. On the other hand, in the case of the B frame, the PSNR value is acceptable.

5   Proposed Method

Our proposed method is an extension of a Leader-based protocol in which there will be one or more receivers of from the multicast group that have been chosen to be the leader for the purpose of supplying CTS packet and ACK packet in response to RTS packet and data packets. There may be some nodes that are not ready for receiving multicast data, and the nodes will send NCTS (Not Clear to Send) packet. On the successful reception of CTS packet from the leader, the sender /base station will send data and wait for the ACK packet. Only the leader will send ACK and the nodes that are not ready will reply with NACK packet. There will be a backup leader, which will take the responsibilities of the leader in case of the leader's mobility, or the leader leaves the group.

Fig. 2(a). I Frame No:287 from "Carphone_qcif" [Transmitted frame]

Fig. 2(b). I Frame No: 287 from "Carphone_qcif" [Received frame]

Fig. 2(c). B Frame No: 288 from "Carphone_qcif" showing Propagation effect

Fig 2(d). B Frame No: 294 from "Carphone_qcif" showing Propagation effect

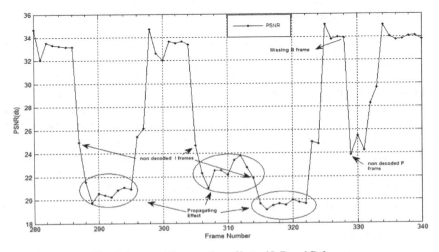

Fig. 3. Loss and Propagation effect of I, P and B frames

Our proposed Leader-based protocol for MPEG-4 multicasting is specified as follow:

1. Sender→ Receivers
                              Send RTS packet
2. Receivers→ Sender
              Leader: If ready to receive data, send CTS packet
                              If not ready to receive data, do nothing
                              If move or leaves group, inform to backup leader
              Others: If ready to receive data, do nothing
                              If not ready to receive data, send NCTS packet
3. Sender→ Receiver
                              If CTS packet is heard, start multicast transmis-
                              sion
                              If no CTS packet is heard, back off and go to
                              step 1

   .Receivers→Sender
              Leader: If I frames is received without error, send ACK
                              packet
                              If P and B frames received without error, no ACK
                              packet
                              If I frames received with error send NACK packet

              Others: If I, P and B frames are received without error, do
                              nothing
                              If I frames are not received, send NACK packet.
4. Sender→Receiver
                              If ACK packet is not received for I frames,
                              retransmit I frame.
                              If NACK packet is received for I frames, retrans-
                              mit I frames

The proposed protocol reduces the number of retransmissions as compared to LBP, because only the missing I frames will be retransmitted, and there is no retransmission for P and B frames. Chan et al [19] experimental results show that when the traffic load is near or exceed the network capacity, retransmissions cause erratic video quality and tremendously increase the end-to-end delay. They also show that, when the best-effort traffic coexists, increasing the number of retransmissions degrades the good-put of best-effort traffic and increases the end-to-end delay of video streaming. Retransmissions add reliability and increase the video streaming quality only when the traffic volume is far below the network capacity limit. We have already showed that P and B frames are less important than I frames are, and wireless channels are mostly suffering from low bandwidth and high bit error rates due to the noise, interference, and multipath fading channels[20]. Therefore, when traffic volume is very high, retransmissions of P and B frames can significantly reduce the throughput and have less impact on video quality.

The proposed protocol also reduces the number of RTS/CTS and ACK packets comparing to LBP, so the probability of collision is less. Only a leader will transmit ACK packet on successful reception of I frames, there will be no ACK packet for P and B frames. MPEG-4 traffic is generated as shown by Fig. 1. GOP pattern can varied with different values of P and B frames. However, in one GOP, the first frame is always an I frame called a reference frame, and there is only one I frames in one GOP followed by B and P frames. We can consider that an error in the I frame will affect N (distance of I frames) frames in the actual GOP and M-1 frames in the previous one. Therefore, the distortion level is the highest when I frame is damaged. If I frame is dropped, then following B and P frames are useless, so the retransmission of I frame can enhance the video quality.

6   Conclusion

We have two main contributions in this paper. Firstly, we analyze the impact of different frame losses on PSNR values. Our simulations results show that, I frames are more important that P and B frames and have significant impact on video quality. Secondly, we propose an extension to the leader-based protocol for reliable multimedia multicasting over mobile ad-hoc networks. The proposed protocol reduces the number of retransmission as compared to leader-based protocol, and increased the system throughput when the traffic volume exceeds the network capacity. Implementation of proposed idea is as future work to provide detail results.

Acknowledgement. This research is supported in part by the National Research Foundation of Korea (NRF) grant funded by the Korea government (MEST) (2012-0003609) and in part by Basic Science Research Program through the National Research Foundation of Korea (NRF) funded by the Ministry of Education, Science and Technology (2012000536).

References

1. Deering, S.: Multicast routing in a datagram Network. Ph.D. Dissertation Standford University (1991)
2. Cordeiro, C.M., Gossain, H., Agrawal, D.P.: Multicast over wireless mobile ad hoc networks: present and future directions. IEEE Network, Special Issue on Multicasting: An Enabling Technology 17(1) (2003)
3. Molteni, M., Villari, M.: Using SCTP with Partial Reliability for MPEG-4 Multimedia Streaming. In: Procs. of BSDCon, Europe, pp. 1–8 (2002)
4. Xiao, Y., Zhang, Y., Nolen, M., Deng, J.H., Zhang, J.: A cross layer approach for Prioritized Frame Transmissions of MPEG-4 over the IEEE 802.11 and IEEE 802.11e wireless local area networks. IEEE System Journal 5, 474–485 (2011)
5. Kuri, J., Kasera, S.K.: Reliable multicast in multi-access wireless LANs. Wireless Networks 7(4), 359–369 (2001)

6. Gupta, S.K.S., Shankar, V., Lalwani, S.: Reliable Multicast MAC Protocol for wireless LANs. In: IEEE International Conference on Communication, vol. 1, pp. 93–97 (2003)
7. Yu, K., Choi, W.C.: A Reliable Multicast MAC Protocol Using Busy-Tone for the IEEE 802.11-Based Wireless Networks. Info. Sci. and App. (ICISA), 1–7 (2011)
8. Lee, K.-H., Cho, D.H.: A Multiple Access Collision Avoidance Protocol for Multicast Service in Mobile Ad Hoc Networks. IEEE Communication Letters 7(10) (2003)
9. Jain, S., Das, S.R.: MAC layer Multicast in wireless Multihop Networks. In: First International Conference on Communication System Software and Middleware, pp. 1–10 (2006)
10. Campolo, C., Molinaro, A., Casetti, C., Chiasserini, C.F.: An 802.11-Based MAC Protocol for Reliable Multicast in Multihop Networks. In: IEEE Vehicular Technology Conference, pp. 1–5 (2009)
11. IEEE 802.11 Part 11: Wireless LAN Medium Access Control (MAC) and Physical Layer (PHY) specifications, Standard. IEEE (2007)
12. Ke, C.-H., Shieh, C.-K., Hwang, W.-S., Ziviani, A.: An Evaluation Framework for More Realistic Simulations of MPEG Video Transmission. J. of Info. Sci. and Eng. 24, 425–440 (2008)
13. http://www.isi.edu/nsnam/ns
14. ITU-R Recommendation BT.500-10. Methodology for the subjective assessment of the quality of television pictures (2000)
15. ITU-T Recommendations P.910 P.920 P.930. Subjective video quality assessment methods for multimedia applications, interactive test methods for audiovisual communications, principles of a reference impairment system for video (1996)
16. ISO-IEC/JTC1/SC29/WG11. Evaluation methods and procedures for mpeg-4 tests (1996)
17. ANSI T1.801.01/02-1996. Digital transport of video teleconferencing/video telephony signals. ANSI (1996)
18. ANSI T1.801.03-1996. Digital transport of one-way video signals - parameters for objective performance assessment. ANSI (1996)
19. Chan, A., Lee, S.-J., Cheng, X., Banerjee, S., Mohapatra, P.: The impact of link-layer retransmissions on video streaming in wireless mesh networks. In: Proceedings of the 4th Annual International Conference on Wireless Internet, WICON (2008)
20. AL-Suhail, G.A.: Impact of packet size on the temporal quality of video transmission over wired-to-wireless network. In: Proceedings of the 6th International Conference on Advances in Mobile Computing and Multimedia, pp. 94–101 (2008)

On Action Permutation and Progress for Partially Commutative Asynchronous Binary Sessions*

Zhenguo Yang, Farong Zhong**, Jinfang Zhang, and Tiantian Song

Department of Computer Science, Zhejiang Normal University,
Jinhua 321004, Zhejiang Province, P.R. China
{yangzhenguo1988,zjfcathy}@126.com, zfr@zjnu.cn, 373636796@qq.com

Abstract. A theory of asynchronous binary sessions is generalized by asynchronous communication subtyping, which actually permutates and optimizes the actions on each participant. With the types of messages distinguished between dependent and independent types, a series of action asynchronous subtyping rules for the two kinds of message types are proposed, respectively. To make such action permutations automatic, an algorithmic asynchronous subtyping is presented, associating the subtyping for session types with asynchronous communication subtyping. In addition, action permutation and optimization will change the sequence and structure of messages sent and received. To ensure runtime safety, the cases of communication errors that may occur in asynchronous sessions are revealed by examples. What's more, the type compliance we defined assures the progress property, i.e., once a communication has been established, well-formed programs will never starve at communication points. Finally, we conclude and discuss some possible future work in this area.

Keywords: Communication-Centered Programming, Session Types, Subtyping, Bounded Polymorphism, Partial Commutativity, Progress.

1 Introduction

Programs which communicate by asynchronous message passing are abundant in distributed computing scenes, from simple web-service applications between two parties to networks hosting thousands of nodes. The actual development of such applications, which may be developed in geographically disparate sites, still leaves to the programmer much of responsibility in guaranteeing that the sequence and structure of messages are correct according to the protocol.

---

* This work has been supported by the Natural Science Foundation of China under grant 60873234 and Top Key Discipline of Computer Software and Theory in Zhejiang Provincial Colleges at Zhejiang Normal University.
** Author to whom correspondence should be addressed.

Y. Xiang et al. (Eds.): IDCS 2012, LNCS 7646, pp. 120–133, 2012.

Session types [9–11] are one of the formalisms that have been proposed to structure interactions and reason over communicating processes and their behaviors. They were first proposed in the context of a language based on Pi-calculus [14, 18]. The flexibility and expressive power of session types were enhanced by defining a notion of subtyping for session types [5], whose main contribution is to make the participants following different protocols compatible in a conversation. A notion of bounded polymorphism [6, 8] was first proposed to make the range of such compatibility clear. Further, The solution was extended in [19] by introducing a recursive session types [7] to describe protocols with an indefinite number of repetitive behaviors. In addition, the type system of MOOSE [3] has been designed not only to assure the type safety of the communication protocols, but also the progress property, i.e. once a session has been initiated, well-typed processes will never starve at session channels. In binary synchronous interleaving sessions, a type system with progress was proposed in work [4, 20].

In asynchronous communications, the progress was proved by introducing an effect system in work [2]. Asynchronous communication subtyping was first presented for binary sessions in an unpublished manuscript [15], where the treatment for recursive types and branching/selection types is left open. The subtyping for recursive types and branching/selection types in binary session types was first studied in work [7]. Further, top-down and bottom-up approach in multiparty sessions was integrated seamlessly by introducing asynchronous communication subtyping [13] over local types. In practical communications, messages in the channels could be dependent, in which case the result of composition using action asynchronous subtyping rules in work [13], will not be as expected, which is revealed by $P_3 \mid Q_3$ in the present work.

This work generalizes a theory of partially commutative asynchronous binary sessions, where the types of messages are distinguished between dependent and independent types, and a series of action asynchronous subtyping rules are proposed for the two kinds of types, respectively. The subtyping rules actually permutate and optimize the actions in asynchronous partially commutative binary sessions. An algorithmic asynchronous subtyping which associates the subtyping for session types with asynchronous communication subtyping is presented, making such action permutations automatic. In addition, action permutation and optimization will change the previous sequence of actions in sessions. To ensure runtime safety, the cases of communication errors that may occur in asynchronous sessions are revealed by examples, and progress property is assured by defining type compliance and some related lemmas. Let us assume the following processes.

$$P_1 = x?[a]; y![7]; end \ Q_1 = y?[b]; x![5]; end$$

$P_1 \mid Q_1$ will cause a dead-lock. To execute the two processes safely, they might be locally optimized in asynchronous communications. The resulting processes given below still preserve linearity and proper communication structures.

$$P_2 = y![7]; x?[a]; end \ Q_2 = x![5]; y?[b]; end$$

Asynchronous communication subtyping specifies safe action permutations, by which the processes can be locally optimized. For example, P_2 is abstracted to type $y![int]; x?[int]; T$, which is a subtype of $x?[int]; y![int]; T$, and such optimizations can be checked locally. This is the idea of partial commutativity, which is defined between a sequence of actions. The calculation can be made automatic by algorithmic subtyping to characterize the semantic notion of subtyping. However, such a subtyping cannot simply making action permutations as by instinct. Let us assume the following processes.

$$P_3 = x?[a]; y![a \times 2]; end \ Q_3 = x![5]; y?[b]; end$$

Assuming the initial value of a is 0, $P_3 \mid Q_3$ first upgrades the variable a by value 5, and then upgrade the variable b by double of 5. After the communication completes, the result will be $a = 5$ and $b = 10$. However, if we use the action permutation directly as previously discussed, the processes P_3 will turn to P_4 as follow.

$$P_4 = y![a \times 2]; x?[a]; end \ Q_3 = x![5]; y?[b]; end$$

The composition $P_4 \mid Q_3$ still can proceeds well without violating the progress property, while the result could be $a = 5$ and $b = 0$, which is against the previous. To deal with the problem, we distinguish such types by defining the dependent types, and define related action asynchronous subtyping rules associating subtyping for session types with asynchronous communication subtyping.

The remainder of the work is organized as follows. Section 2 reviews the session types and progress property through simple examples. Section 3 defines the syntax and operational semantics for asynchronous sessions. Section 4 presents the subtyping for non-recursive and recursive types in asynchronous partially commutative sessions. In addition, such action permutations are automatic by the algorithmic asynchronous subtyping. Section 5 shows the type soundness, and the runtime safety is ensured by type compliance and the related lemmas. Finally, we conclude and indicate our plans in Section 6.

2   Session Types and Progress

2.1   Session Types and Subtyping

A session, starting after a connection has been established between two participants, is a sequence of messages exchanged through the connection following a fixed protocol. Session types have been proposed, aiming to characterize such sessions, in terms of the types of messages received or sent by a participant. For example, the session type $begin.![int].?[bool].end$ expresses that an integer is sent first, and then a boolean value is expected to be received before the protocol completed.

$$P_5 = \&\{go :?[int].![int], quit : end\} \ Q_4 = \oplus\{go :![int].?[int], quit\}$$

Naturally, $P_5 \mid Q_4$ can communicate well without an error, which reveals general binary sessions. However, we have to face the case that the P_5 has updated to the type $P_6 = \&\{go :?[real].![nat], quit : end\}$, while Q_4 stays the same. How to deal with $P_6 \mid Q_4$?

Gay and Hole [5–8] addressed the problem by defining the subtyping for session type, where the input, branch and continuation types are covariant while the output and choice types are contravariant. The subtyping for session type could be a session type where receipt is replaced by sending with a smaller type, and vice versa. After the update, P_6 can receive and send more numbers than P_5, and the composition $P_6 \mid Q_5$ will be compatible and proceed well.

2.2   Progress Property

We have to distinguish *shared channels* and *live channels*, which are ignored in the above examples such that we can illustrate the session types and polymorphism more explicitly. Shared channels have not yet been connected; they are used to decide if two threads can communicate, in which case they are replaced by fresh live channels. After a connection has been created, the channel is live. And data may be transmitted through such active channels only. We present the progress by analyzing the following examples.

Example 1. (Bounded Shared Channels) A bounded shared channel not having a dual to start a session can block the communication on live channels forever, as in

$$P_7 = va(a(x).(x?[real].end))$$

The problem does not arise if the shared channel a is free, since we can always compose with a dual process e.g. with

$$Q_5 = \bar{a}(x).(x![int].end)$$

Note that the protocols followed by the two processes are different, yet they can be compatible in our type system by introducing subtyping for session types. This situation is solved well with definition of relaxed duality [19] for both non-recursive and recursive session types.

Example 2. (Type Compliance) Though we introduce the subtyping for session types, yet the protocols followed by the two processes can be incompatible.

$$P_8 = a(x).b(y).(x![nat]; y?[int].end) \quad Q_6 = \bar{a}(x).\bar{b}(x).(x?[nat]; y![real].end)$$

As $P_8 \mid Q_6$ shows, such incompatibility prevents the composition from going. To cope with such kind of misbehaviour, in [1], Acciai et al. incorporated *type compliance* in the theory of session types. Further, we integrate it with the relaxed duality for non-recursive and recursive session types, which is defined in Definition 8. As a result, we consider P_8 and Q_7 are in type compliance.

$$Q_7 = \bar{a}(x).\bar{b}(y).(x?[real]; y![nat].end)$$

Example 3. (Circularity of Channels)

$$P_9 = a(x).b(y).(x![int]; y?[real].end) \quad Q_8 = \bar{a}(x).\bar{b}(x).(y![real] : x?[int].end)$$

These processes use the channels bound by a and b in reverse order, which is blocked in synchronous communication. However, $P_9 \mid Q_8$ will proceed well in asynchronous communications. However, consider $P_{10} \mid Q_9$, which will lead to a deadlock and such a case will be prevented by type compliance we defined.

$$P_{10} = a(x).b(y).(y?[real]; x![int].end) \quad Q_9 = \bar{a}(x).\bar{b}(x).(x?[int]; y![real].end)$$

Example 4. (Bilinearity)

$$P_{11} = a(x).b(y).(x![int]; y?[real].end) \quad Q_{10} = \bar{a}(x).\bar{b}(x).(x?[real].end)$$

The $P_{11} \mid Q_{10}$ cannot complete the communication and such a case will be prevented by introducing the bilinearity condition, i.e. there are exactly two threads that contain occurrences of the same live channel.

3   Asynchronous Sessions

3.1   Syntax

We use Pi-calculus with output prefixing [14], omitting polyadicity and delegation for simplicity. Generally, we use a, b for shared channels, x, y for live channels, P, Q for processes, $l_1,, l_n$ for labels of choices, U_d for dependent types and U_i for independent types. In order to layout aesthetics, in the present work, $i \in \{1,, n\}$, $j \in \{1,, m\}$, $m \le n$ and $i \le j$. Recursive types are contractive, containing no subexpressions of the form $\mu X.\mu X_1 \mu X_n.X$. Each session type S has a dual type $\bar{S}$, defined for non-recursive session types in Figure 2. We introduce the relaxed duality relation [19, 20] as follows, where for any recursive type T, $unfold(T)$ is the result of repeatedly unfolding the top level recursion until a non-recursive type constructor is reached.

$$
\begin{array}{lll}
\text{Session Types} \quad S ::= & X & \text{type variable} \\
& \mid \; end & \text{terminated session} \\
& \mid \; ?[T].S & \text{input} \\
& \mid \; ![T].S & \text{output} \\
& \mid \; \&\{l_i : S_i\} & \text{branch} \\
& \mid \; \oplus\{l_i : S_i\} & \text{choice} \\
& \mid \; \mu X.S & \text{recursive session} \\
\text{Message Types} \; M ::= & U_d & \text{dependent type} \\
& \mid \; U_i & \text{independent type}
\end{array}
$$

Fig. 1. Types

$$\overline{?[T].S} =![T].\overline{S} \quad \overline{\&\{l_i : S_i\}} = \oplus\{l_i : \overline{S_i}\} \quad \overline{end} = end$$
$$\overline{![T].S} =?[T].\overline{S} \quad \overline{\oplus\{l_i : S_i\}} = \&\{l_i : \overline{S_i}\} \quad \overline{X} = \overline{Y}(if \ Y \leq X)$$

Fig. 2. Relaxed Duality for Non-Recursive Types

Definition 1. *A relation $R_1 \subseteq Type \times Type$ is a relaxed duality relation if $(T, U) \in R_1$ implies the following conditions:*

1. *If $unfold(T) =?[T_1].S_1$ and $unfold(U) =![U_1].S_2$, then $(S_1, S_2) \in R_1$ and $U_1 \leq_c T_1$.*
2. *If $unfold(T) =![T_1].S_1$ and $unfold(U) =?[U_1].S_2$, then $(S_1, S_2) \in R_1$ and $T_1 \leq_c U_1$.*
3. *If $unfold(T) = \&\{l_1 : S_1, ..., l_n : S_n\}$, $unfold(U) = \oplus\{l_1 : V_1, ..., l_m : V_m\}$, then $(S_i, V_i) \in R_1$.*
4. *If $unfold(T) = \oplus\{l_1 : S_1, ..., l_m : S_m\}$, $unfold(U) = \&\{l_1 : V_1, ..., l_n : V_n\}$, then $(S_i, V_i) \in R_1$.*
5. *If $unfold(T) = end$, then $unfold(U) = end$.*

Definition 2. *The coinductive relaxed duality relation $\perp_c$ is defined by $T \perp_c U$ if and only if there exists a type simulation R_1 such that $(T, U) \in R_1$.*

3.2 Processes

The syntax of processes is defined in Figure 3. Names may be *polarized*, occurring as x^+ or x^- or simply as x. We write x^p for a general polarized name, where p represents an optional polarity. $\mathbf{0}$ is the inactive process and | is parallel composition. In $(vx^\pm : S)P$, both x^+ and x^- in P are bound. The process $x^p?[y : T].P$ inputs the names along the port x^p and then executes P. The process $x^p![y].P$ outputs the names y along the port x^p and then executes P. Process offers a choice of the labels l_i and an accompanying type T. Process $x^p \lhd l.P$ selects and sends the label l along port x^p, and then executes P.

$$
\begin{array}{llll}
P ::= \ \mathbf{0} & \text{inaction} & | \ P \mid Q & \text{parallel} \\
\quad | \ a(x).P & \text{accept} & | \ \bar{a}(x).P & \text{request} \\
\quad | \ x^p?[y : T].P & \text{input} & | \ x^p![y].P & \text{output} \\
\quad | \ (vx)P & \text{hiding} & | \ x^p \rhd \{l_i : P_i\} & \text{branch} \\
\quad | \ x^p \lhd l.P & \text{choice} & &
\end{array}
$$

Fig. 3. Processes

3.3 Operational Semantics

Structural congruence $\equiv$ is the smallest congruence relation on processes that includes the equations in Figure 4, which are standard as [12]. The operational semantics is given by the reduction relation, denoted by $P \to Q$, the smallest relation closed under the rules in Figure 5. R-COM is a standard rule for communication, where the channel on which communication takes place are polarized and the names received are substituted in the continuation process P. R-SELECT is a rule for selection from labeled processes. R-TRUE and R-FALSE are standard, defining reduction in conditional expressions. R-PAR and R-CONG are also standard, defining reduction in parallel composition and structural congruence. Finally, R-NEW is standard, defining reduction for processes under v bindings.

$$P \mid \mathbf{0} \equiv P \qquad P \mid Q \equiv Q \mid P \qquad (P \mid Q) \mid R \equiv P \mid (Q \mid R)$$
$$(vnn')P \equiv (vn'n)P \qquad (vn)\mathbf{0} \equiv \mathbf{0} \qquad (vn)P \mid Q \equiv (vn)(P \mid Q) \; if \; n \notin fn(Q)$$

Fig. 4. Structural Congruence

$$x^p?[y:U].P \mid x^{\bar{p}}![z].Q \to P\{z/y\} \mid Q \quad \text{R-COM}$$

$$x^p \rhd \{l_i : P_i\} \mid x^p \rhd l_i.Q \to P_i \mid Q \quad \text{R-SELECT}$$

$$\frac{P \to P'}{P \mid Q \to P' \mid Q}\text{R-PAR} \qquad \frac{P' \equiv P \quad P \to Q \quad Q \equiv Q'}{P' \to Q'}\text{R-CONG}$$

$$\frac{P \to P'}{(vx^\pm : S)P \to (vx^\pm : S)P'}\text{R-NEW}$$

Fig. 5. Reduction Rules

3.4 Subtyping for Session Types

The subtyping rules for non-recursive types are defined in Figure 6, which show the key features of subtyping for session types. If T is a subtype of U, denoted by $T \leq U$, then a channel of type T may safely be used wherever a channel of type U as expected.

Rules S-IN and S-OUT specify covariance and contravariance, respectively, in the message type, and covariance in the continuation type. Rule S-CHAN specifies invariance in the message type. The variance of message type in these cases is the same as in Pierce and Sangiorgi's system of input/out subtyping in Pi-calculus [16]. Rules S-BRANCH and S-CHOICE specify covariance and contravariance, respectively, in the set of labels, and covariance in the continuation type. This is as expected if a branch is viewed as an input and a choice as an output.

What's more, to extend subtyping for recursive types, we introduce the coinductive subtyping relation [7] in a similar way to the coinductive duality relation.

Definition 3. *A relation $R_2 \subseteq Type \times Type$ is a type simulation if $(T, U) \in R_2$ implies the following conditions:*

$$\frac{}{end \leq end}\text{S-End} \quad \frac{T_i \leq U_i \quad V \leq W}{?[T].V \leq ?[U].W}\text{S-In} \quad \frac{T_i \leq U_i \quad V \leq W}{![U].V \leq ![T].W}\text{S-Out}$$

$$\frac{R_j \leq S_j}{\&\{l_j : R_j\} \leq \&\{l_i : S_i\}}\text{S-Branch} \quad \frac{R_j \leq S_j}{\oplus\{l_i : R_i\} \leq \oplus\{l_j : S_j\}}\text{S-Choice}$$

Fig. 6. Subtyping for Non-Recursive Types

1. If $unfold(T) = ?[T_1].S_1$ and $unfold(U) = ?[U_1].S_2$, then $(S_1, S_2) \in R_2$ and $(T_1, U_1) \in R_2$.
2. If $unfold(T) = ![T_1].S_1$ and $unfold(U) = ![U_1].S_2$, then $(S_1, S_2) \in R_2$ and $(U_1, T_1) \in R_2$.
3. If $unfold(T) = \&\{l_1 : S_1, ..., l_m : S_m\}$, $unfold(U) = \&\{l_1 : V_1, ..., l_n : V_n\}$, then $(S_i, V_i) \in R_2$.
4. If $unfold(T) = \oplus\{l_1 : S_1, ..., l_n : S_n\}$, $unfold(U) = \oplus\{l_1 : V_1, ..., l_m : V_m\}$, then $(S_i, V_i) \in R_2$.
5. If $unfold(T) = end$, then $unfold(U) = end$.

Definition 4. *The coinductive subtyping relation $\leq_c$ is defined by $T \leq_c U$ if and only if there exists a type simulation R_2 such that $(T, U) \in R_2$.*

4 Asynchronous Partially Commutative Sessions

4.1 Asynchronous Commutative Subtyping: Non-recursive Types

This section introduces and studies a basic theory of asynchronous sessions subtying $\ll$. The dependent types U_d and independent types U_i are distinguished in Figure 1, where dependent types deal with the dependence of one message on other messages, yet it does not necessarily imply causation. For a message U, U_d indicates its messages use a message U while U_i does not. However, for most of the action asynchronous subtyping rules, it makes no difference whether the relation between the messages is dependent or not, which is revealed by U_c. Similarly, the suffix i or c of a rule name indicates the range of its applicability. As an example, OIi indicates that a rule is only applicable to the case that the types of messages are independent.

Note that we cannot exchange an input and output in IOc even for different channels. Consider two processes $P_{12} = s?[\ ]; r![\ ]$ and $Q_{11} = s![\ ]; r?[\ ]$, which interact smoothly. If we permute the output and input of Q_{11}, we get $Q_{12} = r?[\ ]; s![\ ]$. Then the parallel composition $P_{12} \mid Q_{12}$ will cause a deadlock. For the same reason, BOc, ISc, and BSc are prohibited. In addition, the rule OId is not allowed. For example, $P_3 \mid Q_3$ shows that we can get P_4 by applying OId rule to P_3. Though $P_4 \mid Q_3$ can proceed without any communication errors, the result could be totally different. We also prohibit IIc, because it violates the sequence construct of messages.

$$k![U_i]; k'?[U]; T \ll k'?[U]; k![U_i]; T \qquad \text{OI}i$$
$$k![U]; k'\&\{l_j : T_j\} \ll k'\&\{l_j : k![U]; T_j\} \qquad \text{OB}c$$
$$k \oplus \{l_j : k'?[U]; T_j\} \ll k'?[U]; k \oplus \{l_j : T_j\} \qquad \text{SI}c$$
$$k \oplus \{l_i : k'\&\{l'_j : T_{ij}\}\} \ll k'\&\{l_j : k \oplus \{l'_i : T_{ij}\}\} \qquad \text{SB}c$$
$$k![U]; k'![U_c]; T \ll k'![U_c]; k![U]; T \qquad \text{OO}c$$
$$k \oplus \{l_j : k'![U]; T_j\} \ll k'![U]; k \oplus \{l_j : T_j\} \qquad \text{SO}c$$
$$k'![U]; k \oplus \{l_j : T_j\} \ll k \oplus \{l_j : k'![U]; T_j\} \qquad \text{OS}c$$
$$k \oplus \{l_i : k' \oplus \{l'_j : T_{ij}\}\} \ll k' \oplus \{l'_j : k \oplus \{l_i : T_{ij}\}\} \qquad \text{SS}c$$

Fig. 7. Action Asynchronous Subtyping Rules ((BIc, IBc, BBc) are omitted)

4.2   Asynchronous Commutative Subtyping: Recursive Types

For handling recursive types in asynchronous subtyping, we need to introduce the unfolding definition. For any recursive types T, $unfold^n(T)$ is the result of inductively unfolding the first recursion (even under guarded types) up to a fixed level of nesting. In addition, since the introduction of bilinearity condition, the channel will be subscribed by a number indicating the times of unfolding. For example, $unfold^2(s?[T]; \mu t.r![U]; t) = s?[T]; r_1![U]; r_2![U]; \mu t.r![U]; t$. As our recursive types are contractive, $unfold^n(T)$ terminates.

Definition 5. *A relation $R_3 \subseteq Type \times Type$ is an asynchronous subtyping relation if $(T, U) \in R_3$ implies the following conditions:*

1. *If $unfold(T) = ?[T_1].S_1$ and $unfold(U) \gg ?[U_1].S_2$, then $(S_1, S_2) \in R_3$ and $(T_1, U_1) \in R_3$.*
2. *If $unfold(T) = ![T_1].S_1$ and $unfold(U) \gg ![U_1].S_2$, then $(S_1, S_2) \in R_3$ and $(U_1, T_1) \in R_3$.*
3. *If $unfold(T) = \&\{l_1 : S_1, ..., l_m : S_m\}$, $unfold(U) \gg \&\{l_1 : V_1, ..., l_n : V_n\}$, then $(S_i, V_i) \in R_3$.*
4. *If $unfold(T) = \oplus\{l_1 : S_1, ..., l_n : S_n\}$, $unfold(U) \gg \oplus\{l_1 : V_1, ..., l_m : V_m\}$, then $(S_i, V_i) \in R_3$.*
5. *If $unfold(T) = end$, then $unfold(U) = end$.*

Definition 6. *The coinductive asynchronous subtyping relation $\ll_c$ is defined by $T \ll_c U$ if and only if there exists a type simulation R_3 such that $(T, U) \in R_3$.*

4.3   Algorithmic Asynchronous Subtyping

To obtain an algorithm for checking the subtyping relation, Gay and Hole [7] follow the approach taken by Pierce and Sangiorgi [16] in their system of input/output subtyping for Pi-calculus. Algorithmic issues in subtyping recursive types are discussed at greater length by Pierce [17]. With the incorporation of asynchronous permutation and n-time unfolding in the type simulation, we need to update the algorithmic subtyping for session types. We first list some selected rewriting rules $\overset{k}{\mapsto}$ which move the types with channel k to the head applying the action asynchronous subtyping rules.

$$k'?[U]; k![U_i]; T \overset{k}{\mapsto} k![U_i]; k'?[U]; T \text{ OI} \qquad \frac{T \overset{k}{\mapsto} T'}{k'![U]; T'} \text{CO}$$

$$\frac{T_j \overset{k}{\mapsto} T_j'}{k'\&\{l_1 : T_1, ..., l_j : T_j\} \overset{k}{\mapsto} k'\&\{l_1 : T_1', ..., l_j : T_j'\}} \text{CB} \qquad \frac{T_1 \overset{k}{\mapsto} T_2 \ T_2 \overset{k}{\mapsto} T_3}{T_1 \overset{k}{\mapsto} T_3} \text{Tr}$$

We omit the similar rules using other previous rules. Obviously, $T \overset{k}{\mapsto} T'$ implies $T' \ll T$. If $T' \ll T$, then we have $T' \overset{k_1}{\mapsto} ... \overset{k_n}{\mapsto} T$, where $k_1 k_n$ are a (possible empty) subsequence of channels occurring in T'.

The inference rules in Figure 8 define judgments $\Sigma \vdash T < U$, in which T and U are types Σ is a sequence of assumed instances of the subtyping relation, and $<$ is a combination of subtyping for session types and action asynchronous subtyping. We use n-hole type contexts $(C, C', ...)$ where $[\ ]^{h \in H}$ denote a hole with index h.

$$C ::= [\ ]^{h \in H} \mid k![U]; C \mid k?[U]; C \mid k \oplus \{l_i : C_i\}_{i \in I} \mid k\&\{l_i : C_i\}_{i \in I}$$

For example, with $H = 1, 2$ and $C = k \oplus \{l_1 : k_1?[U_1]; [\ ]^{i \in H}, l_2 : [\ ]^{2 \in H}\}$, we have $C[T_i]^{i \in H} = k \oplus \{l_1 : k_1?[U_1]; T_1, l_2 : T_2\}$.

$$\frac{}{\Sigma \vdash end < end} \text{END} \qquad \frac{T < T' \in \Sigma}{\Sigma \vdash T < T'} \text{ASMP}$$

$$\frac{\Sigma \vdash U_1 \le U_2 \quad \Sigma \vdash T_1 \le C[T_k']^{k \in H} \quad C[k![U_2]; T_k]^{k \in H} \overset{k}{\mapsto} k![U_2]; C[T_k']^{k \in H}}{\Sigma \vdash k![U_2]; T_1 < C[k![U_1]; T_k]^{k \in H}} \text{OUT}$$

$$\frac{\Sigma \vdash T_1 \le C[T_k']^{k \in H} \quad C[k \oplus \{l_i : T_i\}]^{i \in H} \overset{k}{\mapsto} k \oplus \{l_i : C[T_i]^{i \in H}\} \quad i \le j}{\Sigma \vdash k \oplus \{l_j : T_j\} < C[k \oplus \{l_i : T_i\}]^{i \in H}} \text{SEL}$$

$$\frac{\Sigma, \mu t.T < T' \vdash unfold(\mu t.T) < T'}{\Sigma \vdash \mu t.T < T'} \text{REC}$$

Fig. 8. Algorithmic Subtyping Rules

In Figure 8, ASMP and END are standard. Rule OUT first fixes the subtype and applies to $\overset{k}{\mapsto}$ to place $k![U]$ to the top level, and then indicates the contravariance of output and the covariance of the continuation type. Rule SEL is defined similarly. Rule REC is defined for recursive session types. The rule for input/branch is defined like OUT/SEL, respectively.

Theorem 1. (Soundness and Completeness of the Algorithmic Subtyping) *For all closed types T an T', $T \ll_c T'$ if and only if $T < T'$.*

The if direction is by Lemma 12 in [7] and the only-if direction by constructing a relation following Theorem 4 in [7].

5   Type Soundness and Communication Safety

5.1   Subject Congruence and Reduction

The judgment of the form $\Sigma \vdash P$ means that process P uses channels as specified by the types in Σ, which is a map from names to value types and from process variables to sequences of value types and session types.

Theorem 2. (Subject Congruence) *If $\Sigma \vdash P$ and $P \equiv Q$, then $\Sigma \vdash Q$.*

Proof. The proof follows the same routine as in [7, 12].

Theorem 3. (Subject Reduction) *If $\Sigma \vdash P$ and $P \to Q$ and Σ is balanced, then $\Sigma \vdash Q$.*

Proof. The proof is specified in our earlier work [19], and we omit the details.

Before we proceed, we need the following notion: an x-process is a prefixed process with subject x. Next, an x-redex is the parallel composition of a pair of dual x-processes. Then P is an error, if the parallel composition of either two x-processes that does not form a x-redex, or three or more x-processes.

Theorem 4. (Type Safety). *A typable program never reduces to an error.*

Proof. The proof is by reduction to absurdity, assuming error processes typable. Suppose that $\Sigma \vdash P \mid Q$. There are two cases of an error in a typable program. **Case 1.** $P = P_1 \mid P_2$ is the parallel composition of two x-processes that do not form an x-redex. There are several subcases will occur, yet they are alike. Therefore, we only consider one subcases, for example, the pair output/label-select. $P_1 = x^{\bar{p}}![y]$ while $P_2 = x^p \rhd \{(l_i : P_i)\}$, from which we can conclude their types on the two ports of a channel are $x^{\bar{p}} :![\alpha]$ and $x^p : \oplus\{l_i : \alpha_i\}$ respectively. Obviously, the composition $P \mid Q$ is not typable. **Case 2.** $P = (P_1 \mid P_2) \mid P_3$ is the parallel composition of three or more x-processes, it will be against the bilinearity condition, If $P_1 \mid P_2$ is not an x-redex, it just is the Case 1 above.

In both cases, we conclude a contradiction.

5.2   Runtime Safety

Definition 7. (Progress Property) *A process P has the progress property if $P \to P'$ implies that either P' does not contain live channels or $P' \mid Q \to$ for some Q such that $P' \mid Q$ is well-typed and $Q \nrightarrow$.*

A process P has the progress property if it is not blocked, and a process is blocked if it is some "bad" normal form. Even an irreducible process can have progress whenever it is able to interact in parallel with an irreducible process Q. In addition, The function $head(P)$ is to get the head prefixed subprocess in P.

Definition 8. (Type Compliance) *Type compliance is the largest relation on types such that whenever S is compliant with T, written $S \propto T$, and there are $S' \ll S$ and $T' \ll T$ by action-asynchronous subtyping rules. It holds that either $head(S) = \alpha \neq ?[\,]$ or $head(T') = \beta \neq ?[\,]$, such that $S' \xrightarrow{\bar{\alpha}} S''$, $T' \xrightarrow{\bar{\beta}} T''$, it holds that $S' \propto T'$.*

The duality relation is relaxed, aiming to combine subtyping for both recursive and non-recursive session types, which allows communications between participants following different protocols.

Lemma 1. *For communications occur in binary sessions, both non-recursive and recursive sessions must keep the following rules:*

1. *The shared channels are free, without using shared channel hiding.*
2. *The session types on the dual channels are in the relaxed duality relation.*
3. *The session types on the two ports satisfy the type compliance.*
4. *The live channels satisfy the bilinearity condition.*

Theorem 5. (Progress) $P \mid Q$ *keeps the progress property if it follows the Lemma 16.*

Proof. Let $P_0 = P \mid Q$ be a process and $P_0 \to^* P_1$. There are three cases about process P_1 as discussed below.

Case 1. P_1 does not contain live channel or it $P_1 \to P'$. There is nothing to prove.

Case 2. P_1 is irreducible and its head prefixed subprocess is an accept/request on a free shared channel a. Naturally, we can build an irreducible Q_2 as a request process on a according to the relaxed duality for non-recursive or recursive session types. This is why we do not consider any irreducible process as blocked, rather we say that even a irreducible P_1 has the progress whenever it is able to interact in parallel with some Q_2 such that $P_1 \mid Q_2$ is well-typed.

Case 3. P_1 does not contain an accept/request on a shared channel as head subprocess, but contains a live channel k^p. Since live channels satisfy the bilinearity condition and type compliance, $k^{\bar{p}}$ must occur in P_1, which means it follows that P_1 reduces.

6   Conclusions and Future Work

In the present work, a theory of asynchronous binary sessions is generalized through asynchronous communication subtyping, which actually permutate and optimize the actions on each participant. With the types of messages distinguished between dependent and independent types, a series of action asynchronous subtyping rules for the two kinds of message types are proposed, respectively. Partial commutativity is actually a definition of permutations among actions. To make action permutations automatic, the algorithmic asynchronous subtyping is presented, associating the subtyping for session types with asynchronous communication subtyping. However, such permutations will change the previous sequence and structure of messages. As a result, the communication safety of processes using the action asynchronous subtyping rules has to be assured. To solve the problem, the cases of communication errors that may occur in asynchronous sessions are revealed by examples, and progress property is assured by defining type compliance and some related lemmas.

However, two participants is the focus of the present work, with no treatment in the context of multiparty session types [12, 13]. Clearly, there is scope for further work in this area. On the other hand, the syntax of the present work does not define session delegation [3, 12], which allows transmissions of channels. We hope to touch on these aspects in our future study.

Acknowledgement. We would like to thank Simon Gay, Mario Coppo, Mariangiola Dezani-Ciancaglini, Lucia Acciai, Nobuko Yoshida and Dimitris Mostrous for their valuable guidance on subtyping for session types, the progress property and action permutations.

References

1. Acciai, L., Boreale, M.: A Type System for Client Progress in a Service-Oriented Calculus. In: Degano, P., De Nicola, R., Meseguer, J. (eds.) Montanari Festschrift. LNCS, vol. 5065, pp. 642–658. Springer, Heidelberg (2008)
2. Coppo, M., Dezani-Ciancaglini, M., Yoshida, N.: Asynchronous Session Types and Progress for Object Oriented Languages. In: Bonsangue, M.M., Johnsen, E.B. (eds.) FMOODS 2007. LNCS, vol. 4468, pp. 1–31. Springer, Heidelberg (2007)
3. Dezani-Ciancaglini, M., Mostrous, D., Yoshida, N., Drossopoulou, S.: Session Types for Object-Oriented Languages. In: Hu, Q. (ed.) ECOOP 2006. LNCS, vol. 4067, pp. 328–352. Springer, Heidelberg (2006)
4. Dezani-Ciancaglini, M., de'Liguoro, U., Yoshida, N.: On Progress for Structured Communications. In: Barthe, G., Fournet, C. (eds.) TGC 2007. LNCS, vol. 4912, pp. 257–275. Springer, Heidelberg (2008)
5. Gay, S., Hole, M.: Types and Subtypes for Client-Server Interactions. In: Swierstra, S.D. (ed.) ESOP 1999. LNCS, vol. 1576, pp. 74–90. Springer, Heidelberg (1999)
6. Gay, S., Hole, M.: Bounded polymorphism in session types. Technical Report, Department of Computing Science, University of Glasgow (2003)
7. Gay, S., Hole, M.: Subtyping for session types in the Pi-calculus. Acta Informatica 42(2/3), 191–225 (2005)
8. Gay, S.J.: Bounded polymorphism in session types. Mathematical Structures in Computer Science, vol. 18, pp. 895–930. Cambridge University Press (2007)
9. Honda, K.: Types for Dyadic Interaction. In: Best, E. (ed.) CONCUR 1993. LNCS, vol. 715, pp. 509–523. Springer, Heidelberg (1993)
10. Honda, K., Kubo, M., Takeuchi, K.: An Interaction-Based Language and Its Typing System. In: Halatsis, C., Philokyprou, G., Maritsas, D., Theodoridis, S. (eds.) PARLE 1994. LNCS, vol. 817, pp. 398–413. Springer, Heidelberg (1994)
11. Honda, K., Vasconcelos, V.T., Kubo, M.: Language Primitives and Type Discipline for Structured Communication-Based Programming. In: Hankin, C. (ed.) ESOP 1998. LNCS, vol. 1381, pp. 122–138. Springer, Heidelberg (1998)

12. Honda, K., Yoshida, N., Carbone, M.: Multiparty asynchronous session types. In: POPL 2005, pp. 273–284. ACM Press, New York (2008)
13. Mostrous, D., Yoshida, N., Honda, K.: Global Principal Typing in Partially Commutative Asynchronous Sessions. In: Castagna, G. (ed.) ESOP 2009. LNCS, vol. 5502, pp. 316–332. Springer, Heidelberg (2009)
14. Milner, R., Parrow, J., Walker, D.: A calculus of mobile processes, I and II. Information and Computation, pp. 1–77 (1992)
15. Neubaure, M., Thiemann, P.: Session types of asynchrionous communication. University Freiburg (2004)
16. Pierce, B.C., Sangiorgi, D.: Typing and subtyping for mobile processes. Mathematical Structures in Computer Science 6(5), 409–453 (1996)
17. Pierce, B.C.: Types and programming languages. MIT Press (2002)
18. Sangiorgi, D., Walker, D.: The Pi-calculus: a theory of mobile processes. Cambridge University Press (2001)
19. Yang, Z., Zhong, F. and Zhang, J.: A bounded polymorphic type system for client-server interactions. In: ICNDS 2012, Journal of Digital Content Technology and its Application (to appear, 2012)
20. Yang, Z., Zhong, F., Zhang, J.: A Polymorphic Type System with Progress for Binary Sessions. In: Philips, W.F.L. (ed.) WISM 2012. LNCS, vol. 7529, pp. 451–461. Springer, Heidelberg (2012)

A NetFlow v9 Measurement System with Network Performance Function

Guang Cheng[1,2] and Hua Wu[1,2]

[1] School of Computer Science and Engineering,
Southeast University, Nanjing 210096, P.R. China
[2] Key Laboratory of Computer Network and Information Integration,
Ministry of Education, P.R. China
gcheng@njnet.edu.cn

Abstract. Netflow can be employed for accounting, anomaly detection and network monitoring, and can bring new data source for network management. But most IPv6 routers in CERNET2 backbone network don't provide IPFIX or NetFlow flow record function. Netflow flow records don't have the network performance information, such as RTT and packet loss ratio, so we hardly use the Netflow data to analyze the network performance. In this paper, we designs a NetFlow v9 measurement system (N9MS) which converts IPv6 packet headers into the Net-Flow v9 flow records and monitors the link performance with these flow records. The N9MS has two improvements to the traditional Cisco's sampled NetFlow feature. Firstly, the Cisco's sampling strategy is to sample packets, while that in the N9MS is flow sampling which can keep all packets in the sampled flows to infer network performance based on these sampled packets. Secondly, N9MS directly uses these sampled packets to calculate these performance metrics, such as round trip time (RTT) and packet loss ratio. We also define both RTT and packet loss ratio fields in the scalability NetFlow v9 template format. In this paper we also use the N9MS to monitor a 10Gbps backbone link between Nanjing site and the CNGI-CERNET2 backbone, and give some experimental results.

Keywords: IPv6, NetFlow V9, Packet Loss Rate, Round Trip Time, CERNET2.

1 Introduction

Internet has become increasingly complex and it's data transmission speed keeps growing. Internet operators are demanding efficient and dependable tools to manage and monitor network. In recent years, Netflow implemented in Cisco routers has established as the main solution for flow-level measurements. Netflow reports aggregated information on network traffic in the form of flow-records, which can be employed for accounting, anomaly detection and network monitoring. Most IPv4 core routers provide generally IPFIX or NetFlow[1] functionality, and IPFIX or NetFlow can bring new data source for network management. We have developed a network behavior observed system (NBOS) with the NetFlow

Y. Xiang et al. (Eds.): IDCS 2012, LNCS 7646, pp. 134–145, 2012.

v5 data from the core routers in the CERNET backbone[2]. CERNET, an IPv4 network, is the abbreviation of China Education and Research Network. However most IPv6 routers in CERNET2 backbone network don't provide IPFIX or NetFlow flow record, we split packet traffic from CERNET2 backbone link directly and convert the packet traffic into NetFlow v9[3] format to observe and manage the IPv6 network.

CERNET2, which is one of the backbone networks of China Next Generation Internet project (CNGI), is undertaken by the network center of CERNET, jointly with 25 universities. CERNET2 backbone runs IPv6 protocol and connects 25 PoPs distributed in 20 cities in China with the speed of 2.5Gbps and 10Gbps. Meanwhile, the transmission rate of Beijing-Wuhan-Guangzhou and Wuhan-Nanjing-Shanghai is 10Gbps. Since 2004, CERNET2 backbone has connected more than 200 IPv6 access networks of universities and R&D institutes in China, supported technical trials and application demonstration, and provided excellent environment for world-wide next generation Internet research. CERNET2 has become the key fundamental infrastructure for Chinese next generation Internet technology research, key applications development, core equipments of next generation Internet industrialization.

However Netflow don't have the performance informance, such as RTT and packet loss ratio. The sampling strategy in Cisco Routers is packet sampling[4] to sample 1 in N packets. Packet sampling makes the flow information be lost, so we can not assess the network performance from NetFlow data directly. In order to solve the above problem, this paper proposes a NetFlow v9 Measurement System (N9MS), which output flow records obeyed the NetFlow v9 format. N9MS has two improvements comparing to the Cisco's NetFlow. Firstly, N9MS use flow sampling to keep all packets in the sampled flows, so we can infers network performance with the sampled packets. Secondly, N9MS calculates performance metrics, such as RTT and packet loss ratio, and we also define both RTT and packet loss rate field in the new NetFlow v9 format.

The remainder of this paper is organized as follows. Section 2 discusses the related work. Section 3 gives the system architecture of N9MS. Section 4 presents the key technologies in N9MS system. Section 5 defines the performance template in NetFlow v9. In Section 6, we test N9MS to monitor a backbone link in the CERNET2 backbone network. We finally conclude our paper in Section 7.

2   Related Works

NetFlow[1] is a network protocol developed by Cisco Systems for collecting IP traffic information. Routers that support NetFlow can collect IP traffic statistics on all interfaces and export those statistics as NetFlow records. Netflow is designed to employ for accounting, anomaly detection and network monitoring, such as the Network Management Research Group (NMRG)[5] organized in 2010 is a one-day workshop for discussing the use of NetFlow/IPFIX in Network Management, and Idilio Drago [6] summarized the presentations and the main conclusions of the NMRG workshop. Carrie Gates[7] also gives a suite of tools with network security analysis for saving and analyzing NetFlow data. Dario Rossi[8] presented a behavioral algorithm which exploited Netflow records for traffic classification. Since their classifier identified an application by means of the simple counts of received packets and bytes, Netflow records contained all information required. Valentin Carela-Espaol [9] analyzed the performance of current machine learning methods with NetFlow by adapting a popular machine learning-based technique. Until to now, we don't find any papers about analyzing network performance with network data.

IPv6 [10] was developed by the Internet Engineering Task Force (IETF) to deal with this long-anticipated IPv4 address exhaustion, and is described in Internet standard document RFC 2460, published in December 1998. While IPv4 allows 32 bits for an IP address, and IPv6 uses 128-bit addresses, for an address space of 2^{128} addresses. 6QM[11] developed a comprehensive approach to monitor the QoS of the traffic of IPv6 services exchanged between the points of measures. 6QM provided not only usage data but also QoS metrics (delay, loss, jitter and so on) for IPv6 traffic by analyzing the collected information through the measurement device. Google [12][13] has been measuring the availability of IPv6 connectivity among Google users since September 2008. Their studies showed the percentage 0.5% of users that would access Google over IPv6 if www.google.com had an IPv6 address, and the result is updated periodically. Myungjin Lee[14] measured the intermediate delay between two different routers or more any segment along an end-to-end path to maintain the same flows and timestamps for the same first and last packets.

Hao [15] proposed two passive measurement algorithms to estimate the round trip time (RTT) for the TCP connections that flowed through a network link. The first algorithm is applicable to TCP 3-way handshake messages. The second algorithm is applicable to these flows, when the sever transfers a number of MSS segments to the client, and it is the slow-start phase of TCP. Peter Benko [16] presented a passive end-to-end loss monitoring method, which relied on traffic monitoring at a core or ingress router interface to estimate the loss ratios based on the seen sequence number pattern. Per Hurtig [17] observed traffic in 70 measurements on backbone links from 2006 and 2009. They looked at out-of-sequence TCP segments, and observed a significant decrease in OOS due to packet reordering from 22.5% to 5.2% of all OOS segments.

3   System Architecture

Figure 1 is the architecture of the NetFlow v9 Measurement System (N9MS) which is running on the Jiangsu broader of CERNET2 backbone. N9MS aims to collect the Netflow v9 flow records collected IPv6 packets with flow sampling. It also monitors the performance and correctness of the data process procedure. In Figure 1, the two thicker lines represent two 10Gbps fibres which connect two backbone routers. The optical splitter gets part of the energy from the target fiber with all information in the original signal. A corresponding equipment transfers the splitted signal into the electrical signal. The data acquisition

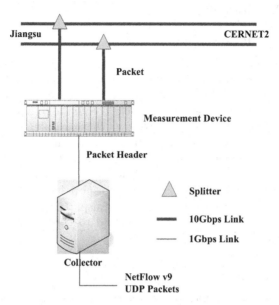

Fig. 1. Architecture of NetFlow v9 Measurement System

program in the collector reads the data from the network interface card, and analyzes the IPv6 packets. The collector exports these flow records with NetFlow V9 format encapsulated in UDP packets to the process program.

The collector in N9MS is divided into 4 module: packet capture module, flow export module, flow sampling modules and flow records transfer and forward module. A signal monitor thread continually listens to the termination signal. The packet capture module is responsible for reading packets from the network interface card. The flow export module analyzes the packets. The flow sampling module samples and saves these flow records into the intermediate queues. The flow records transfer and forward module transforms the flow records which are exported by the flow export module to a NetFlow v9 format, and encapsulate these flow records into UDP packets, then send these UDP packets.

N9MS includes three threads, those are the signal thread, the main processing thread, and the analyzing thread. The signal thread controls the system. The analyzing thread measures these packets from flow sampling queue and analyzes it. The main processing thread does all other works.

N9MS includes the following three functions, such as to capture the packets, to export netflows, and to encapsulate UDP packets. The captured packets function receives the IPv6 packets with flow sampling, and resolves the packet header. The exported flows function clusters the IPv6 packets and stores flow records correctly. The encapsulated flows function encapsulates the exported flows into NetFlowv9 flow records which are transfered into UDP packets. The input data in N9MS is the IPv6 packets from the optical splitter, and the output data is the Netflowv9 flow records.

4   Key Technologies

4.1   Header Resolution

IPv6 header is composed by 40 bytes basic header and variable length extended header. The field next protocol in the basic header indicates the type of the extension header followed by the basic header or the type of the upper layer protocol. For example, the next protocol field is equal to 0 that means a hop-by-hop expansion header. The next protocol is 44 that indicates a fragment header. Each extension header except encryption header also has a next protocol field, and the length of the current extension header. The IPv6 header resolving process is similar to have access to a link, and gradually jump backward according to the next protocol and length, until to the transport layer. For example, if the next protocol is 6, then we arrive to a TCP transport layer.

The encryption headers can not be resolved to cluster into flows, so these encryption packet will be clustered as IP packets.

4.2   Flow Sampling

Flow sampling module samples packets with a flow sampling algorithm. Flow sampling module samples the flow according to the default defined sampling ratio. In N9MS, the sampling ratio is set to 1/32. The first step of the sampling algorithm is to compute a hash value based on the four-tuple of source IP address, source port, destination address, destination port. In order to guarantee the TCP bidirectional flow, the source IP address and the destination IP address, the source port and the destination port are needed to do bitwise exclusive-or operation, so that the packets in the same TCP flow will have the same hash value. For example, a hash value is equal to 10101, and is stored in a circular queue. The consequent processing thread reads packets from the circular queue one by one and computes the RTT and packet loss ratio of the TCP flow. A mutex operation process in the queue prevents the data to be out of synchronization.

4.3   Estimating Performance

In this paper, we use the SYN-ACK algorithm to estimate the RTT. When the monitor sees a flow from a TCP client to a server, the RTT can be estimated according to three packets during the three-way handshake. The RTT can be estimated from the time interval between the last-SYN packet and the first ACK packet that the client sends to the server.

Figure 2 describes the RTT measurement algorithm in this paper. This algorithm is the main advantage of a reverse ACK packet in the TCP three-way handshake packet. In Figure 2, the first RTT, named RTT_1, is the time interval which the client sent the server a SYN and an ACK. The second RTT named as RTT_2 is the estimation of the value between the last SYN-ACK and the first ACK which the server sends to client. In order to ensure the estimated accuracy, and take full advantage of a two-way message, this paper uses both RTT_1 and RTT_2 to estimate the TCP RTT.

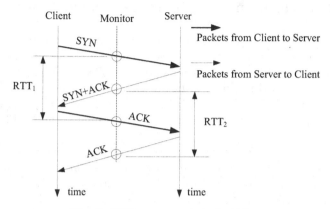

Fig. 2. RTT measurement algorithm

In the actual network, the lost packet will certainly lead to erroneous measurement results. If the SYN-ACK packet is lost, the measured values of RTT_1 would contain the retransmission time of the lost packets. As soon as the sever finishes handshake messages, it will immediately start sending data generally. But in some cases, after the TCP connection is established server does't send data immediately with a long wait time, that will increase RTT_2 measured values.

N9MS will address these problems to improve RTT_1 estimated accuracy by Eq. 1. RTT_2 is computed by Eq. 2. We can compute the RTT by Eq. 3.

$$RTT_1 = (ack_{first} - syn_{first}) - (synack_{first} - synack_{last}) \qquad (1)$$

In Eq. 1, the value in the first parenthesis is the time difference between the client issued an ACK packet and the last SYN packet. The value in the second parenthesis is time delay due to SYN-ACK packet loss. The estimated RTT_1 in Eq. 1 eliminate the delay due to the packet loss.

$$RTT_2 = (ack_{first} - synack_{last}) - (ack_{last} - ack_{first}) \qquad (2)$$

In Eq. 2, the value in the first parenthesis is the time difference between the first ACK packet and the last SYN-ACK packet which the client sent. The value in the second parenthesis is the delay produced by the sever. The difference between the two brackets is the estimated value of RTT_2.

$$RTT = min(RTT_1, RTT_2) \qquad (3)$$

N9MS uses the Peter Benko algorithm[15] to compute the packet loss ratio. N9MS records both the serial number of each TCP packets and the total number of TCP packets, and computes the reverse serial number of each packets. The packet loss ratio is equal to the ratio between the reverse serial number and the total number of packets.

5   Define Performance Template in NetFlow v9

NetFlow v9 (Version 9) export format is flexible and extensible, which provides the versatility needed to support new fields and record types. NetFlow v9 can carry NetFlow records from a network node to a collector. NetFlow v9 has definable record types and is self-describing for easier NetFlow Collection Engine configuration. In NetFlow v9, record formats are defined using templates, and template descriptions are communicated from the router to the NetFlow Collection Engine.

The main feature of NetFlow v9 export format is that it is template-based. A template describes a NetFlow record format and attributes of the fields (such as type and length) within the record. The monitor in N9MS, that converts the packets into NetFlow v9 flows, assigns each template an ID, which is communicated to the NetFlow processor along with the template description. The template ID is used for all further communication from the monitor to the Net-Flow processor.

N9MS adds the definition of two template fields in the NetFlow v9 to record both RTT and packet loss ratio. In the template of Netflow v9, the Field Type field represents the type of the field, and these possible numeric values of the field type are vendor specific. Cisco supplied values are consistent across all platforms that support NetFlow Version 9. The number in the Field Length gives the length of the above-defined field in bytes. The information on the field types with the numbers between 1 and 127 has reserved or used by Cisco, and the numbers between 128 and 346 can refer to the IANA registry of IPFIX information elements[18]. The numbers between 347 and 32767 is unassigned.

N9MS adds to define the Field Type 30000 for RTT with its field length 4 bytes, and the Field Type 30001 for Packet Loss Ratio with its field length 4 bytes. The NetFlow v9 flow format is as following.

NetFlow v9 Flow Format

```
L1 \\ Netflow v9 header(32bits*5)
L2 \\ Template FlowSet
L3 \\ Template Record
L4 \\ Record FlowSet
L5 \\ Data Record(first)
L6 \\ Data Record(second)
L7 \\ Data Record(third)
Following repeated L2-L7 records
```

The Template FlowSet and Template Record is defined as following.

Template FlowSet and Template Record

```
FlowSet ID = 0(16bits) // 0 is Template definition fields
Length = 44 bytes // Template FlowSet length
Template ID = 256 // larger than 255
```

```
Field count = 9 // the number of following fields
sourceIPv6Address(27) // 27 means the source address of IPv6
Length = 16 // IPv6 address length
destinationIPv6Address(28) // 28 means the destination address of IPv6
Length = 16 // IPv6 address length
PacketCount(2) // the number of packets
Length = 4
BytesNumber(1) // the number of bytes
Lenrth = 4
tcpSourcePort(182) // TCP source port
Length = 2
tcpDestinationPort(183) // TCP destination port
Length = 2
tcpControlBits(6) // TCP control field
Length = 1
tcpRTT(30000) // 30000 is defined by N9MS to record the RTT.
Length = 4 // the record unit is millisecond for RTT.
tcpPacketLoss (30001) // 30001 is to record packet loss ratio
Length = 4 // the value is equal to PLR multiplied by 1000000.
```

We define tcpRTT(30000) to record the RTT, which is record with 4 bytes and its unit is millisecond. tcpPacketLoss (30001) field type is defined by N9MS to record the packet loss ratio. N9MS uses 4 bytes to record packet loss ratio, and its value is equal to the value of the packet loss ratio multiplied by 1000000. For example, if the packet loss ratio of a TCP flow is 0.01, then its tcpPacketLoss value is 10000.

The following example gives three flow records using the new netflowv9 template.

an Example with Three NetFlow v9 Flow Records

```
Src IP addr. | Dst IP addr. | PacketNo | BytesNo | SPort | DPort
2001:250:202:: | 2001:0da8:1001:: | 5009 | 5344385 | 8000 | 9000
2001:250:203:: | 2001:0da8:1002:: | 748 | 388934 | 8001 | 9001
2001:250:204:: | 2001:0da8:1003::| 5 | 6534 | 8002 | 9002
tcpControlBits | RTT | Packet Loss Ratio
FIN(1) | 300 | 1000
RST(4) | 210 | 0
FIN(1) | 113 | 0
```

The example uses the NetFlow v9 Template FlowSet and Template Record with 9 fields, which is source IP address, destination IP address, the number of packets, the number of bytes, source port, destination port, control bits in TCP fields, the estimated value of the round trip time in the TCP flow, and the estmated value of packet loss ratio.

6   Experimental Evaluation

The collector server in Figure 1 is equipped with CPU P4 Xeron2.4*2, memory 2GB, hard disk 1.2TB, NIC 1000G, operating system Readhat. The Measurement Device in Figure 1 is a device that can capture packets traffic in 10Gbps links and keep packet header of all packets and then transfer these packet headers to collector server. In this paper, we only test the performance of collector server in Section 6.1, and then in Section 6.2 we analyze IPv6 statistics and TCP performance in CERNET2 backbone according to the NetFlow v9 data that are produced by N9MS.

6.1   Performance Testing

In Linux system, The subdirectory /proc/net/dev includes the statistical information of all the NICs from one moment to the current time, such as the amount of data, the number of packets, bytes, and so on. In order to get all the data throughout the time when the program is running, we can read the NIC statistical information $info\_begin$ at the beginning of the process, and then read the NIC statistical information $info\_end$ at the end of the process. $send\_data = info\_end - info\_begin$ is all the data which go through the NIC during the process running time. We can compare $send\_data$ with the statistical data $info\_proc$ in the process, the packet loss of the process can be obtained. After joining flow exporting and other process function, under the normal traffic intensity of NIC (1Gbps), with the repeated testing, after the system is running stabilized, packet loss rate is less than 0.05%, generally between 0.001% and 0.03%.

The files in the /proc/net/dev subdirectory is not updated in real time, and the system updates these files about every 0.1-1 seconds, so the equation $info\_end - info\_begin$ will cause the maximum traffic error of one second. The NIC normal packet rate is tested to be about 10-200 000 pps. To limit the error in 0.01%, N9MS should be tested continuously for at least 10,000 seconds with over 10-20 billion packets.

Figure 3 is the test statistics from December 18, 2011 0:00 to December 19, 2011 0:00. Figure 3 shows that the system has a certain amount of packet loss in

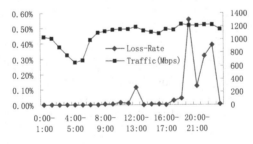

Fig. 3. IPv6 traffic rate and packet loss ratio for one day in the CERNET2 backbone link

the peak traffic period (from 19:00 to 23:00). Under the ordinary traffic density, packet loss rate is very low. Figure 3 shows that N9MS has a very high packet loss rate during 19:00 to 23:00. During this period of time, the byte rate and packet rate handled by the system is almost unchanged, while the packet loss rate has fluctuated, indicating that it has close to the maximum processing capacity of the system. This maximum traffic rate is from 135000 pps to 140000pps. Its maximum byte rate is 152MBps-154MBps, that is 1216Mbps-1232Mbps. Figure 3 also shows that the performance is not stable and its packet loss rate is big during the peak processing rate. The recommended packet rate is not more than 130,000 pps, and the recommended byte rate is not more than 145MBps, that is 1160Mbps.

6.2   IPv6 Result Analysis

Figure 4 is the IPv6 traffic rate and packet length for one day in the CERNET2 backbone link from December 18, 2011 0:00 to December 19, 2011 0:00. Figure 4 shows that the average packet length is more than 1000 bytes. During 2:00-4:00 the average packet length is over 1400 bytes, however the average length of the packets in the CERNET IPv4 network is about 500 bytes at the same time. According to our analysis of traffic in the CERNET2 IPv6 network, we know that the P2P traffic CERNET2 occupies more than 90% of the total traffic.

Figure 5 is the RTT for one day from Nanjing site to Beijing site and USA site. The RTT value of each points in Figure 5 means the average value of all measured RTT in every 5 minutes. X-axis is time for one day from 0:00 to 23:55 on December 18, 2011. The Y-axis is RTT, and its unit is milliseconds. Figure 5 shows that the TCP average RTT between Beijing nodes and Beijing nodes in the CERNET2 is about from 200 to 300 milliseconds. the average RTT for one day is 260 ms, and its standard deviation is 90.5. However the results from Nanjing nodes to the USA's nodes is discrete, that its average RTT is 676.9 milliseconds, and its standard deviation is 336.8 ms.

Figure 6 is the results of packet loss ratio (PLR) for one day from Nanjing node to node in Beijing and USA . The PLR value of each points in Figure 5 is the average value of all measured PLR in every 5 minutes. X-axis is time for one day from 0:00 to 23:55 on December 18, 2011. The Y-axis is PLR, and its unit is

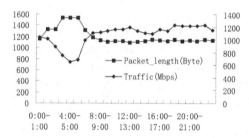

Fig. 4. IPv6 traffic rate and packet length for one day in the CERNET2 backbone link

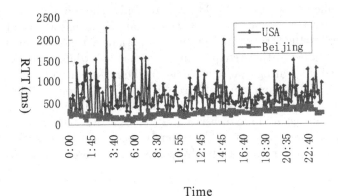

Fig. 5. RTT from Nanjing to Beijing and USA

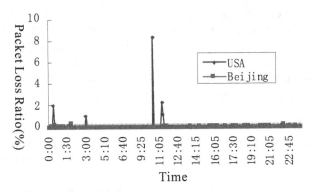

Fig. 6. Packet Loss Ratio from Nanjing to Beijing and USA

percent (%). Figure 6 shows that the TCP average PLR between Nanjing nodes and Beijing nodes in the CERNET2 is about 0%. The average PLR between Nanjing nodes to the USA's nodes is also close to 0, except the packet loss ratio reaches about 9% in one 5 minutes.

7   Conclusion

This paper splits packet traffic from CERNET2 backbone link directly and converts the packet traffic into NetFlow v9 format to observe and manage the IPv6 network. The sampling strategy in N9MS is flow sampling, which can keep all packets in the sampled flows. N9MS can infer network performance information with the sampled packets. N9MS also directly uses these packets of sampled flow to calculate the RTT and packet loss ratio. We define and record both RTT and packet loss ratio field in the NetFlow v9 format. We test and analyze N9MS in a 10Gbps backbone link between Nanjing site and the CNGI-CERNET2 backbone. In the future, we will put N9MS in the distrbuted CERNET2, and improve its function to help us to manage the CERNET2 network.

Acknowledgment. This work was sponsored by the National Grand Fundamental Research 973 program of China under Grant No. $2009CB320505$, the National Nature Science Foundation of China under Grant No. 60973123, the Technology Support Program (Industry) of Jiangsu Province under Grant No. $BE2011173$, the Qing Lan Project of Jiangsu Province, the Six major talent Summit Project of Jiangsu Province, and Jiangsu Provincial Key Laboratory of Network and Information Security under Grants No. BM2003201.

References

1. Cisco IOS NetFlow Introduction,
   http://www.cisco.com/en/US/products/ps6601/products_ios_protocol_group_home.html
2. Key Lab of Computer Network Technology in Jiangsu Province,
   http://www.jslab6.edu.cn/
3. NetFlow v9 Export Format,
   http://www.cisco.com/en/US/docs/ios/12_3/feature/gde/nfv9expf.html
4. Sampled NetFlow Documentation,
   http://www.cisco.com/univercd/cc/td/doc/product/software/ios120/120newft/120limit/120s/120s11/12s_sanf.htm
5. Network Management Research Group (NMRG), http://irtf.org/nmrg
6. Report of the Third Workshop on the Usage of NetFlow/IPFIX in Network Management. Journal of Network System and Management (August 2011)
7. Gates, C., Collins, M., Duggan, M., Kompanek, A., Thomas, M.: More Netflow Tools: For Performance and Security. In: Proceedings of LISA 2004: Eighteenth Systems Administration Conference (November 2004)
8. Rossi, D., Valenti, S.: Fine-grained traffic classification with Netflow data. In: IWCMC 2010, June 28-July 2 (2010)
9. Carela-Espaol, V., Barlet-Ro, P., Cabellos-Aparicio, A., Sole-Pareta, J.: Analysis of the impact of sampling on NetFlow traffic classification. Computer Networks 55(5), 1083–1099 (2011)
10. What is IPv6?, http://en.wikipedia.org/wiki/IPv6
11. Overview - 6QM - IPv6 QoS Measurement, http://www.6qm.org/overview.php
12. IPv6 Statistics, http://www.google.com/intl/en/ipv6/statistics/
13. Colitti, L., Gunderson, S.H., Kline, E., Refice, T.: Evaluating IPv6 Adoption in the Internet. In: Krishnamurthy, A., Plattner, B. (eds.) PAM 2010. LNCS, vol. 6032, pp. 141–150. Springer, Heidelberg (2010)
14. Lee, M., Duffield, N., Kompella, R.R.: Two Samples are Enough: Opportunistic Flow-level Latency Estimation using NetFlow. In: IEEE INFOCOM 2010 Proceedings (2010)
15. Jiang, H., Dovrolis, C.: Passive Estimation of TCP Round Trip Times. ACM Computer Communication Review 32(3) (2002)
16. Benko, P., Veres, A.: A Passive Method for Estimating End-to-End TCP Packet Loss. In: Global Telecommunications Conference, GLOBECOM 2002. IEEE (2002)
17. Hurtig, P., John, W., Brunstrom, A.: Recent Trends in TCP Packet-Level Characteristics. In: The Seventh International Conference on Networking and Services, ICNS 2011 (2011)
18. IP Flow Information Export (IPFIX) Entities,
    http://www.iana.org/assignments/ipfix

Efficient Ciphertext-Policy Attribute Based Encryption with Hidden Policy

Xiaohui Li[1], Dawu Gu[1], Yanli Ren[2], Ning Ding[1], and Kan Yuan[1]

[1] Department of Computer Science and Engineering,
Shanghai Jiao Tong University, Shanghai, China
{shininglxh,dwgu,dingning,heroutman}@sjtu.edu.cn
[2] School of Communication and Information Engineering,
Shanghai University, Shanghai, China
ryl1982@shu.edu.cn

Abstract. In an anonymous ciphertext-policy attribute-based encryption (CP-ABE) scheme, the encryptor-specified access structure is hidden in ciphertexts. The decryptor gets his secret key from a trust authority according to his attributes. However, he cannot decrypt any ciphertext or guess even what access structure was specified by the encryptor if his attributes do not satisfy the access structure associated with the ciphertext. All previous anonymous CP-ABE schemes are inefficient in that each ciphertext grows linearly with the number of attributes. In this paper, we propose an efficient anonymous CP-ABE scheme that reduces both the length of each ciphertext and the number of pairing operations to a constant level, but still leverages a hidden policy to keep recipients' privacy preserved. Furthermore, our scheme is fully secure in the standard model based on the decisional Bilinear Diffie-Hellman (DBDH) assumption in composite order groups. We remark that in our security definition, only the legitimate decryptor knows access structures associated with ciphertexts.

Keywords: Attribute-Based Encryption, Ciphertext-Policy, Constant Size Ciphertext, Recipient Anonymity, Fully Secure.

1   Introduction

With the development of cloud computing in both academic and industrial worlds, there is a trend for the sensitive user data to be stored by third parties (cloud service providers) on the Internet. For example, personal emails, data and personal preferences are stored on web portal sites such as Google and Yahoo. However, cloud service providers cannot be completely trusted in practice. One method of protecting the privacy of user data is to store data in the encrypted form. Thus if the storage is compromised, the amount of information loss will be limited. One disadvantage of encrypting data is that it severely limits the ability of users to selectively share their encrypted data at a fine-grained level. If an user wants to share data with others, he either needs to act as an intermediary and decrypt all relevant data for other users or encrypts his data by using

Y. Xiang et al. (Eds.): IDCS 2012, LNCS 7646, pp. 146–159, 2012.
© Springer-Verlag Berlin Heidelberg 2012

other users' public key respectively, and thus may lead to low efficiency when the number of users becomes larger and larger. So it can be seen that neither one of these options is particularly appealing.

Sahai and Waters [1] made initial steps to deal with this problem by introducing the notion of Attribute-Based Encryption (ABE). To further protect user's privacy in an access structure itself, anonymous ABE was introduced in [11,15] and further improved by [4]. Anonymous ABE has a wide range of applications. For example, in some military circumstances, an access structure itself could be sensitive information. Therefore, to share data with users possessing certain attribute-policy, anonymous ABE schemes can be applied to encrypt data while keeping the access structure hidden in the ciphertext. Compared with [4], Lai et al.[8] applied the dual system encryption methodology [17] to obtain full security. But in all these anonymous CP-ABE schemes [11,15,4,17], the size of each ciphertext is growing linearly with the number of attributes, so is the number of pairing computations.

To improve the efficiency of previous ABE schemes [1,2,3,4,7,16], in which the length of each ciphertext and the number of pairing computations depend on the number of attributes, Emura et al. [6] for the first time proposed a CP-ABE scheme with a constant ciphertext length and a constant number of pairing computations with a restricted access structure. Zhou [14] proposed a new construction of CP-ABE with a constant size ciphertext length. However, neither of these two schemes achieves anonymity, and the access structure is left in a plain text form.

In a summary, all the existing anonymous CP-ABE schemes are inefficient in the aspects of storage (the size of each ciphertext) and computation (the number of pairing computations), and all the existing efficient CP-ABE schemes do not hide access structures.

Our Contribution. In this paper, we propose an efficient ciphertext-policy attribute based encryption scheme with hidden policy in the standard model. Our scheme is an improvement of Waters' scheme in [5], which is the first fully secure Identity-Based Encryption (IBE) scheme without random oracles, and is efficient in that each ciphertext is of constant size and the number of pairing computations is also constant. We transform his IBE scheme into an ABE scheme, since ABE schemes are more flexible and applicable, while maintaining the prominent feature of the original IBE scheme – high efficiency. That is to say, in our scheme, the size of every ciphertext and the number of pairing computations are both constant too.

Furthermore, we achieve anonymity of access structures by applying composite order bilinear groups. As we will point out in Section 3, the original IBE scheme is not anonymous, and the identity v which has the authority of decryption of ciphertext CT is easily to be revealed from the ciphertext CT and public parameters (published to everyone). That is, identity is not hidden in ciphertexts. However, our scheme is an anonymous CP-ABE scheme, and no one can disclose ciphertext-policy through the ciphertext and public parameters only. The anonymity is very useful in the circumstances that data are stored in untrusted servers. Not only the contents of data, but also the access control policy should be hidden from the untrusted servers.

[5] is fully secure in the standard model under DBDH assumption, more stronger than the selective secure model, but it is not anonymous. Since our scheme is anonymous, we need to prove both the indistinguishability of ciphertexts and the indistinguishability of access structures. Thus, we modify the common security model [7,8] for CP-ABE, and add one more parameter to portray the indistinguishability of access structures, some proof techniques and results in [5] are used in our proof. Naturally, our scheme is also proven fully secure.

1.1 Related Work

The first fully functional Identity-Based Encryption (IBE) scheme was proposed in [18]. In IBE, an identity or ID is a string one-to-one mapped to each user. An user can acquire a private key corresponding to his ID in an off-line manner from trusted authority and the ID is used as public key. The ciphertext encrypted by a particular ID can only be decrypted by the user with the corresponding private key, i.e., the encryption is one-to-one. Boneh and Boyen [25] described a scheme proven to be fully secure without random oracles but the efficiency was too bad to be of practical use. Waters [5] presented an efficient IBE scheme in the same security model as [25].

ABE was generalized from IBE. It was first proposed as fuzzy version of IBE [1] which supports a threshold policy. There are two kinds of ABE schemes which are key-policy and ciphertext-policy ABE schemes. In a key-policy ABE scheme (KP-ABE) [2], every ciphertext is associated with a set of attributes, and every user's secret key is associated with an access structure on attributes. Decryption can succeed if and only if the ciphertext attribute set satisfies the access structure associated with the user's secret key. In a ciphertext-policy ABE scheme (CP-ABE) [3], the situation is reversed. That is, attributes are associated with user's secret keys and access structures are within the ciphertext.

First KP-ABE [2] made the access structure more expressive that it supports a tree-based access structure, in which an attribute is one-to-one corresponding to a leaf node and internal nodes are threshold gates like n-of-n (AND), 1-of-n (OR) and m-of-n, which is also called the monotonic access structure. To enable more flexible access control policy, Ostrovsky et al. [19] presented a KP-ABE supporting a non-monotonic access structure by adding NOT gate. Goyal et al. [2] gave a general way to transform KP-ABE into CP-ABE. First CP-ABE [3] also supported the monotonic access structure. However, this construction is only secure under the generic group model. To overcome this weakness, Cheung et al. [7] presented another construction that is secure under the standard model. But it only supports the type of access structures that are represented by AND-gate on positive and negative attributes with wildcards. CP-ABE is more appealing since it is conceptually closer to the Role Based Access Control (RBAC) [20] model.

To further achieve anonymity, Boneh and Waters [9] proposed a predicate encryption scheme based on the primitive called Hidden Vector Encryption. The scheme also realizes the anonymous CP-ABE by using the opposite semantics of subset predicates. Katz et al. [21] proposed a novel predicate encryption scheme supporting inner product predicates which can achieve KP-ABE and anonymous CP-ABE. However, both [21] and [22] are inefficient compared with [4]. Nishide et al. [4] introduced the notion of ciphertext-policy hiding CP-ABE and proposed two concrete constructions. The admissible access structure in their schemes can expressed as AND-gates on multi-valued attributes with wildcards. Some other ciphertext-policy hiding CP-ABE construction were proposed in [22,23]. However, all these anonymous CP-ABE schemes were only proven selectively secure. Lai et al. [8] first described a construction of hiding CP-ABE from attribute-hiding inner-product PE formally and proposed a concrete construction proven fully secure and their scheme's access structure is the same as [4]. The fully secure CP-ABE systems for expressive access structures were proposed in [16,24].

For efficiency consideration, Emura et al. [6] reduced the ciphertext length to a constant level and so did the number of pairing computations, but the admissible access structure is restricted to AND-gates on multi-valued attributes. [13,14] also proposed two CP-ABE schemes with constant ciphertext length. The only difference between these two schemes is access structures. However, none of these schemes can achieve recipient anonymity as our scheme does.

1.2   Organization

The rest of this paper is organized as follows. In Section 2 we give some preliminaries. In Section 3, we first describe Waters' scheme , and then present our scheme in details. The security proof will be given in Section 4. In Section 5, we compare our scheme with previous works in multiple aspects. Finally, we conclude our work in Section 6.

2   Preliminaries

This section presents the preliminaries used throughout this paper. The notation $x \in_R S$ means x is randomly chosen from a set S.

2.1   Composite Order Bilinear Groups

Composite order bilinear groups were first introduced in [10]. We use bilinear groups whose order is the product of two distinct primes.

Let $\mathcal{G}$ be an algorithm that takes as input a security parameter 1^λ and outputs a tuple $(p, r, \mathbb{G}, \mathbb{G}_T, e)$, where p, r are distinct primes, and $\mathbb{G}, \mathbb{G}_T$ are cyclic groups of order $N = pr$, and $e : \mathbb{G} \times \mathbb{G} \to \mathbb{G}_T$ is a map such that

1. (Bilinear) $\forall g, h \in \mathbb{G}, a, b \in \mathbb{Z}_N^*, e(g^a, h^b) = e(g, h)^{ab}$;
2. (Non-degenerate) $\exists g \in \mathbb{G}$ such that $e(g, h)$ has order N in $\mathbb{G}_T$.

We assume that multiplication in $\mathbb{G}$ and $\mathbb{G}_T$, as well as the bilinear map e, are computable in time polynomial in λ. We use $\mathbb{G}_p, \mathbb{G}_r$ to denote the subgroups of $\mathbb{G}$ having order p, r respectively. Let $\mathbb{G} = \mathbb{G}_p \times \mathbb{G}_r$ observe that the rule holds that if $h_p \in \mathbb{G}_p$ and $h_r \in \mathbb{G}_r$, then $e(h_p, h_r) = 1$. In fact, g, g_p, g_r be the generator of $\mathbb{G}, \mathbb{G}_p, \mathbb{G}_r$ respectively, then g^r generates $\mathbb{G}_p$, and g^p generates $\mathbb{G}_r$. Hence, for some α_1, α_2, we have $h_p = (g^r)^{\alpha_1}, h_r = (g^p)^{\alpha_2}$, then $e(h_p, h_r) = e((g^r)^{\alpha_1}, (g^p)^{\alpha_2}) = e(g^{\alpha_1}, g^{\alpha_2})^{pr} = 1$.

2.2 Complexity Assumption

We state the DBDH complexity assumption shown in [26].

DBDH assumption: Let $e : \mathbb{G} \times \mathbb{G} \to \mathbb{G}_T$ be an efficiently computable bilinear map, where $\mathbb{G}$ has composite order $N = pr$. We use $\mathbb{G}_p, mathbb{G}_r$ to denote the subgroups of $\mathbb{G} = \mathbb{G}_p \times \mathbb{G}_r$ having prime order p and r, respectively. Choose generators $g_p \in \mathbb{G}_p, g_r \in \mathbb{G}_r$ and random numbers $a, b, c \in_R \mathbb{Z}_N^*$. The Decision Bilinear Diffie-Hellman (DBDH) problem in $\mathbb{G}, \mathbb{G}_T$ is a problem that for a tuple $(g_p, g_r, g_p^a, g_p^b, g_p^c, Z)$ as input to decide $Z = e(g_p, g_r)^{abc}$ or not. An algorithm $\mathcal{B}$ has advantage ϵ in solving DBDH problem in $\mathbb{G}, \mathbb{G}_T$ if $Adv(\mathcal{B}) = |Pr[\mathcal{B}(g_p, g_r, g_p^a, g_p^b, g_p^c, e(g_p, g_p)^{abc}) = 0] - Pr[\mathcal{B}(g_p, g_r, g_p^a, g_p^b, g_p^c, e(g_p, g_p)^z) = 0]| \geqslant \epsilon(\kappa)$ We say that the DBDH assumption holds in $\mathbb{G}, \mathbb{G}_T$ if no PPT algorithm has an advantage of at least ϵ in solving the DBDH problem in $\mathbb{G}, \mathbb{G}_T$.

2.3 Access Structure

Several access structure such as the threshold structure [11,13], the tree-based access structure [3,12], AND-gates on positive and negative attributes with wildcards [7], AND-gates on multi-valued attributes with wildcards [4] and AND-gates on multi-valued attributes [6] were used in previous ABE schemes. In our scheme, we use the same access structure as [6].

Definition 1. Let $\mathcal{U} = \{att_1, \ldots, att_n\}$ be a set of attributes. For $att_i \in \mathcal{U}, S_i = \{v_{i,1}, \ldots, v_{i,m}\}$ is a set of possible values, and m is the number of possible values for each att_i. Let $L = \{l_1, \ldots, l_n\}, l_i \in S_i$ be an attribute list for a user, and $W = \{w_1, \ldots, w_n\}, w_i \in S_i$ be an access structure. The notation $L \vDash W$ expresses that an attribute list L satisfies an access structure W, namely, $l_i = w_i (i = 1, 2, \ldots, n)$.

2.4 Syntax of CP-ABE

An CP-ABE scheme consists of four algorithms, introduced in [7].

Setup(1^λ). This algorithm takes the security parameter λ as input and generates a public key PK used for encryption and a master secret key MK held by the central authority for generating user secret keys.

KeyGen(MK, L). This algorithm takes MK and an attribute list L as input and generates a secret key SK_L associated with L.

Encrypt(PK, W, M). This algorithm takes as input the public key PK, an access structure W and a message M. It returns a ciphertext CT such that a secret key generated from user attribute list L can be used to decrypt CT if and only if S satisfies W.

Decrypt(CT, SK_L). This algorithm takes CT and SK_L associated with L as input and returns the message M if the attribute list L satisfies the ciphertext policy W specified for CT, that is, $L \models W$.

2.5   Security Model

The full security model is described as a security game between a challenger and an adversary A. This CPA security game refers to [8]. The game proceeds as follows:

Setup. The challenger runs Setup(1^λ) to obtain a public key PK and a master secret key MK. It gives the public key PK to the adversary $\mathcal{A}$ and keeps MK to itself.

Phase 1. The adversary $\mathcal{A}$ adaptively queries the challenger for secret keys corresponding to sets of attributes $L_{t1}, \ldots, L_{tq}$. In response, the challenger generates the secret key S_{L_i} using $KeyGen$ and gives them to $\mathcal{A}$, for all i in set $\{t1, \ldots, tq\}$.

Challenge. The adversary $\mathcal{A}$ submits two (equal length) messages M_0, M_1 and two access structure W_0, W_1, subject to the restriction that, W_0 and W_1 cannot be satisfied by any of the queried attribute sets. The challenger selects two random bits (β, γ), where $\beta, \gamma \in \{0, 1\}$, sets $c^* = Encrypt(PK, W_\beta, M_\gamma)$, and returns c^* to the adversary as its challenge ciphertext.

Phase 2. The adversary $\mathcal{A}$ continues to adaptively query the challenger for secret keys corresponding to sets of attributes with the added restriction that none of these satisfies W_0 and W_1.

Guess. The adversary $\mathcal{A}$ outputs its guess (β', γ') where $\beta', \gamma' \in \{0, 1\}$ for (β, γ) and wins the game if $(\beta', \gamma') = (\beta, \gamma)$, that is $\beta' = \beta, \gamma' = \gamma$.

The advantage of the adversary in this game is defined as $|Pr[(\beta', \gamma') = (\beta, \gamma)] - \frac{1}{4}|$ where the probability is taken over the random bits used by the challenger and the adversary.

Definition 2. *(Semantic Security)*. *A ciphertext-policy attribute-based encryption scheme with hidden policy is (t, q, ϵ) - semantically secure if all t - time adversaries making at most q private key queries have at most an ϵ advantage in breaking our scheme.*

3   The Proposed Scheme

In this section, we present our scheme that achieves recipient anonymity and extends access structures to AND-gates on multi-valued attributes.

In Section 3.1, we first show Waters' construction and then explain why this scheme is not anynomous, which means all the decryptors, no matter legal or illegal, can reveal the identity that the message is encrypted for from the cipher-text and public parameters. In Section 3.2, we give our construction in details. In Section 3.3, we explain the intuition behind our approach we take to achieve anonymity, which means all the illegal decryptors are unable to reveal information about who can do successful decryption.

3.1   Waters' Construction

Identities will be represented as bitstrings of length n, also, we can let identities be bitstrings of arbitrary length and n be the output length of a collision-resistant hash function, $H : \{0,1\}^* \to \{0,1\}^n$. The construction follows.

Setup(1^λ). The system parameters are generated from the security parameter 1^λ as follows. $\mathbb{G}$ and $\mathbb{G}_T$ are groups of prime order, p, for which there exists an efficiently computable bilinear map $e : \mathbb{G} \times \mathbb{G} \to \mathbb{G}_T$, g is the generator of group $\mathbb{G}$. A secret $\alpha \in_R \mathbb{Z}_p$ is chosen, we set $g_1 = g^\alpha$ and choose $g_2 \in_R \mathbb{G}$. Additionally, the authority chooses $u' \in_R \mathbb{G}$ a random n-length vector $U = (u_i)$ where $u_i \in_R \mathbb{G}, 1 \leq i \leq n$. The published public key is $PK = < g, g_1, g_2, u', U >$, and the master secret key is $MK = < g_2^\alpha >$.

KeyGen(v, MK, PK). v is an n-bit string representing an identity, v_i denotes the i-th bit of v, and $V \subseteq \{1, \ldots, n\}$ is the set of all i for which $v_i = 1$. (That is V is the set of indicates for which the bitstring v is set to 1.) The authority chooses $r \in_R \mathbb{Z}_p$, then the secret key for identity v is generated as: $d_v = < d_1 = g_2^\alpha (u' \prod_{i \in V} u_i)^r, d_2 = g^r >$.

Encrypt(PK, M, v). A message $M \in \mathbb{G}_T$ is encrypted for an identity v as follows. The encryptor chooses $t \in_R \mathbb{Z}_p$, then the ciphertext is constructed as: $C = < C_1 = e(g_1, g_2)^t M, C_2 = g^t, C_3 = (u' \prod_{i \in V} u_i)^t >$.

Decrypt(C, d_v). Let $C = < C_1, C_2, C_3 >$ be a valid encryption of M under the identity v. Then C can be decrypted by $d_v = < d_1, d_2 >$ as:

$$C_1 \frac{e(d_2, C_3)}{e(d_1, C_2)} = (e(g_1, g_2)^t M) \frac{e(g^r, (u' \prod_{i \in V} u_i)^t)}{e(g_2^\alpha (u' \prod_{i \in V} u_i)^r, g^t)}$$

We explain why the above scheme is not anonymous. Some parts of a ciphertext for an identity v, $(C_2, C_3) = (g^t, (u' \prod_{i \in V} u_i)^t)$ is a DDH (Decision Diffie-Hellman) tuple, from which the identity information v can be revealed. Concretely, for an identity v' and $V' \subseteq \{1, \ldots, n\}$ is the set of all i for which $v'_i = 1$, an attacker can run the DDH test $e(C_2, u' \prod_{i \in V'} u_i)) = e(C_3, g)$ since u', u_i, g are all public parameters, then the attacker can determine whether V' is used in ciphertext or not, that is, for identity v' or not. In fact, the number of all possible identities is 2^n, which means that the identity associated with the ciphertext is sure to be revealed through at most 2^n times DDH test attack.

3.2 Our Construction

Without loss of generality, we assume that there are n categories of attributes and every user has n attributes with each attribute belonging to a different category. Let $\mathcal{U} = \{att_1, \ldots, att_n\}$ be a set of attributes; $att_i \in \mathcal{U}, S_i = \{v_{i,1}, \ldots, v_{i,m}\}$ is a set of possible values with $m = |S_i|$; $L = \{l_1, \ldots, l_n\}, l_i \in S_i$ be an attribute list for a user, and $W = \{w_1, \ldots, w_n\}, w_i \in S_i$ be an access structure.

Setup(1^λ). A trusted authority TA first runs $\mathcal{G}(1^\lambda)$ to obtain $(p, r, \mathbb{G}, \mathbb{G}_T, e)$ with $e : \mathbb{G} \times \mathbb{G}_p \to \mathbb{G}_r$ where $\mathbb{G}$ and $\mathbb{G}_T$ are cyclic groups of order $N = pr$. Let g_p, g_r be the generator of $\mathbb{G}_p, \mathbb{G}_r$ respectively. TA chooses $\alpha \in_R \mathbb{Z}_N^*, a', g_2 \in_R \mathbb{G}_p, R_0, R' \in_R \mathbb{G}_r$ and calculates $g_1 = g_p^\alpha$, then TA uniformly chooses $a_{i,j} \in_R \mathbb{Z}_N^*, R_{i,j} \in_R \mathbb{G}_r (1 \leq i \leq n, 1 \leq j \leq m)$. The public key is:

$$PK = <\; g_p, g_r, A' = a'R', \{A_{i,j} = g_p^{a_{i,j}} \cdot R_{i,j}\}_{1 \leq i \leq n, 1 \leq j \leq m},$$
$$A_0 = g_p \cdot R_0, Y = e(g_1, g_2) \;>$$

and the master secret key is

$$MK = <\; a', \alpha, g_2, \{a_{i,j}\}(1 \leq i \leq n, 1 \leq j \leq m) \;>$$

KeyGen(PK, MK, L). For a certain user attribute list $L = \{l_1, \ldots, l_n\} = \{v_{1,t_1}, \ldots, v_{n,t_n}\}$ with $t_j \in \{1, \ldots, m\}(1 \leq j \leq n)$. TA chooses $r \in_R \mathbb{Z}_N^*$, and computes the user's secret key as follows:

$$SK_L = <\; D_0 = g_p^r, D_1 = g_2^\alpha (a' \cdot g_p^{\sum_{v_{i,j} \in L} a_{i,j}})^r \;>$$

Encrypt(PK, M, W). Let an access structure be $W = \{w_1, \ldots, w_n\}$ with $w_i \in S_i$. The encryptor chooses $s \in_R \mathbb{Z}_N^*$ and $R_0', R_1' \in_R \mathbb{G}_r$, for a message $M \in \mathbb{G}_T$, then it outputs the ciphertext:

$$CT = <\; \tilde{C} = M \cdot Y^s, C_0 = A_0^s \cdot R_0', C_1 = (A' \prod_{v_{i,j} \in W} A_{i,j})^s \cdot R_1' \;>$$

Correctness. Let SK_L and CT be as shown above. Let the access structure associated with the ciphertext be W. If $L \vDash W$. Then

$$\tilde{C} \cdot \frac{e(D_0, C_1)}{e(D_1, C_0)} = M \cdot Y^s \cdot \frac{e(g_p^r, (A' \prod_{v_{i,j} \in W} A_{i,j})^s \cdot R_1')}{g_2^\alpha (a' \cdot g_p^{\sum_{v_{i,j} \in L} a_{i,j}})^r, A_0^s \cdot R_0'}$$
$$= M \cdot Y^s \cdot \frac{g_p^r, (A' \prod_{v_{i,j} \in W} A_{i,j})^s}{g_2^\alpha (a' \cdot g_p^{\sum_{v_{i,j} \in L} a_{i,j}})^r, g_p^s} = \frac{M \cdot Y^s}{e(g_2^\alpha, g_p^s)} = M$$

Note that in KeyGen algorithm, we assume $\forall L, L'(L \neq L'), \sum_{v_{i,j} \in L} a_{i,j} \neq \sum_{v_{i,j} \in L'} a_{i,j}$ because the parameter r has no effect on decryption. If the above condition is not assumed, various users associated with attribute list L, L' will have the same decryption ability. Emura et al. [6] gave the result that this assumption holds with overwhelming probability $P_{assump}(> 1 - \frac{N_0^2}{N})$, where $N_0 = m^n$.

3.3 Analysis

In our construction, we achieve recipient anonymity by applying composite order bilinear groups. The key point is that we change two parts of ciphertext (C_0, C_1) by adding a "tail", respectively. That is one more multiplication with element in group $\mathbb{G}_r$. Actually, we set $C_0 = A_0^s \cdot R_0', C_1 = (A' \prod_{v_{i,j} \in W} A_{i,j})^s \cdot R_1'$ instead of $A_0^s, (A' \prod_{v_{i,j} \in W} A_{i,j})^s$ although R_0', R_1' have no effect on decryption. The changes are necessary, because if we do not make these changes and remove the "tail", that is $(C_0, C_1) = (A_0^s, (A' \prod_{v_{i,j} \in W} A_{i,j})^s)$, then for some access structure W', the attacker can still run the DDH test $e(C_0, A' \prod_{v_{i,j} \in W} A_{i,j}) = e(C_1, A_0)$, to determine whether the encryptor uses the access structure W' or not. The "tail" can help us to avoid this DDH test attack. It is not hard to find that the identity can be seen as a special case of the attribute list. If we set m to 2, i.e. the attribute value could only be 0 or 1, then it is the identity case.

4   Proof of Security

We now prove the security of our scheme.

Theorem 1. *Our scheme is (t, q, ϵ) secure assuming the $(t + O(\epsilon^{-2}ln(\epsilon^{-1})\lambda^{-1} ln(\lambda^{-1})), (1 - \frac{N_0^2}{N})\frac{\epsilon}{32(n+1)q})$ DBDH assumption holds, where $N_0 = m^n$ is the number of all possible expressed access structures and $\lambda = \frac{1}{8(n+1)q}$.*

Proof. We suppose there exists a (t, q, ϵ) adversary $\mathcal{A}$ against our scheme. Then we can construct a simulator that breaks the DBDH assumption with the advantage at least $(1 - \frac{N_0^2}{N})\frac{\epsilon}{32(n+1)q}$. The DBDH challenger $\mathcal{B}$ selects $a, b, c \in_R \mathbb{Z}_N^*, v \in_R \{0, 1\}$, and g_p, g_r where $< g_p >= \mathbb{G}_p, < g_r >= \mathbb{G}_r$. If $v = 0$, then $Z = e(g_p, g_p)^{abc}$. Otherwise, if $v = 1$, then $Z = e(g_p, g_p)^z$. The simulator will take the challenge tuple $(g_p, g_r, A = g_p^a, B = g_p^b, C = g_p^c, Z)$ and outputs a guess v'.
The desired simulator is constructed as follows:

Setup. The simulator first sets an integer $u = 4q$, chooses an integer $k \in_R \{0, \ldots, n\}$, and then chooses an integer matrix $x = (x_{i,j})_{n \times m}, 1 \leq i \leq n, 1 \leq j \leq m$, where $x_{i,j} \in_R \{0, \ldots, u - 1\}$ and $x' \in_R \{0, \ldots, u - 1\}$. Additionally, the simulator chooses $y' \in_R \mathbb{Z}_N^*$ and a matrix $y = (y_{i,j})_{n \times m}, 1 \leq i \leq n, 1 \leq j \leq m$ where $y_{i,j} \in_R \mathbb{Z}_N^*$. All these values are kept internal to the simulator.

For an attribute list L, we define two functions, $F(L) = (N - uk) + x' + \sum_{v_{i,j} \in L} x_{i,j} (mod N)$, $J(L) = y' + \sum_{v_{i,j} \in L} y_{i,j} (mod N)$, and a binary function $B(L) = 0$ if $x' + \sum_{v_{i,j} \in L} x_{i,j} \equiv 0 (mod u)$ or $B(L) = 1$ otherwise.

The simulator assigns $g_1 = A, g_2 = B$, chooses $r' \in_R \mathbb{Z}_N^*$ and $r_{i,j} \in_R \mathbb{Z}_N^*$ and $R_1 \in_R \mathbb{G}_r$, outputs the PK parameters $A_0 = g_p \cdot R_1, A' = g_2^{p-uk+x'} g_p^{y'} g_r^{r'}, A_{i,j} = g_2^{x_{i,j}} g_p^{y_{i,j}} g_r^{r_{i,j}} (1 \leq i \leq n, 1 \leq j \leq m)$. Here PK implies that $a_{i,j} = bx_{i,j} + y_{i,j}$.

Phase 1. In private key query phase, suppose the attribute list is $L = \{v_{1,t_1}, \ldots, v_{n,t_n}\}$ with $t_j \in \{1, \ldots, m\}(1 \le j \le n)$. If $B(L) = 0$, the simulator aborts and randomly chooses its guess v' of the challenger's value v. Otherwise, it chooses a random $r \in_R \mathbb{Z}_N^*$ and computes $D_0 = g_1^{\frac{-1}{F(L)}} g_p^r$, $D_1 = g_1^{\frac{-J(L)}{F(L)}} \cdot (a' \cdot g_p^{\sum_{v_{i,j} \in L} a_{i,j}})^r$. Let $a' = g_2^{F(L) - \sum_{v_{i,j} \in L} x_{i,j}} g_p^{y'}$, which in fact is easy to compute. It is easy to see both D_0 and D_1 are efficiently computable. Let $\tilde{r} = r - \frac{a}{F(L)}$.

Then we have $D_1 = g_1^{\frac{-J(L)}{F(L)}} \cdot (a' \cdot g_p^{\sum_{v_{i,j} \in L} a_{i,j}})^r = g_1^{\frac{-J(L)}{F(L)}} \cdot (g_2^{F(L)} g_p^{J(L)})^r = g_2^a (g_2^{F(L)} g_p^{J(L)})^{\frac{-a}{F(L)}} (g_2^{F(L)} g_p^{J(L)})^r = g_2^a (g_2^{F(L)} g_p^{J(L)})^{r - \frac{a}{F(L)}} = g_2^a (a' \cdot g_p^{\sum_{v_{i,j} \in L} a_{i,j}})^{\tilde{r}}$.

Then verify if $D_0 = g_1^{\frac{-1}{F(L)}} g_p^r = g_p^{r - \frac{a}{F(L)}} = g_p^{\tilde{r}}$. The simulation will be able to perform this computation if and only if $F(L) \ne 0 \bmod N$. For convenience, the game will only continue in the condition that $B(L) \ne 0 (B(L) \ne 0$ implies $F(L) \ne 0)$.

Challenge. The adversary $\mathcal{A}$ will submit two (equal length) messages M_0, M_1 and two access structure W_0, W_1. The simulator flips a fair coin twice, and gets (β, γ), where $\beta, \gamma \in 0, 1$, if $x' + \sum_{v_{i,j} \in W_\beta} x_{i,j} \ne uk$, the simulator will abort and submit a random guess of v'. Otherwise, we have $F(W_\beta) \equiv 0 (\bmod N)$. Next, the simulator chooses $R_0 \in_R \mathbb{G}_r$ and $r_c \in_R \mathbb{Z}_N^*$, r_c can be written in the form $r_c = cr'' + r_0$ for some unknown r_0, in which $c, r'' \in \mathbb{Z}_N^*$ and $r'' = r' + \sum_{v_{i,j} \in W_\beta} r_{i,j}$, and we let $g_r^{r_0} = R_1'$ (we cannot get r_0, but it does not matter, since R_1' is randomly chosen), the ciphertext is constructed as follows:

$$CT = < \tilde{C} = M_\gamma \cdot Z, C_0 = C \cdot R_0, C_1 = C^{J(W_\beta)} g_r^{r_c} >$$

Now we check the validity of the ciphertext, $C_0 = g_p^c R_0$ and

$$C_1 = C^{J(W_\beta)} g_r^{r_c} = (g_2^{F(W_\beta)} g_p^{J(W_\beta)} g_r^{r''})^c R_1' = (g_2^{F(W_\beta) - \sum_{v_{i,j} \in W_\beta} x_{i,j}} g_p^{y'} g_r^{r'}$$
$$\prod_{v_{i,j} \in W_\beta} (g_p^{a_{i,j}} g_r^{r_{i,j}}))^c R_1' = (a' g_r^{r'} \prod_{v_{i,j} \in W_\beta} A_{i,j})^c \cdot R_1' = (A' \prod_{v_{i,j} \in W_\beta} A_{i,j})^c \cdot R_1'$$

We see that CT is a valid encryption of M_γ under access structure W_β.

Otherwise, we have that Z is a random element of $\mathbb{G}_p$. In that case, the ciphertext will give no information about the simulator's choice of γ.

Phase 2. The simulator repeats the same strategy it used in Phase 1.

Guess. The adversary $\mathcal{A}$ output a guess (β', γ') of (β, γ).

Suppose the simulator has not aborted at this point. Then check if the adversary's guess $(\beta', \gamma') = (\beta, \gamma)$. The challenger $\mathcal{B}$ outputs $v' = 0$ if $(\beta', \gamma') = (\beta, \gamma)$, or outputs $v' = 1$ if $(\beta', \gamma') \ne (\beta, \gamma)$.

Analysis. If $Z = e(g_p, g_p)^{abc}$ then $\tilde{C} = M_\gamma \cdot e(A, B)^c$. The CT shown above is a valid ciphertext associated with W_β. Therefore, $\mathcal{A}$ has advantage ϵ by assumption. Hence, $Pr[(\beta', \gamma') = (\beta, \gamma) | e(g_p, g_p)^{abc}] = \frac{1}{4} + \epsilon$. Otherwise, if $Z = e(g_p, g_p)^z$, $\mathcal{A}$ has no advantage to distinguish two bits (β, γ). Hence, $Pr[(\beta', \gamma') = (\beta, \gamma) | e(g_p, g_p)^z] = \frac{1}{4}$. We can see that the game will not abort if $x' + \sum_{v_{i,j} \in L} x_{i,j} \ne 0 (\bmod u)$ and $x' + \sum_{v_{i,j} \in W_\beta} x_{i,j} = uk (\bmod N)$. We share the same not-aborting condition with [5] in guess and challenge phase. Combining with the probability analysis result in Section 3.2, we have that $\mathcal{B}$'s advantage in the DBDH game is at least $(1 - \frac{N_0^2}{N})\frac{\epsilon}{32(n+1)q}$. Also, we share the same time complexity $O(\epsilon^{-2}ln(\epsilon^{-1})\lambda^{-1}ln(\lambda^{-1}))$ with [5].   □

5   Performance Comparison

In this section, we compare our work with previous work to expound our scheme's advantages. For convenience, we denote by PK, MK, SK and CT the size of the public key, of the master key, of the secret key, and the ciphertext length excluding the access structure, respectively. Besides, Enc. and Dec. are the computational times of encryption and decryption, respectively. The terms that DBDH, D-Linear [4] and BDHE [14] are short for the Decision Bilinear Diffie-Hellman assumption, the Decision Linear assumption and the Bilinear Diffie-Hellman Exponent assumption, respectively.

Let n be the number of all attributes in universe, m be the number of all possible values for each attribute and $N' = mn$ represent the number of all possible combinational values for all attributes. The notation $|\mathbb{G}|$ is the bit-length of the element which belongs to $\mathbb{G}$. Let the notation $k\mathbb{G}$ and kC_e (where $k \in \mathbb{Z}_{>0}$) be k-times calculations over the group $\mathbb{G}$ and pairing, respectively. N is the order of bilinear group. Generally speaking, it is a big prime number , but in [8] and our scheme, it is a composite number, pqr and pr, where p, q, r are prime numbers respectively. Other equal notations are $\mathbb{G} = \mathbb{G}_p \times \mathbb{G}_q \times \mathbb{G}_r$ and $\mathbb{G} = \mathbb{G}_p \times \mathbb{G}_r$.

Our scheme is efficient in that the ciphertext length, the secret key length and the costs of decryption do not depend on the number of attributes. Especially, the number of pairing computations is constant. Only [6] scheme shares more or less the same high efficiency with ours, but [6] also pointed out that their scheme did not provide recipient anonymity, an attacker can run the DDH test to determine the policy used. We address this problem by using the composite order bilinear groups. Furthermore, our scheme is proven fully secure in the standard model. To the best of our knowledge, this is the first scheme providing these properties simultaneously.

Table 1. Size of each parameter

	PK	MK	SK	CT
NYO08[4]	$(2N'+1)|\mathbb{G}| + |\mathbb{G}_T|$	$(2N'+1)|\mathbb{Z}_N|$	$(3n+1)|\mathbb{G}|$	$(2N'+1)|\mathbb{G}| + |\mathbb{G}_T|$
Emura09[6]	$(2N'+3)|\mathbb{G}| + |\mathbb{G}_T|$	$(N'+1)|\mathbb{Z}_N|$	$2|\mathbb{G}|$	$2|\mathbb{G}| + |\mathbb{G}_T|$
Zhou10[14]	$(6n+2)|\mathbb{G}|$	$2|\mathbb{Z}_N|$	$(2n+1)|\mathbb{G}|$	$2|\mathbb{G}| + |\mathbb{G}_T|$
Lai11[8]	$(N'+1)|\mathbb{G}| + |\mathbb{G}_T|$	$|\mathbb{G}_p| + (N'+1)|\mathbb{Z}_N^*|$	$(n+1)|\mathbb{G}_p|$	$(N'+1)|\mathbb{G}| + |\mathbb{G}_T|$
Ours	$(N'+4)|\mathbb{G}| + |\mathbb{G}_T|$	$2|\mathbb{G}_p| + (N'+1)|\mathbb{Z}_N^*|$	$2|\mathbb{G}_p|$	$2|\mathbb{G}| + |\mathbb{G}_T|$

Table 2. Computational time of Encryption and Decryption

	Enc.	Dec.
NYO08[4]	$(2N' + 1)\mathbb{G} + \mathbb{G}_T$	$(3n + 1)C_e + (3n + 1)\mathbb{G}_T$
Emura09[6]	$(n + 1)\mathbb{G} + 2\mathbb{G}_T$	$2C_e + 2\mathbb{G}_T$
Zhou10[14]	$(n + 2)\mathbb{G} + 2\mathbb{G}_T + C_e$	$(n + 1)C_e + (n + 1)\mathbb{G}_T$
Lai11[8]	$(2N' + 2)\mathbb{G} + \mathbb{G}_T$	$(n + 1)C_e + (n + 3)\mathbb{G}_T$
Ours	$(n + 3)\mathbb{G} + 2\mathbb{G}_T$	$2C_e + 2\mathbb{G}_T$

Table 3. Security Properties of CP-ABE

	Order of Bilinear Groups	Security Model	Recipient Anonymity	Assumption
NYO08[4]	$N = p$	Selective	Yes	DBDH,D-Linear
Emura09[6]	$N = p$	Selective	No	DBDH
Zhou10[14]	$N = p$	Selective	No	K-BDHE
Lai11[8]	$N = pqr$	Fully	Yes	Non-standard*
Ours	$N = pr$	Fully	Yes	DBDH

Table 4. Expressiveness of Policy

NYO08[4]	AND-gates on multi-valued attributes with wildcards
Emura09[6]	AND-gates on multi-valued attributes
Zhou10[14]	AND-gates on positive and negative attributes with wildcards
Lai11[8]	AND-gates on multi-valued attributes with wildcards
Ours	AND-gates on multi-valued attributes

*Subgroup decision problem and others problems, please refer to [8].

6   Conclusions

In this paper, we present an efficient ciphertext-policy attribute based encryption scheme with hidden policy. Both the length of each ciphertext and each secret key are constant. Additionally, the number of pairing computations in decryption is independent of the number of attributes. We also prove the proposed scheme achieves the full security in the standard model. Access structures are hidden such that any storage service provider knows nothing about access structures from ciphertexts and public parameters only.

However, our scheme only supports a restricted access structure, which is AND-gates on multi-valued attributes. This work motivates an open problem of how to make access structures more expressive while still maintaining high efficiency in a relative stronger security model.

References

1. Sahai, A., Waters, B.: Fuzzy Identity-Based Encryption. In: Cramer, R. (ed.) EUROCRYPT 2005. LNCS, vol. 3494, pp. 457–473. Springer, Heidelberg (2005)

2. Goyal, V., Pandey, O., Sahai, A., Waters, B.: Attribute-based encryption for fine-grained access control of encrypted data. In: Proc. ACM Conference on Computer and Communications Security (CCS), pp. 89–98 (2006)

3. Bethencourt, J., Sahai, A., Waters, B.: Ciphertext-policy attribute-based encryption. In: Proc. IEEE Symposium on Security and Privacy, pp. 321–334 (2007)

4. Nishide, T., Yoneyama, K., Ohta, K.: Attribute-Based Encryption with Partially Hidden Encryptor-Specified Access Structures. In: Bellovin, S.M., Gennaro, R., Keromytis, A.D., Yung, M. (eds.) ACNS 2008. LNCS, vol. 5037, pp. 111–129. Springer, Heidelberg (2008)

5. Waters, B.: Efficient Identity-Based Encryption Without Random Oracles. In: Cramer, R. (ed.) EUROCRYPT 2005. LNCS, vol. 3494, pp. 114–127. Springer, Heidelberg (2005)

6. Emura, K., Miyaji, A., Nomura, A., Omote, K., Soshi, M.: A Ciphertext-Policy Attribute-Based Encryption Scheme with Constant Ciphertext Length. In: Bao, F., Li, H., Wang, G. (eds.) ISPEC 2009. LNCS, vol. 5451, pp. 13–23. Springer, Heidelberg (2009)

7. Cheung, L., Newport, C.: Provably secure ciphertext policy ABE. In: Proc. ACM Conference on Computer and Communications Security (CCS), pp. 456–465 (2007)

8. Lai, J., Deng, R.H., Li, Y.: Fully Secure Cipertext-Policy Hiding CP-ABE. In: Bao, F., Weng, J. (eds.) ISPEC 2011. LNCS, vol. 6672, pp. 24–39. Springer, Heidelberg (2011)

9. Boneh, D., Waters, B.: Conjunctive, Subset, and Range Queries on Encrypted Data. In: Vadhan, S.P. (ed.) TCC 2007. LNCS, vol. 4392, pp. 535–554. Springer, Heidelberg (2007)

10. Boneh, D., Goh, E.-J., Nissim, K.: Evaluating 2-DNF Formulas on Ciphertexts. In: Kilian, J. (ed.) TCC 2005. LNCS, vol. 3378, pp. 325–341. Springer, Heidelberg (2005)

11. Kapadia, A., Tsang, P.P., Smith, S.W.: Attribute-based publishing with hidden credentials and hidden policies. In: Proc. Network and Distributed System Security Symposium (NDSS), pp. 179–192 (2007)

12. Goyal, V., Jain, A., Pandey, O., Sahai, A.: Bounded Ciphertext Policy Attribute Based Encryption. In: Aceto, L., Damgård, I., Goldberg, L.A., Halldórsson, M.M., Ingólfsdóttir, A., Walukiewicz, I. (eds.) ICALP 2008, Part II. LNCS, vol. 5126, pp. 579–591. Springer, Heidelberg (2008)

13. Herranz, J., Laguillaumie, F., Ràfols, C.: Constant Size Ciphertexts in Threshold Attribute-Based Encryption. In: Nguyen, P.Q., Pointcheval, D. (eds.) PKC 2010. LNCS, vol. 6056, pp. 19–34. Springer, Heidelberg (2010)

14. Zhou, Z., Huang, D.: On efficient ciphertext-policy attribute based encryption and broadcast encryption. In: Proc. ACM Conference on Computer and Communications Security (CCS), pp. 753–755 (2010)

15. Yu, S., Ren, K., Lou, W.: Attribute-based content distribution with hidden policy. In: Proc. Workshop on Secure Network Protocols (NPSEC), pp. 39–44 (2008)

16. Waters, B.: Ciphertext-Policy Attribute-Based Encryption: An Expressive, Efficient, and Provably Secure Realization. In: Catalano, D., Fazio, N., Gennaro, R., Nicolosi, A. (eds.) PKC 2011. LNCS, vol. 6571, pp. 53–70. Springer, Heidelberg (2011)

17. Waters, B.: Dual System Encryption: Realizing Fully Secure IBE and HIBE under Simple Assumptions. In: Halevi, S. (ed.) CRYPTO 2009. LNCS, vol. 5677, pp. 619–636. Springer, Heidelberg (2009)

18. Boneh, D., Franklin, M.: Identity-Based Encryption from the Weil Pairing. In: Kilian, J. (ed.) CRYPTO 2001. LNCS, vol. 2139, pp. 213–229. Springer, Heidelberg (2001)
19. Ostrovsky, R., Sahai, A., Waters, B.: Attribute-based encryption with non-monotonic access structures. In: Proc. ACM Conference on Computer and Communications Security (CCS), pp. 195–203 (2007)
20. Sandhu, R.S., Coyne, E.J., Feistein, H.L., Youman, C.E.: Role-based access control models. Computer 29(2), 38–47 (1996)
21. Katz, J., Sahai, A., Waters, B.: Predicate Encryption Supporting Disjunctions, Polynomial Equations, and Inner Products. In: Smart, N.P. (ed.) EUROCRYPT 2008. LNCS, vol. 4965, pp. 146–162. Springer, Heidelberg (2008)
22. Balu, A., Kuppusamy, K.: Ciphertext policy attribute based encryption with anonymous access policy. International Journal of Peer-to-Peer networks (IJP2P) 1(1), 1–8 (2010)
23. Li, J., Ren, K., Zhu, B., Wan, Z.: Privacy-Aware Attribute-Based Encryption with User Accountability. In: Samarati, P., Yung, M., Martinelli, F., Ardagna, C.A. (eds.) ISC 2009. LNCS, vol. 5735, pp. 347–362. Springer, Heidelberg (2009)
24. Lewko, A., Okamoto, T., Sahai, A., Takashima, K., Waters, B.: Fully Secure Functional Encryption: Attribute-Based Encryption and (Hierarchical) Inner Product Encryption. In: Gilbert, H. (ed.) EUROCRYPT 2010. LNCS, vol. 6110, pp. 62–91. Springer, Heidelberg (2010)
25. Boneh, D., Boyen, X., Shacham, H.: Short Group Signatures. In: Franklin, M. (ed.) CRYPTO 2004. LNCS, vol. 3152, pp. 41–55. Springer, Heidelberg (2004)
26. Ren, Y., Gu, D., Wang, S., Zhang, X.: Anonymous Identity-Based Encryption scheme without Random Oracles. Journal of University of Science and Technology of China (to appear, 2012) (in Chinese)

MashStudio: An On-the-fly Environment for Rapid Mashup Development

Jianyu Yang, Jun Han, Xu Wang, and Hailong Sun

School of Computer Science and Engineering,
Beihang University, Beijing, 100191 China
{yangjy,hanjun,wangxu,sunhl}@act.buaa.edu.cn

Abstract. Mashup is a new application development pattern that integrates different resources such as data, service or api to construct application. Despite the emergence of mashup platforms like YahooPipes or Popfly, current platforms aim toward users with some programming knowledge. When facing a lot of components in the platform, common users without any programming knowledge always don't know how to begin. MashStudio aims to provide interactive assistance at every step during the development, in order to significantly improve the development efficiency and quality. To achieve this goal, we created a repository with collected mashup process (the composition logic information of a mashup) and analyzed these processes to find meaningful mashup process fragments, which are reusable and will be interactively recommended to users when building mashup. Moreover, MashStudio can provide the function of "just in time compilation" to help user find mistakes in time instead of after accomplished the whole mashup. Finally, the experimental evaluation demonstrates the efficiency and utility of our method.

Keywords: mashup, end user, recommendation, process fragments reuse.

1 Introduction

As a new application development pattern, mashup supports the integration of different resources provided by third parties and available from the Internet to help end user rapidly build personalized application. Meanwhile, with the rapid development of the Web 2.0 technologies, more and more opened user interfaces or web services are published in the Internet. Agenzy[1], a website that combines 8 open APIs provided by Amazon, Brightcove, LinkShare and contrasts products from different suppliers, is a typical application built by mashup technologies. So far, there are about 5800 APIs and 6600 mashup applications listed in ProgrammableWeb[2], from where users can register new mashups and access these data through the Internet freely. YahooPipes[3] provides an online development

---

[1] http://www.agenzy.com/
[2] http://www.programmableweb.com/
[3] http://pipes.yahoo.com/

Y. Xiang et al. (Eds.): IDCS 2012, LNCS 7646, pp. 160–173, 2012.
© Springer-Verlag Berlin Heidelberg 2012

tool to help users build their own applications on the web, and almost 36,000 mashups have been created with this tool. Moreover, with the development of mobile Internet, mobile terminals become more powerful than before, and more people are willing to use mobiles for its portability, people can access Internet with mobile at anytime and anywhere. All these make mobile terminal become a new platform for all kinds of applications.

Currently, many existing popular mashup editors like YahooPipes, Microsoft Popfly[4], IBM Damia[5] can further make it easy for end users to build mashup applications through simple direct drag and drop manipulation or UI operator components. Yet, although these advances in graphical development environment, building a mashup application with the above editors is still not easy for end users, especially for the users who just begin to use these editors and don't familiar with the details. Facing with many different modules in the editor, users have to perform some unpleasant steps when building mashup applications, such as finding a suitable module for their situational needs, reading its specification and figuring out the parameters. Even so, users may still make some mistakes like connecting unmatched modules together, and they always don't realize this situation during development. Finally, when accomplished the mashup, they may found that the mashup application can't give the right results as their expectations, but locating the mistakes in the complex mashup process is a difficult task for end users.

To figure out the above problems, we build an on-the-fly development environment, named MashStudio, that can provide design-time assistance by recommending connectable components or process fragments to end-user and making in time response to give correctness verification in every step. By leveraging the power of collective intelligence, MashStudio collected real mashups from the Internet, we created a repository to analyze the internal structure of the collected mashups and compute the connectable components based on a probabilistic model. Compare with other mashup tools, MashStudio has the following four features which make it more efficient and convenient for end-user.

1. Unicursal Development. To simplify the development and improve development efficiency, MashStudio provide design-time assistance at every step. After dragging and dropping a component, the user just needs to click current component, MashStudio will interactively return a list of recommended items, and the alternative items will be classified and ranked for the users' convenience. The user just needs to click the required item, it will be automatically connected to current partial mashup process. The whole development procedure just like painting a unicursal, what the users need to do is no more than "select" and "click".

2. On-the-fly Development. To detect potential errors without delay, MashStudio don't distinguish design-time and run-time. That is to say, MashStudio can get the intermediate state and validate the correctness of the user's action

---

[4] http://www.popfly.com/Overview/

[5] http://www.damia.alphaworks.ibm.com/

in real time, and it may alert user whenever user makes mistakes. If not the on-the-fly environment, when the user accomplished the whole mashup, he may find that the mashup can't execute at all, but locating this bug and repairing this complex mashup process may be not that easy.

3. Process Fragment Reuse. As we all know, reusing existing mashups that basically match user's need is much easier than creating the whole mashup application from scratch. On the other hand, reusing process fragment and considering the fragment as a single component will significantly reduce the complexity of the mashup process, meanwhile the development efficiency will been significantly improved.

4. Develop on PC and Use on Mobile. With the development of mobile Internet and mobile devices, people can access Internet at anytime and anywhere, which brings great convenience for people's lives. So we combine the traditional personal computer and mobile device together, users can build their own mashup applications on PC and access them from their mobile devices freely. MashStudio provides programming interfaces for third-party devices. When accessing mashup application from mobile, MashStudio's background engine will execute this mashup and return the result.

The rest of this paper is organized as follows. Section 2 describes a typical scenario to illustrate the features mentioned above. Section 3 gives a detailed description of our approach. In Section 4, we will evaluates MashStudio with experiments. Related works are summarized in Section 5. Finally, we will conclude with future works in Section 6.

2   Motivation Scenario

We describe a typical scenario to illustrate how MashStudio provide assistances for end users. In this scenario, Tom is a sports fan, he wants to create a mashup application that aggregates sports news RSS information and shows the news on google map. Without MashStudio, Tom has to pick up components such as "fetch feed", "google map", "extract location" and "union", and then connects them together to build mashup application. When building the mashup, Tom has to read their specifications to figure out all these components first. However, with MashStudio, the building procedure is much easier:

(1) Tom drags and drops a "google map" component on the edit panel, MashStudio recommends a list of components that can be connected to it.
(2) In the recommended list, Tom finds a "breaking news" component that supports sports information from several famous sports websites. Moreover, this news component also provides coordinate information for map display.
(3) Tom selects the "breaking news" component, then the "breaking news" component automatically connects to "google map".
(4) Tom just wants to see the latest news, so he needs to modify this mashup. He clicks the output point of "breaking news" component, MashStudio recommends a component list.

(5) Tom selects a "sort filter" component to sort the sports news, but mistakenly configures the component parameter to sort news by wrong time format. Because of this component doesn't match "breaking news" component. MashStudio validates Tom's action and alerts him.

(6) Tom reselects "sort by date", and MashStudio automatically connects it to "breaking news".

(7) Then, Tom clicks the "sort filter" component, and selects "truncate" to keep the latest 20 sports news. Then he saves this mashup and access the news from his mobile freely.

In step 2, without MashStudio, Tom has to select interested news sources by himself, and connects them together in appropriate order, then extracts location information. Now MashStudio can help Tom accomplish all these tasks by recommending a single component based upon the information already exist in editor panel and the mashup process repository from real users. Because of replacing the complex task with a single component, the mashup process becomes much simpler. Moreover, MashStudio provides an on-the-fly environment to realize real-time verification. In step 5, Tom can find the mistake in time, rather than waiting until he accomplished the whole mashup.

3   The MashStudio Platform

MashStudio can provide design-time assistance by recommending components based upon the partial process already exist in editor panel and the mashup process repository collecting from real users. So far, we collected 6000 real mashup processes from YahooPipes and analyzed their internal structure to extract meaningful knowledge as the basis for recommendation. The following sections first describe the overall architecture of MashStudio, then explain the details of how to deal with collected data and the recommendation strategy.

3.1   System Architecture

The structure of MashStudio is depicted in Figure 1. The main components of MashStudio include Visual Editor, Data Source Register, Mobile Client Access, Execution Engine, Mashup Repository, and Recommendation Server.

Visual Editor: MashStudio provide a visual drag and drop development environment, the end user can use the visual editor through their browser software to develop their personal mashup applications and save them in server.

Data Source Register: MashStudio provides many kinds of data sources to users, but this may not meet user's need. Therefore, MashStudio provides this browser plugin to scrape the information on the screen when the user browses web pages.

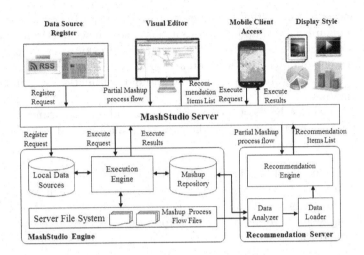

Fig. 1. System Architecture

Mobile Client Access: MashStudio provides access APIs for mobile clients, so users can trigger a request from their mobile phones to execution engine and get the execution results at anytime and anywhere.

Execution Engine: The execution engine can analyze the mashup process, and then access and integrate data in accordance with the process logic. Moreover, whenever users take any action in Visual Editor, the action will be sent to execution engine. The engine will put this change into practice in realtime and return the intermediate results immediately.

Mashup Repository: When the user accomplished the mashup application, the process file of this application will be saved to mashup repository. This repository also provides initial materials for recommendation server to support the recommendation engine.

Recommendation Server: As previously mentioned, MashStudio needs to provide design-time assistance for user, so the response time is very import for user experience. The recommendation server loads the initial data in mashup repository and analyzes them off-line. The recommendation engine is the core of the recommendation server, and it performs a recommendation algorithm to realize rapid recommendation based upon existing partial process.

3.2 The Execution Engine

The execution engine provides support for the on-the-fly environment. It extracts logic information based upon the input mashup process coming from the Mash-Studio Web Server, and then executes the operations in the process according to the logic information. The requests to the engine may come from Visual Editor or Mobile Client, and the purposes of the requests are different. The Visual

Editor needs to get the intermediate data in the editing process to provide assistance for modeling, therefore, the request is in debug mode. However, Mobile Client needs to obtain the final implementation results of the mashup process, so its request is in the execution mode.

The process file to Visual Editor contains UI information and execution logic. First, the execution engine preprocesses the process information to extract logic information and establish the run-time object (MashStudio Execution Object, MEO for short). In fact, MEO is a tree consisted of operator nodes and data flow edge, and it is transferred with XML file. Then the execution engine maps the operator nodes in MEO to a collection of object instances in the memory and analyzes the data flow.

Definition 1. *Data Flow Object (DFO for short): DFO is intermediate data in the flow, and it stands for the edge of the flow. DFO = (Id, Status, Value), where Id is the unique identifier for DFO, Status is the state of the DFO and contains the following three states: 1. Not running, 2. Normal, 3. Exception, Value is the data value of DFO and Value is effective only when the status is 2.*

Definition 2. *Data Operator Object (DOO for short): DOO is executable node in the flow, and it consists of operator nodes that obtain data and process data. DOO = (Id, InFlowSet, OutFlowSet, Type), where Id is the unique identifier for DFO, InFlowSet is a set of input DFO, OutFlowSet is a set of output DFO, Type is the operator object specific type.*

The implementation condition of the DOO depends on the status of the DFOs in InFlowSet. Some DOOs, such as Sort, can't achieve the implementation condition until all the DFOs in InFlowSet have reached status 2, while some others just need status 2 or status 3. As defined above, we can convert the flow into graph G = (Vo, Ef, Vn, Ve)

where $Vo = \{o_i \ (oId, \ oInFlowSet, \ oOutFlowSet, \ oType) \mid oInFlowSet,$ $oOutFlo \in Ef, \ 1 \le i \le n\}$ and Vo is a set of DOO, $Ef = \{f_i \mid f_i \in DFO, \ 1 \le i \le n\}$, $V_n = \{o_i \mid o_i \in Vo, 1 \le i \le n\}$ and Vn stands for a set of not running DOOs, $Ve = \{o_i \mid o_i \in Vo, 1 \le i \le n\}$ and Ve stands for a set of running DOOs. Then the execution engine traverses the collection Vo to get the execution path, and the core algorithm of execution engine is described as algorithm 1.

Algorithm 1 searches not-running nodes to check if they satisfy execution condition, and then call the function of execute(O_i,type(O_i)) to execute them until the above process is over. In execution mode, we just need to return the final results of the implementation. But in debug mode, we need to gain the intermediate results and states, so we return DFO collection Ef.

3.3   The Data Analyzer

The data analyzer aims to find meaningful mashup process fragments, which can be recommended as a whole. Elmeleegy et al. in [1] recommend components based upon co-occurrence, because several components always occur together means that they have special relevance.

Algorithm 1. Execution Engine

Input:
    a graph G = (Vo, Ef, Vn, Ve);
1: start:
2: **for** each $O_i \in V_n$ **do**
3:     **if** satisfyExecutionConditions(O_i,type(O_i),InFlowSet(O_i)) **then**
4:         $V_n = V_n - O_i$;
5:         $V_e = V_e \bigcup O_i$;
6:     **end if**
7: **end for**
8: **if** size(V_e) > 0 **then**
9:     **while** size(V_e) > 0 **do**
10:         $V_e \leftarrow V_e - O_i$;
11:         execute(O_i,type(O_i)); // execute not-running DOO nodes;
12:         setDFO(O_i,OutFlowSet(O_i)); // update status and value of DFO in Ef;
13:     **end while**
14:     goto start;
15: **end if**
16: Output G;

We collected 6000 mahup processes from YahooPipes. The data analyzer needs to pre-process these mashups to convert them into our weighted directed graph. Figure 2 shows two mashup applications' structure, and the parts in the dashed line both occur in the two structures. Our goal is to find frequent co-occurrence parts, which we called "clique", in the 6000 mashup processes. First, each kind of component has the unique identifier id, and then we convert the 6000 mashup processes into a weighted directed graph. Figure 3 demonstrates how to convert structure 1 and structure 2 into a weighted directed graph, the attributes on the edges show which structure the record comes from. For example, the attribute < 1, 2 > at the edge of node 1 to node 4 shows that this edge both occurred in structure 1 and structure 2. Then, we process the weighted directed graph in accordance with the following five steps to discover meaningful clique. The five steps can be summed up to algorithm 2.

Definition 3. *The complex weighted directed graph $G = (V, E, A)$, where V is the set of nodes, E is the set of edges, and A is the attributes set at edge set E. For each $e \in E$, $A(e)$: $v_1 \rightarrow v_2$, $< s_1, s_2, s_3 >$. $A(e)$ means edge e is from node v_1 to node v_2 and edge e occurs in structure $s_1 s_2 s_3$, and $Num(A(e))$ is the occurrence number of edge e. For each $v \in V$, $Output(v) = < e_1, e_2, e_3 >$ means node v has output edges $e_1 e_2 e_3$ in the weighted directed graph, and $Input(v) = < e_4, e_5, e_6 >$ means node v has input edges $e_4 e_5 e_6$.*

(1) In this step we set a threshold T, for each $v_i \in V$, BFSGen(G,T,v_i) will execute the bread-first search from v_i to find components that always occur together. If the times that these components occur in the same mashup process is more than T and these components are connected, BFSGen will return them as a domain. Finally BFSGen extracts a domain list $D =< d_1, d_2, \ldots >$, $di \in D$ is a connected domain.

(2) For each $d_i \in D$, we search the leaf nodes V_{leaf} in domain d_i. For every node v in domain d_i, $v \in V_{leaf}$ if only Num(Output(v)) = 0.

(3) In every domain $di \in D$, ReverseTraverse(d_i,v) starts from each leaf node $v \in V_{leaf}$, then traverse the domain d_i along the edges pointing to current node. Each traversal, we can gain a sub-domain, and these sub-domains may contain repeated parts.

(4) In this step, we take the attributes at the edges into account. For each edge e in the sub-domain of step c, if more than half of the occurrences in $A(e) :< s_1, s_2, \ldots >$ are the same, then the edges belong to the same type. After the treatment of ExtractConnectedArea(sub-domain), we divide the sub-domain into different connected areas according to the edges' type.

(5) The set of connected areas obtained from previous step may exist duplicated items. After the operation of duplicate removal, we get the final outputs.

3.4   The Data Loader

To save the recommendation response time, the Data Loader needs to preload the weighted directed graph which we constructed in the section of the data analyzer, as well as the cliques that we have obtained from algorithm 2. In this section we will also accomplish some statistical works and load the statistical results into the memory in advance, in order to further reduce response time delay of the recommendation engine.

3.5   Recommendation Engine

Given the current partial mashup, the recommendation engine will return a list of ordered cliques leveraging on the conditional probability calculation. Due to the preprocessing in the previous section, the candidate components and basic statistical results can be fast retrieved from the data loader. The cliques list L in the data loader is $\{S_1, S_2, \ldots S_k\}$. Now we suppose that the current component is C and the recommendation engine needs to recommend candidate component C^* connected to C, in the meanwhile, the input components connected to C is $\{I_1, I_2, \ldots I_i\}$, the output components connected to C is $\{O_1, O_2, \ldots O_j\}$.

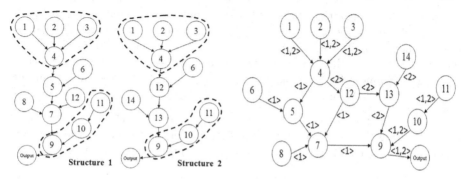

Fig. 2. Mashup Structure   **Fig. 3.** Weighted Directed Graph

---

Algorithm 2. Clique Search
___
Input:
    a weighted directed graph G = (V,E,A) , a threshold T;
1: Init a domain array D, a leaf node set V_{leaf}, a clique array Out;
2: **for** each $v_i \in V$ **do**
3:     connected domain $di \leftarrow BFSGen(G, T, v_i)$;
4:     add d_i to D;
5: **end for**
6: **for** each $d_i(V, E, A) \in D$ **do**
7:     **for** each $v_i \in V$ **do**
8:         **if** Num(Output(v_i))=0 **then**
9:             add v_i to set V_{leaf};
10:         **end if**
11:     **end for**
12:     **for** each $v_j \in V_{leaf}$ **do**
13:         sub-domain(V,E,A)←ReverseTraverse(d_i, v_j);
14:         areasList←ExtractContectedAreas(sub-domain(V,E,A));
15:     **end for**
16: **end for**
17: Out←DuplicateRemoval(areasList);
18: Output Array Out;
___

If $C \in S_i$, that is, C occurred in S_i as a node. Then recommendation engine return the components connected to C in clique S_i. If $C \notin S_i$, we calculate the probability that candidate C^* can be connected to component C as the following inclusion and exclusion principle formula.

$$
\begin{aligned}
&P\left(C^* | \bigcup_{m=1}^{i+j+1} A_m\right) \\
&= \sum_{m=1}^{i+j+1} P\left(C^* | A_m\right) - \sum_{1 \le m1 < m2 \le i+j+1} P\left(C^* | A_{m1} \cap A_{m2}\right) \\
&\quad + \ldots + P\left(C^* | \bigcap_{m=1}^{i+j+1} A_m\right) \\
&= \sum_{m=1}^{i+j+1} (-1)^{m-1} [\sum_{sub \subset \{1,2,\ldots,i+j+1\}, |sub|=m} P\left(C^* | A_{sub}\right)]
\end{aligned} \tag{1}
$$

Suppose $\{A_1, A_2, \ldots A_{i+j+1}\}$ are component collection that contains current component C, input set I connected to C and output set O connected to C.

After obtaining the probability of the candidate C^*, we search the candidate clique Sc in the clique collection $\{S_1, S_2, \ldots S_k\}$ that contains the candidate C^*. There may be several alternative cliques Sc that all contain the candidate C^*. Suppose Sc is consisted of $\{B_1, B_2, \ldots B_n\}$, we use the formula of $P\left(C^* | \bigcup_{m=1}^{i+j+1} A_m\right) * P(\bigcup_{q=1}^{n} B_q | C^*)$ to measure the probability that S_c should be recommended to user given the partial mashup. $P(\bigcup_{q=1}^{n} B_q | C^*)$ has been calculated during the preprocessing in the data loader. Given the partial mashup, recommendation engine uses algorithm 3 to obtain the ordered candidate cliques.

Algorithm 3. Mashup Recommendation

Input:
    a weighted directed graph WDG and cliques collection L;
    current component C and its input components collection I=$\{I_1, I_2, \ldots I_i\}$ output
    components collection O=$\{O_1, O_2, \ldots O_j\}$;

 1: Init a component collection S, a clique array Out1, a clique array Out2;
 2: S←FindConnectedComponentsInWDG(WDG,C);
 3: **for** each *clique* $\in$ L **do**
 4:    **if** isContained (C, clique) **then**
 5:       $Out1 \leftarrow Out1 + clique$;
 6:    **end if**
 7: **end for**
 8: **for** each *component* $\in$ S **do**
 9:    **if** not isIncluded (component,I,O) **then**
10:       **for** each *clique* $\in$ L **do**
11:          *clique.probability* $\leftarrow$ *calculate(component, I, O, C, clique)*;
12:          $Out2 \leftarrow Out2 + clique$;
13:       **end for**
14:    **end if**
15: **end for**
16: sortByProbability(Out2);
17: Obj.array1= Out1;
18: Obj.array2= Out2;
19: Output Obj;

4 Experiments and Results

In this section we will set up several experiments to test the recommendation performance, recommendation accuracy, rank quality, recommendation coverage and diversity to show that MashStudio can provide an effective environment for rapid mashup development.

4.1 Data Sets and Experiment Setup

We collect 6000 real mashup processes from YahooPipes and divide them into two set. One set contains random selected 500 processes and is used as test set, and the rest processes are used as training set. We use the training set as the repository in MashStudio. For each mashup in the test set, we divide the mashup into two parts, and one part is used as experiment input, then we compare the the other part with the candidates that recommended by MashStudio.

The next experiments are run on a DELL desktop computer OPTIPLEX 790 with 3.10GHz Intel Core i5-2400 CPU and 4GB RAM.

4.2 Recommendation Performance

We have described our recommendation algorithm in section 3.4, the recommendation performance is related to the number of the cliques that we discovered in section 3.3, and the number of the cliques is relevant to the mashup repository scale. Figure 4 shows the average running time condition with the growth of the repository scale. Because we have accomplished some statistical works and loaded the statistical results into the memory in advance, the run time is reduced a lot, but further reduce the run time on large scale repository is necessary.

4.3   Recommendation Accuracy

This experiment is carried out to evaluate the recommendation accuracy. We use the test set to evaluate the accuracy. We divide the 500 test mashup into 5 set and every set contains 100 test mashups. As described in section 4.3, we extract partial mashup process from each test mashup as input and use the rest part RP to test our method. We use the following formula to calculate accuracy:

$$\text{Accuracy} = \frac{1}{M} \sum_{i=1}^{M} \frac{N_i}{L} \tag{2}$$

M is the set size (here is 100), L is the length of recommended items list and Ni is the number of the recommended items that are similar to RP. Then we compare the recommended result of MashStudio with random selection. Figure 5 shows that the recommended results of MashStudio are better than random recommendation. Set 4 is significantly less than the others, because MashStudio uses the repository to calculate current user's recommended list, if test set 4 contains specific users who are different from others, it may result in this condition.

4.4   Rank Quality

Rank quality is important for user experience. We carry out the same experiment as section 4.3, we divide the 500 test mashup into 5 set, then extract partial mashup process from each test mashup as input and use the rest part RP to test rank quality. By counting the RP's ranking in the recommended list to evaluate the rank quality. If RP doesn't exist in the list, we consider its ranking as the list length. We use the average rank score formula to evaluate rank quality:

$$\text{RS} = \frac{1}{M} \sum_{i \in testset} \frac{R_i}{L} \tag{3}$$

M is the size of the test set, L is the recommended item list length, Ri is the ranking of the RP in the recommended list (In fact, the recommended item may not exactly the same as RP, we measure the similarity between recommended item and RP with function $S(\alpha, \beta)$, if the similarity is bigger than a threshold, we consider that they are the same). So the smaller RS value means high quality rank. Figure 6 demonstrated that compared with random recommendation, MashStudio improved the rank quality $40.7\% \sim 52.7\%$.

4.5   Recommendation Diversity

In fact, even a recommendation with high accuracy can't ensure that the user will be satisfied with the recommended results. A good recommendation system

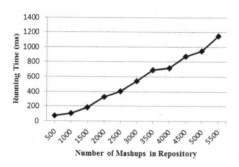

Fig. 4. Recommendation Performance

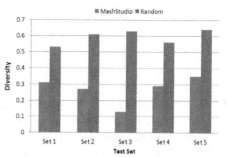

Fig. 5. Recommendation Accuracy

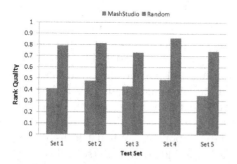

Fig. 6. Rank Quality

Fig. 7. Recommendation Diversity

should supply something new and useful to user. So we bring diversity to measure how many different kinds of items the recommendation system can supply.

$$\text{Div} = \frac{1}{L * (L - 1)} \sum_{\alpha \neq \beta} S(\alpha, \beta) \tag{4}$$

L is the recommendation list length, α and β are different items in the recommendation list, and $S(\alpha, \beta)$ evaluates the similarity between α and β by calculating the different components in them and normalizes the result. Note that $S(\alpha, \beta)$ and $S(\beta, \alpha)$ are equal and we count it twice in the accumulation. Figure 7 illustrates that although MashStudio provides variety of recommended results to some extent, it is still obviously less than random selection. This is because MashStudio always tends to recommend candidates related with current input, and these candidates may have more common parts, while random selection never considers this. In the future, we may make an effort to recommend accurate and diverse results to users, in order to help them create mashup applications with more abundant functions.

5   Related Work

So far, many mashup development tools[2] have been built to provide assistance for non-programmer users, such as YahooPipes, Microsoft PopFly, Intel Mash

Maker and IBM DAMIA. YahooPipes and Microsoft PopFly offer a pipes-like data flow to quickly assemble data feed or other kinds of data sources. Intel Mash Maker[6] provides mashup function as a browser plugin. Mash Maker enables user to create mashup applications when browsing the websites. IBM DAMIA[3][4] is an information integration platform mainly for enterprise users. It offers support to quickly assemble data feeds from the Internet and a variety of enterprise data sources. Other similar platforms also provide visual functions to build mashup applications in various ways, such as Kongdenfha et al.[5] proposed a spreadsheet based web mashup, and Wang et al.[6] use nested tables to construct mashup applications. Recommendation system has been proven an effective way to provide better user experience in many domains like shopping and social network system. But few online mashup development tools, such as mentioned above, can provide recommendation function in the process of building workflow.

In the last several years, a lot of works about mashup recommendation have been done to simplify the mashup development process. Some research efforts focus upon semantic model, such as works in [7][8]. They first build a semantic model based upon annotation in the description and parameters, and then recommend compatible components leveraging on the semantic model. But when the data volume is large, the response real time feature is a big problem. Another related research efforts, such as proposed in [9][10][11], are directed toward the problem of finding connections between the components. When the user provides a set of components, they recommend suitable connector (so-called glue pattern) to connect the components to satisfy user's desire. Elmeleegy et al.[1] recommend components based upon co-occurrence in probability and statistics, because several components always occur together means that they have special relevance. To further simplify data mashup composition, Riabov et al.[12] provide an automatic composition engine and allows users to select tags to describe their goals, then the engine will automatically generates candidate mashups for preview. The users iteratively change the desired tags to refine their wishes until they get the satisfied results. The work presented in [13] integrates the APIs by surfing a web of data APIs to construct mashup process.

Although the above recommendation systems simplify the complexity of the mashup creation procedure in a way, they overlooked that the most users neither received any training nor the domain experts. MashStudio introduces a design-time recommendation mechanism to recommend process fragment, rather than single component, to help user rapidly construct mashup application. MashStudio also provides an on-the-fly environment to validate user's action in time. These mechanisms are significantly different from the other mashup platforms.

6 Conclusion and Future Work

This paper proposed a mashup development platform to provide design-time assistance for end user. The key attributes of this paper lie in the following several points. Firstly, we take the mashup process fragment into account, and

---

[6] http://mashmaker.intel.com/

recommend meaningful fragments to user to improve the development efficiency. Secondly, we provide an on-the-fly environment to validate the correctness of the user's action in real time, in order to help user realize the bug in time rather than accomplishing the whole mashup process. Finally, we introduce the mode of developing mashup on PC and using it on mobile. There is however some future works to be done to improve MashStudio, such as considering the semantic factor to further improve the accuracy of the recommendation; on the other hand, we may make an effort to supply accurate and diverse recommendation to bring something new to user. To further optimize the recommendation performance on large scale repository is also what we want to do in the future.

References

1. Elmeleegy, H., Ivan, A., Akkiraju, R., Goodwin, R.: Mashup advisor: A recommendation tool for mashup development. In: IEEE International Conference on Web Services, ICWS 2008, pp. 337–344. IEEE (2008)
2. Hoyer, V., Fischer, M.: Market Overview of Enterprise Mashup Tools. In: Bouguettaya, A., Krueger, I., Margaria, T. (eds.) ICSOC 2008. LNCS, vol. 5364, pp. 708–721. Springer, Heidelberg (2008)
3. Simmen, D., Altinel, M., Markl, V., Padmanabhan, S., Singh, A.: Damia: data mashups for intranet applications. In: Proceedings of the 2008 ACM SIGMOD International Conference on Management of Data, pp. 1171–1182. ACM (2008)
4. Altinel, M., Brown, P., Cline, S., Kartha, R., Louie, E., Markl, V., Mau, L., Ng, Y., Simmen, D., Singh, A.: Damia: a data mashup fabric for intranet applications. In: Proceedings of the 33rd International Conference on Very Large Data Bases, pp. 1370–1373. VLDB Endowment (2007)
5. Kongdenfha, W., Benatallah, B., Vayssière, J., Saint-Paul, R., Casati, F.: Rapid development of spreadsheet-based web mashups. In: Proceedings of the 18th International Conference on World Wide Web, pp. 851–860. ACM (2009)
6. Wang, G., Yang, S., Han, Y.: Mashroom: end-user mashup programming using nested tables. In: Proceedings of the 18th International Conference on World Wide Web, pp. 861–870. ACM (2009)
7. Carlson, M.P., Ngu, A.H.H., Podorozhny, R., Zeng, L.: Automatic Mash Up of Composite Applications. In: Bouguettaya, A., Krueger, I., Margaria, T. (eds.) ICSOC 2008. LNCS, vol. 5364, pp. 317–330. Springer, Heidelberg (2008)
8. Melchiori, M.: Hybrid techniques for web apis recommendation. In: Proceedings of the 1st International Workshop on Linked Web Data Management, pp. 17–23. ACM (2011)
9. Greenshpan, O., Milo, T., Polyzotis, N.: Autocompletion for mashups. Proceedings of the VLDB Endowment 2(1), 538–549 (2009)
10. Greenshpan, O.: Harnessing data management technology for web mashups development. Proceedings of the VLDB Endowment 2(1), 96–101 (2010)
11. Deutch, D., Greenshpan, O., Milo, T.: Navigating in complex mashed-up applications. Proceedings of the VLDB Endowment 3(1-2), 320–329 (2010)
12. Riabov, A., Boillet, E., Feblowitz, M., Liu, Z., Ranganathan, A.: Wishful search: interactive composition of data mashups. In: Proceeding of the 17th International Conference on World Wide Web, pp. 775–784. ACM (2008)
13. Chen, H., Lu, B., Ni, Y., Xie, G., Zhou, C., Mi, J., Wu, Z.: Mashup by surfing a web of data apis. Proceedings of the VLDB Endowment 2(2), 1602–1605 (2009)

BSU: A Biased Seed Unchoking Algorithm for P2P Systems

Xianglin Wei[1,2], Guomin Zhang[2], Jianhua Fan[1], and Ming Chen[2]

[1] Nanjing Telecommunication Technology Institute, Nanjing 210007, China
[2] Institute of Command Automation, PLA Univ. of Sci. & Tech., Nanjing 210007, China
`wei_xianglin@ieee.org`

Abstract. As the source of the content in P2P systems, the main objective of the seed is to help deliver the content to all peers as soon as possible and to ensure the quality of service of the peers as well as to stimulate them to contribute resources to the system. Recent researches mostly concentrate on either the unchoking algorithms of the leechers or the scheduling algorithms of the seed. In contrast, the unchoking algorithms of the seeds have drawn little attention. Experimental results have shown that the unchoking algorithm of the seeds may have a remarkable impact on the performance of the system, especially when there are a large amount of free-riders in the system. Firstly, a P2P content delivery model based on the fluid model is established in this paper. Secondly, a biased seed unchoking algorithm (BSU) is put forward. Finally, a series of experiments in both homogeneous and heterogeneous environments are conducted to investigate the performance of BSU. Experimental results show that BSU may achieve better performance than existing algorithm used in BitTorrent-like systems remarkably.

Keywords: P2P, Seed, Unchoking algorithm.

1 Introduction

P2P based applications such as file sharing, live streaming and video on demand have been widely deployed and are popular with users due to their higher quality of service than traditional Client/Server model. This makes P2P based content delivery technologies attract continuous attention from the researchers.

Current researches on P2P content delivery mainly focus on such aspects as the promotion of the delivery efficiency, management and security issues. Therefore, peer scheduling becomes an important issue since it is the key component to boost the efficiency of P2P content dissemination. There are two types of peers in the system, i.e. seeds (peers with full content) and leechers (peers with part of or no content). During the content delivery, the seeds and the leechers choose leechers for unchoking firstly (unchoking process), and then decide which pieces to upload for the unchoked leechers (scheduling process). Current researches mainly focus on the scheduling algorithms of the peers and the unchoking algorithm of the leechers. In contrast, the unchoking algorithms of the seeds have drawn little attention. In fact, as the source of

Y. Xiang et al. (Eds.): IDCS 2012, LNCS 7646, pp. 174–187, 2012.

the content, the seeds play the key role during the content delivery process especially in the initial delivery phase [1]. The impact of the seeds' unchoking algorithm is more prominent when there are many free-riders in the system or when the heterogeneity of the peers is obvious. This paper focuses on the seeds' unchoking algorithm in BitTorrent-like systems since BitTorrent is actually one of the most popular P2P applications today.

The current adopted Fair Seed Unchoking (FSU) algorithm (see Section 2 for detail) can to some extent improve the fairness of distribution of the seeds' upload bandwidth as well as constrain the free-riders. However, FSU pays much attention to the download speed of the leechers other than their contribution to the system. In other words, the seed cannot tell free-riders from honest peers if they have similar download speeds. This will impair the efficiency of the delivery. Based on this observation, a novel biased seed unchoking algorithm is proposed in this paper.

The contributions of this paper are threefold. First, a P2P content delivery model based on the fluid model is proposed, and then the impact of the seeds' unchoking algorithm is analyzed. Second, a Biased Seed Unchoking algorithm (BSU) is put forward to promote the performance of the system. Finally, simulation results show that the performance of BSU is better than that of FSU.

The rest of the paper is organized as follows. Section 2 summarizes related work. The P2P content delivery model is built in Section 3. Section 4 introduces BSU. In Section 5 several experiments are conducted to evaluate the performance of BSU. Finally, we conclude our main work and further research in Section 6.

2   Related Work

As reciprocity is not relevant for the seeds, their unchoking algorithm is different from the leechers'. In early versions of BitTorrent [1], seeds simply uploaded to the peers that downloaded the fastest. Since Version 4.0.0 [11, 12] however, a more sophisticated unchoking algorithm is in place to make the seeding process more 'fair' and to reduce free-riding based on available seeding capacity. In this algorithm, a certain number v of random unchoked leechers is spread over three consecutive rounds, again performed in a round-robin fashion. For a particular seed, this number is computed as follows: $v = \lfloor u + 2 \rfloor / 3$, where u is the number of upload slots of the seed. For instance, if $u = 4$, a total of two unchoked leechers are spread over three rounds, i.e., a pattern of 1-1-0 unchoked leechers is followed repeatedly. During each round, the seed allocates its remaining upload slots in the following order: First, all leechers that went from choked to unchoked during the last two rounds remain unchoked; Second, the leftover slots are allocated to the fastest remaining leechers (based on a moving average of their download rate).

The above policy ensures that every three rounds, v new peers are unchoked, and that a peer which is unchoked will stay unchoked for at least three rounds. For the sake of simplicity, this unchoking algorithm of the seeds will be referred to as Fair Seed Unchoking algorithm (FSU) in the following analysis. As mentioned above, FSU cannot ensure the efficiency of the system when there are many free-riders. This is also our motivation in this paper.

3   P2P Content Delivery Model and Problem Formulation

A P2P content delivery model based on fluid model is established firstly, and then the seed unchoking algorithm is analyzed based on it. Then the problem is formulated and an intuitionist example is illustrated in this section.

3.1   A Fluid Model Based P2P Content Delivery Model

3.1.1   Definitions and Notations

Definition 1 (Seed). The seeds refer to those peers which have all the pieces of the content delivered in the system. Other peers except the seeds are referred to as leechers.

Definition 2 (Interested neighbors). A peer's neighbors are those peers who are connected to it. The interested neighbors of a peer are those neighbors who are interested in its pieces.

Definition 3 (Homogeneous and heterogeneous environments). In homogeneous environment, all the leechers have the same upload bandwidths. On the contrary, the leechers have different upload bandwidths in heterogeneous environment.

Definition 4 (Seed unchoking algorithm). A seed unchoking algorithm decides leechers that should be unchoked in each round.

The fluid models are widely adopted in modeling BitTorrent-like file sharing systems [1-3]. Based on these models, we establish a P2P content delivery model here in the heterogeneous environment. The peers are classified into several categories according to their upload bandwidths, and the peers of some particular categories have the same upload bandwidths. Moreover, the upload bandwidths are assumed to be the bottleneck for content delivery. Table 1 contains the notations in our model, which is consistent with the notation in [2][3].

3.1.2   Fluid Model

The number of downloads completed per second in class i is determined by the total upload bandwidth that class i receives from all classes in the swarm, divided by the file size. This can be described in Fig. 1.

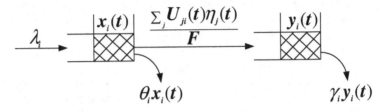

Fig. 1. The fluid model of the leechers and seeds in class i

Therefore, the evolution of $x_i(t)$ and $y_i(t)$ can be described as Formula (1).

Table 1. The notations used in the P2P content delivery model

Symbol	Meaning
μ_i	The upload bandwidth of a peer in class i.
$x_i(t)$	# of leechers in class i at time t.
$y_i(t)$	# of seeds in class i at time t.
$\eta_i(t)$	The upload bandwidth utilization ratio of the peers in class i at time t.
λ_i	The arrival rate of leechers in class i.
γ_i	The rate at which seeders in class i leave the system.
θ_i	The probability that a peer in class i aborts its downloading at time t.
$\omega_{ij}(t)$	The fraction of upload slots of the leechers in class i that is allocated to leechers in class j at time t.
$\sigma_{ij}(t)$	The fraction of upload slots of the seeders in class i that is allocated to leechers in class j at time t.
F	The size of the file being downloaded.
N	The total number of peers' categories in the system.
π_i	The fraction of leechers in class i
μ	The number of upload slots of each peer
Δ_i	The time a seeder in class i stays in the system.
$U_{ij}(t)$	The total upload bandwidth in class i allocated to leechers in class j at time t.

$$\begin{cases} \dfrac{dx_i}{dt} = \lambda_i - \dfrac{\sum_j U_{ji}(t)\eta_j(t)}{F} - \theta_i x_i(t) \\ \dfrac{dy_i}{dt} = \dfrac{\sum_j U_{ji}(t)\eta_j(t)}{F} - \gamma_i y_i(t) \end{cases} \qquad (1)$$

where λ_i is the arrival rate of the leechers, and $\dfrac{\sum_j U_{ji}(t)\eta_j(t)}{F} + \theta_i x_i(t)$ is the departure rate of the leechers. Therefore, $\lambda_i - \dfrac{\sum_j U_{ji}(t)\eta_j(t)}{F} - \theta_i x_i(t)$ is the change rate of the leechers in class i. With similar method, the change rate of the seeds in class i can be drawn.

As the total upload bandwidth of class j allocated to class i consists of the upload bandwidth of the seeders and the upload bandwidth of the leechers, $U_{ji}(t)$ is derived as follows:

$$U_{ji}(t) = (\omega_{ji}(t)x_j(t) + \sigma_{ji}(t)y_j(t))\mu_j \qquad (2)$$

where $\omega_{ji}(t)$ and $\sigma_{ji}(t)$ depend on the specifics of BitTorrent's unchoking algorithm.

3.1.3   Steady State Analysis

Assume that the swarm is in a steady state, i.e., while peers are arriving and departing, the total number of leechers and seeds in each class are constant. In a steady state, Formula (3) holds.

$$\frac{dx_i}{dt} = \frac{dy_i}{dt} \equiv 0 \tag{3}$$

The equilibrium values of $x_i(t)$, $y_i(t)$, $U_{ji}(t)$, $\eta_i(t)$, $\omega_{ij}(t)$ and $\sigma_{ij}(t)$ are denoted by $\bar{x}_i$, $\bar{y}_i$, $\bar{U}_{ji}$, $\bar{\eta}_i$, $\bar{\omega}_{ij}$ and $\bar{\sigma}_{ij}$ respectively. Formula (1) can be reduced to Formula (4):

$$\begin{cases} \lambda_i = \dfrac{\sum_j \bar{U}_{ji}\bar{\eta}_j}{F} + \theta_i \bar{x}_i \\[4mm] 0 = \dfrac{\sum_j \bar{U}_{ji}\bar{\eta}_j}{F} - \gamma_i \bar{y}_i \end{cases} \tag{4}$$

After applying Little's Law to the number of seeders, yielding $\bar{y}_i = \dfrac{\sum_j \bar{U}_{ji}\bar{\eta}_j}{F}\Delta_i$.

Therefore, combining this with Formula (4), it therefore has to hold that $\Delta_i = 1/\gamma_i$.

From Formula (4), Formula (5) and Formula (6) can be obtained.

$$\bar{x}_i = \frac{\lambda_i - \gamma_i \bar{y}_i}{\theta_i} \tag{5}$$

$$\bar{y}_i = \frac{\sum_j \bar{U}_{ji}\bar{\eta}_j}{F\gamma_i} \tag{6}$$

After applying Little's Law to the number of leechers, we have Formula (7).

$$T_i = \bar{x}_i / \lambda_i \tag{7}$$

where T_i is the download time of a leecher in class i.

Combining Formula (5) with Formula (7), Formula (8) can be obtained.

$$T_i = \frac{\lambda_i - \gamma_i \bar{y}_i}{\lambda_i \theta_i} \tag{8}$$

When the abort downloading probability equals to 0, we can apply Little's Law to the number of seeds, yielding $\bar{y}_i = \lambda_i \Delta_i$. Moreover, Formula (4) can be reduced to:

$$\begin{cases} \lambda_i = \dfrac{\sum_j \bar{U}_{ji}\bar{\eta}_j}{F} \\[4mm] \dfrac{\sum_j \bar{U}_{ji}\bar{\eta}_j}{F} = \gamma_i \bar{y}_i \end{cases} \tag{9}$$

Combining Formula (9) with $\bar{y}_i = \lambda_i \Delta_i$ yields

$$\lambda_i F = \sum_j (\bar{\omega}_{ji} \bar{x}_j + \bar{\sigma}_{ji} \lambda_j \Delta_j) \mu_j \bar{\eta}_j \qquad (10)$$

When there is only one class of leechers in the system (i.e. $N=1$), combining Formula (7) with Formula (10), the downloading time can be illustrated as Formula (11).

$$T = \frac{F}{\mu \eta} - \frac{1}{\gamma} \qquad (11)$$

From Formula (11), we can see that the higher η, the lower the downloading time of the system.

3.2   Seed Unchoking: Problem Statement and an Example

3.2.1   Problem Statement
Assume there is only one seed and a number of leechers in the system, and they join the system simultaneously. Given some particular seed S, let S's pieces be $\{P_1, P_2, ..., P_F\}$, and the leechers are referred to as $L_1, L_2, ..., L_C$, where F stands for the number of pieces in system and C is the number of unchoked leechers. The seed unchoking algorithm can be described as the way that deciding which leechers should be unchoked to deliver all the pieces to each leecher as soon as possible.

3.2.2   An example
To help understand the seed unchoking algorithm, typical examples of the seed unchoking algorithms are given in Fig. 2 and Fig. 3 respectively. In Fig. 2 and Fig. 3, S is the seed while L_1 and L_2 are leechers. There are two pieces $\{P_1, P_2\}$ for delivery. In each round, S, L_1 and L_2 can upload 2, 2 and 0 pieces to the system respectively. In Fig. 2 and Fig. 3, S adopts different unchoking algorithm and it will unchoke only one leecher in each round.

In Fig. 2(a), S sends *Have* message to both L_1 and L_2, notifying them it has $\{P_1, P_2\}$. When L_1 and L_2 need the blocks, they tell S that they are *"Interested"* in the pieces in Fig. 2(b). In Fig. 2(c), S decides to unchoke L_2, accepts its requests for $\{P_1, P_2\}$ in Fig. 2(d), and then sends them to it in Fig. 2(e). The second round is composed of Fig. 2 (f), (g), (h), (i) and (j). Notice that in the second round of Fig. 2, L_2 cannot upload any piece to L_1 although it has $\{P_1, P_2\}$ since its upload bandwidth is 0. Moreover, L_1's upload bandwidth cannot be used since it does not have any pieces for uploading. Therefore, L_1 will send request and download $\{P_1, P_2\}$ from S from Fig. 2(f) to Fig. 2(j).

As in Fig. 2(a), S sends *Have* message to both L_1 and L_2, notifying them it has $\{P_1, P_2\}$ in Fig. 3(a). In Fig. 3(b), L_1 and L_2 send *Interested* to S. Unlike those steps from Fig. 2(c) to Fig. 2(e), S unchokes L_1 and uploads $\{P_1, P_2\}$ to it from Fig. 3(c) to Fig. 3(e) in the first round. Therefore, in the second round in Fig. 3, L_1 can upload $\{P_1, P_2\}$ to L_2 since it has $\{P_1, P_2\}$ as well as the upload bandwidth to upload them. Concretely speaking, L_1 sends Have message to L_2 in Fig. 3(f). In Fig. 3(g), L_2 sends *Interested* message to L_1. L_1 unchokes L_2 in Fig. 3(h). L_2 requests pieces to L_1 in Fig. 3(i). L_1 uploads $\{P_1, P_2\}$ to L_2 in Fig. 3(j). Notice that in this unchoking manner, the seed only uploads two pieces to the system in all other than four pieces as it uploads in Fig. 2, and it can leave the system at the end of the first round since there are full pieces in the system. Moreover, the upload bandwidths of L_1 can be utilized during the second round to alleviate the load on the seed S.

Therefore, S can identify those free-rider leechers from honest ones and promote the efficiency of the system if S can obtain the upload bandwidth of the leechers when deciding which leechers for unchoking.

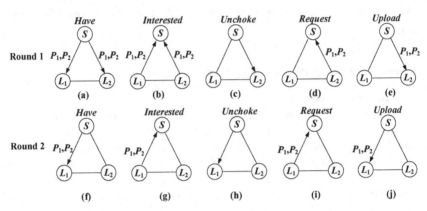

Fig. 2. The first example of the seed unchoking algorithm

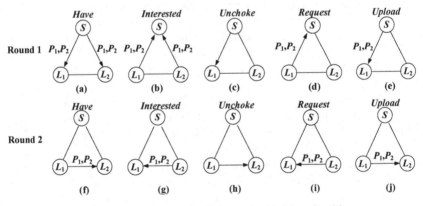

Fig. 3. The second example of the seed unchoking algorithm

4   A Biased Seed Unchoking Algorithm

Inspired by the example in Section 3.2, we introduce a biased seed unchoking (BSU) algorithm in this section. Section 4.1 describes the fundamental idea of BSU. BSU is illustrated in Section 4.2. The complexity analysis of BSU is given in Section 4.3.

4.1   Fundamental Idea

A good seed unchoking algorithm should fulfill three requirements: First, it should make the newly involved leechers be unchoked in time since they do not have any pieces for exchanging with other leechers through Tit-For-Tat policy adopted by Bit-Torrent; Second, it should prefer to unchoke those leechers which upload more pieces to the system to provide to some extent fairness to them as well as to promote the delivery efficiency of the system; Third, to use all the leechers' upload bandwidth as much as possible, it should try to unchoke different leechers in different rounds.

Based on these principles, BSU is proposed in this section. Firstly, BSU will prefer those newly joined leechers to those elder ones to fulfill the first requirement. Secondly, to fulfill the second requirement, BSU will unchoke those peers who upload the most content to the system in priority. Finally, if BSU need to unchoke C leechers, it will choose them from the first ρC ones randomly rather than the first C leechers determinately.

4.2   The Biased Seed Unchoking Algorithm

The pseudo code of BSU algorithm is illustrated in Fig. 4, in which S is the seed and r is the current round. Note that BSU algorithm concentrate on the unchoking algorithm of the seed, leaving the scheduling algorithm of the seed untouched. In the first round, i.e. $r=1$, S unchokes C leechers from its interested neighbors since it has no knowledge of the leechers' contribution to the system. These unchoked leechers are named as S's *unchoking set* U in line 5. In line 6, S records the unchoking time of these leechers as T, and it increases r by 1 in line 7. If $r> 1$, S will remove the eldest leecher from U (i.e. the leecher with the lowest unchoking time) in line 9. Moreover, those c peers who become seeds in the last round will also be deleted from U in line 10 since they are not interested in S's content anymore. After removing the eldest leechers and deleting those leechers who become seeds, S needs to unchoke another $c+1$ leechers and add them to U.

In line 11, S judges whether there are more than $c+1$ leechers in its interested neighbors for unchoking. If there are enough interested neighbors, in line 12, S will further calculate h, i.e. the number of leechers who had never been unchoked before. If h is larger than $c+1$, S will unchoke $c+1$ leechers from these h leechers in line 14, otherwise, S will unchoke all these h leecehrs in line 16 and have to choose $c-h+1$ leechers for unchoking form the leftover g leechers in its interested neighbors. If $\rho \times g \geq c - h + 1$, S will rank these g leechers in descending order according to their contribution to the system and unchoke $c - h + 1$ leechers randomly from the first $\rho \times g$ ($\rho \geq 1$) leecehrs in line 19 and 20, otherwise, S will randomly choose $c - h + 1$ from these g leechers in line 22. If the number of S's interested neighbors is less than $c+1$, S will unchoke all of its interested neighbors in line 26. At last, in line 28, S records the unchoking time for the newly unchoked leechers.

Algorithm 1. Biased Seed Unchoking algorithm, BSU

Input: rechoking time interval T_{rc}, current time T, current round r, the chosen ratio $0 < \rho \leq 1$

Output: current round r

1: **if** Re-choking interval time T_{rc} expires **do**

2: // the seed unchoking part

3:   **if** r equals to 1 **do**

4:     S randomly selects C leechers to unchoke from its *interesting neighbors*

5:     These C leechers are referred to as S's *unchoking set* $U=\{L_1,L_2,...,L_C\}$

6:     S records the unchoking time of these leechers as T

7:     $r = r + 1$

8:   **elseif** r is large than 1 **do**

9:     S removes the eldest leecher in U, i.e. the leecher with the lowest unchoking time

10:     S removes c leechers, who become seeds in last round, from U

11:   **if** there are more than $c+1$ leechers in S's *interesting neighbors* **do**

12:       Assume there are h leechers which have not been unchoked before

13:       **if** $h \geq c + 1$

14:         S selects $c+1$ leechers randomly from these h leechers and adds them to U

15:       **else**

16:         S unchokes all these h leechers which have not been unchoked before

17:         Assume there are g choked leechers remain in S' *interesting neighbors*

18:       **if** $\rho \times g \geq c - h + 1$

19:         S ranks these g leechers in an descending order by their upload rate to the system

20:         S unchokes $c - h + 1$ leechers from the first $\rho \times g$ leechers randomly

21:       **else**

22:         S unchokes $c - h + 1$ leechers from all these g leechers randomly and adds them to U

23:       **end if**

24:       **end if**

25:     **else**

26:       S unchokes all the leechers in its *interesting neighbors* and adds them to U

27:   **endif**

28:   The unchoking times of those newly selected leechers are set to be T

29: **endif**

30: **end if**

Fig. 4. The pseudo code of BSU

4.3   Complexity Analysis

In comparison with the original unchoking algorithm, BSU introduces extra $2N$ storage overhead to record all leechers' contributions and unchoking time. In order to obtain a leecehr's contribution or upload bandwidth, there are two feasible ways. On the one hand, the seed can try to download some pieces from the leecher to evaluate its upload bandwidth and its willingness to contribute resources to the system as Smartseed [6] does. On the other hand, S can obtain this information via deploying some reputation mechanism, such as ratio incentive [7] and iRep [8], in which those leechers with the highest reputation will be treated as the ones contributing more resources to the system. In this paper, we focus on the unchoking algorithm, and use the second way in the evaluation of BSU algorithm.

5   Evaluation and Results

In both homogeneous and heterogeneous environments, the performance of BSU algorithm is evaluated based on two sets of experiments, and FSU algorithm is chosen as the comparison benchmarks. Section 5.1 describes the experimental context. The evaluation metrics are illustrated in Section 5.2. Section 5.3 presents the experimental results in both homogeneous and heterogeneous environments.

5.1   Experimental Context

The simulator implemented in literature [5] is used as the basic platform. To fulfill the requirements in this work, BSU and FSU algorithm are implemented on the simulator. Moreover, the arrival process of the peers in the simulator is also modified to flash crowd (i.e. all the peers arrive at the system simultaneously). Besides, an information statistical module is also added to the simulator. The default common parameters are listed in Table 2, which are also the default parameters in mainline BitTorrent version. In order to keep the simulation results similar to the measurement ones [11], the leechers will stay in the system for a random short additional time after downloading completion. N peers arrive at the system simultaneously, in which one peer is the seed and the others are leechers. Each round is set to be 10 seconds.

Table 2. SimulationParameters

Symbol	Meaning	Base Value
N	# of peers	varies
P	# of pieces in the file	varies
U_S	Upload bandwidth of the initial seed	varies
U_{max}	The highest upload bandwidth of the leechers	varies
U_{min}	The lowest upload bandwidth of the leechers	varies
N_{Max}	Maximum number of neighbors	80
N_{Min}	Minimum number of neighbors	20
C	The number of leechers chosen for uploading during each round	4
R_f	The ratio of free-riding peers to total peers in the system	varies
ρ	The chosen ratio	varies

5.2   Evaluation metrics

In order to compare these different algorithms mentioned above, two metrics, i.e. the downloading time and the average downloading time are used, and they are defined as follows.

Downloading Time (DT): The downloading time of a peer i is defined as the time interval between the time it arrives at the system and the time it obtains all the pieces of the content.

Average Downloading Time (ADT): The average downloading time of a system refers to the average value of all the leechers' downloading times in the system.

5.3   Simulation Results

5.3.1   Simulation Results in Homogeneous Environment

Firstly, the downloading time of BSU and FSU algorithms are compared with $N=38$, $F=100$, $U_S = U_{max} = U_{min} = 4$ pieces/round, $\rho = 0.5$, and $R_f=0.1$, 0.2, 0.3 and 0.4 respectively. Under this setting, the results are shown in Fig. 5. The ADTs of these two algorithms are presented in Table 3.

In Fig. 5, the downloading time of the first peer is 0 since it is the initial seed. From Fig. 5, we can see that with various parameter settings, the downloading times of the leechers in BSU algorithm are lower than those in FSU algorithm. And the benefit of BSU algorithm is more prominent as R_f increases from 0.1 to 0.4. Fig. 5 tells us that the ADTs of both FSU and BSU increase as R_f increases. We owe this phenomenon to the fact that large R_f will decrease the total upload bandwidths of the system, which will take more time to deliver the same amount of pieces. Besides, we also compare the ADTs of BSU and FSU algorithms when $R_f = 0$. The ADTs of BSU and FSU are 337.89s and 335s respectively. Therefore, BSU will not sacrifice the performance of the system when there are no free-riding peers.

Table 3. The ADTs of FSU and BSU algorithms in homogeneous environment with various R_f (in second)

ADT Algorithm R_f	FSU	BSU
0.1	362.10	338.42
0.2	382.36	375.26
0.3	470.78	373.15
0.4	514.47	432.36

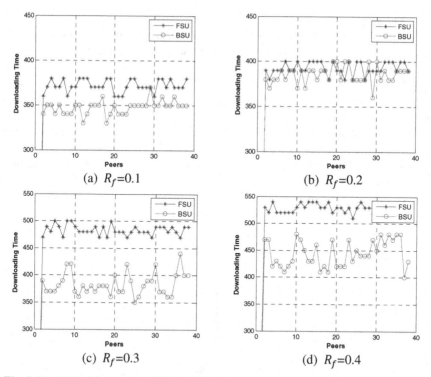

Fig. 5. The DTs of the peers in FSU and BSU in homogeneous environment with various R_f

5.3.2 Simulation Results in Heterogeneous Environment

Firstly, the performance of BSU and FSU algorithm are compared with $N = 38$, $F = 100$, $U_{min} = 4$ pieces/round, $U_S = U_{max} = 8$ pieces/round, $\rho = 0.5$ and $R_f = 0.1$, 0.2, 0.3 and 0.4 respectively. Under this setting, the ADTs of BSU and FSU are listed in Table 4.

As in the homogeneous context, the first peer is the seed whose downloading time is 0. From Table 4, we can obtain similar observations to those in the homogeneous setting. First, the ADTs of BSU with different parameter settings are less than those of FSU algorithm. Second, the benefit of BSU algorithm is more prominent as R_f increases

Table 4. The ADTs of FSU and BSU algorithms in heterogeneous environment with various R_f (in second)

R_f	FSU	BSU
0.1	332.36	310
0.2	342.89	313.11
0.3	400	330.26
0.4	441.57	369.73

5.3.3   The Impact of ρ

From the pseudo code of BSU algorithm, we can see that ρ may influence the performance of BSU. $\rho=1.0$ means that BSU will choose the unchoking leechers from all its interested neighbors randomly which does not constrain the free riders in the system. When $N=38$, $F=2000$, $U_S = U_{max} = U_{min} = 10$ pieces/round, $R_f=0.3$ and $\rho=0.1, 0.2, 0.3, 0.4, 0.5, 0.6, 0.7, 0.8, 0.9$ and 1.0 respectively, Fig. 6 shows the ADTs of the free riders and non free-riders in the system with various ρ.

Fig. 6 tells us that the ADT of the free riders decreases as ρ increases while the ADT of the non free-riders increases as ρ increases. Therefore, in order to provide fairness to the leechers and to promote the efficiency of the system, ρ should neither be too large nor too small.

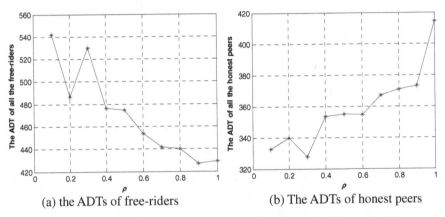

(a) the ADTs of free-riders   (b) The ADTs of honest peers

Fig. 6. The ADTs of free-riders and honest peers with various ρ

6   Conclusion and Future Works

A biased seed unchoking (BSU) algorithm is proposed in the environment where there are many free-riding peers in the system. BSU's designation detail is given and its performance is evaluated in both homogeneous and heterogeneous environments. The evaluation results show that BSU can improve the performance of the system. Moreover, the benefit of BSU algorithm is more prominent as the ratio of free riders of all peers in the system increases.

There are many types of malicious peers in P2P system while this paper focuses on the free riders. In the future, we will take other types of malicious peers into consideration [9].

References

1. Esposito, F., Matta, I., Bera, D., Michiardi, P.: On the impact of seed scheduling in peer-to-peer networks. Computer Networks (2011)
2. Qiu, D., Srikant, R.: Modeling and Performance Analysis of BitTorrent-like Peer-to-Peer Networks. SIGCOMM (September 2004)

3. Meulpolder, M., Pouwelse, J.A., Epema, D.H.J., Sips, H.J.: Modeling and Analysis of Bandwidth-Inhomogeneous Swarms in BitTorrent. IEEE P2P (September 2009)

4. Kamvar, S., Schlosser, M., Garcia-Molina, H.: The EigenTrust Algorithm for Reputation Management in P2P Networks. In: Proc. of the Twelfth International World Wide Web Conference (2003)

5. Al-Hamra, A., Legout, A., Barakat, C.: Understanding the properties of the bittorrent overlay. INRIA, Tech. Rep. (2007), http://arxiv.org/pdf/0707.1820

6. Bharambe, A., Herley, C.: Analyzing and Improving BitTorrent Performance. Technical Report MSR-TR-2005-03, Microsoft Research (2005)

7. Liu, Z., Dhungel, P., Wu, D., Zhang, C., Ross, K.: Understanding and improving ratio incentives in private communities. In: Proc. IEEE Int. Conf. on Distributed Computing Systems (ICDCS), Genoa, Italy (August 2010)

8. Wei, X., Chen, M., Tang, C., Bai, H., Zhang, G., Wang, Z.: iRep: Indirect Reciprocity Reputation based Efficient Content Delivery in BT-like Systems. Telecommunication Systems (accepted)

9. Wei, X., Ahmed, T., Chen, M., Pathan, A.-S.: PeerMate: A malicious peer detection algorithm for P2P Systems based on MSPCA. In: Proc. IEEE Int. Conf. on Computing, Networking and Communications (ICNC), Lahaina, HI, USA (January 2012)

10. BitTorrent, http://www.bittorrent.com

11. Bharambe, A.R., Herley, C., Padmanabhan, V.N.: Analyzing and improving a bittorrent networks performance mechanisms. In: INFOCOM 2006, 25th IEEE International Conference on Computer Communications, pp. 1–12 (April 2006)

12. Cuevas, R., Kryczka, M., Cuevas, A., Kaune, S., Guerrero, C., Rejaie, R.: Is content publishing in BitTorrent altruistic or profit-driven? In: Proceedings of the 6th International Conference (Co-NEXT 2010). ACM, New York (2010)

Towards a Secure and Available Smart Grid Using Intrusion Tolerance

Maryam Tanha and Fazirulhisyam Hashim

Department of Computer and Communication Systems Engineering,
Universiti Putra Malaysia,
43400 UPM Serdang, Selangor, Malaysia
maryam.tanha@ieee.org,fazirul@eng.upm.edu.my

Abstract. In this paper, we propose an intrusion tolerant architecture to enhance the security of smart grid control centers. The proposed architecture is mainly composed of several modules, including replication and diversity, auditing, compromised/faulty replica detector, reconfiguration and proxy. These modules attempt to enhance the service continuity and availability of critical components in smart grid control centers due to far-reaching, economic and destructive effects of failure, malfunction, power brownout or outage on the normal operation of societies. By adopting a combination of proactive and reactive security measures to tolerate and mitigate the impacts of intrusions, the presented intrusion tolerant system shows improved availability in case of DoS attacks when analytically evaluated and compared with two well-known intrusion tolerant architectures.

Keywords: Smart Grid Security, Availability, Intrusion Tolerance, Critical Infrastructure, SCADA.

1   Introduction

The integration of electrical power grid and data communication in a smart grid network introduces various advantages such as greenness, the 2-way communication between energy suppliers and customers, real-time pricing, load shedding and consumption management [1]. Besides these environmental and technical benefits, such integration may expose smart grid to various Information and Communication Technology (ICT) security threats [2-3]. However, maintaining the same level of security as the ICT for smart grid is not sufficient. Smart grid is a critical infrastructure, so its high complexity and heterogeneity may result in new security challenges as well as its societal and economic impacts that mandate a more resilient and durable security level. Owing to its criticality, security requirements for smart grid are normally in reverse order of importance compared to the ICT security properties. In general, availability is regarded as the top security priority in smart grid, whereas message confidentiality and integrity are the principal security properties for ICT [3-4]. Thus, a smart grid should be able to provide services to users even with the existence of network intrusions.

Y. Xiang et al. (Eds.): IDCS 2012, LNCS 7646, pp. 188–201, 2012.

One possible approach to address the aforementioned issues is having an Intrusion Tolerant System (ITS) in the smart grid. Unlike Intrusion Detection System (IDS) and Intrusion Prevention System (IPS) where their principal operation is to detect and prevent an intrusion from happening, intrusion tolerance is associated with the fact that intrusions are viable to happen even in a protected system. Hence, intrusion tolerance offers a complementary solution for conventional security approaches, i.e., IDS, and IPS. Intrusion Tolerance usually comes on the scene when the fundamental security mechanisms are unable to handle a security problem. In addition, intrusion tolerance provides self-healing capabilities (e.g., by proactive recovery) and resilience to intrusions along with a way to achieve survivability, which is a key feature for smart grid. Since the prime goal of intrusion tolerance is to maintain service despite the presence of intrusions in the system, attacks are tolerated to a certain extent to secure the system while some remedial measures are taken to eliminate the adverse effects of intrusions. Nevertheless, it should be noted that intrusion tolerance techniques may incur considerable costs, so they should be applied to critical components in the smart grid such as control centers. Due to the pivotal role of the control centers in real-time data analysis, control and monitoring of the smart grid, any malfunction of them would lead to adverse effects on the operation of the entire grid.

To the best of our knowledge, the significance of intrusion tolerance for smart grid has only been pointed out in [5]. However, a taxonomy of various existing ITSs for communication systems, their capabilities and differences has been provided in [6]. Several intrusion tolerance components such as redundancy, diversity, rejuvenation, voting, and their respective applications have been covered in [7-9].

In order to highlight the significance of intrusion tolerance as a promising security approach for smart grid, we propose an ITS architecture for securing smart grid control centers, in particular Supervisory Control and Data Acquisition (SCADA) systems. Our proposed ITS architecture incorporates the best features and components of several existing ITSs to make it more tailored to be employed in the smart grid control systems. Then, we model the proposed ITS architecture using a Discrete Time Semi Markov Model (DTSMM) and compare its performance with two existing ITSs.

The remainder of this paper is organized as follows: Section 2 provides an overview of smart grid network and its cyber security issues. Details of the proposed ITS architecture are described in Section 3. The theoretical framework of the proposed ITS is presented in Section 4, while Section 5 presents the results, discussion and comparison with other ITSs. Finally, we conclude the paper in Section 6.

2   Smart Grid and Intrusion Tolerance

2.1   Smart Grid Architecture

The existing electricity grid is composed of three distinct functions: generation, transmission and distribution. Once electricity is generated by power plants it flows through high-voltage transmission lines to local electricity distributors, known as substations. Substations then transform electricity into a medium/low voltage and send it through local distribution lines to industrial, commercial, and residential consumers. Generally, electricity must be generated and consumed almost instantaneously because large amounts of electricity cannot be easily stored [4].

Considering the large communication networks that will exist in the smart grid, most of existing technical papers have emphasized that a smart grid network, in particular the consumption part should be composed of a three-layer network, namely, Home Area Network (HAN) or Business Area Network (BAN), Neighborhood Area Network (NAN), and Wide Area Network (WAN) [4]. As illustrated in Fig. 1, WAN serves as the communication backbone to transmit control and monitoring signals and commands from control centers, SCADA and Energy Management System (EMS) in particular, to electric devices located in substations and also the real-time measurements from electric devices to the control centers. It adopts various broadband wired (e.g., fiber) and wireless (e.g., WiMAX, Wireless LAN) communication technologies. WAN covers several NANs each formed under one substation. NANs (using communication technologies such as Wireless Sensor Network and Wireless Mesh Network) undertake the task of exchanging and sharing information between electricity distribution facilities and consumers premises in smart grid. Each NAN consists of a number of HANs or BANs that are geographically near to each other. Concentrators which collect data from HANs are considered as the point of vulnerability in NANs. HANs (using communication technologies such as 802.15 Zigbee) provide the new functionalities such as demand response in smart grid through the use of smart meters.

2.2   Intrusion Tolerance in Smart Grid

Availability is generally recognized as the most critical security goal due to its greatest impact on the grid reliability [3-4]. This arises from two main factors, namely service continuity and delay sensitivity. The widespread, destructive and economic consequences of service interruption in the power grid, render availability to be the top priority. Moreover, messages transmitted through the smart grid system are time-sensitive in contrast with the Internet in which the data throughput receives special attention.

Although various levels of intrusion tolerance are required in different parts of the smart grid information and communication infrastructure, such a mechanism may impose extra expenses to smart grid communication infrastructure. No expense is spared in developing stringent and resilient security technologies such as intrusion tolerance for the smart grid. However, we believe the intrusion tolerance should be at least applied to the most critical elements of smart grid such as the control centers. Control centers act as the heart of the smart grid. They include SCADA and EMS as main components. The SCADA is a distributed measurement and control system responsible for data collection, control and real-time monitoring of the electricity delivery network. The EMS is a system of computer-aided tools utilized by power grid operators for monitoring, control, and optimization of the performance of the generation and/or transmission

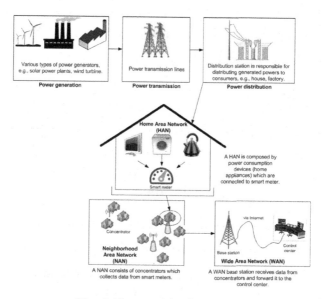

Fig. 1. Smart grid infrastructure

system [10]. Any failure, impairment or abnormal behavior of these two systems will lead to devastating impacts on the operation of the whole power grid and subsequently will affect the industries and societies (e.g., power outage).

In this paper, we place an emphasis on intrusion tolerance for strengthening the security of SCADA systems in smart grid control centers. Therefore, an ITS architecture is proposed and delineated in the following section.

3   The Proposed ITS Architecture

The proposed ITS for SCADA systems in smart grid adopts several working principles from existing ITS architectures, namely Scalable Intrusion Tolerant Architecture (SITAR) [11] and Self-Cleansing Intrusion Tolerance (SCIT) [12]. In contrast to SITAR which is detection triggered, and SCIT which is recovery based [6], our proposed ITS is adaptive and can be considered as a hybrid model, and therefore it somehow inherits the advantages of these two ITSs. As illustrated in Fig. 2, the proposed system consists of five ITS modules, namely replication and diversity module, auditing module, compromised/faulty replica detector module, reconfiguration module and proxy module. The aforementioned modules and their constitutive sub modules will be discussed in the following subsections.

3.1   Replication and Diversity Module

Redundancy is a fundamental technique which enables the designation of additional resources to a system beyond its requirement in normal operating conditions [7]. Replication is a kind of redundancy which involves physical resource

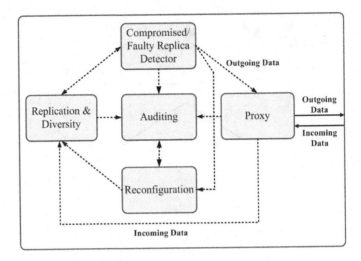

Fig. 2. The proposed intrusion tolerant system architecture

redundancy or the replication of entities in the network to resist faults or intrusions [8]. So, replication module consists of a number of replicas for a critical entity in the SCADA systems of the smart grid such as Master Terminal Unit (MTU). Based on byzantine fault tolerant design, the number of replicas should be $2f + 1$ to tolerate f intrusions. In this module, the number of replicas is assumed to be $2f + 1 + k$ and the value of f and k are indicated in the deployment time. This approach (for the number of replicas) also used in [13] to design a distributed firewall-like protection device named Crutial Information Switch (CIS). The reason why the value of k is added to the number of replicas will be explained in the reconfiguration module section. These replicas have diversity in the operating system. Diversity serves as a complementary intrusion tolerance technique to redundancy for precluding the replicas from facing the same fate [8] and increasing the robustness of the system. For instance, we have adopted operating system diversity. Due to the fact that different vulnerabilities are associated with various operating systems, the probability of being infected by the same attack for the replicas is reduced.

3.2   Compromised/Faulty Replica Detector Module

Compromised/faulty replica detector module aims at carefully examinning the replicas to identify possible faulty ones with the assistance of its three sub modules, including file integrity checker module, acceptance monitor and voting module. This module assissts in identifying and handling attacks both from inside or outside. For instance, if an authenticated but malcious operator (i.e., a malicious insider) tries to infect one or more replicas with a trojan, it is possible that the intrusion detected by the file integrity checker (using detection capabilities) or the voting sub module (due to the fact that the replicas have different operating systems, all of them may not be infected by the same trojan targetted at a special type of vulnerability, and thus the generated responses would be different).

1. File integrity checker: This sub module acts as an intrusion detection system to spot the defective critical system files on the active replicas. This can be achieved through a challenge-response protocol. It keeps records of corresponding responses computed with regard to the challenges for crucial files of each replica. Then, on a periodic basis, random challenges are sent to active replicas and the received responses are compared with the stored ones for each file. More details on the mentioned challenge-response mechanism can be found in [14]. Following the identification of suspected replicas, the file integrity checker signals the reconfiguration module.

2. Acceptance monitor: Acceptance testing is a programmer or developer-provided error detection function in a software module to examine the reasonableness of the generated results [7]. This technique along with other application-specific checks are carried out with regard to the security policy to ensure the sanity of outgoing data from the replicas. Any signs of security compromise will signal the reconfiguration module.

3. Voting: The purpose of this sub module is to mask the impacts of intrusions as a way to withstand them as well as ensuring the integrity of data [7]. It is based on a voting algorithm and seeks for the correct response by comparing the redundant responses from the active replicas that passed the acceptance monitor successfully. It attempts to reach a consensus on the final appropriate and desired output to be passed to the proxy module. This output can be a command or information from the SCADA critical components destined for a particular field device in smart grid.

3.3   Reconfiguration Module

Reconfiguration module comprises of two sub modules namely, automatic rejuvenation and manual restoration. When the proposed ITS is able to mask an intrusion, it leverages the automatic rejuvenation sub module, otherwise it takes advantage of manual restoration which involves human intervention. The latter happens when for instance the system is targeted by DoS attacks and only capable of provisioning the essential services (graceful degradation). The sub modules descriptions are as follows:

1. Automatic rejuvenation: It involves the restoration of a replica to a pristine state to eliminate the likely effects of intrusions or faults. It enables the rejuvenation of at most k (determined at design time) replicas at the same time. A combined rejuvenation approach (i.e., proactive-reactive recovery) will enhance the performance of the system through decreasing the possible duration of time a compromised replica may disrupt the normal operation of the system [9]. Proactive rejuvenation assists in the identification of dormant faults or masking intrusions and should be conducted frequently sufficient to restrain the adversary from infecting more than f (the number of faulty

replicas that can be tolerated by the system) replicas during a recovery period. It is performed periodically through choosing an active replica based on a round robin algorithm. Note that only one replica can be under proactive recovery at a time. Reactive rejuvenation complements the proactive recovery by speeding up the process of handling compromised replicas. It is triggered by compromised/faulty replica detector module. As it has been mentioned earlier, since only one replica can be under proactive recovery at a time, the maximum potential number of available replicas for reactive recovery can be k-1. The number of concurrent rejuvenations (i.e., k) should be added to the number of replicas (i.e., $2f+1$) that conforms to byzantine fault tolerant design. Thus, the availability of the system will not be affected by the rejuvenation process.

2. Manual restoration: As stated before, this sub module is triggered when the detected intrusion is non-maskable (e.g., more than f replicas have been compromised). This may cause the system to be in graceful degradation mode, stopped functioning mode or complete failure mode all of which require manual restoration and corrective measures to return the system to the normal working state.

3.4   Auditing Module

This module maintains audit logs for all modules as well as it procures information associated with the state of replicas (e.g., last rejuvenation timestamp and current status of the replica whether active or under recovery) to be used or updated by rejuvenation module. The logs would be useful for security administrator to monitor and analyze the operation of the system.

3.5   Proxy Module

Proxy module is placed on the boundary of the ITS architecture where the data comes in or goes out. The proxy module shields the internal structure of the ITS from attackers as well as acting as a load balancer. When the state information of field devices or power usage data collected by smart meters gathered in field devices passed to the respective critical components in the control center, it goes through the proxy module as the first layer of defense. The incoming data is then forwarded to the replication and diversity module to be dealt with. Proxy module is composed of several proxies located in different virtual machines that have diversity in their operating systems and are managed by a controller. Proxies can have three modes, namely online, offline, and cleansing. The number of online (i.e., active) proxies can be one or more based on the decision of the controller. Depending on a defined exposure time for proxies and a round-robin algorithm, the controller deals with the rotation and changing turn between proxies [6]. When the exposure time requirement for a proxy is met, it will go through the rejuvenation process (or cleansing process) and will be in cleansing mode. Then, its mode will be altered to offline mode and it will be ready to be chosen by the controller to go online.

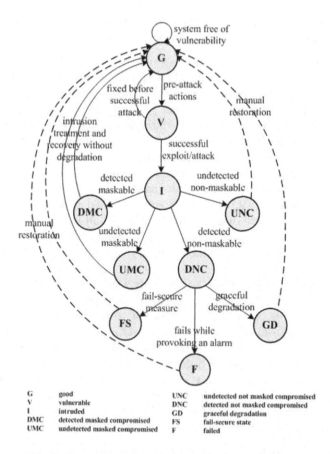

Fig. 3. State transition diagram for the proposed ITS

G	good	UNC	undetected not masked compromised
V	vulnerable	DNC	detected not masked compromised
I	intruded	GD	graceful degradation
DMC	detected masked compromised	FS	fail-secure state
UMC	undetected masked compromised	F	failed

4   System Model

In this paper we model the proposed ITS architecture using State Transition Diagram (STD) [15], as illustrated in Fig. 3. Then, by using the STD we derive the availability performance of the proposed ITS using a DTSMM.

4.1   State Transition Diagram

A system free of vulnerabilities is envisaged as being in good state G. During probing and scanning the system, the identification of vulnerabilities, makes it possible for an adversary to overcome prevention and detection mechanisms, and violate the systems security policy. Consequently, the system state changes from good state G to vulnerable state V. Even if the system possesses potential vulnerabilities that may be abused by the malicious intent, it can be considered as being in the vulnerable state. Discovering a vulnerability (i.e., before an intrusion) and subsequently fixing it brings the system from state V into state G.

Successful exploitation of a vulnerability will result in an intruded state I. At state I, there are four feasible transitions to other states:

1. If the intrusion tolerance techniques employed in the ITS fail to detect the occurrence of the intrusion and mitigate the impacts of an attack (i.e., mask the attack's impacts), the system enters the state UNC (i.e., undetected not masked compromised) with no service guarantee.
2. If the intrusion is detected and the intrusion tolerance techniques succeed in masking the attack's impact, the state of the system will change from I to DMC (i.e., detected masked compromised). In this state, the intrusion is handled by compromised/faulty replica detector module.
3. If the intrusion goes undetected but masked through proactive recovery, a transition to state UMC (i.e., undetected masked compromised) is made. This is where our state diagram differs from [15] in which the ITS architecture did not provide proactive recovery. Subsequently, restoration without any service degradation enables reaching the state G from states UMC or DMC.
4. The last possible transition is to the state DNC (i.e., detected not masked compromised) when an intrusion is identified but the containment of the damage fails. It is possible for an attacker to be able to compromise more than f replicas (e.g., in case of a DoS attack). This may result in complete system failure (transition from DNC to F) or non-failure states (i.e., GD or FS). In GD (i.e., graceful degradation) state the system is only able to provide essential services which might have different definitions in various systems whereas in FS (i.e., fail-secure) state the system would stop functioning. Note that transitions from F, GD, FS and UNC to the state G would involve manual restoration and corrective maintenance.

For the benefits of readers, we explain the proposed ITS by a working example. Assume a possible attack scenario in which an attacker has gained unauthorized access to SCADA system in smart grid, and has compromised one or more replicas of a critical component (recall that the number of compromised replicas are less than or equal to f). Thus, he/she would be able to issue control commands. It is also possible that the adversary makes the replica work not properly (e.g., by running a Trojan or changing some system files) which may result in sending inappropriate commands (in case of automatic operation). However, the command must first pass the compromised/faulty replica detector. It is highly probable that the compromised replica(s) being recognized by voting module or file integrity checker, so the command will not go further and the infected replicas will undergo reactive recovery. Even if the intrusion tolerance mechanisms fail to detect the intrusion, it is possible that the attack's impact is masked through proactive recovery.

4.2   Availability Analysis in Case of DoS Attacks

Denial of Service (DoS) attack is one of the most prevalent attacks targeted at the availability of SCADA systems. DoS attack usually attempts to saturate or consume the victims' resources to disrupt the service which may have adverse consequences for critical infrastructures such as smart grid. Thus, the availability analysis of the intrusion tolerant system in the presence of this security compromise is of great importance.

The STD in Fig. 3 serves as a generic tool to study the behavior of adversaries as well as the system's response. As stated in [15], in the event of DoS attacks, the states DMC and FS are not included in the ITS's reaction to the compromise. This is due to the fact that masking the effects of DoS is not possible through the redundancy, diversity or voting techniques. Also, bringing the system to the state FS would preclude it from functioning which in turn assists the DoS attack to achieve its goal. Therefore, by using a reduced form of the STD presented in Fig. 3, a DTSMM with a discrete state space $X_s = \{$G, V, I, UMC, DNC, UNC, GD, F$\}$ is derived for quantitative analysis of the steady-state availability [15-16].

In this paper, we define the steady-state availability A as the probability that the ITS is in one of normal functioning states. Since the system is unavailable in the states F and UNC, thus, the steady-state availability A can be formulated as,

$$A = 1 - (\pi_{UNC} + \pi_F) \tag{1}$$

where $\pi_i, i \in \{$UNC, F$\}$ denotes the steady-state probability of being in state i for the semi Markov process. This steady state probability can be computed as,

$$\pi_i = \frac{\nu_i h_i}{\Sigma \nu_j h_j}, \quad i, j \in X_s \tag{2}$$

where h_i indicates the mean state holding time in state i (i.e., the time the system spends in state i) and ν_i denotes the embedded Discrete Time Markov Chain (DTMC) steady-state probability in state i. We derive ν_is from the following two equations,

$$\nu = \nu \cdot P \tag{3}$$

$$\sum_i \nu_i = 1, \quad i \in X_s \tag{4}$$

where P is the transition probability matrix of the corresponding DTMC for the proposed ITS,

$$
P =
\begin{array}{c}
\\
G \\
V \\
I \\
UNC \\
UMC \\
DNC \\
GD \\
F
\end{array}
\begin{array}{c}
\begin{array}{cccccccc}
G & V & I & UNC & UMC & DNC & GD & F
\end{array} \\
\left(
\begin{array}{cccccccc}
0 & 1 & 0 & 0 & 0 & 0 & 0 & 0 \\
1-p_I & 0 & p_I & 0 & 0 & 0 & 0 & 0 \\
0 & 0 & 0 & p_{UN} & p_{UM} & p_{DN} & 0 & 0 \\
1 & 0 & 0 & 0 & 0 & 0 & 0 & 0 \\
1 & 0 & 0 & 0 & 0 & 0 & 0 & 0 \\
0 & 0 & 0 & 0 & 0 & 0 & p_{GD} & p_F \\
1 & 0 & 0 & 0 & 0 & 0 & 0 & 0 \\
1 & 0 & 0 & 0 & 0 & 0 & 0 & 0
\end{array}
\right)
\end{array}
$$

In this paper, the mean state holding times h_i for all the states of DTMC have been assumed to have the same values as [15] except for the state UMC which is a new state (corresponding to proactive recovery) for our proposed ITS. From the above mentioned equations, we may compute the π_G,

$$\pi_G = \frac{h_G}{\begin{array}{c} h_G + h_V + p_I(h_I + h_{DNC}p_{DN} + h_{UNC}p_{UN} + \\ h_{UMC}p_{UM} + h_{GD}p_{DN}p_{GD} + h_F p_{DN}p_F) \end{array}} \tag{5}$$

where from (5), we may derive the π_{UNC} and π_F as follows,

$$\pi_{UNC} = h_{UNC}p_I p_{UN} \frac{\pi_G}{h_G} \tag{6}$$

$$\pi_F = h_F p_I p_{DN} p_F \frac{\pi_G}{h_G} \tag{7}$$

Finally, by using (1) and (5)-(7), the steady-state availability A_p of our proposed ITS is derived as,

$$A_p = 1 - \frac{h_F p_I p_{DN} p_F + h_{UNC}p_I p_{UN}}{\begin{array}{c} h_G + h_V + p_I(h_I + h_{UNC}p_{UN} + h_{UMC}p_{UM} + \\ h_{DNC}p_{DN} + h_{GD}p_{DN}p_{GD} + h_F p_{DN}p_F) \end{array}} \tag{8}$$

In a similar fashion, the steady-state availability for SITAR (A_{SITAR}) and SCIT (A_{SCIT}) are computed as,

$$A_{SITAR} = 1 - \frac{h_F p_I p_{DN} p_F + h_{UNC}p_I p_{UN}}{\begin{array}{c} h_G + h_V + p_I(h_I + h_{UNC}p_{UN} + h_{DNC}p_{DN} + \\ h_{GD}p_{DN}p_{GD} + h_F p_{DN}p_F) \end{array}} \tag{9}$$

$$A_{SCIT} = 1 - \frac{h_F p_I p_F}{h_G + h_V + p_I(h_I + h_{UMC}p_{UM} + h_F p_F)} \tag{10}$$

It should be noted that some of the transition probabilities may have different values or even may not be applicable for all three ITSs since they do not possess the same state space.

4.3   Performance Evaluation

In this paper, the availability performance is analyzed according to two decision parameters, namely probability of intrusion (p_I) and the mean time to resist becoming vulnerable to intrusions (h_G). As a proof of concept, we also compare the availability performance under DoS attack for our proposed ITS with SITAR and SCIT.

Fig. 4 illustrates the availability performance of the proposed ITS, SITAR and SCIT with regard to p_I . It can be observed that the steady-state availability is

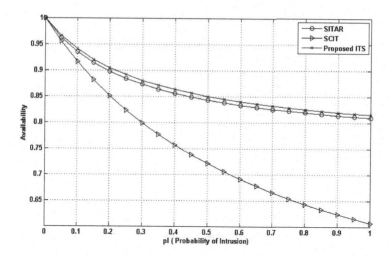

Fig. 4. Availability performance vs p_I

a decreasing function of p_I for all three ITSs. The availability for SCIT reduces markedly when the probability of intrusion increases compared to the other two ITSs. Although it is viable to enhance the availability of SCIT by tuning parameters such as exposure window (i.e., the duration of time that a replica is online) but the exposure window must be larger than the transaction time [16]. The acquired results show 0.7% and 15% availability improvement compared to SITAR and SCIT respectively.

Fig. 5 illustrates the impact of increasing the time that the system is in the good state on the availability performance. It can be seen that the availability rises as the h_G increases. For larger amount of h_G, there is a slight difference in the behavior of the three ITS with regard to availability. The acquired result for the proposed ITS demonstrates 0.4% and 2% availability enhancement compared to SITAR and SCIT respectively.

The results clearly show that the proposed ITS has a more stable working condition as well as a better behavior when facing DoS attacks. This can be mostly due the employment of both timing test (in case of Dos attack, response time from the replicas will exceed the expected value) embedded in the compromised/faulty replica detector as a detection mechanism and periodic rejuvenation as a way to limit the effects of DoS attack. In contrast, SITAR possesses timing test and SCIT leverages the periodic rejuvenation as countermeasures against DoS attacks. By using a combination of these techniques, the security of the proposed ITS has been enhanced. It is also evident that increasing the probability of Intrusion (i.e., DoS attack) has a more negative impact on the availability performance of the other two ITSs.

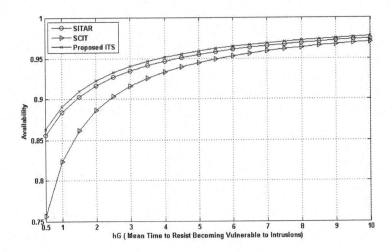

Fig. 5. Availability performance vs h_G

5   Conclusion

An ITS architecture for securing smart grid control centers has been proposed in this paper. It encompasses a number of modules each makes use of different intrusion tolerance techniques to improve the resilience to intrusions, as well as ensuring the availability of smart grid control centers. The availability of the proposed ITS in the event of DoS attacks has been evaluated analytically, and the results have been compared with two existing ITS architectures. In future, we are intended to consider other performance measures reflecting the tolerance of the proposed ITS architecture and make a comparison with other existing architectures.

References

1. Fang, X., Misra, S., Xue, G., Yang, D.: Smart Grid The New and Improved Power Grid: A Survey. IEEE Communications Surveys & Tutorials (2011)
2. Dan, G., Sandberg, H., Bjorkman, G., Ekstedt, M.: Challenges in Power System Information Security. IEEE Security & Privacy 10, 62–70 (2012)
3. Mo, Y., Kim, T.H.-J., Brancik, K., Dickinson, D., Lee, H., Perrig, A., Sinopoli, B.: Cyber-Physical Security of a Smart Grid Infrastructure. Proceedings of the IEEE 100, 195–209 (2012)
4. Wang, W., Xu, Y., Khanna, M.: A survey on the communication architectures in smart grid. Computer Networks 55, 3604–3629 (2011)
5. Overman, T.M., Sackman, R.W., Davis, T.L., Cohen, B.S.: High-Assurance Smart Grid: A Three-Part Model for Smart Grid Control Systems. Proceedings of the IEEE 99, 1046–1062 (2011)
6. Nguyen, Q.L., Sood, A.: A Comparison of Intrusion-Tolerant System Architectures. IEEE Security & Privacy 9, 24–31 (2011)

7. Wang, F., Uppalli, R., Killian, C.: Analysis of techniques for building intrusion tolerant server systems. In: IEEE Military Communications Conference, pp. 729–734. IEEE Press (2003)
8. Sterbenz, J.P.G., Hutchison, D., Çetinkaya, E.K., Jabbar, A., Rohrer, J.P., Schöller, M., Smith, P.: Resilience and survivability in communication networks: Strategies, principles, and survey of disciplines. Computer Networks 54, 1245–1265 (2010)
9. Sousa, P., Bessani, A.N., Correia, M., Neves, N.F., Verissimo, P.: Highly Available Intrusion-Tolerant Services with Proactive-Reactive Recovery. IEEE Transactions on Parallel and Distributed Systems 21, 452–465 (2010)
10. Tranchita, C., Hadjsaid, N., Viziteu, M., Rozel, B., Caire, R.: ICT and Powers Systems: An Integrated Approach. In: Securing Electricity Supply in the Cyber Age, vol. 15, pp. 71–109. Springer, Netherlands (2010)
11. Wang, F., Jou, F., Gong, F., Sargor, C., Goseva-Popstojanova, K., Trivedi, K.: SITAR: a scalable intrusion-tolerant architecture for distributed services. In: Foundations of Intrusion Tolerant Systems, pp. 359–367. IEEE Press (2003)
12. Bangalore, A.K., Sood, A.K.: Securing web servers using self cleansing intrusion tolerance (SCIT). In: 2nd International Conference on Dependability, pp. 60–65. IEEE Press (2009)
13. Bessani, A.N., Sousa, P., Correia, M., Neves, N.F., Verissimo, P.: The Crutial Way of Critical Infrastructure Protection. IEEE Security & Privacy 6, 44–51 (2008)
14. Saidane, A., Nicomette, V., Deswarte, Y.: The Design of a Generic Intrusion-Tolerant Architecture for Web Servers. IEEE Transactions on Dependable and Secure Computing 6, 45–58 (2009)
15. Madan, B.B., Goseva-Popstojanova, K., Vaidyanathan, K., Trivedi, K.S.: A method for modeling and quantifying the security attributes of intrusion tolerant systems. Performance Evaluation 56, 167–186 (2004)
16. Nguyen, Q., Sood, A.: Quantitative approach to tuning of a time-based intrusion-tolerant system architecture. In: 3rd Workshop on Recent Advances on Intrusion-Tolerant Systems, pp. 132–139 (2009)

A Note on Constant-Round Concurrent Zero-Knowledge Arguments of Knowledge for NP

Hongda Li[*], Yang Liu, and Qihua Niu

State Key Laboratory of Information Security,
Institute of Information Engineering, Chinese Academy of Sciences,
Beijing 100093, China
lihongda@iie.ac.cn

Abstract. This paper deals with how to construct a constant-round bounded-concurrent zero-knowledge argument of knowledge with black-box extractors for any NP language under standard complexity assumptions. It is accepted that both constant-round zero-knowledge arguments of knowledge and constant-round bound-concurrent zero-knowledge arguments exist for all NP. But the existence of constant-round bounded-concurrent zero-knowledge arguments of knowledge (with black-box extractors) for NP is still an unsolved question. In this paper, we give a positive answer to this question by constructing a constant-round bounded-concurrent zero-knowledge argument of knowledge with a black-box extractor for any NP under certain standard complexity assumptions.

1 Introduction

Zero-knowledge proofs, first introduced by Goldwasser, Micali, and Rackoff[14], are protocols that allow one party ("the prover") to convince another ("the verifier") that an assertion in question is true without providing the verifier with any additional information about the assertion being proved. The zero-knowledge property is formalized by requiring that whatever the verifier might have learned from interacting with the prover, the verifier could actually have obtained itself. The notion of zero-knowledge arguments are a relaxation of the zero-knowledge proofs, in which the soundness property is required to hold only with respect to a computationally bounded prover.

Proofs of knowledge, defined by Goldwasser, Micali and Rackoff[14], are proofs that allow the prover to convince the verifier that it knows a secret witness w about a given common input x. If the prover is restricted to be strict polynomial-time, it is a argument of knowledge. Analogously to regular interactive proofs, proofs (or arguments) of knowledge should satisfy certain constraints: completeness (if the prover knows w, the verifier should accept) and soundness (for any prover that does not know w, the verifier should almost always reject).

---

[*] This work was supported by the National Natural Science Foundation of China under Grant No.60970139, the Strategic Priority Research Program of Chinese Academy of Sciences under Grant XDA06010702, and IIEs Cryptography Research Project.

Y. Xiang et al. (Eds.): IDCS 2012, LNCS 7646, pp. 202–216, 2012.

To use zero-knowledge proofs in real applications, one need more strong zero-knowledge property, known as "concurrent zero-knowledge", that was first considered by Feige[11], and explored extensively by Dwork, Naor and Sahai[9]. In concurrent setting, many instances of the proof system are executed concurrently, and there exists a concurrent verifier (adversary) that may have control over the scheduling of these instances. Now, concurrent zero-knowledge proofs or arguments (of knowledge) have played a crucial role in the design of cryptographic schemes and protocols.

It is easy to see that some known constructions of zero-knowledge proofs (or arguments), which only consider a single prover and a single verifier working in isolation, are in fact proofs (or arguments) of knowledge. Furthermore, there exist constant-round zero-knowledge arguments of knowledge for any NP-relation in such a restricted scenario (a single prover and a single verifier)[8,10]. By permitting the knowledge extractor to access the description of the prover algorithm (non-black-box extraction), Barak and Lindell[5] gave a relaxed definition of argument of knowledge. If this relaxed definition is adopted, the existence of constant-round concurrent zero-knowledge proofs or arguments of knowledge (with non-black-box extractors) is implied by the result of [2,3,5]. Recently, Pass and Rosen[21] constructed the constant-round zero-knowledge argument of knowledge. Therefore, a natural question is whether or not constant-round concurrent zero-knowledge proofs or arguments of knowledge (under the standard definition, with black-box extractors) exist for all NP under certain assumptions. Recently, [19] showed a construction of constant-round bounded-concurrent zero-knowledge arguments of knowledge under more strong assumptions.

1.1 Our Works

This paper focuses on the existence of constant-round concurrent zero-knowledge arguments of knowledge (with black-box extractors) for NP. The main contribution of this paper is to provide a constant-round zero-knowledge argument for any NP problem with two properties: It is bounded-concurrent zero-knowledge and a argument of knowledge with black-box extractors. Therefore, we prove the following theorem:

Main Theorem: *Suppose that constant-round statistically-hiding commitment schemes and collision-resistant hash functions exist. Then, there exist constant-round bounded-concurrent zero-knowledge arguments of knowledge (with black-box extractors) for any NP.*

Analogously to [2], we use FLS technique of [12] to convert a witness indistinguishable argument of knowledge into a zero-knowledge argument of knowledge. Roughly speaking, Our construction consists of two phase. In phase 1, the prover first sends a commitment to a random string, denote by c_p, by a perfectly hiding commitment scheme. Then, both the parties run a modified coin-tossing protocol to generate a random string τ. In this coin-tossing protocol, the prover first sends his commitment to a random string α. Instead of revealing the commitment after receiving the verifier's response, the prover only sends α' and then proves that the commitment sent before is the commitment to α' by a zero-knowledge argument. In phase 2, instead of proving in possession of a witness for $x \in L$, the prover proves knowing a witness for $x \in L$ or $(c_p, \tau) \in L'$ by a 3-round WI argument of knowledge (here, we denote by $(c_p, \tau) \in L'$ the statement that c_p is a commitment to τ). Note that the statement that $x \in L$ or c_p is a commitment, denote by $(c_p, \tau) \in L'$. It is easy to see that the probability that the prover learns a witness for $(c_p, \tau) \in L'$ is at most negligible. Thus, on the one hand, if the prover can convince the verifier of holding a witness for $(x \in L) \vee ((c_p, \tau) \in L')$, the prover must hold a witness for $x \in L$ with extremely high probability. On the other hand, to give a simulated proof, the simulator first obtains a witness for $(c_p, \tau) \in L'$ by selecting a proper α' in simulation setting, and then can complete the proof in phase 2.

1.2   Related Works

Constant-Round Zero-Knowledge Proofs (Arguments):   Feige and Shamir in [10] showed how to construct constant-round zero-knowledge arguments of knowledge for any NP from one-to-one one-way function. Goldreich and Oren[15] first proved that languages outside of BPP do not exist two-round auxiliary-input zero-knowledge proof systems. Furthermore, Barak et al[6,7] recently proved there does not exist a 2-round zero-knowledge proof system with perfect completeness for an NP-complete language. Goldreich and Kahan[16] first presented a 5-round zero-knowledge proof system for HC (Hamiltonian Cycle) problem under the existence of the claw-free functions. Rosen[22] constructed a 7-rounds zero-knowledge proof system for HC problem. However, these known constant-round constructions are not proof of knowledge.

Concurrent Zero-Knowledge: Concurrent zero-knowledge, which was first considered by Feige[11], and explored extensively by Dwork, Naor and Sahai[9]. The first construction of constant-round bounded-concurrent (non-black-box) zero-knowledge arguments for NP came from [2]. By introducing a new kind of non-black-box simulation technique, [2] provided the constant-round bounded-concurrent zero-knowledge argument system for NP with a strict polynomial-time simulator, assuming the existence of collision-resistant hash function with super-polynomial hardness. Barak and Goldreich later weaken the assumption to the existence of standard collision-resistant hash function with polynomial hardness. However, these constructions is not general arguments of knowledge(only with a weak proof of knowledge property).

Zero-Knowledge Proofs (Arguments) of Knowledge: It is known that constant-round zero-knowledge arguments of knowledge exist for any NP-relation if one-way functions exist [10,8]. However, the known constructions are not concurrent zero-knowledge. [18] gave a 3-round construction of non-black-box zero-knowledge proof of knowledge for all NP (with black-box knowledge extractor). Recently, Lindell presented 5-round black-box zero-knowledge proof of knowledge system for all NP assuming the existence of two-round perfectly-hiding commitment [20]. Following the work of [2,3], [5] showed that there exist constant-round zero-knowledge arguments of knowledge with strict polynomial-time non-black-box simulators and non-black-box extractors. Furthermore, [5] showed that constant-round zero-knowledge argument of knowledge with a strict polynomial-time black-box simulator does not exist for the language out of BPP. The construction in [5] is zero-knowledge argument of knowledge for NP, but not concurrent zero-knowledge.

1.3 Organization

The some standard definitions and cryptographic tools used in our protocols are in section 2. In section 3, we first construct a constant-round WI argument of knowledge for HC problem. The construction of constant-round zero-knowledge argument of knowledge for any language $L \in NP$ is presented in section 4.

2 Preliminaries

In this paper, we use some standard notations. If $A(\cdot)$ is a probabilistic algorithm, $A(x)$ is the result of running A on input x and $y = A(x)$ denote that y is set to $A(x)$. For a finite set S, $y \in_R S$ denotes y is uniformly selected from S. We use $X_n \stackrel{c}{\equiv} Y_n$ to denote two probability ensembles $\{X_n\}$ and $\{Y_n\}$ are computationally indistinguishable. For convenience, we write $poly(\cdot)$ to denote an unspecified polynomial, $\mu(\cdot)$ (sometimes, $\mu'(\cdot)$) to denote an unspecified negligible function, and R_L to denote the corresponding witness relation of any language $L \in NP$.

2.1 Zero-Knowledge Proof

We recall the definitions of zero-knowledge in [14,17]. Let P and V be a pair of interactive Turing machines, $\langle P(y), V(z)\rangle(x)$ be a random variable representing the local output of V when interacting with P on common input x, when the random input to each machine is uniformly and independently chosen, where y, z are auxiliary inputs . Customarily, machine P is called the prover and machine V is called the verifier. For the sake of simplicity, we leave out the auxiliary input in what follows. We denote by $\langle P, V\rangle(x) = 1$ ($\langle P, V\rangle(x) = 0$) that machine V accepts (rejects) the proofs given by the machine P.

Definition 1. *A pair of interactive Turing machines $\langle P, V\rangle$ is called an interactive proof system for a language L if machine V is polynomial-time and the following two conditions hold:*

- *Completeness: there exists a negligible function c such that for every $x \in L$,*
$$Pr[\langle P, V\rangle(x) = 1] > 1 - c(|x|)$$
- *Soundness: there exists a negligible function s such that for every $x \notin L$ and every interactive machine B,*
$$Pr[\langle B, V\rangle(x) = 1] < s(|x|)$$

$c(\cdot)$ is called the completeness error, and $s(\cdot)$ the soundness error. In the case that the soundness condition is required to hold only with respect to a probabilistic polynomial-time prover, $\langle P, V \rangle$ is called an interactive arguments system for L.

An interactive proof is said to be zero-knowledge if the interaction between the prover and verifier reveals nothing beyond the validity of the assertion to be proved to the verifier. This is formalized by requiring that for any polynomial-time verifier V^* (holding auxiliary input z) there exists a polynomial-time algorithm $\mathcal{S}_{V^*}$ (a.k.a the simulator) such that the view of V^* can be simulated by $\mathcal{S}_{V^*}(x)$. We denote by $View_{V^*}^P(x)$ a random variable describing the content of the random tape of V^* and the messages V^* receives and sends during the interaction with P on common input x.

Definition 2. *Let $\langle P, V \rangle$ be an interactive proof system for a language L. $\langle P, V \rangle$ is called a zero-knowledge proof system if for every probabilistic polynomial-time machine V^* there exists a (expected) probabilistic polynomial-time algorithm $\mathcal{S}_{V^*}$ such that $\{View_{V^*}^P(x)\}_{x \in L}$ and $\{\mathcal{S}_{V^*}(x)\}_{x \in L}$ are computationally indistinguishable.*

Black-box zero-knowledge requires that there exists a "universal" simulator $\mathcal{S}$ such that for every $x \in L$ and every probabilistic polynomial-time verifier V^*, the simulator $\mathcal{S}$ can simulate $View_{V^*}^P(x)$ while using V^* in a "black-box" manner.

Definition 3. *Let $\langle P, V \rangle$ be an interactive proof system for a language L. $\langle P, V \rangle$ is called a black-box zero-knowledge proof if there exists a (expected) probabilistic polynomial-time algorithm $\mathcal{S}$ such that for every probabilistic polynomial-time machine V^* $\{View_{V^*}^P(x)\}_{x \in L}$ and $\{\mathcal{S}^{V^*}(x)\}_{x \in L}$ are computationally indistinguishable.*

2.2 Proofs of Knowledge

In a proof of knowledge for a relationship R, the prover, holding a secret input w such that $(x, w) \in R$, and the verifier interact on a common input x. The goal of the protocol is to convince the verifier that the prover indeed knows such w.

The notion of proofs of knowledge is formalized by saying that if a prover can convince the verifier, then there exists an efficient procedure that can "extract" a witness from this prover

Definition 4. *An interactive protocol $\langle P, V \rangle$ is a system of proofs (arguments) of knowledge for a (poly-balanced) relation R with knowledge error κ if the following conditions hold:*

- *Efficiency: $\langle P, V \rangle$ is polynomially bounded, and V is computable in probabilistic polynomial time.*
- *Non triviality: There exists an interactive machine P such that for every $(x, w) \in R$ all possible interactions of V with P on common input x and auxiliary y are accepting.*

- *Validity: Denote by $p(x, y, r)$ the probability that the interactive machine V accepts, on input x, when interacting with the prover specified by $P^*_{x,y,r}$ (the prover's strategy when fixing common x, auxiliary input y and random tape r). If there exists an expected polynomial-time oracle machine $\mathcal{K}$ (known as knowledge extractor) such that, for any prover P^*, on input x and access to oracle $P^*_{x,y,r}$, $\mathcal{K}^{P^*_{x,y,r}}(x)$ outputs w, such that $(x, w) \in R$, with probability at least $(p(x, y, r) - \kappa(|x|))$*

If the prover is restricted to be strict polynomial-time one, $\langle P, V \rangle$ is known as a argument of knowledge.

The definition of proofs (arguments) of knowledge require that the knowledge extractor uses the prover algorithm only as a black-box. This results in a fact that there do not exist constant round proofs of knowledge with strict polynomial-time extractors [5]. To obtain constant round zero-knowledge arguments of knowledge with strict polynomial-time extractors for NP, Barak and Lindell[5] presented a relaxed definition of arguments of knowledge. Comparing with the standard definition, their relaxed definition diffs from Definition 4 only in the validity property. More concretely, the validity of their definition permits that the knowledge extractor $\mathcal{K}$ is given the description of the prover, and so is called non-black-box extraction. Equivalently, $\mathcal{K}$ try to output w upon input $(desc(P)$ and (x, z), where $desc(P)$ is the description of the prover's strategy.

2.3   Concurrent Zero-Knowledge

Informally speaking, concurrent composition of zero-knowledge considers such a setting in which many (or single) honest provers are concurrently running many instance of the same zero-knowledge protocol, meanwhile, a polynomial time concurrent adversary (verifier) V^* controls many verifiers simultaneously. Each instance, consisting of a prover and a verifier, is called a session. This can be also thought of as one prover with many sessions, but the behavior of the prover in any of the copies depends only on the current session.

A zero-knowledge protocol is said to be concurrent zero-knowledge if it remains zero-knowledge under concurrent composition. The zero-knowledge property of a protocol requires that the view of every probabilistic polynomial-time adversary interacting with the prover can be simulated by means of a simulator. In the concurrent setting, a concurrent adversary V^* controls over the scheduling by means of concatenating each message that it sends with the session number, and that the reply sent by the prover should have session and message indices as specified in the message receiving from V^*. As usual, we denote by $View^P_{V^*}(x)$ a random variable describing the content of the random tape and the transcript, which includes all messages that V^* receives during the concurrent interaction with the prover P on some common input.

Let $\langle P, V \rangle$ be an interactive proof protocol. And more generally, we assume $\{(x_i, y_i, z_i)\}_{i=1}^t$ be t inputs to $\langle P, V \rangle$, where y_i, z_i are auxiliary inputs. The concurrent execution of the t instance of $\langle P, V \rangle$ is as follows:

- t independent instances of P get his input respectively (the ith instance gets x_i and y_i as inputs).
- Except for the common input $\bar{x} = (x_1, \cdots, x_n)$, the concurrent verifier V^* (possible adversary) gets $z_1, \cdots, z_t$ as inputs.
- After receiving the reply from some instance, such as i^{th} instance, of P, V^* will outputs a message (j, m) (the jth instance of P is given with the message m) or waits next message from some instance of P. Note that it is permitted that $i \neq j$.
- Any instance of P receiving the reply sent by V^* proceeds honestly as the protocol.

Without loss of generality, we assume that the verifier first sends its message. Thus a transcript of a concurrent interaction is of the form

$$((s_1, v_1), p_1, (s_2, v_2), p_2, ..., (s_q, v_q), p_q)$$

where p_i is the P's message, (s_i, v_i) is the message sent by V^*.

Formally, we define concurrent zero-knowledge as follows:

Definition 5. *Let $\langle P, V \rangle$ be an interactive proof system for a language L. $\langle P, V \rangle$ is called concurrent zero-knowledge proof if for every probabilistic polynomial-time concurrent adversary V^* there exists a probabilistic polynomial-time algorithm $\mathcal{S}_{V^*}$ such that $\{View_{V^*}^P(\bar{x})\}$ and $\{\mathcal{S}_{V^*}(\bar{x})\}$ are computationally indistinguishable.*

2.4   Commitment Schemes

We use two kind of commitment schemes. One is non-interactive perfectly-binding scheme which can be constructed using any 1-1 one-way function (see Section 4.4.1 of [17]). The other is two-round perfectly-hiding commitment schemes that can be constructed using any claw-free collections (see Section 4.8.2 of [17]).

3   Constant-Round WI Arguments of knowledge for NP

Suppose that the language HC consists of all directed graphs that contain a Hamiltonian cycle. For $G = (V, E) \in HC$, let $V = \{v_1, \cdots, v_n\}$. In this section and throughout this paper, we denote by $Com_{pb}(\cdot; \cdot)$ a non-interactive perfectly-binding commitment scheme.

Recall Blum's basic interactive proof for HC [1].

Construction 1 :

- *The prover then sends its commitment c: The prover randomly selects a permutation π over V and $r \in_R \{0,1\}^{poly(|V|)}$, computes $c = Com_{pb}(\pi(G); r)$, the commitments of the adjacency matrix of $\pi(G)$. Sends c to the verifier .*

- *The verifier sends a challenge σ: The verifier uniformly selects $\sigma \in_R \{0,1\}$ and sends it to the prover.*
- *The prover responds to the challenge with a: If $\sigma = 0$, the prover reveals the partial commitments of c corresponding to the edges of a Hamiltonian cycle $\pi(H)$. If $\sigma = 1$ then the prover reveals the all commitments of c and π.*
- *Upon receiving the response a from the prover, the verifier checks whether $Check(c, a, \sigma) = 1$. (Here, we define $Check(c, a, \sigma) = 1$ if that all values revealed by a are 1 and the corresponding edges form a simple Hamiltonian cycle when $\sigma = 0$, or a correctly reveals all the commitments of c and π such that the revealed graph is indeed isomorphic G via π when $\sigma = 1$)*

This construction is a zero-knowledge argument of knowledge with knowledge error $\frac{1}{2}$ for HC. Thus, it is a witness indistinguishable proof [17]. To reduce the knowledge error, one can run the basic protocol n times in parallel.

Construction 2 : *WI argument of knowledge for NP*

- *The prover first sends its commitment $c_1, \cdots, c_n$.*
- *The verifier sends n challenges $\sigma_1, \cdots, \sigma_n$.*
- *The prover responds the challenges with $a_1, \cdots, a_n$.*
- *Upon receiving $a_1, \cdots, a_n$, the verifier checks whether $\bigwedge_{j=1}^{n} Check(c_j, a_j, \sigma_j) = 1$.*

By the parallel-composition lemma for witness indistinguishability (see Section 4.6.2 of [17][24]), Construction 2 is a WI proof with negligible error probability.

Furthermore, this paralleled protocol is a argument of knowledge. In fact, knowledge extractor $\mathcal{K}$ with input G and access to the prover oracle P^* proceeds as follows:

1. Obtain the commitments $C = (c_1, \cdots, c_n)$ from the prover oracle P^*.
2. Randomly selects $\sigma = \sigma_1 \cdots \sigma_n \in \{0,1\}^n$.
3. Invoke P^* with σ and obtain its responses $a_1, \cdots, a_n$. Output $\perp$ and stop if there exits j such that $Check(c_j, a_j, \sigma_j) = 0$.
4. Otherwise, repeat the follows at most $n \cdot 2^n$ times.
   - Randomly select $\sigma' = \sigma'_1 \cdots \sigma'_n \in \{0,1\}^n$.
   - Invoke P^* with σ' and obtain its responses $a'_1, \cdots, a'_n$.
   - If $\sigma' \neq \sigma$ and all P^*'s responses are correct, (that is, $Check(c_j, a'_j, \sigma_j) = 1$, $i = 1, \cdots, n$), find j such that $\sigma_j \neq \sigma'_j$, computes H from a_j and a'_j. And then output H and stop.
   - Otherwise, proceed to the next iteration.
5. In the case that the above repeat ends without any output, output $\perp$ and stop.

It is easy to see that the following two facts must hold: (1) $\mathcal{K}$ runs in expected polynomial time , and (2) if the probability p that P^* gives a correct proof is greater than 2^{-n}, then there exists a negligible function $\mu(n)$ such that $\mathcal{K}$ succeeds in computing an Hamiltonian cycle in G with probability $p - \mu(n)$.

we first show that $\mathcal{K}$ runs in the expected polynomial time. Note that $\mathcal{K}$ clearly runs in (strict) polynomial time when $p = 0$. So consider the case that $p > 0$ in what follows. When P does not respond correctly to the first challenge (which happens with probability $1 - p$), then $\mathcal{K}$ runs in (strict) polynomial time. When P responds correctly to the first challenge, $\mathcal{K}$ repeats the iteration at most $n \cdot 2^n$ times to find δ'. When $p = \frac{m}{2^n} > 2^{-n}$, the expected running time of $\mathcal{K}$ is given by $(1-p) \cdot poly(n) + p \cdot \frac{2^n}{m-1} \cdot poly(n)$. When $p = 2^{-n}$, the expected running time of $\mathcal{K}$ is given by $p \cdot 2^n n \cdot poly(n) = n \cdot poly(n)$. Overall, $\mathcal{K}$ runs in the expected polynomial time.

Next, we consider the probability that $\mathcal{K}$ succeeds in computing an Hamiltonian cycle in G when $p = \frac{m}{2^n} > 2^{-n}$. First, P^* responds correctly to the first challenge σ with probability exactly p. Note that $\mathcal{K}$ stops its execution with output $\perp$ when either (1) P^* does not answer correctly its first query, or (2) $\mathcal{K}$ does not find correct σ' in given time. Let μ be $\mathcal{K}$ does not find correct σ' in given time. It is easy to see that $\mu = (1 - \frac{m-1}{2^n})^{2^n n} < (1 - 2^{-n})^{2^n n}$ is negligible since σ' is uniformly distributed on $\{0,1\}^n$. Thus, the probability that $\mathcal{K}$ succeeds in computing an Hamiltonian cycle is more than $p - \mu$. It follows that Construction 2 is a argument of knowledge for R_{HC} with knowledge error $\kappa = \max(2^{-n}, \mu(n))$.

4 Constant-Round Concurrent Zero-Knowledge Arguments of Knowledge for NP

In this section, we attempt to present a constant-round bounded-concurrent zero-knowledge arguments of knowledge for any $L \in NP$. For simplicity we suppose that $Com_{ph}(\cdot; \cdot)$ is a two-round perfectly-hiding commitment scheme, and denote by $Com_{ph}(s; r)$ the commitment to s. For convenience, define a language

$$L' = \left\{ (c, \tau) : \tau \in \{0,1\}^n, \exists r \in \{0,1\}^{poly(n)} \text{ such that } c = Com_{ph}(\tau; r) \right\}$$

Analogously to [2], our construction utilizes FLS technique, and then consists of two phase. In Phase I, the prover first selects $\rho \in \{0,1\}^n$ and commits to it by $c_p = Com_{ph}(\rho; \cdot)$. Then, both the party run a modified coin-tossing protocol to generate a random string τ. In this coin-tossing protocol, the prover first sends his commitment c_1 to a random string α. Instead of revealing the commitment after receiving the verifier's response β, the prover only sends α' and then proves and then proves that the commitment c_1 is the commitment to α' by a zero-knowledge argument. If the proof is accepted, the two parties set $\tau = \alpha' \oplus \beta$. In Phase II, instead of proving in possession of a witness for $x \in L$, the prover proves the knowledge of witness for $(x \in L) \vee ((c_p, \tau) \in L')$ by a 3-round WI argument of knowledge, where $\tau = \alpha' \oplus \beta$. Obviously, $(c_p, \tau) \in L'$ holds at all time since $Com_{ph}(\cdot; \cdot)$ is perfectly-hiding. However, the probability that the prover learns r such that $c_p = Com_{ph}(\tau; r)$ is at most negligible. Thus, the fact that the prover can convince the verifier of holding a witness for $(x \in L) \vee ((c_p, \tau) \in L')$ implies that, with extremely high probability, the prover must hold a witness for $x \in L$. However, in simulation setting, the simulator can make that $\tau = \rho$ by selecting

α', and then obtains a witness for $((c_p, \tau) \in L')$ to proceed as a honest prover in Phase II. The details are described as follows:

Construction 3 (constant-round zero-knowledge argument of knowledge)
Common input: $x \in L$ ($|x| = n$).
Auxiliary input for the prover's: w, meeting with $(x, w) \in R_L$.

1. Phase I:
   I-1 The verifier sends the first message m of commitment scheme $Com_{ph}(\cdot; \cdot)$ to the prover.
   I-2 The prover selects randomly $\alpha, \rho \in_R \{0, 1\}^n$, $r_1, r_2 \in_R \{0, 1\}^{poly(n)}$. And then, the prover computes $c_1 = Com_{pb}(\alpha; r_1)$ and $c_p = Com_{ph}(\rho; r_2)$, sends c_1, c_p to the verifier.
   I-3 The verifier randomly selects $\beta \in_R \{0, 1\}^n$ and sends it to the prover.
   I-4 The prover sets $\tau = \alpha \oplus \beta$ and sends τ to the verifier.
   I-5 By running a constant-round zero-knowledge arguments, denoted by Σ, with the verifies, the prover convince the verifier of that the value committed by c_1 at step I-2 is indeed $\tau \oplus \beta$. If the proof fails, the verifier abort.
2. Phase II:
   II-1: On common input $(x, (c_p, \tau))$, the prover and verifier execute a constant-round witness indistinguishable proof of knowledge, such that the prover, with auxiliary input w, convince the verifier of $x \in L$ or $(c_p, \tau) \in L'$.
   II-2: The verifier accepts if it accepts at II-1.

Theorem 1. *Construction 3 is a constant-round ZK argument of knowledge system for $L \in NP$.*

Proof. **Completeness:** It follows directly from the completeness of the WI argument.

Stand-alone zero-knowledge: In order to prove the zero-knowledge property, we need to construct a simulator $\mathcal{S}_{V^*}$ for any verifier V^*, such that $\mathcal{S}_{V^*}(x) \stackrel{c}{\equiv} View_{V^*}^P(x)$. Let $\mathcal{O}$ be the simulator of zero-knowledge argument system Σ. $\mathcal{S}_{V^*}(x)$ operates as follows:

- Uniformly select a string $r \in \{0, 1\}^{poly(n)}$ to be used as the content of the local random tape of $V*$.
- Simulates Phase I
  1. Invoke V^*, which responds with m.
  2. Randomly select $\alpha, \rho \in_R \{0, 1\}^n$, $r_1, r_2 \in_R \{0, 1\}^{poly(n)}$, and then computes $c_1 = Com_{pb}(\alpha; r_1)$ and $c_p = Com_{ph}(\rho; r_2)$. Finally, feed V^* with (c_1, c_p).
  3. After receiving $\beta \in \{0, 1\}^n$ from V^*, feed V^* with $\tau = \rho$.
  4. Invoke $\mathcal{O}$ for the statement that there exists a string r such that $c_1 = Com_{pb}(\tau \oplus \beta; r)$. Let $View'$ be the output of the simulator $\mathcal{O}$, that is, $View' = \mathcal{O}(c_1, \tau)$.
- Simulates Phase II. Let $k = |(c_p, \tau)| = poly(n)$.

1. Use the honest prover's algorithm to prove $x \in L$ or $(c_p, \tau) \in L'$, where r_2 is used as an auxiliary. Let $View''$ be the view of V^* in this execution.
2. Output $(r, c_1, c_p, \tau, View', View'')$

Obviously, the simulator's running time is (expected) strict polynomial-time when the simulator of Σ is (expected) strict polynomial-time.

We will use a standard hybrid argument to prove $\mathcal{S}_{V^*}(x) \stackrel{c}{\equiv} View_{V^*}^P(x)$. To this end, define a hybrid simulators $\mathcal{S}'$: $\mathcal{S}'$ follows the simulator's strategy in Phase I, and the honest prover's strategy in Phase II. That is, $\mathcal{S}'$ first runs $\mathcal{S}_{V^*}$ in Phase I. Instead of using r_2, a witness for $((c_p, \tau) \in L'$, $\mathcal{S}'$ uses w as an auxiliary input to prove the statement $(x \in L)$ or $((c_p, \tau) \in L')$ as the honest prover in Phase II.

Let $\mathcal{S}'(x)$ be the distribution produced by the hybrid simulator $\mathcal{S}'$. Thus, the fact that $\mathcal{S}'(x) \stackrel{c}{\equiv} \mathcal{S}_{V^*}(x)$ follows directly from the witness indistinguishability of the proof used in the phase II.

For convenience, define
$$L'' = \{(t_1, t_2) : \exists s, \text{such that } t_1 = Com_{pb}(t_2; s)\}$$
Note that the only difference between $\mathcal{S}'(x)$ and $View_{V^*}^P(x)$ is whether or not $(c_1, \tau \oplus \beta) \in L''$. If there exists a efficient algorithm $\mathcal{D}$ can distinguish $\mathcal{S}'(x)$ from $View_{V^*}^P(x)$, then we can derive a efficient algorithm $\mathcal{D}'$ to distinguish the case $(c_1, \tau \oplus \beta) \notin L''$ from the case $(c_1, \tau \oplus \beta) \in L''$. This contradicts the computationally hiding property of $Com_{pb}(\cdot; \cdot)$. Therefore, $\mathcal{S}'(x) \stackrel{c}{\equiv} View_{V^*}^P(x)$.

Overall, the above facts imply that $\{\mathcal{S}_{V^*}(x)\}_{x \in L}$ and $\{View_{V^*}^P\}_{x \in L}$ are computationally indistinguishable.

validity: Intuitively, if the prover convince the verifier with probability $p > \kappa(k)$ (here, $k = |(x, (c_p, \tau)| = poly(n)$, and $\kappa(k)$ is the knowledge error of Construction 2), there exists a knowledge extractor (of the WI argument of knowledge in Phase II) that can output a witness w' such that $(x, (c_p, \tau), w') \in R_{L \vee L'}$ with probability $p - \kappa(k)$. However, It is not hard to proved that $Pr[((c_p, \tau), w') \in R_{L'}]$ is negligible. Therefore, the probability of $(x, w') \in R_L$ is at least $p - \mu(n)$ (here $\mu(\cdot)$ is a negligible function).

More formally, we need to construct a knowledge extractor $\mathcal{K}$ that, when given access to the prover's strategy, can output a witness for $x \in L$. Let $\mathcal{K}_{II}$ be the knowledge extractor, with negligible knowledge error $\kappa(k)$, of the WI argument of knowledge executed in Phase II. On input x, $\mathcal{K}$ proceeds as follows:

- Act as a honest verifier to run Phase I with P^*. Let (c_p, τ) be the common messages that are generated in Phase I.
- Invoke the extractor $\mathcal{K}_{II}$ with $(x, (c_p, \tau))$ and obtains its output w.
- If w is a witness for $x \in L$, outputs w. Otherwise, fails and outputs $\perp$.

For convenience, we denote the strategies of the prover and verifier in Phase II respectively by P_{II} and V_{II}. Obviously, if $p = Pr[\langle P, V \rangle(x) = 1] > \kappa(k)$, then

$$Pr[\langle P_{II}, V_{II} \rangle(x, (c_p, \tau)) = 1] = p > \kappa(k)$$

Therefore, the extractor $\mathcal{K}_{II}$ can, with the probability $p - \kappa(k)$, output a witness w' for $x \in L$ or $(c_p, \tau) \in L'$ when $p > \kappa$. It follows that $\mathcal{K}$ will output a witness w' for $x \in L$ or $(c_p, \tau) \in L'$ with probability $p - \kappa(k)$.

Next, we will show that $p'' = Pr[((c_p, \tau), w') \in R_{L'}]$ is negligible. Supposed, to the contrary, that $p'' \geq \frac{1}{poly(n)}$. This implies that the prover can find r' with probability $p'' \geq \frac{1}{poly(n)}$ after receiving τ, such that $Com_{ph}(\rho; r_2) = Com_{ph}(\tau; r')$. Since $Pr[\rho = \tau]$ is negligible, we can derive an efficient algorithm $\mathcal{A}$, by combining the prover's strategy and verifier's program, to attack the binding property of $Com_{ph}(\cdot; \cdot)$. This contradicts the assumption that $Com_{ph}(\cdot; \cdot)$ is a computationally-binding commitment scheme.

Overall, there must exist a negligible function μ', such that $\mathcal{K}$ will output a witness w for $x \in L$ with probability $p - \mu'(n)$ when $p > \mu'(n)$.

Theorem 2. *Construction 3 is a constant-round bounded-concurrent ZK argument system for $L \in NP$ if Σ is a constant-round bounded-concurrent ZK argument system.*

Proof. Consider concurrent zero-knowledge when executed up to $t = poly(n)$ times concurrently. In this case, the transcript of a concurrent interaction is of the form $((s_1, v_1), p_1, (s_2, v_2), p_2, ..., (s_{ct}, v_{ct}), p_{ct})$, where c is the number of the message sent by the verifier in Construction 3. Thus, all that we need to do is to construct a concurrent simulator to simulate $View_{V^*}^P(\overline{x}) = (\overline{r}; p_1, p_2, ..., p_{ct})$, where $\overline{x} = (x_1, \cdots, x_t)$ are common inputs and $\overline{r} = (r_1, \cdots, r_t) \in \{0,1\}^{t \cdot ploy(n)}$. Since only languages in BPP have constant-round concurrent black-box zero-knowledge arguments, Σ executing in Phase I must be a non-black-box zero-knowledge argument system.

We define (non-black-box) simulator $\mathcal{S}(V^*, \overline{x})$ as follows:
Step 0 (Initialization:)

1. $\mathcal{S}$ will construct a table $\mathcal{T}$ of length t. Initially this table will be empty.
2. $\mathcal{S}$ randomly selects $\overline{r} = (r_1, \cdots, r_t) \in \{0,1\}^{t \cdot ploy(n)}$. It is used as the content of the local random tape of V^*.

Step 1 (Simulation each prover message:)
    For $j = 1$ to ct, $\mathcal{S}$ generates the jth simulated message p_j after $p_1, p_2, ..., p_{j-1}$ have be computed. $\mathcal{S}$ first feeds V^* with $(p_1, p_2, ..., p_{j-1})$ and obtains the jth verifier message (i, v). And then, $\mathcal{S}$ computes p_j according to (i, v) as follows:

1. if $v = m$ (that is, (i, v) is the first message sent by V^* for the ith instance), $\mathcal{S}$ randomly selects $\alpha, \rho \in_R \{0,1\}^n$ and $r_1, r_2 \in_R \{0,1\}^{poly(n)}$, computes $c_1 = Com_{pb}(\alpha; r_1)$, $c_p = Com_{ph}(\rho; r_2)$, and sets $p_j = (c_1, c_p)$. Finally, $\mathcal{S}$ stores ρ, r_2 in $T[i]$.
2. If $v = \beta$ (that is, v is the second message sent by V^* for the ith instance), $\mathcal{S}$ sets $p_j = \rho$, where ρ was stored in $\mathcal{T}[i]$.
3. If v is any message sent by V^* when running zero-knowledge arguments Σ, $\mathcal{S}$ invokes the concurrent simulator for Σ to compute p_j.

4. If v is any message sent in Phase II, $\mathcal{S}$ computes p_j as the honest prover does. Note that in the WI argument of knowledge in Phase II, $\mathcal{S}$ can use $\mathcal{T}[i]$ as a witness to complete the proof of the corresponding session.
5. In the case of that v is not a correct message, the ith instance aborts.
6. If all the instance have terminated, stops.

Step 2 Outputs: $\mathcal{S}(V^*, x_1, \cdots, x_t) = (\bar{r}, p_1, p_2, ..., p_N)$.

Since the simulator might stop the simulation for some instances, $N = ct$ does not always hold. However, note that the probability that the simulator stops the simulation for some instances is negligibly closed to the probability that the prover stops the execution of these instances in real execution. Thus, we can assume that $N = ct$ always holds.

Now, we use hybrid arguments to prove that $\mathcal{S}(V^*, x_1, \cdots, x_t) \overset{c}{\equiv} View_{V^*}^{P}(\bar{x})$. Analogously, first define hybrid simulator $\mathcal{S}'$: Upon receiving two inputs $\bar{x} = (x_1, \cdots, x_t)$ and V^*, $\mathcal{S}'(V^*, \bar{x})$ follows the same strategy as the simulator $\mathcal{S}(V^*, \bar{x})$, except that when $\mathcal{S}(V^*, \bar{x})$ uses a witness w' for $((c_p, \tau); w') \in R_{L'}$ to complete the proof in Phase II of the ith instance, $\mathcal{S}'$ is given a witness w for $(x_i, w) \in R_L$ and proceeds as a honest prover. We denote by $\mathcal{H}$ the output of the hybrid simulator $\mathcal{S}'$. The following two claims hold:

Claim 1. $\mathcal{H}$ and $\mathcal{S}(V^*, \bar{x})$ are indistinguishable.

In fact, note that the only difference between $\mathcal{H}$ and $\mathcal{S}(V^*, x_1, \cdots, x_t)$ is the witness that is used in Phase II. This claim follows from the concurrent property of WI arguments. More formally, we first order the all instances by the scheduling of the beginning of Phase II. Then, define new hybrid simulator $\mathcal{S}'_i$ which follows the strategy of the simulator $\mathcal{S}'$ in the first i instances and follows the strategy of the simulator $\mathcal{S}$ in the last $t - i$ instances, $i = 0, \cdots, t$. Let $\mathcal{H}_i$ denote the output of the hybrid simulator $\mathcal{S}'_i$. Note $\mathcal{S}(V^*, \bar{x}) = \mathcal{H}_0$ and $\mathcal{H} = \mathcal{H}_t$. It follows that if there exists a probabilistic polynomial-time algorithm $\mathcal{D}$ to distinguish $\mathcal{H}$ from $\mathcal{S}(V^*, x_1, \cdots, x_t)$, then there must exist a probabilistic polynomial-time algorithm $\mathcal{D}'$ and $0 \leq i \leq t$, such that $\mathcal{D}'$ can distinguish the two neighboring distributions $\mathcal{H}_i$ and $\mathcal{H}_{i+1}$. The only difference between $\mathcal{S}'_i$ and $\mathcal{S}'_{i+1}$ is that the respective witness used in the $(i+1)^{th}$ instance is different. Thus, that $\mathcal{D}'$ can distinguish $\mathcal{H}_i$ and $\mathcal{H}_{i+1}$ is contradictory to the property of the WI argument system used in phase II.

Claim 2. $\mathcal{H}$ and $View_{V^*}^{P}(\bar{x})$ are indistinguishable.

Analogously to the proof of Claim 1, the indistinguishability follows directly from the fact that $Com_{pb}(\cdot; \cdot)$ is computationally hiding. It follows from Claim 1 and Claim 2 that $\mathcal{S}(V^*, \bar{x})$ and $View_{V^*}^{P}(\bar{x})$ are indistinguishable.

In the construction two-round perfectly-hiding commitment schemes are used. In fact, we can replace it with any constant-round statistically-hiding scheme. Moreover, there exist bounded-concurrent (non-black-box) zero-knowledge arguments for NP, assuming that collision-resistant hash functions exist[4,3]. Thus, we obtain our main theorem:

Theorem 3. *Suppose that constant-round statistically-hiding commitment schemes and collision-resistant hash functions exist. Then, there exist constant-round bounded-concurrent zero-knowledge arguments of knowledge for any NP.*

References

1. Blum, M.: How to prove a theorem so no one else can claim it. In: Proceedings of the International Congress of Mathematicians, California, USA, pp. 1444–1451 (1986)
2. Barak, B.: How to go beyond the black-box simulation barrier. In: 42th Annual Syposium on Foundation of Computing Science, pp. 106–115. IEEE Computer Society (2001)
3. Barak, B.: Non-black-box techniques in cryptography. Thesis for the Ph. D. Degree, Weizmann Institute of Science, 53–102 (2004),
   http://www.math.ias.edu/~boaz/index.html
4. Barak, B., Goldreich, O.: Universal arguments and their applications,
   http://eprint.iacr.org/2001/063
5. Barak, B., Lindell, Y.: Strict polynomial-time in simulation and extraction. In the SIAM Journal on Computing 33(4), 783–818 (2004); An extended abstract appeared in the 34th STOC, pp. 484–493 (2002)
6. Barak, B., Lindell, Y., Vadhan, S.: Lower bounds for non-black-box zero knowledge. In: 44th Annual IEEE Symposium Foundations of Computer Science, pp. 384–393. IEEE Computer Society (2003)
7. Barak, B., Lindell, Y., Vadhan, S.: Lower bounds for non-black-box zero knowledge. Journal of Computer and System Sciences 72(2), 321–391 (2006)
8. Bellare, M., Jakobsson, M., Yung, M.: Round-Optimal Zero-Knowledge Arguments Based on Any One-Way Function. In: Fumy, W. (ed.) EUROCRYPT 1997. LNCS, vol. 1233, pp. 280–305. Springer, Heidelberg (1997)
9. Dwork, C., Naor, M., Sahai, A.: Concurrent zero-knowledge. In: Proceedings of 30th STOC, Dallas, Texas, USA, 1998, pp. 409–418 (1998)
10. Feige, U., Shamir, A.: Zero Knowledge Proofs of Knowledge in Two Rounds. In: Brassard, G. (ed.) CRYPTO 1989. LNCS, vol. 435, pp. 526–544. Springer, Heidelberg (1990)
11. Feige, U.: Alternative models for zero knowledge interactive proofs. Ph.D., Weizmann Institute of science (1990)
12. Feige, U., Lapidot, D., Shamir, A.: Multiple non-interactive, zero-knowledge proofs based on a single random string. In: Proc. 31th Ann. Symp. on FOCS, pp. 186–189 (1990)
13. Goldreich, O., Krawczyk, H.: On the composition of zero-knowledge proof systems. SIAM Journal of Computing 25(1), 169–192 (1996); Preliminary version appeared in LNCS, vol. 443, pp. 268–282 (1990)
14. Goldwasser, S., Micali, S., Rackoff, C.: The knowledge complexity of interactive proof systems. SIAM Journal on Computing 18(1), 186–208 (1989)
15. Goldreich, O., Oren, Y.: Definitions and properties of zero-knowledge proof systems. Journal of Cryptology 7(1), 1–32 (1994)
16. Goldreich, O., Kahan, A.: How to construct constant-round zero-knowledge proof system for NP. Journal of Cryptology 9(3), 167–189 (1996)
17. Goldreich, O.: Foundations of Cryptography - Basic Tools. Cambridge University Press (2001)

18. Li, H., Xue, H., Li, B., Feng, D.: On constant-round zero-knowledge proofs of knowledge for NP-relations. Science China Information Sciences 53(4), 788–799 (2010)
19. Jiang, S., Li, H., Li, B.: Constant-round bounded concurrent zero-knowledge arguments of knowledge for NP. In: The 7th China Conference on Information and Communications Security, CCICS 2010, pp. 174–191 (2010)
20. Lindell, Y.: Constant-round zero-knowledge proofs of knowledge. ECCC Reports-TR11-003, http://eccc.hpi-web.de/report/2011/003/
21. Pass, R., Rosen, A.: New and Improved Constructions of Non-Malleable Cryptographic Protocols. SIAM Journal on Computing 38(2), 702–752 (2008); In: 37th STOC, pp. 533–542 (2005)
22. Rosen, A.: A Note on Constant-Round Zero-Knowledge Proofs for NP. In: Naor, M. (ed.) TCC 2004. LNCS, vol. 2951, pp. 191–202. Springer, Heidelberg (2004)

On the Checkpointing Strategy in Desktop Grids

Dongping Wang and Bin Gong

Department of Computer Science and Technology, ShanDong University, Jinan, China
wdp2006@gmail.com, gb@sdu.edu.cn

Abstract. Checkpointing is an effective measure to ensure the completion of long-running jobs in Desktop Grids which are subject to frequent resource failures. We focus on checkpointing strategies in the context of Desktop Grids, including volunteer computing systems, where individual hosts follow diverse failure distributions. We propose an algorithm which computes sequence of checkpoint interval lengths for each individual host according to a sample of its availability interval lengths. This algorithm directly approximates the probability distribution of availability interval lengths with the sample, without deriving a closed form of the probability distribution. Through simulations with synthetic trace data and trace data from real volunteer computing project, this sample based strategy shows better performance than periodic strategy in terms of wasted time in most cases.

Keywords: checkpointing strategy, fault tolerance, volunteer computing, resource failures.

1 Introduction

In Desktop Grids, most computing resources are donated by their owners and not dedicated, which are only available when they are not used by their owners. So, resource failure occurs more frequently in Desktop Grids than in other computing systems with dedicated resources. Checkpointing is usually used as fault tolerance measure to accelerate completion of tasks, especially long-running tasks, in Desktop Grids.

Checkpointing strategies, determining when to create checkpoints, are important in using checkpointing. Too frequent checkpoints will cost too much time in creating checkpoints. On the other hand, too infrequent checkpoints will waste too much production time.

Periodic strategy is probably the most widely used checkpointing strategy. Existing researches about this strategy have given estimate of optimum checkpoint interval length in closed form, which is easy to use in real systems. However, periodic strategy is only optimal when interfailure interval length follows exponential distribution. Interfailure interval corresponds to availability interval in Desktop Grids. According to existing researches [1-3], availability interval lengths do not follow exponential distribution for most individual hosts in Desktop Grids. Moreover, availability interval lengths of individual hosts obey diverse distributions and it is difficult to derive closed forms for all these distributions. So, checkpointing strategies based on closed form of distribution can not work well in Desktop Grids.

Y. Xiang et al. (Eds.): IDCS 2012, LNCS 7646, pp. 217–226, 2012.

In this paper, we propose an aperiodic checkpointing strategy which determines sequence of checkpoint interval lengths for each individual host according to a sample of its availability interval lengths. This strategy takes the distribution of availability interval lengths into consideration. It approximates the distribution with the sample directly, without deriving a closed form of the distribution with parameter model fitting method. As many other researches [4, 5], we make an assumption that time cost in creating a checkpoint and in loading a checkpoint are constants. Through simulations with synthetic trace data and trace data from real volunteer computing project, this strategy shows better performance than periodic strategy in terms of wasted time.

The rest of this paper is structured as follows. Related works are reviewed in section 2. The algorithm of sample based checkpointing strategy is described in section 3. Simulations with trace data and results are given in section 4. Last section gives conclusion and future work.

2   Related Works

Many works study the problem of optimizing checkpointing strategy in the context of transactions systems. Chandy [6] and Chandy et al. [7] considered three analytic models of transactions systems. All three models share the assumptions that the inter-failure time is exponentially distributed and the checkpointing time is fixed. Under the assumptions that the checkpointing interval, the production time between failures, and the checkpointing time are independent and exponentially distributed, Gelenbe [8] and Gelenbe et al. [9] considered two problems: the maximization of system availability and the minimization of the mean response time of transactions. Gelenbe [10] showed that the optimum checkpoint interval is a function of the load of the system and proved that the optimum production time between checkpoints should be a deterministic quantity in order to maximize the system availability. Tantawi and Ruschitzka [11] proposed a model which supports general failure distributions and random check-pointing durations. Moreover, failures are allowed during both checkpointing and recovery. With this model, they derived a general expression for system availability. However, evaluating this expression is intractable, since it requires solving an integral equation with infinite number of imbedded integrals. Consequently, one can not compute an optimal policy with this expression. By considering a component of the failure rate depends on the current time in a cyclic way, L'Ecuyer and Malenfant [12] generalized Tantawi and Ruschitzka's model with a Markov Renewal Decision Process, and gave an approach to compute the optimal strategy. Ling et al. [13] intro-duced the continuous checkpointing frequency function and derived an explicit formula which shows that the optimal checkpointing frequency is proportional to the square root of the failure rate. Although mean response time and system availability are most common optimization criteria in the context of transactions systems, Krishna [14] proposed a new optimization criterion and argued that it is better than mean response time and system availability.

Many other works aim at minimizing program execution time. By considering that interfailure interval lengths follows exponential distribution, Young [4] gave a first order approximation to optimal checkpoint interval length of periodic checkpointing strategy. Under the same assumption, Daly [5] extended Young's model and proposed a higher order approximation to optimal checkpoint interval length of periodic checkpointing strategy. Bouguerra et al. [15] proposed a checkpoint scheduling algorithm that is provably optimal for discrete time when failures obey any general probability distribution. Vaidya [16] studied the relation between optimal checkpoint interval and two metrics of a checkpointing scheme: checkpoint overhead and checkpoint latency, and found that optimal checkpoint interval is independent of checkpoint latency. Ziv [17] showed that significant reduction in the execution time can be achieved in checkpointing schemes with task duplication by using two types of checkpoints: compare-checkpoints and store-checkpoints. Ziv and Bruck [18] proposed an on-line algorithm for placement of checkpoints which uses knowledge of the current cost of a checkpoint to decide whether or not to place a checkpoint. In this paper, we propose a strategy which gives dynamic checkpoint interval lengths according to a sample of availability interval lengths for each individual hosts. Availability interval lengths may obey any distribution and no closed form of the distribution is needed.

3   Algorithm

When failure rate is constant for all time, Daly [5] has given high order approximation of optimal checkpoint interval length which relies on failure rate and time cost to create a checkpoint. If time cost to create a checkpoint is fixed, a failure rate uniquely determines an optimal checkpoint interval length. Reciprocal of checkpoint interval length is checkpoint frequency. Consequently, a failure rate uniquely determines an optimal checkpoint frequency. Thus, optimal checkpoint frequencies for all time can be obtained with Daly's method when failure rate varies with time. In this section, we propose an algorithm which generates sequence of checkpoint interval length from a sample of interfailure lengths. This algorithm derives optimal checkpoint frequencies of all time and place checkpoints so that the integral calculus of optimal checkpoint frequency within each checkpoint interval is equal to one. First, time horizon is divided into time segments by members of the sample and failure rate of each time segment is approximately calculated. Mean of interfailure length is the reciprocal of failure rate. Then, optimal checkpoint interval length of each time segment is calculated based on its mean of interfailure length. The reciprocal of optimal checkpoint interval length is optimal checkpoint frequency. With optimal checkpoint frequencies of all time segments, sequence of checkpoint interval length for the whole time horizon is derived. Pseudo code of this algorithm is given by Algorithm 1.

Algorithm 1. Segments-Chk-Freq
Input: a[];// the sample of interfailure lengths
        n; // size of the sample
      δ; //time to create a checkpoint
      bt; //start time of program execution in current availability interval
Output: o[]; // checkpoint interval sequence

```
1 Begin
2 b[]=sort(a[]); //sort the sample in increasing order
3 for(i=1;i<=n;i++)
4   {
5     if(i==1)
6           m[i]=n*b[i];
7     else
8           m[i]=(n+1-i)(b[i]-b[i-1]);
9       c[i]=Daly-Opt-Chk-Int(m[i], δ);
10      f[i]=1/c[i];
11  }
12  off=bt; j=1; d=0; e=0;
13  while(off<b[n])
14  {
15    for(i=1;i<=n;i++) { if(off<b[i]) break; }
16    while(e<1)
17    {
18       if(i>n) { d=d+(1-e)/f[n]; off=off+(1-e)/f[n]; e=1;
break; }
19            p=e+(b[i]-off)*f[i];
20            if(p>1) { d=d+(1-e)/f[i]; off=off+(1-e)/f[i];
e=1; break;}
21            else {d=d+b[i]-off; off=b[i]; e=p; i++;}
22    }
23      o[j]=d; j++; off=off+δ; e=0;
24  }
25  if(j==1) o[1]=1/f[n];
26 End
```

Details about the algorithm are noted here. Line 2 sorts the sample and stores the result in array b. Thus, time horizon is divided into $(n+1)$ time segments: $(0, b[1])$, $(b[1], b[2])$, ... ,$(b[n-1], b[n])$, $(b[n], +\infty)$. Lines 5-8 compute mean of interfailure length for all time segments except the last one. Since the sample is about interfailure length, a single observation of interfailure length will appear in those $(n+1)$ time segments with equal probability, $1/(n+1)$. When n is big enough, it is easy to get the following approximations. Probability density for the ith time segment approximates

$$\frac{1}{(n+1)(b[i]-b[i-1])}.$$ Failure rate for the ith time segment approximates

$$\frac{1}{(n+1-i)(b[i]-b[i-1])}.$$ Line 9 and 10 compute optimal checkpoint interval

length and optimal checkpoint frequency separately. The function called in line 9 computes optimal checkpoint interval length with the following formulation proposed by Daly [5], $\tilde{\tau}_{opt} = \begin{cases} \sqrt{2\delta M}\left[1+\frac{1}{3}(\frac{\delta}{2M})^{1/2}+\frac{1}{9}(\frac{\delta}{2M})\right]-\delta\,, \text{ for } \delta < 2M \\ M\,, \qquad\qquad\qquad\qquad\qquad \text{ for } \delta \geq 2M \end{cases}$. In

this formulation, M is mean of interfailure length and is also reciprocal of failure rate. Since there is not enough information to compute the optimal checkpoint frequency for the last time segment, we take the optimal checkpoint frequency of the nth time segment for it. Lines 12-24 compute sequence of checkpoint interval length. If *off* is the start of the jth checkpoint interval, then the jth checkpoint interval length $o[j]$ should satisfy the equation of $\int_{off}^{off+o[j]} f(t)dt = 1$, where $f(t)$ is the optimal checkpoint frequency function.

At the beginning of this algorithm, a sort operation to the sample is called. Since we use *QuickSort* method, its computational complexity is bounded by $O(n\log n)$. The computational complexity of other part of the algorithm is bounded by $O(nk)$. Here, n is the size of the sample and k is the number of checkpoint interval lengths in result sequence. So, the computational complexity of this algorithm is $O(n\log n+nk)$. When this algorithm is used in practice, each individual host can call the algorithm and calculate its checkpointing strategy by itself. Moreover, checkpointing strategy of each individual host need not be updated too frequently because failure distribution is relatively stable in a short period. So, the computational cost of using this algorithm in practice is ignorable.

As an example, a result of this algorithm is shown here. The result generated with this algorithm is a sequence of checkpoint interval length. The input sample of interfailure lengths in calling the algorithm is a sample of a Weibull distribution. The scale parameter of the Weibull distribution is 6 and the shape parameter is 0.5. Size of the sample is 1000. This algorithm is called with δ being 1/60 and *bt* being 0. The result is plotted in Fig. 1. As can be seen from the figure, the left part (from 1 to 50) fluctuates with smaller amplitude and shows clearly ascending trend. The middle part (from 50 to 150) fluctuates with bigger amplitude and has no obvious ascending trend or descending trend. The right part (from 150 to 250) has only a few changes. Existing researches [11, 13] have shown that optimal checkpoint interval lengths have ascending trend when failure rate is descending. Consequently, the left part fulfills this regularity better than the middle part and the right part do. The reason that causes the differences among these three parts is the amount of information used in computing checkpoint interval lengths. The algorithm shows that more sample members are used in computing earlier checkpoint interval lengths and less sample members are used in computing later ones. Luckily, earlier checkpoint interval lengths are more important than later ones in terms of system performance.

4   Simulations

To evaluate the effectiveness of the algorithm proposed in last section, we compare it with periodic strategy through simulations. The optimal checkpoint interval length of

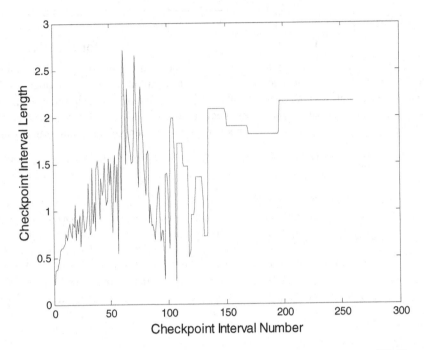

Fig. 1. A sequence of checkpoint interval lengths generated with Segments-Chk-Freq

periodic strategy is computed with the formulation proposed by Daly [5]. In each simulation, we run a task for 10000 times and observe total wasted time which includes time to create checkpoints, time to load checkpoints and rework time. These simulations use not only synthetic trace data but also trace data from real volunteer computing project.

4.1   Simulations with Synthetic Trace Data

Several synthetic data are generated, each of which corresponding to a probability distribution. Parameters of these probability distributions are provided in Table 1. According to [19], availability interval lengths of about 21 percent individual hosts in volunteer computing system are independent and identically distributed (iid), which can be divided into six cluster. Each cluster is modeled with a probability distribution. All these probability distributions are embraced in Table 1. Failure free computation time of a task is 100 hours. Creating a checkpoint and loading a checkpoint both cost 1/60 hour. Sample sizes used in these simulations are all 1000. These simulations are all implemented with Matlab software. Results of simulations with synthetic trace data are shown in Fig. 2.

As can be seen from the figure, sample based strategy leads to less total wasted time for all test distributions except the exponential distribution. For the exponential distribution, sample based strategy causes more total wasted time by about 0.8 percent.

Table 1. Distributions of synthetic trace data

name	Type of distribution	Parameter(s)
exp	Exponential	Rate parameter = 4
wbl	Weibull	Scale parameter = 1.682; shape parameter = 0.431
gam1	Gamma	Scale parameter = 311.711; shape parameter = 0.289
gam2	Gamma	Scale parameter = 152.216; shape parameter = 0.340
gam3	Gamma	Scale parameter = 371.622; shape parameter = 0.357
gam4	Gamma	Scale parameter = 89.223; shape parameter = 0.342
gam5	Gamma	Scale parameter = 43.652; shape parameter = 0.357

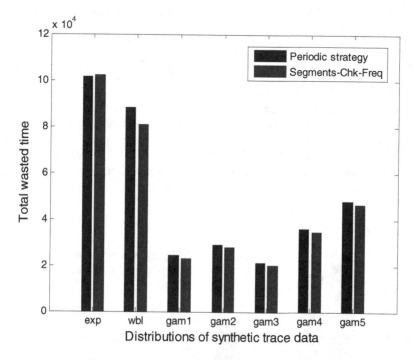

Fig. 2. Results for simulations with synthetic trace data

For other tested distributions, the reduction of total wasted time caused by sample based strategy are by 8 percent, 5 percent, 3.8 percent, 5.8 percent, 3.1 percent and 2.8 percent. Since the exponential distribution is the only one which does not belong to the six probability distributions for availability interval lengths of volunteer computing system, we believe that the sample based strategy can perform well in volunteer computing system which is testified in next subsection.

4.2 Simulations with SETI@home Trace Data

The trace data used here is SETI@home trace data [3] provided by FTA [20]. It is collected using BOINC [21] server of SETI@home from April 1, 2007 to January 1, 2009. It embraces CPU availability trace data from about 230,000 hosts over Internet. Parameters of these simulations are illustrated in Table 2. Three different time of creating checkpoint are considered. For each simulation, a task with given failure free computation time is run for 10000 times. Each task running involves randomly choosing a host and randomly choosing an availability interval whose start is used as the start of current task running. Sample members are fetched from lengths of availability intervals before the chosen one. To ensure enough information in generating checkpoint interval lengths, sample size is limited. If there are not enough availability intervals before the chose one to form a sample, current task running is rerun. These simulations are implemented with C++ language.

Table 2. Parameters for simulations with SETI@home trace data

Minimum sample size	100
Maximum sample size	1000
Time to create/load checkpoint	1/60; 1/120; 1/360
Failure free task computation time	100 hours

Results of these simulations are shown in Fig. 3. It is clearly shown that sample based strategy leads to less total wasted time than periodic strategy does. Particularly, the improvement is 8.4 percent when time to create a checkpoint is 1/60 hour, is 4.5 percent when time to create a checkpoint is 1/120 hour and is 3.7 percent when time to create a checkpoint is 1/360 hour. Obviously, sample based strategy leads to bigger improvement when time to create a checkpoint is bigger.

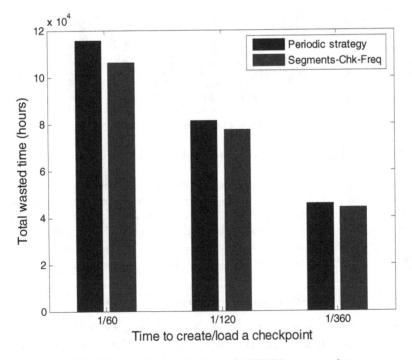

Fig. 3. Results for simulations with SETI@home trace data

5   Conclusion and Future Work

In Desktop Grids, availability interval lengths of individual hosts obey diverse probability distributions. It is difficult to model the probability distribution of availability interval lengths for each individual host. For this case, we propose a checkpointing strategy which computes sequence of checkpoint interval lengths from sample of availability interval lengths. Availability interval lengths may obey any general probability distribution and closed form of the probability distribution is not needed. This strategy is compared with periodic strategy through simulations with synthetic trace data and trace data from real volunteer computing project. As a result, this strategy outperforms periodic strategy in terms of wasted time in most cases.

In volunteer computing system, two or more duplications of each task should be distributed to individual hosts. This measure is for both fault tolerance and anti sabotage. Our future work is to study optimizing checkpointing strategy in such context.

References

1. Nurmi, D., Brevik, J., Wolski, R.: Modeling Machine Availability in Enterprise and Wide-Area Distributed Computing Environments. In: Cunha, J.C., Medeiros, P.D. (eds.) Euro-Par 2005. LNCS, vol. 3648, pp. 432–441. Springer, Heidelberg (2005)
2. Wolski, R., Nurmi, D., Brevik, J.: An Analysis of Availability Distributions in Condor. In: IPDPS 2007: Proceedings of the 21th International Parallel and Distributed Processing Symposium, pp. 1–6. IEEE (2007)
3. Javadi, B., Kondo, D., Vincent, J.-M., Anderson, D.P.: Mining for Statistical Availability Models in Large-Scale Distributed Systems: An Empirical Study of SETI@home. In: MASCOTS 2009: Proceedings of the 17th Annual Meeting of the IEEE/ACM International Symposium on Modelling, Analysis and Simulation of Computer and Telecommunication Systems, pp. 1–10 (2009)
4. Young, J.W.: A First Order Approximation to the Optimal Checkpoint Interval. Commun. ACM 17(9), 530–531 (1974)
5. Daly, J.T.: A higher order estimate of the optimum checkpoint interval for restart dumps. Future Generation Comp. Syst. 22(3), 303–312 (2006)
6. Chandy, K.M.: A Survey of Analytic Models of Rollback and Recovery Strategies. Computer 8(5), 40–47 (1975)
7. Chandy, K.M., Browne, J.C., Dissly, C.W., Uhrig, W.R.: Analytic models for rollback and recovery strategies in database systems. IEEE Trans. Software Eng. SE-1, 100–110 (1975)
8. Gelenbe, E.: A model of rollback recovery with multiple checkpoints. In: Proceedings of the Second International Symposium on Software Engineering, pp. 251–255. ACM (1976)
9. Gelenbe, E., Derochette, D.: Performance of rollback recovery systems under intermittent failures. Commun. ACM 21(6), 493–499 (1978)
10. Gelenbe, E.: On the optimum checkpoint interval. J. ACM 26(2), 259–270 (1979)
11. Tantawi, A.N., Ruschitzka, M.: Performance Analysis of Checkpointing Strategies. ACM Trans. Comput. Syst. 2(2), 123–144 (1984)
12. L'Ecuyer, P., Malenfant, J.: Computing Optimal Checkpointing Strategies for Rollback and Recovery Systems. IEEE Trans. Computers 37(4), 491–496 (1988)
13. Ling, Y., Mi, J., Lin, X.: A Variational Calculus Approach to Optimal Checkpoint Placement. IEEE Trans. Computers 50(7), 699–708 (2001)

14. Krishna, C.M., Shin, K.G., Lee, Y.-H.: Optimization Criteria for Checkpoint Placements. Comm. ACM 27(4), 1008–1012 (1984)
15. Bouguerra, M.-S., Kondo, D., Trystram, D.: On the Scheduling of Checkpoints in Desktop Grids. In: Proceedings of 11th IEEE/ACM International Symposium on Cluster, Cloud and Grid Computing (CCGRID 2011), pp. 305–313. IEEE (2011)
16. Vaidya, N.H.: Impact of checkpoint latency on overhead ratio of a checkpointing scheme. IEEE Transactions on Computers 46(8), 942–947 (1997)
17. Ziv, A., Bruck, J.: Performance Optimization of Checkpointing Schemes with Task Duplication. IEEE Transactions on Computers 46(12), 1381–1386 (1997)
18. Ziv, A., Bruck, J.: An On-Line Algorithm for Checkpoint Placement. IEEE Transactions on Computers 46(9), 976–985 (1997)
19. Javadi, B., Kondo, D., Vincent, J.-M., Anderson, D.P.: Discovering Statistical Models of Availability in Large Distributed Systems: An Empirical Study of SETI@home. IEEE Trans. Parallel Distrib. Syst. 22(11), 1896–1903 (2011)
20. Kondo, D., Javadi, B., Iosup, A., Epema, D.H.J.: The Failure Trace Archive: Enabling Comparative Analysis of Failures in Diverse Distributed Systems. In: CCGRID 2010: Proceedings of the 10th IEEE/ACM International Conference on Cluster, Cloud and Grid Computing, pp. 398–407. IEEE (2010)
21. Anderson, D.P.: BOINC: a system for public-resource computing and storage. In: GRID 2004: Proceedings of the Fifth IEEE/ACM International Workshop on Grid Computing, pp. 4–10 (2004)

A Continuous Reverse Skyline Query Processing Considering the Mobility of Query Objects

Jongtae Lim, Yonghun Park, Kyoungsoo Bok, and Jaesoo Yoo[*]

Department of Information and Communication Engineering, Chungbuk National University,
52 Naesudong-ro, Heundeok-gu, Cheongju Chungbuk, Korea
{jtlim,yhpark1119,ksbok,yjs}@chungbuk.ac.kr

Abstract. With the development of location-based services, various query processing methods for moving objects have been studied. Particularly, a reverse skyline query that is the variation of the skyline query has been receiving much attention these days. However, the existing reverse skyline query processing methods did not consider the mobility of objects. In this paper, we propose a continuous reverse skyline query processing method that considers the mobility of a query object. The proposed method removes the objects that do not affect a query by using a pruning scheme and continuously monitors the areas of candidate objects to update the query result incrementally.

Keywords: Reverse skyline, Moving object, Location-based service, Continuous query.

1 Introduction

In recent, the interests of location-based services (LBS) have been increased [1]. The targets of LBS are the users who use mobile devices such as laptop and smart phone. Users can use the service when they move by using public transport or on foot. To provide the services on this environment, we need a continuous query processing methods for moving objects [2]. Various continuous query processing methods for moving objects have been studied. The major query types studied in the past are the range query [3], the k-Nearest Neighbor query [4] and the Top-k query [5]. In recent, as the demands of customers become various, much research on the skyline query that considers the multi-attribute values and its variation has been done [6, 7]. For example, if a customer wants to find the cheapest and nearest restaurant, the location of the customer is a query point in the space and the restaurants are the target objects of the query. The attributes of the objects are the price and the distance. The result of a skyline query is a set of objects whose attribute vector is not dominated by any other objects. Through the skyline query processing, it becomes possible to provide the service considering multi-attribute values such as the cheapest and nearest restaurant.

---

[*] Corresponding author.

Y. Xiang et al. (Eds.): IDCS 2012, LNCS 7646, pp. 227–237, 2012.

A reverse skyline query (RSL) is one of the variation query types of the skyline query. RSL was proposed for the various LBS services [8-13]. The reverse skyline query finds the objects including the query object as the result of the skyline query. For example, the restaurant is able to retrieve the customers that consider it to be the cheapest and nearest one by the reverse skyline query. We can also provide more useful services through the reverse skyline query. Through the reverse skyline query, the restaurant is able to retrieve the customers that consider it as the cheapest and nearest one. In this case, the restaurant is query and the customers are objects. We can also provide more useful services through the reverse skyline query.

In recent, efficient reverse skyline processing methods have been studied. However, the existing reverse skyline query processing methods did not consider the mobility of objects. Applications such as GPS need a continuous query processing methods in the moving query environment. The existing methods process a continuous query whenever a query object moves or is in a certain period. The existing method spends high costs to process the continuous reverse skyline query.

In this paper, we propose a continuous reverse skyline query processing method that considers the mobility of a query object. The proposed method removes the objects that do not affect a query by using a pruning phase and continuously monitor the areas of candidate objects to update the query result incrementally.

The rest of this paper is organized as follows. Section 2 reviews related work. Section 3 illustrates our proposed method, and Section 4 presents the performance evaluation results of our proposed method. Finally, Section 5 concludes this paper and describes future work.

2   Related Work

2.1   Skyline Query

A skyline query is a specific example of multi-attribute queries, and has been widely studied. The result of a skyline query is a set of objects in the database whose attribute values are not dominated by any other objects. For example, if a customer wants to find the cheapest and nearest restaurant, the location of the customer is a query point in the space and the restaurants are the target objects of the query. The attributes of the objects are the price and the distance.

Figure 1 shows how to process the skyline query. As shown in Figure 1(a), there are certain objects p_1, p_2, p_3, p_4, p_5 and p_6. In the case, there are no objects satisfying the customer's requirements. However, the customer will want some restaurants whose conditions are close to their expectation. In the other words, the customer does not consider objects which have higher price and longer distance than another object. After removing the objects dominated by other objects on all dimensions, the remaining objects are the result of the query. p_3 and p_4 are removed since they are dominated by other objects. That is, p_3 is dominated by p_2, p_4 and p_5, and p_4 is dominated by p_5. The result of the query is shown in Figure 1(b).

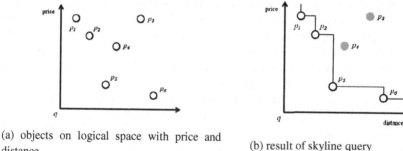

(a) objects on logical space with price and distance

(b) result of skyline query

Fig. 1. Example of skyline query processing

2.2   Reverse Skyline Query

The reverse skyline query is a query type returning a set of objects that includes the query object as the result of the skyline query. For example, when a restaurant wants to advertise a bargain day, the advertisement is more impressive to customers who think the restaurant is cheaper and closer than other restaurants. In this case, the restaurant is a query object issuing a reverse skyline query and the customers are the target objects for the query.

Figure 2 shows the skyline of target objects. Figure 2(a) shows the skyline of c_1. c_1 is the reverse skyline result. In this case, query q is result of skyline. Figure 2(b) shows the skyline of c_2. c_2 is not a reverse skyline result. In this case, query q is not a result of skyline.

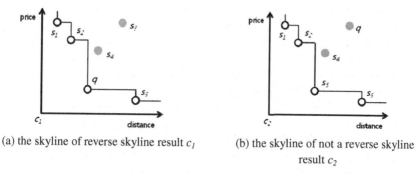

(a) the skyline of reverse skyline result c_1

(b) the skyline of not a reverse skyline result c_2

Fig. 2. The skyline of target objects

Greedy Reverse Skyline (GRSL) is the naive method to process a reverse skyline query. It finds target objects including the query object as a result of a skyline query for each target object [8]. However, the method spends high costs to process the reverse skyline query because it should compute the skyline query results as many as the number of target objects. Recently, the various reverse skyline query processing methods have been studied. E. Dellis [8] proposed Branch and Bound Reverse Skyline (BBRS) and Reverse Skyline Computation Using Skyline Approximations

(RSSA) algorithm. The method adapts Branch and Bound Skyline (BBS) algorithm processed in the range query processing manner. X. Lian [9] proposed a reverse skyline query processing method over uncertain databases. The method considers the rectangle shape as a query. L. Zhu [10] proposed a reverse skyline query processing method processed on data stream. But, they are based on dynamic skyline [14]. The traditional skyline to retrieve skyline points usually assumes static data objects in the database. However, the dynamic skyline focuses on skyline queries with dynamic attributes. The dynamic skyline is specific skyline to process similar query. Thus, existing reverse skyline methods have the limitation of service domains and require the high costs of computation to provide various location-based services. Thus, existing reverse skyline methods have the limitation of service domains and require the high costs of computation to provide various location-based services. So, we proposed an efficient method for processing reverse skyline queries [12]. This method processes a reverse skyline query using the spatial grid indexing method. This method prunes the objects that do not affect a query using skyline dominant relationship during the reverse skyline query processing.

Figure 3 shows the algorithm for processing the reverse skyline query. Figure 3(a) shows all objects in the spatial space. In Figure 3(a), the values in parentheses are the static attributes, and q denotes the query object. First, this method searches for the same type of objects dominating q without the distance attribute in the order of their proximity to q. o_6 is the object first found by the query algorithm, but o_6 does not dominate q. Therefore, the algorithm continues to find the next nearest object until an object dominating q appears. Second, if an object dominating q is found, we draw the bisector between the object and q.

Figure 3(b) shows that o_2 is the object dominating q and the bisector between o_2 and q is drawn. All objects located outside the bisector do not contain q as the skyline

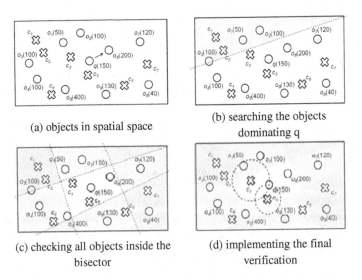

(a) objects in spatial space

(b) searching the objects dominating q

(c) checking all objects inside the bisector

(d) implementing the final verification

Fig. 3. An efficient method for processing reverse skyline queries

result. It is because the objects are always closer to o_2 than q and even o_2 dominates q in static attributes. q is dominated by o_2 on the skyline of both c_1 and c_2. These processes are repeated until all objects inside the bisector are checked. During the processes, we cache different types of objects located inside the bisector and search for objects dominating q as the candidates of the result. In this case, c_3 and c_5 are the candidate object of the query. Finally, we refine the candidate objects by determining whether or not the objects that dominate q and locate closer against q as shown in Figure 3(d). Figure 3(d) shows the final verification. As a result, c_5 is the result of the reverse skyline query.

3   The Proposed Method

In this paper, we propose a continuous reverse skyline query processing method in the moving query objects environment. The proposed method consists of two phases. The first phase prunes the objects that do not affect a query and put the remaining objects into a reference list and candidate list of the query. The second phase makes the monitoring area with the candidate objects.

3.1   Pruning Phase

The first phase prunes the objects that do not affect a query and put the remaining objects into a reference list and candidate list of the query. The pruning algorithm of Reverse Skyline Query Processing in Metric Spaces [12] is used in this phase. Figure 4 shows the proposed pruning method. The proposed pruning method use relative distance between query and target object. In the figure 4(a), the relative distance between query q and target object s_2 present the bisector in fixed location environment. In this case, q is dominated in skyline of s_2. In the figure 4(b), the relative distance between query q and target object s_2 present the parabola in moving query environment.

We search objects in the order of the distance to the query path sequentially. If an object is the same type of the query object, it dominates the all static attributes of the query object and the point that is nearer than other reference objects exists on the query path, the object is put into the reference list. If an object is not the same type of the query object and the point that is nearer than other reference objects exists on the query path, the object is put into the candidate list. There is no need to access all objects because of the pruning phase.

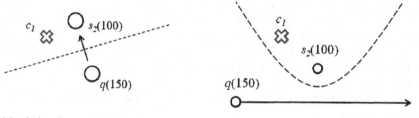

(a) relative distance of point to point   (b) relative distance of point to straight line

Fig. 4. The pruning method using relative distance

3.2   Monitoring Phase

The second phase makes the monitoring area with the candidate objects. Figure 5 shows the proposed monitoring method. In this case, query q has fixed path and another object has fixed location. Figure 5(a) shows the relative distance graph of target object c_1. In the figure 5(a), relative distance between c_1 and q is changed. And relative distance between c_1 and another object is not change. In this example, q is dominated by s_2 before t_0 or after t_1. q is not dominated by s_2 from t_0 to t_1. So, we represent this period in two-dimensional spaces such as figure 5(b).

We draw a circle with the position of each candidate object as the center and the distance to the closest reference object as the radius to make the monitoring area. After that, we monitor the query objects to determine if the query object enters to or leaves from the monitoring area. If a query enters or leaves from the monitoring area, the result of the query is updated. Since the proposed method makes and monitors the monitoring areas, there is no need to reprocess the reverse skyline query redundantly.

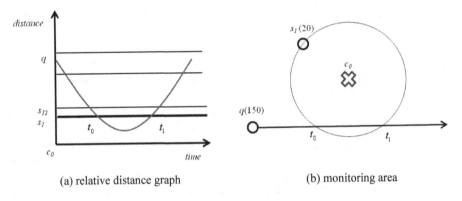

(a) relative distance graph   (b) monitoring area

Fig. 5. The monitoring method

3.3   The Proposed Algorithm

Figure 6 shows the continuous reverse skyline query processing procedure of the proposed method. The proposed method is processed on two-dimensional spaces as shown in Figure 6(a). The circle objects are the same type as the query object and the cross objects are the target objects. When a query is issued, the first phase is performed to prune the objects. The proposed method puts the remaining circle objects into the reference list and the remaining cross objects into the candidate list as shown in Figure 6(b). The drawn parabolas represent the pruning area. As a result, the proposed method gets the candidate object set such as Figure 6(c). Figure 6(d) shows how the second phase is processed. The circles represent the monitoring areas for each candidate object.

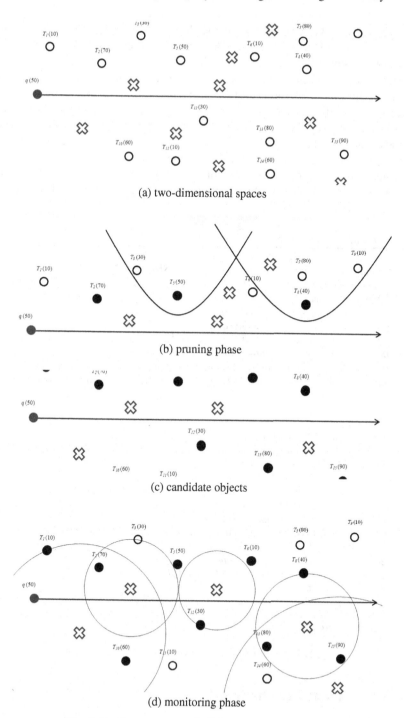

(a) two-dimensional spaces

(b) pruning phase

(c) candidate objects

(d) monitoring phase

Fig. 6. Continuous reverse skyline processing procedure

Figure 7 shows the proposed reverse skyline processing algorithm. The input is query object q and object set $o.queue$. The output is object set that includes the query object as the result of the skyline query. First, the proposed method implements the first phase. The proposed method search the same type object dominating q without the distance attribute in the order of their proximity to q. If an object domination q is found, the proposed method draws the parabola between the object and fix path of q. Through this parabola, the proposed method prunes the objects that do not affect a query and put the remaining objects into a reference list and candidate list of the query (Line 4~10). Second, the proposed method implements the second phase. In the second phase, the proposed method draws the monitoring area of each candidate objects (Line 17~23). Through this monitoring area, the proposed method processes the continuous reverse skyline queries.

ComputeReverseSkyline(q, o.queue)

Input : query object q , object set o.queue
output : object that result of reverse skyline RESULT_SET
01: query q load;
02: while (o.queue is not empty)
03:   o = the object included o.queue;
04:   if (o is same type against q) {
05:   compare the attribute values without location;
06:   if (o is object that can dominate q) {
07:   draw the parabola between q and o;
08:   remove the objects that are not included in pruning area;
09:   }
10:   }
11: }
12: Implement the final verification ;
13: Insert the remaining objects   into c.queue;
14: while (c.queue is not empty) {
15:   c = the object included   in c.queue;
16:   r = search the nearest object that dominates q from the object c;
17:   if (r exists) {
18:   draw the monitoring area;
19:   check the intersection point between path of q and monitoring area;
20:   if (intersection point exists) {
21:   insert the c into RESULT_SET;
22:   }
23:   }
24: }
25: Return RESULT_SET;

Fig. 7. The proposed reverse skyline processing algorithm

4   Experimental Evaluation

All experiments have been performed on a Windows XP operating system with 3.0 GHz CPU and 1 GB main memory. In each experiment, we performed 1K reverse skyline queries in the particular data set that has 1K objects generated in 1024×1024. We also used the R-tree as an index structure and generated all values of the queries and objects randomly.

Table 1. Evaluation parameters

Parameters	Values
Number of objects	1,000
Number of cells	16×16
Number of queries	1,000
Size of space	1,024×1,024

To experimentally evaluate the efficiency of the proposed pruning method, we checked how many objects are pruned during query processing. Figure 8 shows the performance of the proposed pruning method. As a result, the proposed method can process the reverse skyline query using only 5% of all objects.

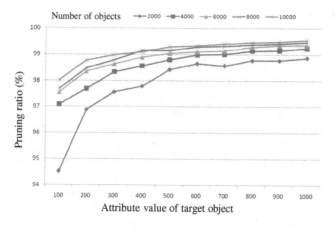

Fig. 8. Performance comparison according to the attribute values of target objects

We experimentally evaluated the efficiency of the proposed method for the reverse skyline computation. We consider three types of query processing method to evaluate the performance according to monitoring time. The first type denoted as "pruning + monitoring" uses both the first and second phase during query processing. The second type denoted as "pruning only" only uses the first phase during query processing. The third type denoted as "monitoring only" only uses the second phase during query processing. Figure 9 shows performance comparison according to monitoring time. For each time unit, the queries are reprocessed. As a result, the "pruning + monitoring" achieves better performance than the method that uses only the first phase and the method that uses only the second phase.

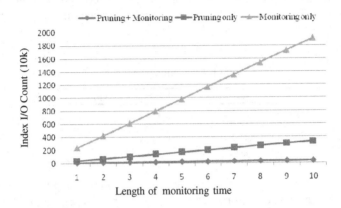

Fig. 9. Performance comparison according to monitoring time

5   Conclusion

In this paper, we proposed a continuous reverse skyline query processing method that considers the mobility of a query object. The proposed method removes the objects that do not affect a query by using a pruning scheme and continuously monitors the areas of candidate objects for incremental query processing. It was shown through the performance evaluation that the method using both phases achieves better performance than the methods using only one of the phases. In our future works, we will study the continuous reverse skyline query processing method in moving object and moving query environments.

Acknowledgments. This work was supported by Basic Science Research Program through the National Research Foundation of Korea(NRF) grant funded by the Koreagovernment(MEST)(No. 2009-0089128)" to "This research was supported by Basic Science Research Program through the National Research Foundation of Korea(NRF) funded by the Ministry of Education, Science and Technology(2012R1A1A2A10042015)

References

1. Lee, D.L., Xu, J., Zheng, B., Lee, W.C.: Data Management in Location-Dependent Information Services. IEEE Pervasive Computing 1(3), 65–72 (2002)
2. Brakatsoulas, S., Pfoser, D., Tryfona, N.: Modeling, Storing, and Mining Moving Object Databases. In: International Database Engineering and Applications Symposium, pp. 68–77 (2004)
3. Papadias, D., Zhang, J., Mamoulis, N., Tao, Y.: Query Processing in Spatial Network Databases. In: International Conference on Very Large Data Bases, pp. 802–813 (2003)

4. Song, Z., Roussopoulos, N.: K-Nearest Neighbor Search for Moving Query Point. In: Proc. of International Symposium on Advances in Spatial and Temporal Databases, pp. 79–96 (2001)
5. Ilyas, I., Beskales, G., Soliman, M.: A Survey of Top-k Query Processing Techniques in Relational Database Systems. ACM Computing Surveys 40(4) (2008)
6. Borzsonyi, S., Kossmann, D., Stocker, K.: The Skyline Operator. In: IEEE International Conference on Data Engineering, pp. 421–430 (2001)
7. Li, C., Ooi, B.B., Tung, A.K.H., Wang, S.: DADA: a Data Cube for Dominant Relationship Analysis. In: ACM SIGMOD International Conference on Management of Data, pp. 659–670 (2006)
8. Dellis, E., Seeger, B.: Efficient Computation of Reverse Skyline Queries. In: International Conference on Very Large Data Bases, pp. 291–302 (2007)
9. Lian, X., Chen, L.: Monochromatic and Bichromatic Reverse Skyline Search over Uncertain Databases. In: ACM SIGMOD International Conference on Management of Data, pp. 213–226 (2008)
10. Zhu, L., Li, C., Chen, H.: Efficient Computation of Reverse Skyline on Data Stream. In: International Joint Conference on Computational Sciences and Optimization, pp. 735–739 (2009)
11. Deshpande, M., Deepak, P.: Efficient Reverse Skyline Retrieval with Arbitrary Non-metric Similarity Measures. In: International Conference on Extending Database Technology, pp. 319–330 (2011)
12. Lim, J., Park, Y., Lee, J., Seo, D., Yoo, J.: An Efficient Method for Processing Reverse Skyline Queries. In: International Conference on Global Mobile Congress, pp. 1–5 (2010)
13. Lian, X., Chen, L.: Reverse skyline search in uncertain databases. ACM Transactions on Database Systems 35(1) (2010)
14. Papadias, D., Tao, Y., Fu, G., Seeger, B.: Progressive Skyline Computation in Database Systems. ACM Transaction Database System 30(1), 41–82 (2005)

Performance Analysis
of Wireless Intrusion Detection Systems

Khalid Nasr[1], Anas Abou-El Kalam[2], and Christian Fraboul[1]

[1] INPT-ENSEEIHT, IRIT, Université de Toulouse, Toulouse, France
{khalid.nasr,christian.fraboul}@enseeiht.fr
[2] OSCARS Laboratory, UCA/ENSA of Marrakesh, Morocco
anas@ensa.ac.ma

Abstract. Wireless Intrusion Detection System (WIDS) is a pivotal element in wireless network security. WIDS monitors the radio spectrum and system activities to detect intrusive events, and then alerts the complementary prevention part to combat the intrusions. Selecting a reliable WIDS system depends significantly on its performance evaluation. Many different attributes judge the WIDS performance such as *effectiveness, efficiency, immunity, interoperability,* etc. We introduce in this paper a novel methodology which consists of sequential tasks that cover all necessary dimensions for a credible evaluation of WIDSs performance. We also introduce a new evaluation metric E_{ID} (*intrusion detection effectiveness*) for evaluating the WIDS effectiveness that is considered the basic factor in evaluating the WIDS performance. Our developed metric E_{ID} manipulates the drawbacks of the previously proposed metrics. We follow our methodology and conduct experimental evaluation tests of two popular WIDSs (Kismet and AirSnare), to demonstrate the utility of E_{ID}.

Keywords: Performance analysis, WIDSs, evaluation methodology, evaluation metrics, wireless attacks.

1 Introduction

Wireless Intrusion Detection System (WIDS) monitors the radio spectrum and system activities to identify malicious activities leaked from the first line of defense such as firewall and encryption, and then alerts the complementary prevention part to combat the intrusions. Despite the importance of WIDSs in wireless network security, their performance is sometimes not satisfying in practice. Thus, WIDSs performance evaluation is a pressing necessity. By evaluation we mean the systematic assessment that measures the ability of a WIDS to meet the intended and expected performance.

This paper introduces a novel methodology for evaluating WIDSs performance. Our proposed methodology covers all necessary dimensions for a credible and comprehensive evaluation of WIDSs. However, this methodology is applicable for wired and wireless intrusion detection systems (IDSs) by considering the concepts and characteristics of each communication medium and characteristics of the IDS

Y. Xiang et al. (Eds.): IDCS 2012, LNCS 7646, pp. 238–252, 2012.

related, but in this paper we concentrate on the WIDSs. One of the focal dimensions in the WIDSs evaluation processes is the evaluation metrics which are the pivot of the evaluation process. Many different evaluation metrics have been proposed; each of them was based on a different approach such as *decision theory* [2], *information theory* [3], *costs* [4], etc. Advantages and disadvantages of the previously proposed metrics will be discussed in details in section 2. As a manipulation of the drawbacks of the previous metrics, we develop a new evaluation metric E_{ID} (*intrusion detection effectiveness*) for evaluating the WIDS effectiveness taking into account all necessary and related parameters. We also describe how we can evaluate the other WIDS performance attributes.

The rest of this paper is organized as follows. Section 2 presents an overview of the previous work on the experimental evaluation of IDSs performance. This section also discusses the previously proposed metrics and their advantages and disadvantages. Section 3 presents a novel methodology for evaluating WIDSs performance. This section explains in details the importance of each dimension in our methodology, with special concern with the evaluation metrics; a new evaluation metric E_{ID} is introduced. Section 4 presents experimental evaluation tests of well-known WIDSs; *Kismet* and *AirSnare*. Finally, section 5 presents our conclusions and future work.

2   Related Work

Most of the previous experimental evaluations of IDSs concerned with the wired IDSs, with a great lack of the wireless IDSs (WIDSs) evaluation. This section presents an overview of the previous work concerned with the experimental evaluation of IDSs performance and the proposed evaluation metrics.

The first introduced IDS evaluation, to our knowledge, is the IDS testing carried out by Puketza et al [5, 6]. They described a methodology and software platform for testing and evaluating IDSs effectiveness. They used simulation scripts for both normal activities (as a background) and intrusive activities. The test procedures concerned with evaluating three objectives: *intrusion identification, resource usage* and *stress* testing. There are no clearly defined metrics used in this work.

Another experimental evaluation of IDSs was performed by IBM Research Division in Zurich [7]. The implemented test-bed consists of several client and server machines managed by a workbench controller. The attacks are obtained from an internally maintained vulnerability database by IBM. Unfortunately, the report presented neither any results obtained nor any metric used.

The most famous evaluations of IDSs are DARPA 1998 [8] and DARPA 1999 [9] evaluations. The implemented test-bed contains generated normal traffic which represents hundreds of users on thousands of hosts. More than 300 instances of 38 different automated attacks were launched against UNIX victim machines in seven weeks of training data and two weeks of test data. Evaluation results were presented by *receiver operating characteristic* (ROC) curve. ROC is used to analyze the trade-off between the *false alarms rate* and the *detection rate*. The main disadvantage in using the ROC curve for evaluating the IDSs is that the IDSs evaluation depends on more parameters than those considered in the ROC. One of the most important parameters that were not considered in ROC is the *base-rate* parameter [1] that reflects the hostility of the operating environment and it is represented by the *prior probability of intrusions*. More details of the critiques of DARPA evaluations are available in [10].

In addition to ROC, there are other valuable metrics have been proposed such as *Bayesian detection rate* [1], *cost-based analysis* [4], *expected cost* [2], *intrusion detection capability* (C_{ID}) [3], and *intrusion detection operating characteristic* (IDOC) [11]. All these metrics concerned with evaluating the IDS effectiveness. These evaluation metrics used one of two approaches: 1) Graphical analysis of the trade-off between the main parameters (e.g., detection rate, false alarms rate, and/or base rate) or their combinations to judge the effectiveness of the IDSs, such as ROC *curve, Bayesian detection rate,* and IDOC, or 2) Analytical analysis by deriving a representative formula or equation that defines the relationship among the effectiveness parameters, such as *cost-base metrics* and C_{ID}. *Expected cost* metric combines these two approaches.

Bayesian detection rate [1] defines a mathematical relation between the main parameters of the IDS effectiveness. Axelsson in [1] demonstrated that due to the base-rate fallacy problem the limiting factor for the IDS performance is not the ability to correctly identify the intrusions, but rather its ability to suppress the false alarms. The drawback of this metric is the unavailability of the prior knowledge of the intrusion probability.

The first *cost-based* metrics were proposed by Stolfo et al. [4] for evaluating the intrusion detection in financial information systems. They argued that ROC analysis is misleading evaluation metric for this application. They defined three types of costs; *operational, damage,* and *challenge costs*. These costs are derived from the credit card fraud case. The drawback of this metric is the difficulty of the prior determining of the costs in some systems.

Another metric that takes the costs into account is the *expect cost* metric which was proposed by Gaffney et al [2]. They argued that both the ROC analysis and cost-based analysis are incomplete metrics. They used decision analysis techniques to combine and extend ROC analysis and cost-based analysis methods to provide an expected cost metric. The unavailability of the prior knowledge of the probability of intrusions and costs are the main difficulties of this metric.

Gu et al [3] proposed another evaluation metric called *intrusion detection capability* (C_{ID}). The authors depended on the notion of having less uncertainty about the IDS input, given the IDS output. The authors introduced C_{ID} metric as the ratio of the mutual information between IDS input and output, and the entropy of the input (as a normalization factor). The C_{ID} is maximized by calculating the operating point that minimizes the uncertainty of the input. We believe that the notion of C_{ID} for minimizing the uncertainty of the input is practically inapplicable for the IDS domain.

Cardenas et al [11] introduced another evaluation metric *Intrusion Detection Operating Characteristic* (IDOC) as a trade-off curve between the *probability of detection* and the *positive predictive value PPV* (or *Bayesian detection rate*) which is the posterior probability of an intrusion given the IDS output is an alarm *P(I|A)*. PPV is a function of the *base-rate (probability of intrusion)*, *probability of benign traffic*, *probability of detection*, and *probability of false alarms*. We believe that there is no novelty in the IDOC curve as an evaluation metric, where it is basically extracted from *Bayesian detection rate* [1]; just the graphical representation curves (which are based on the same equation; *Bayesian detection rate*) are the main difference between the IDOC and Axelsson's proposal in [1]. Axelsson studied graphically the trade-off between the PPV and the false alarms, but Cardenas et al [11] studied the trade-off between the PPV and the probability of detection.

The common main drawback of the previously proposed metrics is that their main notion is based on comparing two or more IDSs to select the best one, although this selected one may be ineffective. For that, we develop a new evaluation metric E_{ID} that is based on comparing the operation curve of an IDS under test with an optimal operation curve (created as a zero reference curve) by calculating the variance between the two curves. The variance value interprets the deviation of the IDS operation from the optimal intended operation.

3   Novel Evaluation Methodology

In this section, we present a novel proposed methodology for evaluating WIDSs performance. In our methodology (Fig. 1), we believe that the premier logical step in any evaluation process is determining the main goals of the evaluation. In this paper, our goal is evaluating wireless intrusion detection systems (WIDSs) performance in wireless networks. It is observed that our evaluation goal consists of three main parts; evaluation, WIDSs performance, and wireless networks. Then, our proposed methodology is fired accordingly from this evaluation goal into three main directions; studying the evaluation challenges, WIDSs performance attributes, and operating environment characterization. By identifying the evaluation challenges, we can extract the satisfactory requirements and take all possible measures to ensure the credibility of the evaluation. In consequence of analyzing the WIDSs performance attributes and the associated limitations, the representative evaluation metrics can be developed and defined. By logic, according to the evaluation metrics and what we need to measure, the helpful and suitable techniques and tools will be selected. As a complement, the wireless networks (operating environment) should be characterized, where it is considered as a foundation for the deployment and configuration of the system under test (WIDS). According to the characteristics of the operating environment and WIDS system, the evaluation workload or dataset can be characterized, and then the suitable workload generation tools can be selected. After that, the test-bed can be designed and configured taking into account the evaluation challenges, the operating environment characterization, the WIDS characterization, and the selected evaluation tools and techniques. Now the evaluator can manage the evaluation tests using the evaluation techniques and tools, and considering the workload characterization. Finally, by the defined evaluation metrics the results can be interpreted and the WIDSs are evaluated. In the following sections, we will discuss each dimension in our methodology in more details.

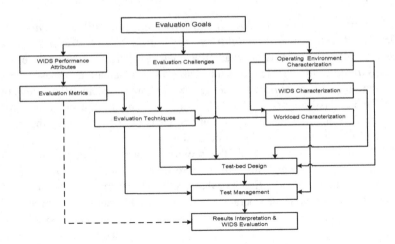

Fig. 1. Evaluation Methodology for WIDSs

3.1   Evaluation Goals

Evaluation goals, in general, interpret the evaluator needs such as evaluating one or more of the WIDS performance attributes in a specific operating environment. According to our goal in this paper, our methodology is fired from three main dimensions as mentioned above. All these dimensions and the related subsequent ones will be explained in details.

3.2   Evaluation Challenges

There are many critical challenges and limitations for evaluating WIDSs in wireless networks. We summarize these challenges as follows.

Openness of Wireless Environment. One of the great problems in WIDSs evaluation is the openness of the wireless environment which is rich in uncontrolled RF (radio frequency) traffic. Due to the continuous broadcasting of the uncontrolled RF traffic from the neighboring nodes in the range of the evaluation test-bed, it is difficult to accurately measure the evaluation parameters such as detection rate, nor false positive rate, nor BW (Bandwidth) utilization that are basically measured under controlled traffic. The only best solution for this problem is managing the evaluation tests through RF isolated box or chamber such as "RF anechoic chamber" [12].

Biased Test-Bed. The second critical challenge that the evaluator faces in WIDSs evaluation is the difficulty of benchmarking different WIDSs in a completely common test-bed. The prominent reasons for that are the restricted compatibility of the WIDS software with a certain determined types of wireless adapters (i.e., usually commercial issue), and the supporting operating systems. This biasing in the evaluation test-bed decreases the fairness of benchmarking and evaluation.

3.3   WIDS Performance Attributes

Many different attributes judge the WIDSs performance: *effectiveness, efficiency, ease of use, interoperability, collaboration* [1], *immunity, redundant alerts correlation, combating the attack ferocity, the impact on the supervised system resources, attack type recognizing, scalability and flexibility, etc.*

Effectiveness. The WIDS effectiveness is considered as the main focal attribute in evaluating the WIDSs performance. Effectiveness reflects the ability of an IDS/WIDS to detect the intrusive traffic into the supervised system, and the absence degree of the false positive alarms. The main challenge associated with the effectiveness attribute is the *false responses* problem which refers to the unexpected response from the IDS. There are two main types of false responses; false alarms (also known as false positives) which occur when the IDS generates alarms for benign activities, and false negatives which refer to the leaked attacks without any raised alerts.

Efficiency. WIDS efficiency includes many parameters related to the WIDS operation such as *real-time detection, operation decay, etc. Real-time detection* evaluates the WIDS ability to detect the intrusive activities in real-time (or near real-time). *Operation decay* is one of the practically observed weaknesses in the WIDS operation in the presence of heavy processing load.

Interoperability. The WIDS interoperability measures the ability of a WIDS to interoperate with other ones. Unfortunately, different WIDSs rarely interoperate with each other. So, it is difficult to consolidate different WIDSs to work together for monitoring the same system. This problem is prominent with the commercial WIDSs.

Collaboration. No doubt that, the additional effectiveness can be achieved when two or more of security mechanisms work together in a synergy manner. WIDS collaboration measures the ability of a WIDS to collaborate with other security mechanisms to achieve the intended level of the effectiveness.

Immunity. It determines and judges the ability of WIDS itself to resist any hostile attack against it, and its ability to quickly recover its activity and functionality from successful attacks.

Redundant Alerts Correlation. WIDS systems may flag a large volume of alerts every day and thus overwhelm the complementary prevention part or annoy the system administrator. A great part of these alerts are redundant and can be neglected, and the whole volume of alerts can be minimized through correlation analysis of intrusion alerts as stated in [13]. Redundant alerts correlation refers to the ability of a WIDS to correlate the redundant alerts that don't indicate significant events.

Combating the Attack Ferocity. Intrusion detection rate is not considered the only criterion for judging the detection ability of WIDS systems, but also it is important to consider the type and ferocity of attacks. However, a WIDS may have a high detection rate, but only for little harm attacks, and in the same time it may not be able to detect the most dangerous attacks such as some nasty types of DoS attacks.

The Impact on the Supervised System Resources. WIDS should not cause a load on the supervised system. The impact of WIDS on the supervised system is reflected by the system resources utilization; e.g., processor and memory usage. For wireless devices with limited biasing power such as wireless sensor nodes in wireless sensor networks (WSNs), it is important to take into account the impact of WIDSs on the power consumption of the sensor nodes. As well as, it is important to consider the network BW utilization by the exchanged traffic between the WIDS entities in the distributed and hierarchical WIDSs architectures.

Attack Type Recognizing. For WIDSs, it is not enough to only notify the intrusion detection, but also the intrusion type must be recognized. The criterion here measures the ability of an IDS to well recognize the type of the detected intrusion. This ability can be clearly observed with the signature-based IDSs than the anomaly-based IDSs.

Scalability and Flexibility. WIDS should be scalable and flexible to accommodate expansion of the networks scale. Expansion can be achieved via clustering, multi-hop delivery, localization of computation and data processing. Also, WIDS should be adaptive to network topologies and configuration changes.

3.4   Evaluation Metrics

In this section we present a new evaluation metric for manipulating the common main drawback of the previously proposed metrics for evaluating the IDS effectiveness, where their notion is based on comparing two or more IDSs to select the best one, although this selected one may not be effective. The effectiveness measured by these metrics can be described as *relative effectiveness*. For measuring the *actual effectiveness* (*effectiveness* for short) we introduce a new metric E_{ID} (*intrusion detection effectiveness*). The notion of E_{ID} is based on comparing the operation curve of an IDS (system under test) with an optimal operation curve (created as a *zero reference curve ZRC*), by calculating the variance between the two curves. The value of this variance interprets the deviation of the IDS operation from the optimal intended operation. E_{ID} can be used for evaluating the effectiveness of the wired or wireless IDSs; our concern in this paper is the WIDSs.

We believe that the main parameters that the WIDS effectiveness depends on are the *detection rate, false alarms rate, and base-rate*. Basically, *detection rate* (or *probability of detection $P(A|I)$*) is the proportion of the malicious activities that are flagged as intrusive, but *false alarms rate* (or *probability of false alarms $P(A|\neg I)$*) is the proportion of the benign activities that are falsely flagged as intrusive. Besides these two important parameters that reflect a significant part of the IDS effectiveness, it is also necessary to consider the hostility of the operating environment that can be represented by the *prior probability of intrusions $P(I)$* (known as the *base-rate*). Where I, $\neg I$, and A denote intrusion, no intrusion, and the output fired alarm respectively. Our proposed metric E_{ID} is based on the *Bayesian detection rate* (Eq. 1), where it includes all the main parameters related to the effectiveness attribute. *Bayesian detection rate* (also known *as Positive predictive value PPV*) is the posterior probability of an intrusion given the IDS output is an alarm $P(I|A)$. *Bayesian detection rate* can be represented graphically versus the *probability of false alarms $P(A|\neg I)$* as shown in [1], or versus the *probability of detection $P(A|I)$* as shown in [11]. In this paper, we use the trade-off between *PPV* and $P(A|\neg I)$, which helps us to develop a more representative metric E_{ID}.

$$PPV = P(I|A) = \frac{P(I) \cdot P(A|I)}{P(I) \cdot P(A|I) + P(\neg I) \cdot P(A|\neg I)} \tag{1}$$

The first step in deriving our metric E_{ID} is calculating and plotting the *zero reference curve ZRC (optimal operation curve)* which is the trade-off between *PPV* and $P(A|\neg I)$ (Eq. 1) with assumption of the optimal operation case of the IDS under test. As we mentioned above, one of the defects of *Bayesian detection rate (PPV)* is the unavailability of the prior knowledge of the probability of intrusions $P(I)$; this is the fact of the real systems, but in the evaluation arena it is easy to control the dataset or workload (background benign traffic with probability $P(\neg I)$ and intrusive traffic with probability $P(I)$) which is injected to the evaluation test-bed). By the same way, the *probability of detection $P(A|I)$* can be calculated by the proportion of the injected intrusions that are detected. With these available values, it is easy to plot the trade-off between *PPV* and $P(A|\neg I)$.

To clarify the idea of calculating and plotting the *ZRC*, we assume that we have an IDS which is tested and evaluated in an operating environment with *base-rate* $P(I)=3*10^{-4}$, and probability of benign traffic $P(\neg I)=1- P(I)=0.9997$. Logically, the effective IDS/WIDS detects most of the intrusive traffic into the supervised system and provides an acceptable level of false alarms. First, we assume that the IDS (under test) operates at the optimal case with *detection rate $P(A|I)=1$*. We use now these three values of $P(I)$, $P(\neg I)$, and $P(A|I)$ to plot the trade-off curve between *PPV* and $P(A|\neg I)$, and consider it as an optimal operation curve (*ZRC*) as shown in Fig. 2 (the axes are in logarithmic scale). In the second step, we plot the real operation curve of the IDS under test with the actual value of the *detection rate $P(A|I)$*; we assume it is 0.1. Now, we have two operation curves; one as a zero reference curve for the optimal operation and another represents the actual operation curve.

In fact, the zero reference curve is not optimal for all the points on it, but just for a certain set of points or, in other words, for a certain values of the false alarms rate; where any secure system accepts a certain level of false alarms (we called it as *false alarms threshold T_{FP}*) according to the system security polices and the costs parameters [4]. For our example, we assume that the *false alarms threshold $T_{FP}=10^{-4}$*; then we have acceptable values of the false alarms rate in the range [0, 10^{-4}]. Thus, the optimal operation on *ZRC* is considered only in the false alarms range [0, 10^{-4}]. For that, our calculation considers only this acceptable range of false alarms. The variance between the two curves is shown in Fig. 2 by the shaded feasible region. We normalize this variance by the area under *ZRC* (only through the interval $P(A|I)=$

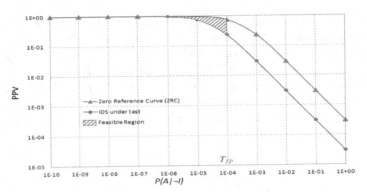

Fig. 2. The trade-off between PPV and $P(A|\neg I)$

[0, T_{FP}]) to have a representative metric E_{ID} has values in the range [0,1]; where "0" indicates zero deviation and then high effectiveness, but "1" indicates the maximum deviation from the optimal intended operation and then zero effectiveness (or ineffectiveness). Also, the IDS which violates the T_{FP} threshold is considered ineffective. Our developed evaluation metric E_{ID} is represented by Eq.2. We replace the parameters notations in Eq.1 by other ones to simplify our equation. PPV_{ZRC} and PPV_{ID} denote the PPV of ZRC and the IDS under test respectively, $P_{ZRC}(A|I)$ and $P_{ID}(A|I)$ denote the *probability of detection* for the ZRC and the IDS under test respectively, and R_{FP} denotes the false alarms rate.

$$E_{ID} = \frac{1}{\int_0^{T_{FP}} PPV_{ZRC}\, dR_{FP}} \left(\int_0^{T_{FP}} PPV_{ZRC}\, dR_{FP} - \int_0^{T_{FP}} PPV_{ID}\, dR_{FP} \right) \tag{2}$$

Where,

$$PPV_{ZRC} = \frac{P(I) \cdot P_{ZRC}(A|I)}{P(I) \cdot P_{ZRC}(A|I) + P(\neg I) \cdot P(A|\neg I)} \tag{3}$$

$$PPV_{ID} = \frac{P(I) \cdot P_{ID}(A|I)}{P(I) \cdot P_{ID}(A|I) + P(\neg I) \cdot P(A|\neg I)} \tag{4}$$

By applying E_{ID} metric on the curves in Fig. 2,

$$E_{ID} = 0.808$$

This value of E_{ID} indicates a great deviation of the operation of the IDS under test from the optimal intended operation, and then it is not effective.

As well as, the attack type recognizing attribute can be represented by a metric R_R (recognizing rate) which measures the proportion of the detected intrusions that are recognized. TP (true positive) *and* TP_R (recognized true positive) denote the truly detected intrusions and the recognized ones respectively.

$$R_R = \frac{TP_R}{TP} \tag{5}$$

3.5   Operating Environment Characterization

According to the evaluator goals, the wireless operating environment can be characterized on the basis of the network type, mode, topology, physical span, and architecture. *1) Network type*: it differentiates between military, commercial, academic networks, etc. Knowing the network type helps in determining the hostility of the operating environment. *2) Network mode*: there are two main modes in wireless networks; wireless infrastructure mode and wireless ad-hoc. In wireless infrastructure mode, the wireless nodes associate themselves with a wireless access point (AP) to get the network services and/or communicate with each other. Wireless Ad-hoc network is a self-organized network which is a collection of autonomous wireless nodes that can be deployed and communicate with each other by forming a multi-hop radio network and maintaining connectivity in a decentralized manner. *3) Network topology*: refers to a specific arrangement of network devices or nodes. The most common network topologies are star, tree, and mesh connection. *4) Physical span*: refers to the network coverage range. *5) Architecture*: wireless networks can be configured as either flat or multi-layered network infrastructure. In flat network infrastructure, all nodes are considered homogeneously equal and may participate in routing functions, while in multi-layered networks, all nodes are not considered equal [14] and they are partitioned in clusters with an elected cluster head for each cluster. The communication between the clusters is performed through the cluster heads.

3.6   WIDS Characterization

The deployment and configuration of the WIDS system depend on the operating environment characterization. For example, in infrastructure wireless networks, WIDS systems are often deployed wherever the access points (APs) are located; where the AP is the most targeted point by attacks. But, in Ad-hoc networks each wireless node may be a target of attacks. For that, the stand-alone architecture of WIDS may be appropriate for infrastructure networks, but WIDS distributed or hierarchical architectures are required for Ad-hoc networks.

Characteristics of wireless IDSs (WIDSs) do not deviate much more from the wired IDSs; just the RF (radio frequency) sensors, wireless communication features and wireless intrusions features are considered for WIDSs. There are a number of proposed classifications for the wired and wireless IDS systems [15, 16, 17], but they did not cover all characteristics of WIDS systems. Some of the previous classifications focused only on some common characteristics such as detection techniques, data collection and the IDS response. Some others considered also the detection time and granularity of data-processing. Besides all these characteristics, it is important to take into account and add two important dimensions related to *WIDS architecture* and *WIDS administration*. We have organized all these metrics in a compressive classification of the WIDSs in [18].

3.7   Workload Characterization and Generation

One of the focal points in our methodology is the characterization of the evaluation workload that includes two main parts of traffic; normal traffic (as background) and malicious traffic. The background traffic, which comprises normal benign activities in the absence of attacks, can be generated using real dataset or synthetic dataset. The real dataset can be captured, for example, using *Airodump-ng* [19] and replayed by *Aireplay-ng* [20]. The synthetic dataset can be generated artificially using tools such as *MGEN* [21] and *Rude/Crude* [22]. The malicious traffic part of the workload is composed of intrusive activities. The most famous tools for generating the malicious traffic are *Metasploit* [23], and *CANVAS* [24].

No doubt that the credibility of the WIDS evaluation test results depends significantly on a holistic characterization of the malicious traffic. This task naturally necessitates taking into account all possible attacks to evaluate comprehensively and fairly the WIDS systems. While this is operationally impossible, it is necessary to develop an attack classification that groups the common attack characteristics under expressive categories. This facilitates generating and extracting the representative attack test cases by combining the terminal classes of the classification. Therefore, we have developed a holistic taxonomy of wireless security attacks in [25] that classifies the attacks from the perspective of the WIDS evaluator.

3.8   Evaluation Techniques

The selection of the right techniques depends on the available tools, resources and the desired level of accuracy. Basically, there are three main techniques for system evaluation; *analytical modeling, simulation,* and *experimental measuring* [26]. *1) Analytical modeling:* It refers to the analytical analysis of the system under evaluation, mainly by mathematically abstracting the features of the system as a set of parameters or parameterized functions. *2) Simulation:* It is the imitative representation of the operation of a system or process by means of the operation of another synthetic tool; software program or simulating device. *3) Experimental measuring:* It refers to the practical measuring of the system features. This can be managed through an actual real system or using a prototype.

The remaining steps in our methodology are a little bit obvious; they are systematic tasks for test management and results interpretation.

4   Experimental Evaluation of WIDSs

In this section, we have followed the above methodology for evaluating experimentally two popular WIDSs; Kismet (for Linux) [27] and AirSnare (for Windows) [28].. The designed test-beds for the WIDSs evaluation tests are shown in Fig. 3. We concern ourselves with wireless infrastructure mode. For this mode,

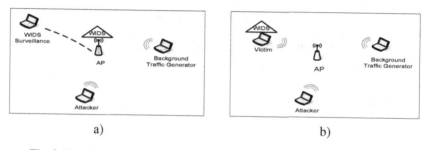

a)   b)

Fig. 3. Test-beds a) WIDS monitors the AP, b) WIDS monitors a terminal host

we have two possible scenarios. Scenario 1, the WIDS was installed on the access point (Fig. 3, a)). Scenario 2, the WIDS was installed on a terminal machine (as a victim) (Fig. 3, b)). The results of these experimental tests are shown in Table 1, Fig. 4, and Fig. 5. Fig.4 shows the Kismet and AirSnare operation curves with a common ZRC curve. For the evaluation workload, we generated real normal traffic by capturing realistic wireless traffic in the space of the laboratory IRIT-ENSEEIHT-INPT, France using Airodump-ng tool, and replayed them through our test-bed using Aireplay-ng tool. For the malicious traffic, we have used Metasploit and Linux Comand Line for generating 18 different wireless attacks. With these simple tests, we have $P(I)=1.63*10-6$, $P(\neg I)=0.99999837$, $P(A|I)=0.44$ for Kismet, and $P(A|I)=0.167$ for AirSnare; we assume that $TFP=10-4$. The evaluation results are interpreted as follows.

Kismet. Compared to AirSnare, Kismet operation doesn't deviate much more from the optimal case *ZRC*. There is no correlation between the generated redundant alarms that are a heavy load on the complementary prevention part. As an advantage, Kismet is considered as light software with little utilization of the supervised system resources in the absence of intrusions, and with little increasing impact according to the attack types (Fig. 5, a)). It has a good ability in attack recognizing besides to the attack detection ability. Also, it has a short processing time. It has a medium immunity against attacks that are directed to it, with a little tie-up of its operation.

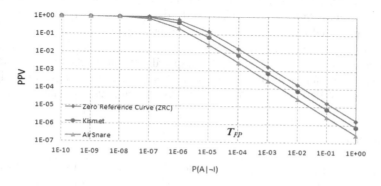

Fig. 4. The trade-off between *PPV* and *P(A|¬I)* of Kismet, AirSnare, and ZRC

Table 1. WIDSs Evaluation

Criteria and Metrics	Kismet	AirSnare
E_{ID}	0.49	0.904
R_R	0.75	0.33
Scalability	x	x
Redundant Alerts Correlation	x	x

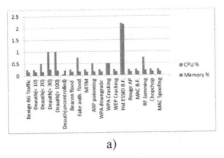   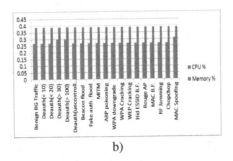

a)   b)

Fig. 5. The impact of WIDSs on the Supervised System Resources, a) Kismet, b) AirSnare

AirSnare. It is ineffective where it has high deviation from the optimal case. As well as, it has a little ability to recognize the intrusion type. It is also considered as light software with nearly the same impact on the system resources in the presence and the absence of attacks (Fig. 5, b)). AirSnare processing time is too short like Kismet. In fact, AirSnare itself is very weak against attacks, specially flooding attack.

5   Conclusions

In this paper we have introduced a novel methodology includes all the necessary and sufficient tasks for comprehensive evaluation of wireless intrusion detection systems (WIDSs). We also developed a new evaluation metric E_{ID} (*intrusion detection effectiveness*) for evaluating the WIDS effectiveness. E_{ID} helps in measuring the actual effectiveness instead of the relative effectiveness which was the concern of the previously proposed metrics. E_{ID} has values in the range [0, 1]; where "0" indicates high effectiveness, but "1" indicates zero effectiveness. E_{ID} is the best way to evaluate the effectiveness of the IDSs/WIDSs. We have followed our methodology to evaluate and test two well-known WIDSs; Kismet and AirSnare. We are working on designing a new effective WIDS to manipulate the defects of the currently available ones.

References

1. Axelsson, S.: The Base-Rate Fallacy and its Implications for the Difficulty of Intrusion Detection. In: Proceedings of the 6th ACM Conference on Computer and Communications Security (CCS 1999), pp. 1–7 (November 1999)

2. Gaffney, J.E., Ulvila, J.W.: Evaluation of intrusion detectors: A decision theory approach. In: Proceedings of the IEEE Symposium on Security and Privacy (S&P 2001), Oakland, CA, USA, pp. 50–61 (2001)
3. Gu, G., Fogla, P., Dagon, D., Lee, W., Skoric, B.: Measuring Intrusion Detection Capability: An Information-Theoretic Approach. In: Proceedings of ACM Symposium on Information, Computer and Communications Security (ASIACCS 2006), Taiwan (2006)
4. Stolfo, S., Fan, W., Lee, W., Prodromidis, A., Chan, P.: Cost-based modeling for fraud and intrusion detection: Results from the JAM project. In: Proceedings of DARPA Information Survivability Conference and Exposition (DISCEX 2000), pp. 130–144 (2000)
5. Puketza, N., Zhang, K., Chung, M., Mukherjee, B., Olsson, R.A.: A Methodology for Testing Intrusion Detection Systems. IEEE Transactions on Software Engineering 22(10), 719–729 (1996)
6. Puketza, N., Chung, M., Olsson, R.A., Mukherjee, B.: A Software Platform for Testing Intrusion Detection Systems. Journal of IEEE Software 14(5), 43–51 (1997)
7. Debar, H., Dacier, M., Wespi, A., Lampart, S.: An Experimentation Workbench for Intrusion Detection Systems. Research Report RZ 2998, IBM Zurich Research Laboratory, Switzerland (1998)
8. Lippmann, R., Fried, D., Graf, I., Haines, J., Kendall, K., McClung, D., Weber, D., Webster, S., Wyschogrod, D., Cunningham, R., Zissman, M.: Evaluating Intrusion Detection Systems: The 1998 DARPA Off-line Intrusion Detection Evaluation. In: Proceedings of the DARPA Information Survivability Conference and Exposition (DISCEX 2000), Los Alamitos, CA, USA, pp. 12–26 (2000)
9. Lippmann, R., Haines, J.W., Fried, D., Korba, J., Das, K.: Analysis and Results of the 1999 DARPA Off-Line Intrusion Detection Evaluation. In: Debar, H., Mé, L., Wu, S.F. (eds.) RAID 2000. LNCS, vol. 1907, pp. 162–182. Springer, Heidelberg (2000)
10. McHugh, J.: Testing Intrusion Detection Systems: A Critique of the 1998 and 1999 DARPA Intrusion Detection System Evaluations as Performed by Lincoln Laboratory. ACM Transactions on Information and System Security 3(4), 262–294 (2000)
11. Cardenas, A.A., Baras, J.S., Seamon, K.: A Framework for the Evaluation of Intrusion Detection Systems. In: Proceedings of IEEE Symposium on Security and Privacy (S&P 2006), pp. 63–77 (2006)
12. Wilkerson, J., Skeen, M., Patrick, D., Hodges, R., Schimizzi, R., Vora, S., Zhiping, F., Gard, K., Steer, M.: Acoustic-RF anechoic chamber construction and evaluation. In: Proceedings of IEEE Radio and Wireless Symposium, pp. 331–334 (2008)
13. Di-Pietro, R., Mancini, L.V.: Intrusion Detection Systems. Advances in Information Security Series, vol. 38. Springer, Heidelberg (2008)
14. Brutch, P., Ko, C.: Challenges in Intrusion Detection for Wireless Ad-Hoc Networks. In: Proceedings of the 2003 Symposium on Applications and the Internet Workshops, Orlando, Florida, USA, pp. 368–373 (2003)
15. Singh, J., Kaur, L., Gupta, S.: Analysis of Intrusion Detection Tools for Wireless Local Area Networks. International Journal of Computer Science and Network Security (IJCSNS) 9, 168–177 (2009)
16. Debar, H., Dacier, M., Wespi, A.: Towards a Taxonomy of Intrusion Detection Systems. International Journal of Computer and Telecommunications Networking 31, 805–822 (1999)
17. Sobh, T.: Wired and Wireless Intrusion Detection System: Classifications, Good Characteristics and State-of-The-Art. Computer Standards and Interfaces 28, 670–694 (2006)

18. Nasr, K., Abou El Kalam, A., Fraboul, C.: A Holistic Methodology for Evaluating Wireless Intrusion Detection Systems. In: Proceedings of International Conference on Network and System Security (NSS 2011), Milan, Italy, pp. 9–16 (September 2011)
19. Airodump-ng, http://www.aircrack-ng.org/doku.php?id=airodump-ng
20. Aireplay-ng, http://www.aircrack-ng.org/doku.php?id=aireplay-ng
21. MGEN, http://cs.itd.nrl.navy.mil/work/mgen/
22. Rude/Grude, http://rude.sourceforge.net/
23. Metasploit, http://www.metasploit.com/
24. CANVAS, http://www.immunitysec.com/products-canvas.shtml
25. Nasr, K., Abou El Kalam, A., Fraboul, C.: An IDS Evaluation-Centric Taxonomy of Wireless Security Attacks. In: Wyld, D.C., Wozniak, M., Chaki, N., Meghanathan, N., Nagamalai, D. (eds.) CNSA 2011. CCIS, vol. 196, pp. 402–413. Springer, Heidelberg (2011)
26. Jain, R.: The Art of Computer Systems Performance Analysis: Techniques for Experimental Design, Measurement, Simulation and Modeling, 1st edn. John Wiley & Sons (1991)
27. Kismet, http://www.kismetwireless.net/
28. AirSnare, http://home.comcast.net/~jay.deboer/airsnare/

Designated Condition One-Time Signatures

Wei Gao[1,2,*], Kefei Chen[1], Guilin Wang[3], and Xueli Wang[4,**]

[1] Department of Computer Science and Engineering, Shanghai Jiao Tong University,
Shanghai 200240, China
sdgaowei@gmail.com, kfchen@sjtu.edu.cn
[2] Department of Mathematics and Informatics, Ludong University,
Yantai 264025, China
[3] School of Computer Science & Software Engineering, University of Wollongong,
Wollongong NSW 2522, Australia
guilin@uow.edu.au
[4] School of Mathematics, South China Normal University,
Guangzhou 510631, China
wangxuyuyan@gmail.com

Abstract. In this paper, a new notion of designated condition one-time signatures (DCOTS) is proposed. For a DCOTS scheme, the signer can generate at most one signature for each condition. For example, the signer can generate at most one signature for each day. If the signer generates two signatures for the same condition, the private key will be severely threatened. Specifically, given two DCOTS signatures for the same condition c and then a DCOTS signature for a new condition c', one can generate the DCOTS signature on any message for the condition c'. We formally define the notion and the security model for DCOTS signatures. We propose a DCOTS signature scheme based on bilinear parings, and prove its security under the CDH assumption in the random oracle model. We show that a k-times signature scheme and a designated condition k-times signature scheme can be easily derived from a DCOTS signature scheme. Some possible applications of DCOTS signatures are discussed.

Keywords: one-time signatures, k-times signatures, designated condition one-time signatures, bilinear pairing.

1 Introduction

Digital signature is one of the most fundamental cryptographic primitives. By a digital signature scheme, a user can uses his secret key to generate the signature on any message, while anybody can use the public key to verify signatures. It is computationally infeasible for the party without knowledge of the secret key to

---

* This work is partially supported by National Natural Science Foundation of China (No. 60973135, No.60970111, No.61133014, No.61202475) and Humanities and Social Science Research Project of the Ministry of Education (11YJCZH039)
** Corresponding author.

Y. Xiang et al. (Eds.): IDCS 2012, LNCS 7646, pp. 253–263, 2012.
© Springer-Verlag Berlin Heidelberg 2012

forge a signature. Various kinds of special signature schemes have been proposed to meet various needs in practical circumstances, such as blind signatures [4], group signatures [3], threshold signatures [7] and so on.

In many practical application circumstances, the number of issued signatures for a certain condition should be restricted. For example, the signer needs to make the verifier believe his promise that the number of his signatures for every day is at most k, through showing that $k+1$ signatures is just enough for exposing the secret signing key. Another example is the proxy signature scheme , where the original signer may want to restrict the proxy signer to generate at most 100 signatures for every week, through letting the proxy signer realize that 101 proxy signatures for one week is just enough for exposing the proxy signing key.

Motivated by the above applications, we propose a new notion of designated condition one-time signatures (DCOTS). For a DCOTS scheme, it is very reasonable to believe that the signer will never generate more than one signatures for each condition, because the price for generating two signatures under one same condition is extremely high. In fact, given two DCOTS signatures for the same condition c, one can forge (1) any DCOTS signature for the condition c, and (2) any DCOTS signature for another condition c' once a DCOTS signature for c' is given. By extending this new notion of DCOTS, it is trivial to get the new notion of designated condition k-times signatures (DCKTS). For a designated condition k-times signature scheme, the signer can generate at most k signatures. Otherwise, the signing power will be severely destroyed as in DCOTS signatures.

There have been some works relative to DCTOTS and DCKTS. Such relative works include one-time signatures [14], k-times signatures [13], k-times proxy signatures [5,11]. For all these kinds of signatures, if the signer generated signatures more than the threshold number, then the signing key will be severely threatened (completely exposed, for example). One-time signature (OTS) schemes can generate at most one signatures, since two OTS signatures corresponding to one public key will expose the signing key. The main application of OTS signatures is the fundamental buiding blocks in many cryptographic primitives such as standard signatures [10], online/offline signatures [8], CCA-secure public key encryption [1] and strongly unforgeable signatures [12]. Here note that there are very few direct applications of OTS in the real world, such as authenticating messages in sensor networks [6]. Motivated by the direct application to restrict the signing ability, Hwang et al. proposed the notion of k-times signatures [13]. For k-times signatures, the signer can generate at most k signatures. Otherwise, the signing key will be exposed. Similarly, for k-times proxy signatures, the proxy signer can generate only k proxy signatures, otherwise $k+1$ signatures will result in the exposure of the proxy signing key.

The organization of this paper is as follows. In section 2, we present the definitions of bilinear pairings and the CDH assumption. In section 3, we formalize the notion and security model of DCOTS signatures. In section 4, we present the DCOTS signature scheme based on bilinear pairings. Then we prove that the proposed DCOTS signature scheme is provably secure in the random oracle model under the CDH assumption. In section 6, we evaluate the efficiency of the proposed DCOTS signature scheme. In section 7, we discuss the extended notions of designated condition k-times signatures and k-times signature. In Section 8, we discuss some possible applications of DCOTS in the real world. At last, we present the conclusion.

2   Preliminaries

In this section, we review the definition of bilinear pairings and the CDH assumption [2].

Definition 1. [Bilinear Pairing] Let G and G_T be two groups of prime order p and let P be a generator of G, where G is additively represented and G_T is multiplicatively. A map $e : G \times G \to G_T$ is said to be a bilinear pairing, if the following three conditions hold:

- e is bilinear, i.e. $e(aP, bP) = e(P, P)^{ab}$ for all $a, b \in Z_p^*$;
- e is non-degenerate, i.e. $e(P, P) \neq 1$, where 1 is the identity of G_T;
- e is efficiently computable.

Definition 2. [Computational Diffie-Hellman Problem/Assumpiton,CDH] Let G be a cyclic group of prime order p with a generator P. Given $aP, bP \in G$ with uniformly random choices of $a, b \in Z_p$, output abP. The CDH assumption means that the probability that any probabilistic polynomial time algorithm solving the CDH problem is negligible.

3   Syntax Definition and Security Model

In this section, we formalize the notion of DCOTS signatures and the security model.

Definition 3. [Syntax] A designated condition one-time signature scheme consists of the following four algorithms.

- GenKey(1^k) $\to$ (pk, sk). Given the security parameter 1^k, this algorithm outputs the public key pk and the secret key sk.
- Sign(sk, c, m) $\to \sigma$. Given the secret key sk, the condition c in the condition space $\mathcal{C}$ and the message m in the message space $\mathcal{M}$, this algorithm outputs the DCOTS signature σ on the message m for condition c.
- Verify(pk, c, m, σ) $\to b$. Given the public key pk, the designated condition c and the message m, this algorithm outputs 1, if σ is the valid DCOTS signature on the message m for the condition c. Otherwise, it outputs 0.
- Forge($pk, (c, m_1, \sigma_1,), (c, m_2, \sigma_2), (c', m_1', \sigma_1'))$ $\to$ (c', m_2', σ_2'). Given two DCOTS signatures σ_1, σ_2 on the messages m_1, m_2 for the same condition, a DCOTS signature on the message m_1' for the condition c', the message m_2', this algorithm outputs the DCOTS signature on the message m_2' for the condition c'.

Remark 1. The algorithm **Forge** means that, after the signer generates two DCOTS signatures σ_1, σ_2 for one condition c, for any condition c' where there is one DCOTS signature, the DCOTS signature σ_1' on any message for c' can be publicly forged. This penalty is severe enough to prevent the signer generating more than one DCOTS signatures for any condition.

The correctness property requires that for any (pk, sk) output by $\mathsf{GenKey}(1^k)$, any condition c, c', any messages m, m_1, m_2, m_1', m_2', and any signatures

$$\sigma = \mathsf{Sign}(sk, c, m),$$
$$\sigma_1 = \mathsf{Sign}(sk, c, m_1),$$
$$\sigma_2 = \mathsf{Sign}(sk, c, m_2),$$
$$\sigma_1' = \mathsf{Sign}(sk, c', m_1'),$$
$$\sigma_2' = \mathsf{Forge}(pk, (c, m_1, \sigma_1,), (c, m_2, \sigma_2), (c', m_1', \sigma_1'), m_2'),$$

we have

$$\mathsf{Verify}(pk, c, m, \sigma) = 1, \ \mathsf{Verify}(pk, c', m_2', \sigma_2') = 1.$$

Definition 4. [Security] Existential unforgeability under a chosen condition and chosen message attack for a designated condition one-time signature scheme (GenKey, Sign, Verify, Forge) is defined using the following game between the challenger $\mathcal{A}$ and the forger $\mathcal{F}$:

- Setup Phase. $\mathcal{A}$ runs $\mathsf{GenKey}(1^k) \to (pk, sk)$ and sends pk to $\mathcal{F}$.
- Queries Phase. $\mathcal{F}$ adaptively makes a series of signature queries. For each signature query, $\mathcal{F}$ sends the message m and the condition c to $\mathcal{A}$. $\mathcal{A}$ responds with the signature $\sigma = \mathsf{Sign}(sk, c, m)$.
- Forgery Phase. $\mathcal{F}$ outputs the forgery (c^*, m^*, σ^*).

$\mathcal{F}$ is said to win the above game if

- $\mathsf{Verify}(pk, c^*, m^*, \sigma^*) = 1$,
- $\mathcal{F}$ has never asked the signature on the message m^* for the condition c^* during the game,
- $\mathcal{F}$ has asked at most one signature for each condition.

The designated condition one-time signature scheme is said to be existentially unforgeable under a chosen condition and chosen-message attack, if the probability that any probabilistic polynomial time forger $\mathcal{F}$ wins the above game is negligible.

4   Designated Condition One-Time Signature Scheme

In this section, we present the designated condition one-time signature scheme which consists of the following algorithms.

- GenKey. Given the security parameter 1^k, this algorithm does as follows.
  (1) Choose two cyclic groups G, G_T of prime order p and the bilinear pairing $e : G \times G \to G_T$, where $p > 2^k$.
  (2) Randomly choose $P_1, P_2 \in_R G$, and $s \in_R Z_p^*$.
  (3) Compute $Q_1 = sP_1$, $Q_2 = sP_2$.
  (4) Choose two cryptographic hash functions:

$$H_1 : \mathcal{C} \to G, H_2 : \mathcal{C} \times \mathcal{M} \to Z_p,$$

where $\mathcal{C}$ is the condition space and $\mathcal{M}$ is the message space.
  (5) Set the private key and the public key

$$sk = (s, Q_2), pk = (G, G_T, p, e, P_1, P_2, Q_1, H_1, H_2).$$

- Sign. To sign the message $m \in \mathcal{M}$ for the designated condition $c \in \mathcal{C}$, this algorithm computes the signature

$$\sigma = sH_1(c) + H_2(c, m)Q_2.$$

- Verify. If

$$e(\sigma, P_1) = e(H_1(c) + H_2(c, m)P_2, Q_1),$$

this algorithm outputs 1. Otherwise, it outputs 0.
- Forge. Given two signatures σ_1, σ_2 on the message m_1, m_2 for the same condition c and the signature σ_1' on the message m_1' for the condition c' which satisfy

$$\sigma_1 = sH_1(c) + H_2(c, m_1)Q_2,$$
$$\sigma_2 = sH_1(c) + H_2(c, m_2)Q_2,$$
$$\sigma_1' = sH_1(c') + H_2(c', m_1')Q_2,$$

then the signature σ_2' under the condition c' for the message m_2' can be generated as follows:

$$Q_2 = (H_2(c, m_1) - H_2(c, m_2))^{-1}(\sigma_1 - \sigma_2),$$
$$sH_1(c') = \sigma_1' - H_2(c', m_1')Q_2,$$
$$\sigma_2' = sH_1(c') + H_2(c', m_2')Q_2.$$

5   Security Analysis

In this section, for the proposed DCOTS signature scheme, we present the security proof in the random oracle model under the CDH assumption.

Theorem 1. *If there exists a forger $\mathcal{F}$ against the above DCOTS signature scheme with running time less than t and success probability greater than ϵ, then we can construct an algorithm $\mathcal{A}$ which solves the CDH problem in the bilinear group G with running time t' and advantage ϵ' where*

$$t' \leq t + c_G(q_{H_1} + 2q_s), \epsilon' \geq \frac{\epsilon}{e(q_s+1)}.$$

Proof. Let G and G_T are two groups of the prime order p, and $e : G \times G \to G_T$ be the bilinear pairing. The attacker $\mathcal{A}$ is given two elements $aP, bP \in_R G$, and uses the forger $\mathcal{F}$ to compute abP. $\mathcal{A}$ simulates the challenger in the game with $\mathcal{F}$ as follows.

- Setup Phase. $\mathcal{A}$ sets $P_1 = P, Q_1 = aP, P_2 = bP$, and then sends the public key $pk = (G, G_T, p, e, P_1, P_2, Q_1, H_1, H_2)$ to $\mathcal{A}$, where the two cryptographic hash functions H_1, H_2 will be simulated in the random oracle model in the following. Here note the secret key $sk = (s, Q_2) = (a, abP)$.
- Queries Phase. During this phase, $\mathcal{A}$ simulates the two random oracles H_1, H_2 and the signing oracles for $\mathcal{F}$ as follows.

  - H_1 queries. For the simulation of the random oracle H_1, $\mathcal{F}$ maintains an initially empty list L_1. On receiving the new H_1 query c, $\mathcal{A}$ randomly chooses $x_1, x_2 \in_R Z_p^*$, and sets $H_1(c) = -x_1 bP + x_2 P$. Then $\mathcal{A}$ adds $(c, H_1(c), x_1, x_2)$ to the list L_1. If this query $H_1(c)$ has been made, $\mathcal{A}$ just finds $H_1(c)$ in the list L_1 and returns it to $\mathcal{F}$.
  - H_2 queries. For the simulation of the random oracle H_2, $\mathcal{F}$ maintains an initially empty list L_2. On receiving the H_2 query (c, m), $\mathcal{A}$ does as follows.
    (1) It first makes the H_1 query c by himself, if this query has not been made before. Now assume that $H_1(c) = -x_1 bP + x_2 P$.
    (2) It generates a random coin $\tilde{b} \in \{0, 1\}$ so that $\Pr[\tilde{b} = 1] = \frac{1}{q_s+1}$.
    (3) It randomly chooses $x_3 \in_R Z_p^*$, and then sets $H_2(c, m) = x_1 + \tilde{b} \cdot x_3$.
    (4) It adds $((c, m), H_2(c, m), \tilde{b}, x_1, x_3)$ to the list L_2 and returns $H_2(c, m)$ to $\mathcal{F}$.
  - Signing queries. On the signing query (c, m), $\mathcal{A}$ does as follows.
    (1) $\mathcal{A}$ makes the query $H_2(c, m)$ and $H_1(c)$ by himself. Assume that $(c, H_1(c), x_1, x_2)$ and $((c, m), H_2(c, m), \tilde{b}, x_1, x_3)$ are the relative records in L_1 and L_2 respectively.
    (2) If $\tilde{b} = 1$, $\mathcal{A}$ reports failure and terminates.
    (3) Otherwise, $\mathcal{A}$ returns the signature $\sigma = x_2(aP)$, since

$$\sigma = sH_1(c) + H_2(c, m)Q_2.$$
$$= a(-x_1 bP + x_2 P) + x_1(abP)$$
$$= x_2(aP).$$

- Forgery Phase. Eventually $\mathcal{F}$ outputs the forgery (c^*, m^*, σ^*). On receiving this forgery, $\mathcal{A}$ does as follows.
(1) $\mathcal{A}$ makes sure that this forgery is legal as required in the security definition. Otherwise, $\mathcal{A}$ reports failure and terminates.
(2) If there is no tuple containing c^* on the list L_1 or tuple containing (c^*, m^*) on the list L_2, $\mathcal{A}$ issues a query itself for $H_1(c^*)$ or $H_2(c^*, m^*)$ to ensure that both tuples exist. Assume that

$$H_1(c^*) = -x_1^* bP + x_2^* P, H_2(c^*, m^*) = x_1^* + \tilde{b}^* \cdot x_3^*,$$

according to these two tuples.

(3) If $\tilde{b}^* = 0$, $\mathcal{A}$ reports failure and terminates.

(4) If $\tilde{b}^* = 1$, $\mathcal{A}$ returns $x_3^{-1}(\sigma^* - x_2^*aP)$ as the answer for the CDH problem instance (P, aP, bP). The correctness can been from

$$\sigma^* = aH_1(c) + H_2(m)abP$$
$$= a(-x_1^*bP + x_2^*P) + (x_1^* + x_3^*)abP$$
$$= x_2^*aP + x_3^*abP.$$

This completes the description of algorithm $\mathcal{A}$. It remains to show that $\mathcal{A}$ solves the given instance of the CDH problem on G with probability at least ϵ'. To do so, we analyze the three events needed for $\mathcal{A}$ to succeed:

- $\mathcal{E}_1$: $\mathcal{A}$ does not abort as a result of any of $\mathcal{F}$'s signature queries.
- $\mathcal{E}_2$: The forgery (c^*, m^*, σ^*) is legal as required in the security definition.
- $\mathcal{E}_3$: $\mathcal{E}_2$ occurs and $\tilde{b}^* = 1$ for the tuple containing (c^*, m^*) on the list L_2.

$\mathcal{A}$ succeeds if all of these events happen. The probability $\Pr[\mathcal{E}_1 \wedge \mathcal{E}_3]$ is:

$$\Pr[\mathcal{E}_1 \wedge \mathcal{E}_3] = \Pr[\mathcal{E}_1] \Pr[\mathcal{E}_2|\mathcal{E}_1] \Pr[\mathcal{E}_3|\mathcal{E}_1 \wedge \mathcal{E}_2].$$

Claim 1. *The probability that algorithm $\mathcal{A}$ does not abort as a result of $\mathcal{F}$'s signature queries is at least $1/e$. Hence, $\Pr[\mathcal{E}_1] \geq 1/e$.*

Proof. Without loss of generality we assume that $\mathcal{F}$ does not ask for the signature of the same condition-message pair twice. We prove by induction that after $\mathcal{F}$ makes i signature queries the probability that $\mathcal{A}$ does not abort is at least $(1 - 1/(q_s + 1))^i$. The claim is trivially true for $i = 0$. Let (c_i, m_i) be $\mathcal{F}$'s i-th signature query and let $(c_i, H_1(c_i), x_{1,i}, x_{2,i})$ and $((c_i, m_i), H_2(c_i, m_i), \tilde{b}_i, x_{1,i}, x_{3,i})$ be the relative records in L_1 and L_2 respectively. Then prior to issuing the query, the bit $\tilde{b}_i$ is independent of $\mathcal{F}$'s view - the only value that could be given to $\mathcal{F}$ that depends on $\tilde{b}_i$ is $H_2(c_i, m_i)$, but the distribution on $H_2(c_i, m_i)$ is the same whether $\tilde{b}_i = 0$ or $\tilde{b}_i = 1$. Therefore, the probability that this query causes $\mathcal{A}$ to abort is at most $1/(q_s + 1)$. Using the inductive hypothesis and the independence of $\tilde{b}_i$, the probability that $\mathcal{A}$ does not abort after this query is at least $(1 - 1/(q_s + 1))^i$. This proves the inductive claim. Since $\mathcal{F}$ makes at most q_s signature queries the probability that $\mathcal{A}$ does not abort as a result of all the signature queries is at least $(1 - 1/(q_s + 1))^{q_s} \geq 1/e$. □

Claim 2. *If algorithm $\mathcal{A}$ does not abort as a result of $\mathcal{F}$'s signature queries then algorithm $\mathcal{F}$'s view is identical to its view in the real attack. Hence, $\Pr[\mathcal{E}_2|\mathcal{E}_1] \geq \epsilon$.*

Proof. The public key given to $\mathcal{F}$ is from the same distribution as a public key produced by algorithm **KeyGen**. Responses to random oracle queries are as in the real attack since each response is uniformly and independently distributed in G or Z_p. All responses to signature queries are valid. Therefore, $\mathcal{F}$ will produce a valid condition-message-signature tuple with probability at least ϵ. Hence, $\Pr[\mathcal{E}_2|\mathcal{E}_1] \geq \epsilon$. $\quad\square$

Claim 3. *The probability that algorithm $\mathcal{A}$ does not abort after $\mathcal{F}$ outputs a valid forgery is at least $1/(q_s + 1)$. Hence, $\Pr[\mathcal{E}_3|\mathcal{E}_1 \wedge \mathcal{E}_2] = 1/(q_s + 1)$.*

Proof. Given that events $\mathcal{E}_1$ and $\mathcal{E}_2$ happened, algorithm $\mathcal{A}$ will abort only if $\mathcal{F}$ generates a forgery (c^*, m^*, σ^*) for which the tuple $((c^*, m^*), H_2(c^*, m^*), \tilde{b}^*,$ $x_1^*, x_3^*)$ on the list L_2 has $\tilde{b}^* = 0$. At the time $\mathcal{F}$ generates its output it knows the value of $\tilde{b}^*$ for those (c^*, m^*) for which it issued a signature query. All the remaining $\tilde{b}^*$'s are independent of $\mathcal{F}$'s view. Indeed, if $\mathcal{F}$ did not issue a signature query for (c^*, m^*) then the only value given to $\mathcal{F}$ that depends on $\tilde{b}^*$ is $H_2(c^*, m^*)$, but the distribution on $H_2(c^*, m^*)$ is the same whether $\tilde{b}^* = 0$ or $\tilde{b}^* = 0$. Since $\mathcal{F}$ could not have issued a signature query for (c^*, m^*) we know that $\tilde{b}^* = 0$ is independent of $\mathcal{F}$'s current view and therefore $\Pr[\tilde{b}^* = 1|\mathcal{E}_1 \wedge \mathcal{E}_2] = 1/(q_s + 1)$ as required. $\quad\square$

Using the bounds from the claims above shows that $\mathcal{A}$ produces the correct answer with probability at least $\epsilon/(e(q_s + 1)) \leq \epsilon'$ as required. Algorithm $\mathcal{A}$'s running time is the same as $\mathcal{F}$'s running time plus the time it takes to respond to $(q_{H_1} + q_s)$ H_1 hash queries, $(q_{H_2} + q_s)$ H_2 hash queries and q_s signature queries. Each H_1 query requires two scalar multiplications in G which we assume takes time c_G. Each signing query requires one scalar multiplication in G. Each H_2 query requires an addition in Z_p which is much more efficient than an scalar multiplication in G and hence can be neglected. Hence, the total running time is at most $t + c_G(q_{H_1} + 2q_s) \geq t'$ as required. This completes the proof. $\quad\square$

6 Efficiency Analysis

First, the signature length is very short, since the signature is only one element in the group G. Just as the short signature scheme due to Boneh et al. [2], with some optimizations, our DCOTS signature length can also be approximately 160 bits and provides a level of security similar to 320-bit DSA signatures.

Second, the signing and verification operation is very efficient. The main operations are one hash function mapping to the group G [9] and two scalar multiplications in the group G. The verification operations mainly consists of two pairings, one scalar multiplication in G and one hash function mapping onto G.

7 Extensions: DCKTS and KTS

In this section, we introduce the new notion of designated condition k-times signatures (DCKTS) and revisit the notion of k-times signatures (KTS) [13]. These two cryptographic primitives can be seen the natural extension of DCOTS signatures. We show that a DCKTS scheme and a KTS scheme can be easily constructed from a DCOTS scheme. Due to the immediate relation between DCOTS and these two notions, this section will omit the formal details.

7.1 Extension I: Designated Condition K-Times Signature (DCKTS)

By slightly modifying the above DCOTS scheme as follows, we get one designated condition k-times signature (DCKTS) scheme.

- First, the public parameter is extended to include the times bound k.
- Second, the signature should be computed by

$$\sigma = sH_1(c, i) + H_2(c, m)Q_2,$$

  where $i \in \{1, 2, \ldots, k\}$ denotes that the current signature is the i-th one under the condition c.
- At last, the verifying algorithm and forging algorithm are trivially modified according to the modification in the signature.

Now we explain the basic construction idea for the above DCKTS signature scheme. For each condition c, the public parameter k ensures that there are only legal k sub-conditions $\{(c, i)\}_{i=1}^{k}$. According to the underlying DCOTS signature scheme, for each sub-condition, the signer can generate at most one signature. Hence, for each condition, the signer can generate at most k signatures.

7.2 Extension II: K-Times Signature (KTS)

By slightly modifying the above DCOTS scheme as follows, we get one designated condition k-times signature (DCKTS) scheme. The construction idea can be easily seen from that for DCKTS and DCOTS, and hence is be omitted here.

- First, the public parameter is extended to include the times bound k which ensures that there are only k valid conditions $\{1, 2, \ldots, k\}$ which can be used for k signatures.
- Second, the signature should be computed by

$$\sigma = sH_1(i) + H_2(i, m)Q_2,$$

  where $i \in \{1, 2, \ldots, k\}$ denotes that the current signature is the i-th one under the condition c.
- At last, the verifying algorithm and disclosing algorithm are trivially modified according to the modification in the signature.

8 Application Examples

In many applications of signatures in the real world, the signature number is expected to be restricted. Now, we present some possible applications.

8.1   Application I: Stronger Prevention on CA's Malicious Behavior

First, designated condition one-time signatures can be used by CA to generated the certificate. Taking the user identity (including some information such as the valid time interval) as the designated condition and the user public key as the message to be signed, CA generates the DCOTS signature as the certificate. In this case, if CA maliciously by himself generates a fake public key and binds this public key with a certain user (who holds the certificate binding her/his identity with other public key) using one certificate (DCOTS), then the private key to generate certificates will be ruined as just previously mentioned for DCOTS. As a result, it is extremely impossible for CA to abuse his power. However, in previous PKI, if CA does the above malicious thing, the price is the proof for CA's illegal behavior which is much more lower than the exposure of the signing key.

8.2   Application II: Monopolistic Purchasing Contract Signing

Second, designated condition one-times signatures can be used in restrictive contract signing. For example, one company A wants to buy one software from the company B which will help them to take advantages over their competitors. Company B is required to sign the sale contract using one DCOTS signature by taking as the condition the time interval when this software will not be sold to any other competitor company. Once B sign the sale contract with other company using DCOTS with this same time interval as the condition, the signing key will be ruined.

8.3   Application III: K-Times Access To Resources

Third, designated condition k-times signatures can be used to restricting a user to access some resources. For example, a student is allowed to access the network database at most k times for every day. To prevent students accessing the resource more than k times, if one student access the database, he is required to generate a DCOTS signature by taking the current date as the condition and the challenge value as the message. Since the signing key will be ruined due to more than k times accesses, it is very impossible for one student to break the times number restriction.

9   Conclusion

This paper proposed the new notion of designated condition one-time signatures (DCOTS). It can be extended to the relative notions of designated condition k-times signatures (DCKTS) and k-times signatures (KTS). With DCKTS signatures, for the condition designated by the signer, the verifier or other accepted entity, the signer can generate at most k signatures, since $k + 1$ signatures will expose the signing key. The new notions of DCOTS and DCKTS has many direct applications in the real world. We constructed one efficient DCOTS signature scheme which is provably secure in the random oracle model.

References

1. Boneh, D., Canetti, R., Halevi, S., Katz, J.: Chosen-ciphertext security from identity-based encryption. SIAM Journal on Computing 36(5), 915–942 (2006)
2. Boneh, D., Lynn, B., Shacham, H.: Short signatures from the Weil pairing. Journal of Cryptology 17(4), 297–319 (2004)
3. Chaum, D., van Heyst, E.: Group Signatures. In: Davies, D.W. (ed.) EUROCRYPT 1991. LNCS, vol. 547, pp. 257–265. Springer, Heidelberg (1991)
4. Chaum, D.: Blind signature system. In: Preceedings of CRYPTO 1983, p. 153. Plenum Press (1984)
5. Choi, C., Kim, Z., Kim, K.: Schnorr signature scheme with restricted signing capability and its application. In: Proc. of CSS 2003, pp. 385–390 (2003)
6. Dahmen, E., Krauß, C.: Short Hash-Based Signatures for Wireless Sensor Networks. In: Garay, J.A., Miyaji, A., Otsuka, A. (eds.) CANS 2009. LNCS, vol. 5888, pp. 463–476. Springer, Heidelberg (2009)
7. Desmedt, Y.: Threshold cryptography. European Transactions on Telecommunications 5(4), 449–457 (1994)
8. Even, S., Goldreich, O., Micali, S.: Online/offline signatures. Journal of Cryptology 9(1), 35–67 (1996)
9. Farashahi, R.R., Shparlinski, I.E., Voloch, J.F.: On hashing into elliptic curves. Journal of Mathematical Cryptology 3(4), 353–360 (2009)
10. Goldwasser, S., Micali, S., Ronald, R.: A digital signature scheme secure against adaptive chosen-message attacks. SIAM Journal on Computing 17(2), 281–308 (1988)
11. Hong, X., Chen, K.F.: Secure Multiple-times proxy signature scheme. Computer Standards and Interfaces 31(1), 19–23 (2009)
12. Huang, Q., Wong, D.S., Zhao, Y.: Generic Transformation to Strongly Unforgeable Signatures. In: Katz, J., Yung, M. (eds.) ACNS 2007. LNCS, vol. 4521, pp. 1–17. Springer, Heidelberg (2007)
13. Hwang, J., Kim, H., Lee, D., Lim, J.: Digital Signature Schemes with Restriction on Signing Capability. In: Safavi-Naini, R., Seberry, J. (eds.) ACISP 2003. LNCS, vol. 2727, pp. 324–335. Springer, Heidelberg (2003)
14. Lamport, L.: Constructing digital signaturs from a one-way function. Technical Report SRI Intl. CSL 98 (1979)

SQL Injection Detection via Program Tracing and Machine Learning

Yi Wang and Zhoujun Li

State Key Laboratory of Software Development Enviroment,
Beihang University, 100191 Beijing, China
wangyi160@hotmail.com, lizj@buaa.edu.cn

Abstract. Database systems are indispensable in modern web applications in order to process and store business information. Due to the contained valuable information, these systems are highly interesting to hackers and their diverse and enormous amount of attacks severely undermine the effectiveness of classical signature-based detection. In this work we propose a novel hybrid approach for learning SQL statements with program tracing techniques in order to detect malicious behavior between the database and application. The approach incorporates the program trace hashing technique and tree structure of SQL queries as well as query name similarity as characteristic to distinguish malicious from benign queries. An prototype learning system integrated in PHP is demonstrated to show the usefulness of our approach on real-world application.

Keywords: SQL injection, web security, machine learning, kernel tricks, program tracing.

1   Introduction

The majority of today's web-based applications does employ the multi-layer infrastructure and rely heavily on database storage for information processing. A lot of attacks against web applications are aimed at injecting commands into database systems in order to gain unprivileged and access to sensitive records stored in these systems. In recent years, SQL injection has become the top cyber security issue and must be treated seriously. Previous approaches of protecting web application include creating detection models on the network layer firewall systems. These systems are equipped with misuse detection engine and try to detect attacks by matching network traffic against known attack patterns. Snort IDS [1] and ModSecurity module[2] are among those popular systems which use rule-based pattern matching techniques.

Besides pattern based approaches, there exists a variety of research on employing anomaly based methods for detecting web-based intrusions [3,4,5] or program analysis on source code of target web application[6,7,8]. The former approaches try to analyze log-files or protocol-level information to detect anomalies based on heuristics or data-mining techniques. The latter ones conduct data flow analysis or model

Y. Xiang et al. (Eds.): IDCS 2012, LNCS 7646, pp. 264–274, 2012.

checking to check possible vulnerability of the program. These approaches are either rooted at the outer network or application protocol layer or only focus on statically analyzing source code. The outer space anomaly detection may not grasp internal weakness of web application and make wrong decisions even with big efforts made in heuristic and mining methods. Statically analyzing source code often generates conservative, inaccurate report and won't predict how program work in dynamic environment.

In this work we focus on the detection at the spot between application and database, while utilizing the program trace from interpreter, in order to understand well the relation between result (SQL query) and reason (program trace). In this way, detecting anomalous SQL statements will be much more accurate as malicious query will be judged based on the fact that they differ from the set of queries normally issued within an application from the same program trace. The main contribution of our work is the use of both SQL syntax structure, i.e. tree-vector-kernel based learning, which became popular within the field of natural language processing (NLP), and program execution context based analysis, Our approach incorporates the parse tree structure of SQL queries as well as query value similarity characteristic to distinguish malicious from benign queries. By applying this kernel trick into the SVM(support vector machine) classifier, we can determine abnormal query accurately and efficiently. The remainder of this paper is organized as follows: Section 2 gives an overview of related work regarding learning SQL injection and tree kernel tricks. Section 3 will explain the need and technique for incorporation of program tracing technique into detection of malicious SQL injection. In Section 4 we give a short introduction to kernel tricks in SVM in general and tree vector kernel for structured data. After that we define our kernel function and describe its rational in SQL injection learning in Section 5. Finally we present the whole system and test on real-world application as well as make comparisons with other variants in Section 6.

2   Related Works

For structural kernel tricks, several tree kernels have been designed. In the following, we highlight their differences and Properties. In [9], the SST tree kernel was experimented with the Voted Perceptron for the parse-tree reranking task. The combination with the original PCFG model improved the syntactic parsing. In [10], a linear complexity algorithm for the computation of the ST kernel is provided (in the worst case). The main idea is the use of the suffix trees to store partial matches for the evaluation of the string kernel [11]. In [12], two kernels over syntactic shallow parser structures were devised for the extraction of linguistic relations. To measure the similarity between two nodes, the contiguous string kernel and the sparse string kernel [11] were used. In [13], it provide a simple algorithm to compute tree kernels in linear average running time and show that kernel combinations always improve the traditional methods.

There have been approaches to apply data-mining and machine learning methods to detect SQL injection in databases. Lee et al [14] suggest learning fingerprints of access patterns of genuine database transactions (e.g. read/write sequences) and using them to identify potential intrusions. SQL queries are summarized in fingerprints (regular expressions) by replacing the constants with variables or wild-cards. Such fingerprints capture some structure of the SQL queries. A drawback of this approach is its inability to correlate and identify fingerprints with applications. In [15] the authors tries to detect SQL injections by a kind of fingerprints. They use parse trees of queries as fingerprints for the queries structure. The main idea is to compare the parse tree of an SQL statement before and after user variables have been inserted. Injected SQL fragments will typically significantly change the trees structure. A similar grammar-based approach has been used in [16], which studied the use of syntax-aware analysis of the FTP protocol using tree-kernel methods on protocol parse-trees. The approach taken in [17] is a little different where the parse tokens are used along with their values to detect anomalies in HTTP traffic. The latter approach does not use the full parse tree but its leaves.

In [18], the authors propose an approach which incorporates the parse tree structure of SQL queries as characteristic for detecting SQL injection and make comparison with n-gram and term vector. Our work is comparable to their work in the way of parsing tree structure and adopting ST or SST tree kernel functions in SVM framework. But we take program context (program trace at the point where SQL query happens) into consideration, as we need a way to learn queries from the same environment. We also add vector characteristic to supplement tree kernel in order to increase accuracy in classification. Finally, we build the system into PHP mysqlnd module for it to work between PHP application and database so that it can identify SQL query for individual http request instead of making classification on all SQL queries.

3   SQL Query Program Tracing

Web application is always a complex system, which may interact with its backend database system heavily. That is to say, a single program will contain many SQL queries and may generate different kind of queries under different circumstances. When we apply anomaly detection or machine learning methods on SQL queries, we first need to tell what kind of normal queries will be like and how to group those similar ones from same origin. Many researches on the detection of malicious SQL query seems to group queries based on program file. We argue that this kind of grouping is very inaccurate and inefficient as it is normal that a single program contains many different kind of queries. It will be very hard to build good model on those internally different queries and classification according to the model may generate many false positives.

In this paper, we would instead group similar queries based on program trace. We collect program trace as the program runs and when there is a SQL query, the trace together with the query will be recorded, thus generate <trace, query> pair. This is reasonable as same program context will generate similar/same SQL queries. As an example shown in Figure 1, the program contains two "mysql_query" statements and they are used for different purpose. So the two queries are quite different in their structure and database table name. It is natural to group queries from the two statements separately and only in this way can we classify malicious from normal according to their structure or table name. For query statement in Line 2, the corresponding program trace is {1,2} and query string is "select categorie from shopprod where activ like 'First Page' group by categorie;". While for query statement in Line 7, the corresponding program trace is {1,2,3,4,5,6,7} and query string is "select * from shopprod where categorie like '".$row["categorie"]."' and activ like 'First Page';", where $row["categorie"] is a variable. It should be noted that same query statement may be represented by several traces caused by loop rewinding. For example, line 7's trace can also be {1,2,3,4,5,6,7,8,15} or {1,2,3,4,5,6,7,8,9,10,11,12, 13,14,15} and only trace before line 7 will be recorded as later lines won't determine line 7' execution. In this way, we can reduce the quantity of recorded traces. The drawback of this approach is that it needs source code available and program tracing will introduce some performance overhead.

```
1 $sql="select categorie from shopprod where activ like
'First Page' group by categorie;";
2 $result = mysql_query($sql, $link);
3 while($row = mysql_fetch_array($result))
4 {
5     $sql="select * from shopprod where categorie like
'".$row["categorie"]."' and activ like 'First Page';";
6     $coloana=0;
7     $result1 = mysql_query($sql, $link);
8     while($row1 = mysql_fetch_array($result1))
9     {
10            $coloana=$coloana+1;
11            if($coloana>$nrrowfp) {
12                    $coloana=0;
13            }
14     }
15 }
```

Fig. 1. PHP program containing more than one SQL query

For the learning phase, trace will be used to group those queries from same trace. For the classification phase, trace will be used as hash to match against learning models. If the trace cannot be found in the learning models, it shows a sign that abnormal behavior happens or there is not sufficient testing in learning phase. In both cases, there will be a warning showing the trace with query and it leave the developers to determine whether it is really a successful SQL injection or add it as normal <trace, query> into learning models.

4   SVM Kernel Tricks and Tree-Vector Kernel

Kernel tricks in general have gained increased attention in recent years, partly due to the grown of popularity of the Support Vector Machines. Support Vector Machines are linear classifiers and regressors that can reproduce Kernel Hilbert spaces through the kernel trick and are thus able to perform non-linear classification and regression in their input space. As in this work we are dealing with the detection of malicious database queries, we choose a tree-vector based approach to represent SQL queries for making it suitable for machine learning.

4.1   SVM Kernel Trick

The Kernel trick is a very interesting and powerful tool. It is powerful because it provides a bridge from linearity to non-linearity to any algorithm that solely depends on the dot product between two vectors. It comes from the fact that, if we first map our input data into a higher-dimensional space, a linear algorithm operating in this space will behave non-linearly in the original input space.   It   is   really   useful because that mapping does not need to be ever computed. If the algorithm can be expressed only in terms of a inner product between two vectors, all we need is replace this inner product with the inner product from some other suitable space. That is where resides the "trick": wherever a dot product is used, it is replaced with a Kernel function. The kernel function denotes an inner product in feature space and is usually denoted as:

$$K(x, y) = <\varphi(x), \varphi(y)>$$

Using the kernel function, the algorithm can then be carried into a higher-dimension space without explicitly mapping the input points into this space. This is highly desirable, as sometimes the higher-dimensional feature space could even be infinite-dimensional and thus infeasible to compute.

4.2   Tree-Vector Kernel for Structured Data

Exploit the syntactic parse tree information is considered most useful tools for structured data processing. For example, the learning models for automatic Word Sense Disambiguation or Co-reference Resolution would benefit from syntactic tree features but their design and selection is not an easy task.

Convolution kernels are an alternative to the explicit feature design. They measure similarity between two syntactic trees in terms of their sub-structures. These approaches have given optimal results when introducing fast kernel computation. Moreover, combination models between tree kernels and feature vectors are recommended for more accurate classification.

*Definition 1 (**vector sets**):* Given two objects, O_1 and O_2, described by two sets of feature vectors, $\{\vec{v_1}, \vec{v_2}, ..., \vec{v_{n_v}}\}$ and $\{\vec{u_1}, \vec{u_2}, ..., \vec{u_{n_u}}\}$, several kernels can be defined:

$$K(o_1, o_2) = K(\{\vec{v_1}, \vec{v_2}, ..., \vec{v_{n_v}}\}, \{\vec{u_1}, \vec{u_2}, ..., \vec{u_{n_u}}\})$$

*Definition 2 (**Tree forests**):* Given O1 and O2, described by two sets of trees, $\{T_1, T_2, ..., T_n\}$ and $\{T_1', T_2', ..., T_n'\}$, two type of tree kernels, SubSet Tree kernel (SST) and Subtree kernel (ST) can be defined on:

$$K(o_1, o_2) = K(\{T_1, T_2, ..., T_n\}, \{T_1', T_2', ..., T_n'\})$$

*Definition 3 (**Combinations of Trees and vectors**):*

(1) *sequential summation,* the kernels between corresponding pairs of trees and/or vectors in the input sequence are summed together. The τ parameter rules the contributions of tree kernels K_t with respect to the feature vector kernel k_b. Each of the two types of kernels can or cannot be normalized according to a command line parameter. More formally:

$$K_s(o_1, o_2) = \tau \times \sum_{i=1,...,min(n,n')} k_t(T_i, T_i') + \sum_{i=1,...,min(n_v,n_u)} k_b(\vec{v_i}, \vec{u_i}) \tag{1}$$

K_t can be either the SST or the ST kernel whereas k_b can be one of the traditional kernels on feature vectors, e.g. gaussian or polynomial kernel.

(2) *all vs all summation,* each tree and vector of the first object are evaluated against each tree and vector of the second object:

$$K_a(o_1, o_2) = \tau \times \sum_{\substack{i=1,...,n \\ j=i,...,n'}} k_t(T_i, T_j') + \sum_{\substack{i=1,...,n \\ j=i,...,n'}} k_b(\vec{v_i}, \vec{u_j}) \tag{2}$$

5   Kernel Function for SQL Query

In this section we will introduce the related kernel functions specific to SQL query respectively.

5.1   Tree Kernel Function

Malicious SQL query often contains carefully prepared user string input in order to change the normal database behavior by different command or condition checking. This may lead to syntax change from benign SQL query in most cases. For example, by appending "' OR 1=1 --" into "age" value will cause the original query "Select * from user where name='john' and id='1001' into different tree structure "Select * from user where name='john' and id='1001' OR 1=1 ==', as shown in Figure 2.

The main idea of tree kernels is to compute the number of the common substructures between two trees T1 and T2 without explicitly considering the whole fragment space. For this purpose, we need to define the tree kernel function in order to compute the similarity of two trees.

$$K_t(T_1,T_2)= \sum_{n_1 \in N_{T_1}} \sum_{n_2 \in N_{T_2}} \Delta_k(n_1,n_2) \qquad (3)$$

where N_{T_1} and N_{T_2} are the sets of the T_1's and T_2's nodes, respectively. By adopting the concept of tree kernel from [13], we can define

$$\Delta_k(n_1,n_2)=\begin{cases} 0 & \textit{if } prod(n_1) \neq prod(n_1) \\ \lambda & \textit{if } height(n_1)=height(n_2)=1 \\ \lambda \prod_{j=1}^{|n_1|}(\sigma + \Delta(c_{n_1}^j,c_{n_2}^j)) & \textit{otherwise} \end{cases} \qquad (4)$$

where λ is the decay factor and $\sigma \in [0,1]$ is the counting factor, $|n|$ is the number of the children of node, for the last condition, $|n_1|=|n_2| \triangleright$

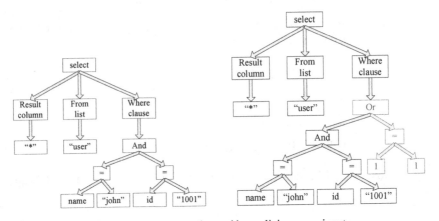

Fig. 2. Tree structure changed by malicious user input

5.2   Vector Kernel Function

In normal web application program, it is always correlated with several fixed table and column names, which will be used in SQL queries. They will influence the program logic and seldom change under different user input, while parameter value may always vary according to user input in where clause. Thus, it is naturally to assume that there exists strong relation between query and the appearing names and this will also be an important factor in deciding the difference between malicious from benign queries. For the purpose of that, we extract appearing names in query, $\{u_1,u_2,...,u_n\}$.

Traditional methods for calculating string similarity Δ_b can be roughly separated into two groups: character-based techniques and vector-space based techniques. The former rely on character edit operations, while the latter transform strings into vector representation on which similarity computations are conducted. The best-known character-based string similarity metric is Levenshtein distance(LD), defined as the minimum number of insertions, deletions or substitutions necessary to transform one string into another. For our case, we adopt this simple algorithm for comparing difference between names from same query point. In order to make measurement for similar strings bigger than different strings, we define:

$$K_b(u,v) = \frac{1}{1 + LD(u,v)}$$
(5)

By introducing +1 into the denominator, we can avoid the divide by zero error.

6   System Design and Evaluation

We present our prototype system SQLLEARN as a mysqlnd extension integrated in PHP interpreter. It functions as a SQL proxy with the ability of query learning and anomaly detection between PHP application and Mysql database. Several vulnerable PHP content management system applications are tested within this framework, the results show that our system can provide accurate and complete protection against SQL injection attacks.

6.1   System Design

For program tracing, we install Xdebug extension into PHP interpreter which support instrumenting the PHP opcode and recording program execution. By calling "xdebug_get_code_coverage" after every "mysql_query", we can know which program lines are executed and which file it belongs to. By making a hash on all these information, we can store the <hash(trace), query> pair in log files and analyze in learning or classification phase.

We then utilize the internal SQL parser in open source Apache Derby database to generate the parse tree of SQL query. Using the tree-interface of the parser, we can create a tree-inspection tool which traverses the tree object of a query and writes out the corresponding node information. Next, we build extension on mysqlnd(a PHP module which communicate with mysql database) to capture http request parameter. By combining the two tools, we can gather the information needed for calculating kernel function both in training phase and testing phase. The tree structure data together with vector pairs will be write in input format for SVM-LIGHT-TK (tree kernel extension of a popular SVM solver) so as to reuse its optimized implementation to compute the kernel value. Finally, the precomputed kernel value will be used as input for LIBSVM (another SVM solver) and reuse its one-class classifier to learn and the model for later testing. The system architecture is shown in Figure 3.

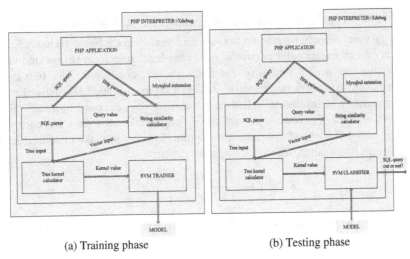

(a) Training phase   (b) Testing phase

Fig. 3. SQLLEARN system architecture

6.2   Evaluation Results

In order to test that our approach can accurately record and analyze program traces, we conduct research on "index.php" of CompactCMS 1.4.1(a complex open source

```
(/usr/local/apache2/htdocs/CompactCMS/lib/config.inc.php :
[5 6 7 8 9 10 11 12 13 14 15 16 17 18 19 20]
/usr/local/apache2/htdocs/CompactCMS/lib/languages/en.inc.php :
[33 34 35 36 37 38 39 40 41 42 43 44 45 46 47 ... 291]
/usr/local/apache2/htdocs/CompactCMS/lib/sitemap.php :
[38 41 42 45 48 49 53 54 55 56 60 61 73 75 79 80 84 92]
/usr/local/apache2/htdocs/CompactCMS/index.php :
[0 33 39]
/usr/local/apache2/htdocs/CompactCMS/lib/class/mysql.class.php :
[35 87 88 89 90 91 93 94 97 958 959 1040 ... 1820 ])
SET CHARACTER SET 'utf8'
...
(/usr/local/apache2/htdocs/CompactCMS/lib/config.inc.php :
[5 6 7 8 9 10 11 12 13 14 15 16 17 18 19 20 ]
/usr/local/apache2/htdocs/CompactCMS/lib/languages/en.inc.php :
[33 34 35 36 37 38 39 40 41 42 43 44 45 46 47 ... 291 ]
/usr/local/apache2/htdocs/CompactCMS/lib/sitemap.php :
[38 41 42 45 48 49 53 54 55 56 60 61 73 75 79 80 ... 168 ]
/usr/local/apache2/htdocs/CompactCMS/index.php :
[0 33 39 ]
/usr/local/apache2/htdocs/CompactCMS/lib/class/mysql.class.php :
[35 87 88 89 90 91 93 94 97 958 959 1040 1043 ... 1820 ])
SELECT * FROM `ccms_pages` WHERE `urlpage` = 'home'
```

Fig. 4. Program trace for SQL query in index.php of CompactCMS

CMS PHP application). Due to its complexity, there are a lot of different SQL statements in the program with multi-level file inclusion so that program trace for single file will still be big. Figure 4 demonstrates a small part of traces while executing "index.php" which reflects the fact that internal different normal queries can be separated by program trace. Otherwise, it is hard or impossible to classify attacks from benign queries from the mixed repository.

In order to test that our approach can accurately detect malicious SQL queries, we used "Damn Vulnerable Web Application"(DVWA) [19] as the test application with security level medium. First, we make 1000 random benign string user inputs as GET parameters and send HTTP request to the application to train the model. After that, by modifying SQLMAP[20] (a penetration testing tool for web application), we make another 1000 benign and 1000 malicious HTTP request to the same application and measure the accuracy of detection.

Table 1. Detection and false positive rate of the different models based on SVM

Kernel Type	TPR	FPR	Time(ms)
3-gram	0.640	0.000	0.233
4-gram	0.453	0.002	0.193
Vector	0.560	0.000	0.450
Tree-vector	0.982	0.000	3.862

We choose ST kernel K_s for the test case, as SQL query and table or column's sequence in real life nearly never change and SST kernel K_a will only bring more computation burden. By using different values of λ, σ, γ and τ, we come to the optimized combination as 1, 0.6, 1 and 0.5 respectively in order to achieve the best detection rate (TPR) and fraction of false positive rate (FPR). Moreover, we compare the tree-vector kernel with nGram and vector kernel alone to show that the combination kernel surpass any singleton kernel and obtain the best result, as show in table 1. This reflect the fact that both syntax and application context play important role in the detection of malicious SQL injection.

7   Conclusion

We presented an approach using tree-vector-kernels in SVM for SQL statements to prevent SQL injection in web applications. The results confirm the benefit of incorporation of syntax information of query and program context from application in analyzing SQL queries. Compared to previous approaches, the combination gains more accuracy than using syntax or context analysis alone as it brings more information into classification. Although tree kernel calculation is a time consuming task, we can separate the classification into sub-task according to request URL and program trace, which will make efficient online testing possible. With the system integrated into PHP interpreter, no modification is needed for web application to gain extra protection against SQL injection attacks. As far as we know, this is the first practical, light-weight learning solution to fight against such attacks. In future works we plan to improve the string similarity calculator and tree kernel functions in both accuracy and efficiency in order to make it suitable in commercial product.

References

1. Roesch, M.: Snort: Lightweight intrusion detection for networks. In: Proc. of LISA, pp. 229–238. USENIX (1999)
2. Ristic, I.: ModSecurity - A Filter-Module for the Apache web server (1998)
3. Kruegel, C., Vigna, G.: Anomaly Detection of Web-based Attacks. In: Proc. of ACM CCS, pp. 251–261. ACM Press, New York (2003)
4. Kruegel, C., Vigna, G., Robertson, W.: A Multi-model Approach to the Detection of Web-based Attacks. Computer Networks 48(5), 717–738 (2005)
5. Cova, M., Balzarotti, D., Felmetsger, V., Vigna, G.: Swaddler: An Approach for the Anomaly-Based Detection of State Violations in Web Applications. In: Kruegel, C., Lippmann, R., Clark, A. (eds.) RAID 2007. LNCS, vol. 4637, pp. 63–86. Springer, Heidelberg (2007)
6. Wassermann, G., Su, Z.: Sound and Precise Analysis of Web Applications for Injection Vulnerabilities. In: Conference on Programming Language Design and Implementation, PLDI (2007)
7. Wassermann, G., Su, Z.: Static detection of cross-site scripting vulnerabilities. In: ICSE (2008)
8. Martin, M., Lam, M.S.: Automatic generation of XSS and Sql injection attacks with goal-directed model checking. In: 17th USENIX Security Symposium (2008)
9. Collins, M., Duffy, N.: New ranking algorithms for parsing and tagging: Kernels over discrete structures, and the voted perceptron. In: ACL (2002)
10. Vishwanathan, S.V.N., Smola, A.J.: Fast kernels on strings and trees. In: Proceedings of Neural Information Processing Systems (2002)
11. Lodhi, H., Saunders, C., Shawe-Taylor, J., Cristianini, N., Watkins, C.: Text classification using string kernels. In: NIPS 2002, Vancouver, Canada (2000)
12. Zelenko, D., Aone, C., Richardella, A.: Kernel methods for relation extraction. Journal of Machine Learning Research (2003)
13. Moschitti, A.: Making tree kernels practical for natural language learning. In: Proceedings of the Eleventh International Conference on European Association for Computational Linguistics, Trento, Italy (2006)
14. Lee, S.-Y., Low, W.L., Wong, P.Y.: Learning Fingerprints for a Database Intrusion Detection System. In: Gollmann, D., Karjoth, G., Waidner, M. (eds.) ESORICS 2002. LNCS, vol. 2502, pp. 264–280. Springer, Heidelberg (2002)
15. Buehrer, G., Weide, B.W., Sivilotti, P.A.G.: Using parse tree validation to prevent sql injection attacks. In: Proc. of SEM, pp. 106–113. ACM, New York (2005)
16. Gerstenberger, R.: Anomaliebasierte Angriffserkennung im FTP-Protokoll. Master's thesis, University of Potsdam, Germany (2008)
17. Düssel, P., Gehl, C., Laskov, P., Rieck, K.: Incorporation of Application Layer Protocol Syntax into Anomaly Detection. In: Sekar, R., Pujari, A.K. (eds.) ICISS 2008. LNCS, vol. 5352, pp. 188–202. Springer, Heidelberg (2008)
18. Bockermann, C., Apel, M., Meier, M.: Learning SQL for Database Intrusion Detection Using Context-Sensitive Modelling (Extended Abstract). In: Flegel, U., Bruschi, D. (eds.) DIMVA 2009. LNCS, vol. 5587, pp. 196–205. Springer, Heidelberg (2009)
19. Dewhurst, R.: Damn Vulnerable Web Application, DVWA (2012), http://www.dvwa.co.uk/
20. Bernardo Damele, A.G., Stampar, M.: Sqlmap: automatic SQL injection and database takeover tool (2012), http://sqlmap.sourceforge.net/

Limitation of Listed-Rule Firewall and the Design of Tree-Rule Firewall

Thawatchai Chomsiri, Xiangjian He, and Priyadarsi Nanda

School of Computing and Communications,
Faculty of Engineering and Information Technology,
University of Technology, Sydney, Australia
Thawatchai.Chomsiri@student.uts.edu.au,
{Xiangjian.He,Priyadarsi.Nanda}@uts.edu.au

Abstract. This research will illustrate that firewalls today (Listed-Rule Firewall) have five important limitations which may lead to security problem, speed problem, and "difficult to use" problem. These limitations consist of, firstly, limitation about "Shadowed rules" (the rule that cannot match with any packet because a packet will be matched with other rules above) which can lead to security and speed problem. Secondly, limitation about swapping position between rules can bring a change in firewall policy and cause security problem. The third limitation is about "Redundant rules" which can cause speed problem. Next, limitation of rule design; firewall administrators have to put "Bigger Rules" only at the bottom or lower positions that can result in a "difficult to use" problem. Lastly, limitation from sequential computation can lead to speed problem. Moreover, we also propose design of the new firewall named "Tree-Rule Firewall" which does not have above limitations.

Keywords: firewall, rule list, rule conflict, tree rule, network security.

1   Background and Related Works

Firewalls are important devices that can improve network security. A firewall's security level does not depend on its cost, but rather comes from the secure rules inside it. While configuring the firewall, we should focus on creating accuracy and non-conflicting rule sets. There are many studies about firewall rule conflicts (anomalies) that occur within rule sets. E-hab Al Shaer et al [1] propose several anomaly definitions including "Shadowing anomaly". He defined the "Shadowed Rule" as the rule that cannot match with any packet. For example, rule number 4 (see Table1) is a shadowed rule. This type of rule can be removed from the rule list without any change of policy. Moreover, they have applied their definitions and theories for analyzing a distributed firewall [2]. In [1-3], authors focused on mathematics for analyzing firewall rules. Scott Hazelhurst [4] uses Binary Decision Diagrams (BDDs) to present and analyze rule sets. Pasi Eronen[5] proposed an Expert System that is based on Constraint Logic Programming (CLP) for users to write higher-level operations to detect common configuration mistakes and find packet matched on each rule.

Y. Xiang et al. (Eds.): IDCS 2012, LNCS 7646, pp. 275–287, 2012.

Table 1. An example of rules on the Listed-Rule Firewall

```
========================================================================
No.  Protocol Source IP      Destination IP  Dest. Port    Action
========================================================================
1    TCP     10.1.1.1         20.1.1.1        80            Accept
2    TCP     10.1.1.2         20.1.1.1        80            Deny
3    TCP     10.1.1.0/24      20.1.1.1        80            Deny
4    TCP     10.1.1.3         20.1.1.1        80            Accept
5    TCP     10.2.2.0/24      20.2.2.5        80            Deny
6    TCP     10.2.2.5         20.2.2.0/24     80            Deny
7    TCP     10.3.3.0/24      20.3.3.9        80            Accept
8    TCP     10.3.3.9         20.3.3.0/24     80            Deny
9    IP      0.0.0.0/0        0.0.0.0/0       0-65535       Deny
========================================================================
```

Lihua Yuan et al. proposed Fireman Toolkit [6] which can help administrators to design and analyze firewall rules. However, their toolkit only mitigates some problems of traditional firewall, and Fireman Toolkit is not a new type of firewall. Our research presents limitations of the traditional firewall and also propose a new type of firewall which has different mechanism inside. We use the tree-shape rule which is also hierarchical. Although the phrase "hierarchical rule set" [7] have been appeared in manuals of CSS (Cisco Services Switch), those are relevant to load-balancing devices in the network but not in firewall (describes which content (for example, .html files) is accessible by visitors to the Web site). Alex Liu and Mohamed Gouda proposed "Diverse Firewall Design" [8] using tree structure rule translated from rule list to discover and eradicate some of the rule conflictions. However their work still focuses on the traditional firewall, and they did not propose a new type of firewall.

2   Limitations of Listed-Rule Firewall

In this section, we propose our solution to the five limitations of Listed-Rule Firewall (today's firewall). We begin with the model explaining the Listed-Rule Firewall. We designed a model, namely the 2D-Box Model for explaining a matching between packets and firewall rules as shown in Figure 1. Suppose there are two source IP addresses ('a' and 'b'), two destination IP addresses ('x' and 'y'), and two port numbers ('1' and '2') in the system. For understanding this model easily, we did not mentioned other attributes yet (such as source port and protocol types).

Note:

SIP: Source IP Address
DIP: Destination IP Address
DPT: Destination Port

Considering the 2D-Box Model (Figure 1- left), incoming packets will be matched with Rule-1 first. In this case, Rule-1 will 'accept' two packets. The remaining packets will continue to fall down to Rule-2 that has a 'deny' action. After that, the remaining packets will continue to fall down to other rules below until they reach the last rule or match with some rules.

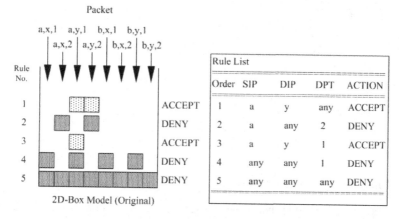

Fig. 1. The 2D-Box Model (left) and rules of Listed-Rule Firewall (right)

As we can see, matched packets of each rule are subsets of SIP × DIP × DPT (ACTION will be excluded), where "×" is an operator for computing the 'Cartesian product' [9]. The result from the Cartesian product is called a Relation [9]. For example (see Figure 1),

Rule Number 1 (Rule-1)
a × y × any = { (a,y,1), (a,y,2) }. The notation representing this relation is ' R_1 '

Rule Number 4 (Rule-4)
any × any × 1 = { (a,x,1), (a,y,1), (b,x,1), (b,y,1) }. The notation representing this relation is ' R_4 '

We can apply the 2D-Box Model to the firewall rules. For example we can define a range of IP address = {0.0.0.0 – 255.255.255.255}, and a range of port number = {0 – 65535} in IPv4. Moreover, the 2D-Box Model can also be extended and applied on IPv6.

Notation:

Rule-i denotes Rule number i.

R_i denotes the relation mapped from Rule-i (ACTION will be excluded).

R denotes sample relation.

Note: 'Relation' is subset of Cartesian product of domain. For example, suppose Rule-x is:

```
===============================================================
Rule No.   Source IP      Dest IP        Dest Port   ACTION
===============================================================
    x        10.1.1.1      20.2.2.0/30     80-81       Accept
===============================================================
```

Therefore, R_x is

```
{ ( 10.1.1.1, 20.2.2.0,  80 ),
  ( 10.1.1.1, 20.2.2.0,  81 ),
  ( 10.1.1.1, 20.2.2.1,  80 ),
  ( 10.1.1.1, 20.2.2.1,  81 ),
  ( 10.1.1.1, 20.2.2.2,  80 ),
  ( 10.1.1.1, 20.2.2.2,  81 ),
  ( 10.1.1.1, 20.2.2.3,  80 ),
  ( 10.1.1.1, 20.2.2.3,  81 ) }
```

2.1   Limitations on Shadowed Rule

"Shadowed rule" is the rule that cannot match with any packet because a packet will be matched with other rules above. Examples of Shadowed rules are Rule-4 in Table1, and Rule-3 in Figure1 (right). This limitation can cause security and speed problem.

Security problems are likely to be occurred, especially in enterprise networks which have a large number of rules in the firewall. For example, suppose that a new worm is sending packets to attack the network. After this attack was detected, the firewall administrator will add new firewall rule for protection against such attack. If this added rule is not in the first order and be shadowed by old rules above which allow attacking packets, then the security problem is absolutely occurred.

Speed problem can be occurred because many shadowed rules can waste firewall processing time on useless rules. Because of most of packets will be matched with the last rule (the rule that deny all packets); as a result, these rules have to be compared with all shadowed rules that are located above the last rule. This can generate the low throughput to the firewall.

We analysed the theory behind such limitations and proved that Shadowed rules are not necessary for firewall and can be deleted without any change to firewall policy.

Theorem 1. If Rule-i has no chance to match with any packet (due to all packets being already matched with other rules above it) then we can remove Rule-i without any change of policy. In this theorem, we call Rule-i a "Shadowed Rule".

For example, we can remove Rule-4 (in Table 1) from rule set without any change of policy.

Proof of Theorem 1. We can prove Theorem 1 using the 2D-Box Model (see Figure 1). However, we will prove it using SET and Relational operations as be shown below:

Denote "-" is a Difference operation of SET theory (this operation can be used for manipulating Relations too).

If p is a packet matched with Rule-1,
    we find that $p \in R_1$ .... (can be proved by using 2D-Box Model)

If p is a packet matched with Rule-2,

we find that $p \in R_2 - R_1$ ... (can be proved by using 2D-Box Model)

If p is a packet matched with Rule-3, we find that $p \in R_3 - R_2 - R_1$

If p is a packet matched with Rule-i, we find that $p \in R_i - R_{i-1} - R_{i-2} - ... - R_1$

From the properties of SET, thus $p \in R_i - (R_{i-1} \cup R_{i-2} \cup ... \cup R_1)$

Before deleting Rule-i,

Packet that fell on rules above Rule-i was $p \in R_{i-1} \cup R_{i-2} \cup ... \cup R_1$

Packet that fell on Rule-i was $p \in \phi$ (because Rile-i is a Shadowed rule)

After deleting Rule-i,

Packet that fell on rules above Rule-i was

$$p \in R_{i-1} \cup R_{i-2} \cup ... \cup R_1 \quad .... \text{(same value)}$$

Packet that used to match with Rule-i ($p \in \phi$) and switched to match with the other rules below was $p \in \phi$

Therefore, deleting Rule-i cannot caused on changes of the policy.

From Theorem 1, we found that Shadowed rules can be occurred on the Listed-Rule Firewall.

2.2   Limitation about Swapping Position between Rules

Swapping position of two rules can cause policy changing on firewall if the two rules are in different actions, and both of them can be matched with the same packet. For example, swapping between Rule-7 and Rule-8 (see Table 1) will change the packet (with Source IP=10.3.3.9, Destination IP=20.3.3.9, Destination Port=80) from being accepted to be denied, and can cause a Shadowed rule.

In this limitation, security problems are likely to be occurred if denied dangerous packets change to be accepted. Moreover, changing the packets from being accepted to be denied can also be considered as security problem. For example, if packets which send / receive between clients and servers are blocked, it can be referred as security problem because of the lack of "Availability" (ready to use). Above limitations are proved as following.

Theorem 2. If $(R_i \cap R_{i+1}) \neq \phi$ and both rules (Rule-i and Rule-i+1) have different actions, swapping the positions of Rule-i and Rule-i+1 may cause some changes of policy.

For example, if we swap positions of Rule-7 and Rule-8 (in Table 1) the policy may be changed.

Proof of Theorem 2

Let

R_u be R_x before swapping position
R_v be R_y before swapping position
K be $(R_{x-1} \cup R_{x-2} \cup ... \cup R_1)$ (it is the group of packets that already match with previous rules above)

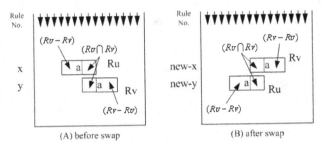

(A) before swap   (B) after swap

Fig. 2. The results from Difference and Intersection operation of Relations

Note: Operation without brackets means operating from the left to right hand. For example, A-B-C means (A-B)-C.

Consider packet (p) that will fall down to Rule-x
Before swapping (see Figure 2-A)

$$p \in R_u - K$$
$$p \in (R_u - R_v) \cup (R_u \cap R_v) - K \qquad (1)$$

After swapping, consider the Rule-x (old) that was changed to the 'Rule-new-y' (Figure 2-B).

Consider packet (p) that will fall down to 'Rule-new-y'

$$p \in R_u - R_v - K$$
$$p \in (R_u - R_v) - (R_u \cap R_v) - K \qquad .(2)$$

Consider packet (p) that will fall to Rule-y (Figure 2)
Before swapping (Figure 2-A)

$$p \in R_v - R_u - K$$
$$p \in (R_v - R_u) - (R_u \cap R_v) - K \qquad (3)$$

After swapping, consider the Rule-y (old) that was changed to the 'Rule-new-x' (Figure 2-B)

$$p \in R_v - K$$
$$p \in (R_v - R_u) \cup (R_u \cap R_v) - K \tag{4}$$

These are the assumptions that will be used for proving the theorems 2 in the next step.

In this case, two rules have different action and $R_u \cap R_v \neq \phi$

Consider packet (p) that will fall to Rule-x (see Figure 2)
    Before swapping: from (1) $p \in (R_u - R_v) \cup (R_u \cap R_v) - K$ (Figure 2-A)
    From the properties of sets, $(B \cup C) - A = (B - A) \cup (C - A)$

Thus $p \in ((R_u - R_v) - K) \cup ((R_u \cap R_v) - K) \tag{5}$

After swapping: from (2) $p \in (R_u - R_v) - (R_u \cap R_v) - K$
    Because $(R_u - R_v)$ does not overlap with $(R_u \cap R_v)$

Thus $p \in (R_u - R_v) - K \tag{6}$

From (5) and (6), we find that the decreased packets (matched with Rule-x) are

$$p \in (R_u \cap R_v) - K \tag{7}$$

Consider packet (p) that will fall to Rule-y (see Figure 2)
    Before swapping: from (3) $p \in (R_v - R_u) - (R_u \cap R_v) - K$
    Because $(R_u - R_v)$ does not overlap with $(R_u \cap R_v)$

Thus $p \in (R_v - R_u) - K \tag{8}$

After swapping: from (4) $p \in (R_v - R_u) \cup (R_u \cap R_v) - K$
    From the properties of sets, $(B \cup C) - A = (B - A) \cup (C - A)$

Thus $p \in ((R_v - R_u) - K) \cup ((R_u \cap R_v) - K) \tag{9}$

From (8) and (9) we find that the increased packets (matched with Rule-y) are

$$p \in (R_u \cap R_v) - K \tag{10}$$

From (7) and (10), $p \in (R_u \cap R_v) - K$ are the packets which changed from being matched with Rule-x to be matched with Rule-y, while both rules have the different action. Therefore, if we swap the positions of the both rules, it causes a change in the policy.

2.3   Limitation about Redundant Rules

Redundant rules mean the rule that is redundant to other rule below with same action. For example, Rule-8 (Table1) is redundant to Rule-9. Another example, Rule-4

(Figure1) is redundant to Rule-5. If we remove the redundant rule, a firewall policy will not be changed. This is because packets which use to match with the redundant rule will change to match with next rules below which have same action.

In this limitation, a speed problem can be occurred because many redundant rules can waste firewall processing time. We prove that redundant rules are not necessary and can be deleted without any change to firewall policy.

Theorem 3. Suppose Rule-i, Rule-(i+1), Rule-(i+2), ..., Rule-(i+n) all have the same action (where 'n' is a positive integer). If $R_i \subset R_{i+1} \cup R_{i+2} \cup ... \cup R_{i+n}$, then removing Rule-i can be done without any change of policy.

Proof of Theorem 3. It was defined that $R_A = R_i \cup R_{i+1} \cup R_{i+2} \cup ... \cup R_{i+n}$
Before removing Rule-i, the packets that will fall to Rule-i are

$$p \in R_i - (R_{i-1} \cup R_{i-2} \cup ... \cup R_1) \tag{11}$$

After removing Rule-i, these packets will fall to the next rules below such as Rule-(i+1), Rule-(i+2), ..., and Rule-(i+n).
But $R_i \subset R_A$, thus

$$R_i - (R_{i-1} \cup R_{i-2} \cup ... \cup R_1) \subset R_i \subset R_A$$
$$R_i - (R_{i-1} \cup R_{i-2} \cup ... \cup R_1) \subset R_A \tag{12}$$

From (11) and (12),

$$p \in R_i - (R_{i-1} \cup R_{i-2} \cup ... \cup R_1) \subset R_A$$

After removing Rule-i, therefore, packets that used to match with Rule-i will fall down to match with Rule-(i+1) or Rule-(i+2), ..., or Rule-(i+n). Due to Rule-i, Rule-(i+1), ..., Rule-(i+n) having the same action, there are no changes to the policy.

2.4   Limitation of Rule Design

In the rule design process, firewall administrators have to put "Bigger Rule" at only bottom or lower positions.

Note

- "Bigger Rule" is the rules that can be mapped into a "Bigger Relation"
- "Bigger Relation" is the relation that is bigger than other relations (super set of other relations) when comparing between two rules (or relations).

An example of a Bigger rule is the last rule (Rule-18 of Table2) which is bigger than every rules above. We cannot move this rule to the first position because it can shadow all other rules.

Another example of Bigger rule, if we want to prevent normal users from attacking the servers in DMZ (see Figure 3) but allow admin to manage servers through port 22, we have to prevent normal users using Rule-14 (in Table2) but allow admin by using

Rule-1 and Rule-2. As a result, Rule-14 is a bigger rule comparing to Rule-1 (and Rule-2), and we have to put Rule-14 under Rule-1 (and Rule-2).

Thus, with this limitation, designing rule on Listed-Rule Firewall can be done hardly because rule positions of each rule are not independent. Moreover, in the Listed-Rule Firewall, the rules that will be matched almost all packets (such as rule number 18) cannot be moved upward to other positions above. This also cause speed problem.

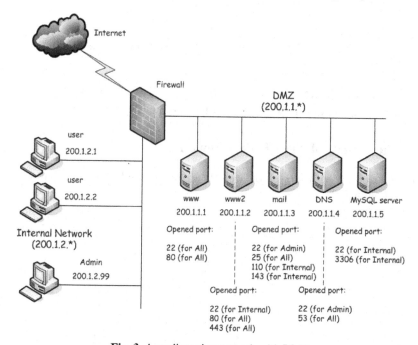

Fig. 3. A medium size network with DMZ

Table 2. An example of rules on a medium size network

No.	Source_IP	Dest_IP	Dest_Port	Action
1	200.1.2.99	200.1.1.3	22	Accept
2	200.1.2.99	200.1.1.4	22	Accept
3	200.1.2.*	200.1.1.2	22	Accept
4	200.1.2.*	200.1.1.5	22	Accept
5	200.1.2.*	200.1.1.3	110	Accept
6	200.1.2.*	200.1.1.3	143	Accept
7	200.1.2.*	200.1.1.5	3306	Accept
8	*	200.1.1.1	22	Accept
9	*	200.1.1.1	80	Accept
10	*	200.1.1.2	80	Accept
11	*	200.1.1.2	443	Accept
12	*	200.1.1.3	25	Accept
13	*	200.1.1.4	53	Accept
14	200.1.2.*	200.1.1.*	*	Deny
15	200.1.2.*	*	*	Accept
16	200.1.1.3	*	25	Accept
17	200.1.1.4	*	53	Accept
18	*	*	*	Deny

2.5   Limitation from Sequential Computation

Rule computing for packet decision on Listed-Rule Firewall is a sequential process. Consequently, it may cause speed problem. Especially, the firewall which has a large number of rules may work with a slow speed. The time used for rule computation would be depended on number of rules.

Let

> Number of rules is N
> Number of rules (in average) that will be compared with packets is N/2

Thus

> In Big O aspect, the time which will be used to compute each packet is $t \in O_{(N)}$
> In the next section, we will propose a new type of firewall which has a better Big O.

3   The Design of Tree-Rule Firewall

We have designed the new type of firewall which is called "Tree-Rule Firewall" as shown in Figure 4.

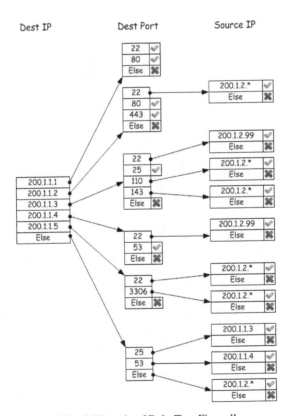

Fig. 4. The rule of Rule-Tree Firewall

This design can avoid limitations occurring on Listed-Rule Firewall. In this section, we will explain many advantages of Tree-Rule Firewall such as:

- No shadowed rule
- No swapping rule (the rule will be sorted automatically)
- No redundant rule
- Easy to design its rules (with independent rule path)
- High speed for packet decision

Rule-Tree Firewall is the new kind of firewall in which the rules are presented in a tree form (Figure4) instead of list of lines. Its processing (in a kernel level) is processed from its Tree Rule. This firewall will read attribute information from packet header and compare first packet's attribute with data in the root node of Tree Rule. After that, the firewall will check next packet's attribute by searching only on relevant node. As a result, the packet will be decided with specific action within a short time. For example, from the Figure 4, when the packets arrived at Tree-Rule Firewall, the Tree-Rule Firewall will consider Dest IP (destination IP address), Dest Port (destination port), and Source Port respectively until packets will be decided by a predefined action.

As we can see, the Tree-Rule Firewall has no security problem because the user cannot swap rule positions (Tree-Rule Firewall has no rules number, but we call each path of tree "Rule Path"). Data in each node will be sorted in ascending order.

Rule designers are not necessary to have any skill. They need only basic concept of Tree-Rule Firewall designing. This means that Tree-Rule Firewall's rules are is easy to design.

Moreover, the rules that will be matched almost all packets (such as the rule on the bottom path that show "Else->Else->Else->Deny") will take time of packet decision (Accept or Deny) equivalent to other rule paths. Each rule (each decision path) will take the same interval of time to decide packet.

With regards to performance, Big O of a decision time in Listed-Rule Firewall is $O(n)$; where n is number of rules. While Big O the decision time in Tree-Rule Firewall is logarithm. For example, in average case of Listed-Rule Firewall, if we assume that the chance of matched packets are equal for each rule in Table 2 (N=18, compare with 3 attributes (Source IP address, Destination IP address, and Destination Port)), we found that it will takes $(18/2) * 3 * C = 27C$ (where C is the time interval that is used for comparing between "1 attribute of packet header" and "1 attribute of rule"). While Tree-Rule Firewall in Figure 4 (Dest IP = 6 lines, Dest Port = 4 lines (in average), Source IP = 2 lines (in average)) will takes a time less than $C*Log\ 8 + C*Log\ 4 + C*Log\ 2 = C*(3+2+1) = 6C$.

Note: All "Log" values are base 2 logarithm.

When we conduct our survey on some enterprise networks that consists of approximately 100 servers, each server open about 20 ports, and has approximately 5 groups of users which need to access DMZ and Internet, we found that there are at least 200 rules on Listed-Rule Firewall which have to be defined for dealing with this condition. In average case, it has takes time about (200/2)*3*C = 300C to decide 1 packet, and requires 200*3*C = 600C in the worst case. While the time taken for 1 packet in Tree-Rule Firewall is less than C*Log 128 + C*Log 32 + C*Log 8 = C*(7+5+3) = 15C in both average case and the worst case scenarios.

Note:

> 128 is the number of destination IP addresses rounded up from 100.
> 32 is the number of destination Port rounded up from 20.
> 8 is the number of source IP addresses rounded up from 5.

As we can see, the Big O of Tree-Rule Firewall is obviously different from Listed-Rule Firewall's Big O. This is similar to a comparison between "Binary Search Tree" [10], and "Linear Search" [11] in an Array.

Considering the "security" aspect, Listed-Rule Firewall in enterprise networks (that has many rules) is likely to encounter with rules confliction of rules. Our scheme can address such conflictions including problems of shadowed and redundant rules. The rule path of Tree-Rule Firewall has no rule conflict within its rule base, because Tree-Rule Firewall does not have any Shadowing, Correlation or Redundancy anomaly.

In the "easy to use" aspect, it is very difficult to design rule in Listed-Rule Firewall following the policy of a corporate. Because, even we write many lines of rule, it will be difficult to check and test working of each rule. On the contrary, Tree-Rule Firewall can be designed easily, because every rule sentence (rule paths) of Tree-Rule Firewall are walk in separate paths obviously.

4   Conclusion

In this paper, we identified five important limitations on Listed-Rule Firewall which may lead to security problem, speed problem, and "difficult to use" problem. These limitations consist of (1) limitation about "Shadowed rules" which can lead to security and speed problem, (2) limitation about swapping position between rules which cause security problem, (3) limitation about "Redundant rules" which can cause speed problem, (4) limitation of rule design that can result in a "difficult to use" problem, and (5) limitation from sequential computation that can lead to speed problem. We presented various theories and their proof to validate our arguments for the above limitations. We developed the Tree-Rule Firewall which will be fast, secure, and easy to use. In our future work, we will discover equation of Big O precisely for comparing its performance with Listed-Rule Firewall. We will also study other factors that may impact the speed and security of Tree-Rule Firewall.

References

1. Al-Shaer, E., Hamed, H.: Firewall Policy Advisor for anomaly Detection and Rule Editing. In: IEEE/IFIP Integrated Management, IM 2003 (March 2003)
2. Al-Shaer, E., Hamed, H., Boutaba, R., Hasan, M.: Conflict classification and analysis of distributed firewall policies. IEEE Journal on Selected Areas in Communications (JSAC) 23(10), 2069–2084 (2005)
3. Haded, H., Al-Shaer, E.: Taxonomy of conflicts in network security policies. IEEE Communications Magazine 44(3), 134–141 (2006)
4. Hazelhusrt, S.: Algorithms for Analyzing Firewall and Router Access Lists. Technical Report TR-WitsCS-1999, Department of Computer Science, University of the Witwatersrand, South Africa (July 1999)
5. Eronen, P., Zitting, J.: An Expert System for Analyzing Firewall Rules. In: Proceedings of 6th Nordic Workshop on Secure IT-Systems (NordSec 2001), pp. 100–107 (2001)
6. Lihua, J.M., Su, Z.: FIREMAN: A toolkit for Firewall modeling and analysis. In: Proceedings of the 2006 IEEE Symposium on Security and Privacy (2006)
7. Cisco Content Services Switch Basic Configuration Guide,
   `http://www.cisco.com/en/US/docs/app_ntwk_services/`
   `data_center_app_services/css11500series/v7.10/`
   `configuration/basic/guide/basicgd.pdf`
8. Liu, A., Gouda, M.: Diverse Firewall Design. IEEE Transaction on Parallel and Distributed Systems 19(9) (September 2008)
9. Pornavalai, C., Chomsiri, T.: Firewall Policy Analyzing by Relational Algebra. In: Proceeding of the 2004 International Technical Conference on Circuits/Systems, Computers and Communications (ITC-CSCC 2004), pp. 214–219 (2004)
10. `http://en.wikipedia.org/wiki/Binary_search_tree`
11. `http://en.wikipedia.org/wiki/Linear_search`

Author Index

Author Index